The Daily Telegraph
CRICKET
YEAR
BOOK
'82

Michael Melford
E.W. Swanton
Bill Frindall
Michael Carey

A complete account of the 1981/82 Season

Consultant editor:	Michael Melford
Special articles:	E.W. Swanton
Statistics:	Bill Frindall
Home Test reports:	Michael Carey
County coverage:	D.J. Rutnagur
Other contributors:	George Abbott, Rajan Bala, Donald Cameron, Tony Cozier, Rachel Heyhoe Flint, John Fogg, Neil Hallam, Majid Khan, Terry Power, Alan Shiell, Darrell Thomson, A.S.R. Winlaw

Editor:	Norman Barrett
Designer:	Martin Bronkhorst
Artist:	Dennis Curran

Most of the photographs appearing in this book were
supplied by Adrian Murrell and Bill Smith. Other picture
acknowledgements are due to Colorsport, Syndication
International, Keystone, and Universal Pictorial Press.

Published by the Daily Telegraph
135 Fleet Street, London EC4P 4BL

First Published 1982
© Daily Telegraph 1982
Scorecharts © Bill Frindall 1982
ISBN 0 901684 79 1 paperback
ISBN 0 901684 81 3 hardback

Printed in Great Britain
by Biddles Limited, Guildford, Surrey
Typeset by Shanta Thawani, London

Contents

Foreword

One particularly annoying facet of growing old is a tendency to imagine that everybody else has lived as long. It should really have come as no surprise to me that, when I mentioned recently, in not-very-ancient company, the fact that 50 years had elapsed since 'the Bodyline series', I was asked what it was — was it a range of torso-hugging underwear? Equally, I suppose, I should have been less than astounded that Ian Botham, on being invited, on 'A Question of Sport', to identify two batsmen *en route* for the wicket, failed to recognize either Denis Compton or Pat Hendren. Fame is, indeed, fleeting. Or time is a great healer. Or something.

I would like to think that the events of the winter of 1932-33 have already been forgotten by Australians. But I cannot be sure, largely because I have not had the courage, when in Australia, to test the temperature of the water. I do, however, vividly remember Sir Donald Bradman's providing me, some years ago, with what came very close to a ball-by-ball commentary of that fateful season. In any event, the point may prove to be of no more than academic interest, because it appears that an action replay of the whole Bodyline saga will soon become available in the shape of a new film from the *Chariots of Fire* team. How about Vincent Price as Douglas Jardine and Robert Redford as Gubby Allen? I can't wait. But I hope the Aussies can, because we shall have our hands quite full enough this winter without having to defend the old country in arguments that began half a century ago.

Not, I imagine, that the new *Daily Telegraph Cricket Year Book* will be too anxious to dwell on the past when there is so much requiring comment or explanation happening here and now in the cricket world. It is a great pleasure to be able to welcome a new cricket publication, and I hope that the very fact of its arrival on the scene may be taken as an indication that interest in the game is high.

There is certainly no shortage of thought-provoking subjects for discussion. Quite apart from such basic topics as over-rates, 'neutral' umpires, dissent and the like, there are even more fundamental matters such as political influence, commercial involvement, and the overall question of the future pattern of international cricket, which merit consideration.

The tour of Australia this winter will help to answer some questions for our cricket administrators, particularly in respect of the desirability or otherwise of the enormous amount of 'international' cricket being played. It is tempting to pack a programme with Test and one-day international matches in order to maximize revenue from gates, sponsorship, and television. But it is pertinent to ask to what extent that revenue is being used to benefit the game at large, and whether we are, in the process, burning up the energies of our leading players too quickly. Playing five Test matches by the end of the first week in January and at least ten one-day internationals over the following three weeks should give us a clue as to the kind of physical and mental strain involved. And, if past experience is anything to go by, the manager will be more exhausted than anybody. Well, almost. With Bob Willis on board, there must, I suppose, be some doubt. He is as hard-working and whole-hearted a cricketer as there is in the land, and a great travelling companion to boot. Like his predecessor he can be less than tolerant of carping media representatives, and is somewhat less adept at disguising the fact. But a measure of hypnotherapy and regular injections of valium, together with an occasional victory, will, I am sure, make for an enjoyable tour, win or lose.

My previous tour of duty as manager in Australia was with Michael Brearley as captain, and, on his retirement as a player, I would like to add my two penn'orth of appraising comment. 'Brears' is a significant figure in several respects, but particularly, in my opinion, because he epitomizes the absolutely crucial and all too often underrated importance of captaincy in cricket — a point also emphasized, in a different way, by the recent transmogrification of Raymond Illingworth. Michael strove as hard as any man can to achieve recognition on the basis of his ability as a Test batsman, and sometimes looked the part completely. But he was unduly sensitive about it — on one occasion to the point of suggesting to me that he should leave himself out of the side. For my money he could have batted at number 11 and still been the first name on the team sheet. He has not infrequently written about his cricketing philosophy, but there are two important aspects of his captaincy to which he has, either modestly or unknowingly, given less than adequate emphasis. First, his tactical approach was quite outstanding in my experience as a player and selector. I know that he has a high IQ, but many highly intelligent people have been unable to achieve the degree of common sense necessary to understand cricket tactics. Second, he was not nearly as soft a touch as he sometimes appeared. He consulted, he listened, he was considerate, but on the field he was the undisputed 'guvnor'. I hope, both from personal and cricketing points of view, that his knowledge and experience will not now be lost to the game.

I hope, too, that this Year Book will survive the inadequacy of its first foreword and provide winter enjoyment for literate followers of cricket for many a long year.

Doug Insole

Looking back

1982 - Not All Anticlimax

After the historic events of the 1981 season in England, with its unforgettable Test matches at Headingley and elsewhere, the next year was certain to have an element of anticlimax about it. With an unexciting England tour of India and the subsequent banning from Test cricket for three years of 15 English cricketers for making a tour of South Africa, the starry-eyed enthusiasm for cricket existing in the autumn of 1981 was soon replaced by a more familiar pattern of criticism, controversy, and financial concern.

As always, some pessimism was unfounded. An English summer of much fine weather and a closely fought series between England and Pakistan improved things. But many problems remain unsolved — the slow over-rate, the isolation of South Africa and its consequences, umpiring, behaviour, and the differing views in England and Australia on the place of Test cricket in the modern game. Anyone who sits through a month of one-day matches with all their prolonged repetitiveness and lack of variety deserves the Australian equivalent of the Purple Heart.

The Over-Rate. One good thing to come out of a not untypical but over-publicized tour of India was the eventual agreement by England and India, and later England and Pakistan, to play a minimum of 96 overs a day in Test matches in England. For a time this worked well. Play usually had to be extended by only about 15 minutes, and the knowledge that the overs had to be bowled seemed to prompt a brisker approach early on.

It was less satisfactory in the Pakistan series, partly because there were fewer slow bowlers in action, partly because the matches were more sternly contested, partly because in the second half of an English summer bad light will often limit any extension of play. However, the great thing was that action had been agreed and taken by three countries, even if the modest success of the innovation had to be qualified by the reminder that, unless a much earlier start is made, the light in many parts of the world will not allow any extension at all. Disappointing, too, was the refusal of West Indies at the ICC to co-operate in the attack on slow over-rates. Many West Indians believe that this is merely a ruse to undermine their strength in fast bowling.

10.00 a.m. Start. The experiment of starting the NatWest Bank Trophy matches from the quarter-finals onwards at 10 o'clock met widespread condemnation for reasons given elsewhere in these pages. Whether there would have been much difference on misty August mornings if the starting time, as before, had been 10.30 is uncertain, but the fuss did draw attention to two contradictions.

It is illogical that the Benson and Hedges Cup should be played over 55 overs a-side in high summer when the NatWest Bank Trophy occupies 60 overs as the days grow shorter. It also makes no sense, at a time when efforts to improve the over-rate in first-class cricket are being intensified, that the limited-over matches, except in the John Player League, are allowed to meander on interminably with changes of field several times an over in the later stages.

In any case, I have thought for 20 years that to attack slow over-rates and time-wasting while still letting quite medium-paced bowlers walk back 40 to 50 paces was like putting patients on a slimming diet while not curbing their passion for potatoes.

The Ban. Those who savour, albeit sadly, the paradoxes and hypocrisy of the cricket world's attitude to South Africa had some rich dishes in 1982. A tour such as the one undertaken in March by the subsequently banned players had long been recognized as inevitable if the subject of the isolation of South Africa continued to be swept under the carpet and if liberal and painstaking representatives of the South African Cricket Union, who had made their country's cricket totally non-racial, continued to be sent home from London empty-handed and discredited in their own country.

Frustration would erupt and, through the sponsors who had long been waiting to back South African cricket at international level, organizers would offer English players sums that certainly those near retirement would not be expected to refuse.

The former president of the SACU, Rashid Varachia, until his death in December 1981, and the vice-president Boon Wallace, until his retirement three months earlier, may have put unreasonable faith in the sense of fair play of some member-countries of the International Cricket Conference. Politics have too strong a hold to allow such sentiments. Even Australia, who did not mind playing in South Africa when cricket was segregated there, shudder at doing so now that it is non-racial.

If that sounds cock-eyed (and, of course, highly racist), the TCCB's three-year ban has it beaten on several counts. Though the players ignored the unspecific warning of August 1981, the Board admitted that they had broken no rule and said that the ban was not a punishment but a move to avoid the loss of revenue that cancellation of the Indian and Pakistan tours to England would entail. This line of reasoning would be appreciated by the Mafia, which lives, as I understand it, on people who pay a relatively small price to avoid greater damage.

At the same time that the TCCB was imposing bans to appease the Indian and Pakistan governments, the ICC was endorsing its admirable agreement of 1981, reached after the England exodus from Guyana, that member-countries should not influence the selection of each other's teams.

Simple observers would have thought, both now and in October 1981 when the acceptability of Boycott and Cook to the Indian government was questioned, that this was exactly what *was* happening. No, said the Board, India and Pakistan were not influencing our selection. We were doing it ourselves in order to protect our financial interests.

This seemed a particularly nice distinction, for, whoever wielded the chopper, it was still the policies of other governments that threatened the Board's finances. The Board, moreover, had done nothing of which to feel culpable, for it had faithfully followed the British government's interpretation of the obscure Gleneagles Declaration by trying to persuade players not to go to South Africa.

There followed such droll paradoxes as the inclusion of a South African, Allan Lamb, in the England team for which Graham Gooch was ineligible; the inclusion, too, in county teams opposing the tourists of South Africans and of English players who had spent the whole winter in South Africa, but not of any of the 15 who had taken part in the brief operations of the SA Breweries XI. The South Africans had fanned the flames by treating the matches as representative and awarding Springbok colours. To the charge that this, and the furtive organization of the tour and the importing of what was by no means a glamorous English team, was unwarranted, the South Africans reply that it was necessary if something positive were to be done for a starved cricket public and to maintain enthusiasm for the game.

It may be that some world-shattering event — someone suggested a take-over by Colonel Gaddafi — will make South Africa *persona grata* at the United Nations again. The mere dismantling of apartheid will not do it, for it suits too many factions to have South Africa isolated. Any cricket initiative will have to come from England, with New Zealand support, and no one has envied the Cricket Council their acutely difficult situation, unable to treat South Africa's cricket as they would that of other countries without upsetting the Foreign Office, some member-countries of ICC and English cricket's own prosperity.

The severity of the ban, and the subsequent rejection of the players' appeal for a reduction of it, have complicated rather than eased the position in which English cricket has put itself by not trying to honour the implied promises of 1970. Then the Cricket council broke Test relations until 'South African cricket is played and teams are selected on a multi-racial basis'. That promise is now said to be dead in this country. But it is considered very much alive in South Africa, something that may not have prompted all their progress but has never been out of mind.

Whereas the SACU was patient while it, and its cricket public, thought that the much respected English cricket authorities were doing what they could to help in a difficult world situation, now it sees English cricket as weak and subservient to nations ignorant of and openly hostile to South Africa. The danger therefore is that there will be more unofficial tours, bigger than that of 1982, more lucrative offers to players, more divisiveness ....

Umpires and Behaviour. One of the year's less attractive developments has been the increase in public criticism of umpires. England objected to an umpire in India. India did the same in England. This has always been the right of the visiting side. What is different is that it is now done publicly. The Pakistan captain and manager in England carried the practice even further by criticizing specific decisions during matches.

This is surely not acceptable. Nor are the extra burdens being put on umpires by the captains' failure to maintain discipline. Ineffectual though the ICC may be in reaching decisions that stick in all countries, they can at least urge all countries playing Test series to agree beforehand two things: one, that, as used to happen, objections to umpires are kept strictly confidential; the other, that captains are constantly reminded that theirs should be the responsibility for stamping out bad behaviour and excessive appealing.

Bad Light. Nothing irritates the public more than the apparent readiness of umpires and batsmen to stop play for bad light, especially if the bowling is only medium-paced and the light no worse than that in which many club cricketers play most evenings. Light meters may have helped, but have not completely solved the problem.

I believe that, as an experiment, umpires should be instructed that there should be no stoppage for bad light for cricketing reasons; but only if players are being put in physical danger. Not everything is fair and equal in cricket, and if one side bats in poor light it is no more unfair than if it bats on a damp pitch; and not all batsmen have exactly the same eyesight in a good light.

Weak Teams Against Tourists. Even the Holt Trophy awards, the useful brainchild of Ted Dexter, had not wholly stopped the practice of fielding below-strength sides against the tourists, and with the end of the awards after the 1981 season, many county teams became so weak that they were swamped by the Pakistanis.

There is a case to be made for resting vital fast bowlers of suspect fitness, though less so now that many counties have gaps in their programmes in August. There is a case for trying out young players in a rather less competitive atmosphere. The TCCB ban, of course, put many leading players out of matches against the tourists in 1982. But fielding weak teams can be carried too far. It does no credit to English cricket, it is a discourtesy to the tourists, and it is not appreciated by England teams overseas when it happens to them.

Memorabilia of 1982. I have always admired 'Memorabilia' sections because, it seems, almost anything goes — from batsmen objecting to the colour of the ball to spectators chewing their umbrellas. The year 1982 had a modest share of qualifiers.

Glenn Turner became the 19th batsman to make 100 first-class hundreds in an innings of 311 not out against Warwickshire at Worcester in May, which was also his highest innings. A boost was given to University cricket by the selection for England during the summer of no fewer than five players from recent Oxford and Cambridge sides.

A stimulating change in world cricket was underlined by the feats in England of Kapil Dev and Imran Khan. With Ian Botham and Richard Hadlee, they give the lie to the theory that modern pressures, which take the blame for almost everything nowadays, are such that no one can be expected to be worth his Test place any longer as both batsman and bowler.

Then there was the singular performance of Mike Gatting in the

English season. He was the top batsman available for England in the first-class averages, the top English bowler in the bowling averages, the second most prolific catcher — and yet he failed to be selected for the tour of Australia, where in 1979-80 aged 22 he won the prize for the most successful player in Sydney Grade cricket, usually regarded as the strongest of its type in the world. Such apparently is the strength of current English cricket!

Michael Melford

Cricket's Deeper Crisis

Cricket and crisis of one sort or another are almost inseparable. In 1982 the first-class game in England is beset by a financial crisis. There is a crisis of manners and behaviour in Test cricket the world over, involving the pressuring of umpires, the stretching of the laws beyond their intention, and a general deterioration in plain honesty. The older generation may well ponder sadly on the days when the captain was king and the word cricket was synonymous with fair play. We sigh for the acceptance and implementation of a code of discipline at the top as the only hope of enforcing standards lower down.

The title of my piece, however, concerns not these aspects but something more profound, something that has been rooted in the game from its infancy. In the age-long conflict between bat and ball, the prime object of the batsman has been to score runs, of the bowler to get him out. Today, in England at least, and to a modified degree in other countries as well, the aim of the bowler in most of the cricket played up and down the country, from one-day internationals, through the limited-over county competitions, down to the humble village leagues, is less to take wickets than to contain.

In a nutshell, the man who in 10 overs takes 2 for 35 has probably been of less value to his side than he who in the same number of overs has allowed only 15 runs without dismissing anyone. The taking of wickets in limited-over cricket is not, of course, irrelevant, but it is secondary to the need to keep a brake on the scoring.

The difference is fundamental because, naturally, it has produced a chain reaction. The most important thing in limited-over bowling is accuracy, and a negative accuracy at that. This puts a premium on the dullest sort of bowler, the medium-pacer. The extremes, of speed at one end of the scale and genuine spin and flight at the other, both essentially attacking weapons, are at a discount. The techniques are more difficult to acquire, so why bother?

There is (to me) a particular abomination in the cultivation by bowlers around fast-medium of the ball slightly short of a length fired just outside the batsman's legs but not far enough to be called a wide. There is scarcely a stroke to be made against this coveted 'dot ball' — a phrase in modern dressing-room usage iterating the scorer's mark. It is the antithesis of attack, and, similarly, of entertainment.

The field-setting for containing cricket needs different aptitudes. The wicket-keeper usually acts as a glorified long-stop and first slip combined, so agility on his part counts for much more than the classical skills of the job standing up to the stumps. The stopping at middle range and the throwing from all distances is exhilarating to watch, but much of it is necessarily at the expense of close catching. Slips and short-legs are a luxury outside the normal plan.

The limited-over game, needless to say, has likewise adulterated the art of batting, especially in encouraging the off-glide with angled bat and the leg-side heave across the line of the ball: both fundamental sins against orthodox belief. Again, there are compensations. The modern county batsman needs to be more flexible in his approach than the average old-timer, who tended more to a settled style and tempo, too often a safe, unadventurous one.

It was this aspect which, twenty years ago, helped to determine my welcome to the one-day idea as introduced by Gillette. Incidentally, it is worth remembering that the first and best of the knock-out cups was originally contested over a maximum of 65 overs each, not 60. The more overs there are, naturally, the less artificial the contest. However, there followed the Benson and Hedges with 55 overs a side and the John Player League with only 40.

Yes, it will be rightly said, and it is these competitions, along with the major sponsorship of Test and one-day international matches, that have saved the counties (so far) from bankruptcy. The paradox is that the version of cricket that has preserved them economically has dealt such a heavy blow at the aesthetics of the game. What in its higher expressions has been an art-form rich in beauty and fascination to the watcher tends now to become a pedestrian exercise, wherein the development of the higher skills seems to be of less account than fitness, stamina, and general athleticism.

It would be foolish to say that the day of the great English cricketer is over when we have the star quality of an Ian Botham to admire. Yet is it not the writing on the wall when Bob Willis, at 33, is the only genuine fast bowler, when in his absence England can go into the field with four bowlers of medium-pace or a little more and one 'flat' off-spinner, and when the selectors can sit down to pick a team for Australia with scarcely half a dozen certainties around whom to build?

The ultimate in defensive thinking surely was reached when in the second of the Lord's Tests England from the first ball of Pakistan's second innings tried to prevent their making 76 runs in the available 18 overs — that is, a mere 4 an over — by splitting the field with not a man in a close catching position. Nor did the critics seem to think it noteworthy that England did not adjudge that the much likelier way of avoiding the probable was to bowl to take wickets, aiming just outside the off-stump with a strong off-side field.

How can the bowling side be induced to attack rather than to contain? There is no single ready answer. A premium on getting wickets in limited-over cricket would be difficult for the hard-pressed TCCB to concoct, but the experts, I suggest, should consider it. A statutory maximum run-up for a proportion of the overs due to be bowled — say 6 yards — would be hatefully artificial, but it might be salutary nevertheless. Cash bonuses for wickets taken? A second fielding circle well inside the current one? A reversion to uncovered county pitches? Ah, that at least is a positive note to end on. Hasten the day!

E.W. Swanton

Daily Telegraph 'Twin Hundreds'

With the inauguration of the Daily Telegraph Trophy for the first bowler to take a hundred wickets — with which, may I say, I am proud to be associated — the English season is now enlivened by two 'races', the new trophy complementing the traditional one for the scorer of the summer's fastest hundred, which was first put up by the late Sir Walter Lawrence back in 1934.

For upwards of four months, the leader for the Lawrence was Paul Todd of Notts, who at Fenner's on a brisk spring afternoon smote the aspiring University bowlers for a hundred in 75 minutes. Attention being thus focused upon him, Todd proceeded to Lord's, there to collect a 'king pair'. Other failures reduced Todd to the 2nd XI, for whom he promptly made a double hundred, and on his return reached three figures with fine panache against Yorkshire.

The Lawrence Trophy is designed to encourage the likes of Todd. Unluckily for him, though, at almost the last hurdle, there emerged Ian Botham, the like of no-one in modern cricket and mighty few in times past. On Friday, September 3, on his home patch at Taunton, Botham took charge of Somerset's daunting job of getting 309 in the fourth innings on a turning pitch, making 131 not out in 70 minutes to win the game with 80 minutes to spare.

As David Green — himself no mean hitter of the ball — told us next morning, Botham spent half an hour in wary reconnaissance for 17 runs before letting fly. Despite this, he reached his hundred in 52 minutes, and in his last 40 minutes scored 114, 'a rate of progress with few parallels in cricket history'. Few indeed! Of all the bygone heroes who come to mind, the name that sticks is that of G.L. Jessop. Only one point have I room for: neither of these powerful men were just sloggers. Jessop flaunted the orthodox, yes, but his hitting had a scientific basis. Of Botham, exactly the same is true: may he long continue to delight us!

If Botham is one worthy winner, so, emphatically, is Malcolm Marshall, Hampshire's 24-year-old fast bowler from the uniquely prolific nursery of Barbados. Jumping well ahead of the field in early August, he reached his 100th wicket on August 25, and finished with 134, the highest since the advent of the John Player League reduced the championship programme in 1969. Marshall gives his all, day in and day out, is cheerful about it, and does not, as I see him, seek to intimidate. These are three important attributes not in evidence by a long chalk with all fast bowlers. They have helped greatly to make Hampshire a happy and successful side, and they will make the presentation of the trophy a pleasure unalloyed.

It would have been good, naturally, if the winner had been an Englishman, either a fast bowler or a spinner. Alas, English bowling is in a trough from which may Providence deliver it. At least, however, there is one new face among the leaders, that of Nicholas Cook, Leicestershire's slow left-armer, whose 90 wickets are second in aggregate to Marshall's. Next year, perhaps, for him.   E.W. Swanton

Daily Telegraph Cricketers of the Year

A new Annual — so a selection of Cricketers of the Year in a novel form would seem appropriate. Hence our correspondents in the seven Test-playing countries and South Africa have been invited to nominate each his own man, the choice to be based on performance in the home domestic season and, of course, on Test matches both at home and away.

The result is intriguing, both individually and collectively. All-rounders take the palm without question in 1981/2: four men of sterling merit and performance, I.T. Botham (England), Kapil Dev (India), R.J. Hadlee (New Zealand), and Imran Khan (Pakistan). There is among the four of them a significant similarity, since three are fast bowlers and the fourth, Botham, above medium in pace. All are forceful batsmen, and on their day devastating hitters.

Next come two spinners, B. Yardley (Australia) and D.S. de Silva (Sri Lanka). Nothing in the selection is more extraordinary than that Australia, of all places, rate an off-spinner as their man of the season. They used scarcely to be reckoned there as bowlers at all. And how good that the high art of wrist-spin is represented by the youngest of the Test countries!

Our eight include only two batsmen, and neither of those a figure of world stature, H.A. Gomes (West Indies) and P.N. Kirsten (South Africa). Not an opener in sight!

To go into brief detail, Michael Carey felt he could not look beyond Ian Botham, while recognizing that he does not often repeat for Somerset his great deeds in Test cricket. Alan Shiell nominates Bruce Yardley, 'a tall, lean, happy-go-lucky character nicknamed "Roo"', on the incontrovertible evidence of 51 Test wickets in 9 matches at 22 apiece in the last Australian season. (What will be English off-spin's answer to that?)

Tony Cozier points to the fact of the likeable Larry Gomes' being far and away the most successful West Indian bat in last winter's Australian Tests (average 78), and notes his admirable captaincy of a weak Trinidad side in the Shell Shield. Kapil Dev's 'charismatic appeal' is mentioned by Rajan Bala, apart from his all-round record which, after his most recent nine Tests against England, has given him figures that no Indian in history has approached, let alone a 23-year-old. Terry Power settles for Richard Hadlee, citing his 59 wickets at 14 each for Canterbury.

Imran Khan, Pakistan's captain, was the only possible choice as his country's Cricketer of the Year. If there were several contenders for the Sri Lankan nomination, few will quibble with the choice of the greatly respected de Silva, who with his leg-breaks and googlies had 19 wickets in the first three Tests ever played by his country. Lastly, Darrell Thomson names Peter Kirsten, who, apart from being the best of the younger South African batsmen, in his first season as Western Province captain brought them the double of Currie Cup champions and Datsun Shield winners — an achievement indeed.

E.W. Swanton

England's winter tour 1981-82

England in India

England's tour of India last winter, in which they were beaten by 1-0 in the six-Test series, was frequently a daunting and frustrating affair, dogged by some of the slowest over-rates of all time, beset by doubts about umpiring, and with a demanding itinerary that even Marco Polo might have rejected.

From the moment that Keith Fletcher's team lost the first Test in Bombay on what was, by some measure, the most sporting pitch of the tour, it became an uphill struggle for parity in conditions that were mostly all against an outright result.

Even though the tour party's morale was not noticeably shaken by the early return home of Geoffrey Boycott through illness, the tempo of the matches was such that India, who had probably been underestimated by their opponents before the tour started, had little difficulty in holding on. They also came from behind to win the three-match one-day series.

When the tour ended, Fletcher was relieved of the England captaincy by the new panel of selectors. Although no official explanation was forthcoming, it was probably felt that they were seeking more positive leadership, with perhaps a greater attention to discipline.

Any Indian tour, however, has its own little local difficulties, and those present mostly felt that Fletcher handled his awkward, first venture reasonably well. The presence of an assistant-manager well versed in cricketing matters, such as the late Ken Barrington, might have enabled him to steer clear of some pitfalls.

Among these were an increased nervousness about Indian umpiring, which clearly communicated itself to the rest of the side and was a factor in losing the first Test. At times, too, the standard of behaviour both on and off the field left much to be desired. And while neither side exactly bustled through their overs, it was England who touched the nadir with nine in one hour at Madras.

Long before that, the shape of the series had been decided at the Wankhede Stadium, in Bombay, where a variable pitch resulted in a compelling match, albeit not for England, who were beaten well inside four days. Their second-innings total was only one higher than their lowest-ever against India.

There were various moments when England looked capable of winning this Test. On the second afternoon, however, they succumbed to a series of hairline decisions given against four successive sweep shots, an episode that provoked a subsequent complaint about the standard of umpiring.

This was just as quickly rejected by the Indian Board of Cricket Control because, they said, the English tour management did not provide any specific instances. But England's frustration probably had more to do with decisions that were not upheld. This was crucial in a game where the bowlers held sway.

There was no doubt that many England players had got it into their minds that justice was not being done. Right or wrong, this attitude clearly affected their concentration in the fourth innings, and a highly inadequate batting performance resulted.

The rumblings about umpiring were to continue, officially and otherwise, throughout the tour. Before the third Test, in Delhi, England lodged an official complaint that resulted in one of the umpires being replaced. It was probably also one reason for England reducing their chances of victory, on more than one occasion, by playing an extra batsman to insure against another Bombay-type disaster.

As it happened, no more pitches similar to the one at the Wankhede were encountered. And although there were occasional compulsive moments, the series droned on at a sluggish tempo. More than once the fifth day of a Test arrived without first innings being completed.

That was one problem. Boycott's malaise was another — although there was no healthier specimen in the English side at Delhi when, to his undisguised delight, he overtook Sir Garfield Sobers' record aggregate of runs in Tests.

Later, he complained of sickness and debility, and eventually the tour management decided to send him home. This decision followed quickly upon Boycott's appearance on a golf course in Calcutta at a time when a substitute was fielding in his place in the fourth Test. Moreover, he had actually asked two or three other England players, not involved in the match, if they cared to join him!

Though it was denied that the decision to allow him to return was in any way connected with the golf 'incident', it was clear to most observers that Boycott's appetite for the game appeared to have diminished after Delhi.

After Boycott's departure, the side applied themselves to trying to save the series. It was not to be. In Madras they might have embarrassed India — rather than been highly embarrassed themselves — if they had held their catches. But on that excellent pitch, anyway, it would have been hard to bowl them out twice.

In Kanpur, they found another mild pitch and, worse, weather that belonged in the middle of a season at home. So the series was lost. But many people wondered, validly, how England would have fared if they had been battle-hardened when confronted with that Bombay pitch, instead of meeting it in their first Test match.

First Test: Bombay, November 27, 28, 29, December 1.
India won by 138 runs.
India took what was to be a conclusive lead in the series with a day to spare, after a match that reverberated with controversy. The Indian Board of Cricket Control rejected England's complaints about the umpiring and, with less conviction, the pitch, on which the ball moved about at varying heights with an increasingly low bounce. Batting was thus never straightforward, and on the first day India were dismissed for 179, largely thanks to Botham, who bowled 28 overs unchanged, and Dilley.

When England reached 95, with Boycott and Tavaré together, they held hopes of the lead that was necessary in these conditions. But they lost their last 9 wickets for 71. India were then reduced to 157 for 8, but Kapil Dev ensured the fourth-innings target would be more substantial by making 45 from 31 balls. And on the fourth day England were bowled out in just over two hours by Kapil Dev and Madan Lal.

Second Test: Bangalore, December 9, 10, 12, 13, 14.
Drawn.
After a first day that produced only 181 runs from 81 overs, anything other than a draw was unlikely on a mild pitch. Indeed, the match was into the final day before first innings had been completed.

There was an incident on the second day when Fletcher, the captain, flicked the bails off with his bat after being adjudged caught behind. Although both he and tour manager Raman Subba Row made light of the incident, calling it a gesture of disappointment rather than dissent, Fletcher later sent a note of apology to the Indian Board of Control.

It took England two days to make 400, the nadir being one afternoon session when 46 runs were scored from 30 overs. Gavaskar then frustrated England by playing the longest innings ever by an Indian. It lasted 708 minutes, and he was on the field for all but four balls. It was also, unsurprisingly, the slowest Test century by an Indian.

Third Test: Delhi, December 23, 24, 26, 27, 28.
Drawn.
An official objection by England to one of the umpires, Mohammed Ghouse, resulted in his being replaced by Swaroop Kishen on the eve of what proved to be another largely desultory Test. On the first day, sundry interruptions and stoppages resulted in only 78 overs being bowled. England reached 190 for 1.

The only high point was when Boycott overtook Sir Garfield Sobers as the highest run-maker in Test cricket. When Boycott was dismissed on the second day, he had batted for 7 hours 20 minutes. It was not until the third morning that England were able to declare. Much depended on whether India could avoid the follow-on, which they did with seven wickets down. After that, everything was highly academic.

Fourth Test: Calcutta, January 1, 2, 3, 5, 6.
Drawn.
There were times when England held hopes of winning and squaring the series. But India were able to deny them comfortably enough in the end, aided by the loss of 70 minutes at the start of the last day while the umpires waited for morning mist to lift from the ground.

Official crowd figures were unobtainable, but it was thought that the match was watched by a world-record 400,000 spectators. They saw England recover from a modest start, thanks to Fletcher and Botham, and then bowl well enough to obtain a first-innings lead. India were eventually required to make 306 or, more probably, bat for six hours. This they did after Gavaskar had survived two early appeals for lbw, going on to make an exemplary unbeaten 83.

Fifth Test: Madras, January 13, 14, 15, 17, 18.
Drawn.
Sensing that this might be England's last opportunity of levelling the series, Fletcher put India in on a pitch that encouraged their fast bowlers. But England dropped two early catches on the first day, and suffered great humiliation on the second, when they did not take a wicket.

The combined efforts of Vengsarkar, who retired hurt after being struck on the helmet, Viswanath and Yashpal added 415 for India's third wicket. It was only the second time that England had failed to take a wicket in a full day's play (the first was at Bridgetown in 1960).

Viswanath's 222 was the highest score of his career and only 9 short of Vinoo Mankad's 231, the record Test innings for India. Surprisingly, perhaps, Gavaskar declared when 19 short of 500. Gooch, now partnered by Tavaré, played an innings full of exhilarating, powerful strokes, making 100 out of 126 from 139 balls, and the follow-on was later comfortably avoided.

Sixth Test: Kanpur, January 30, 31, February 1, 3, 4.
Drawn.
Notwithstanding an excellent innings of 142 by Ian Botham, England's remote hopes of bowling India out twice on the mildest of pitches, and saving the series, were frustrated by the weather. There was only one hour's intermittent play on the second day, and by the time England were in a position to declare, the third day was almost over.

When the last day began — after yet another delay for the weather — India had lost only three first-innings wickets. Willis took 3 wickets in 18 balls in a lively spell, and the latter stages were further enlivened by Kapil Dev.

In a controlled piece of aggression, he made 50 from 39 deliveries, and went on to reach 116 from only 98 balls, with 16 fours and 2 sixes.

India v England 1981-82 1st Test
India won by 138 runs
Played at Wankhede Stadium, Bombay, November 27, 28, 29, December 1
Toss: India. Umpires: K.B. Ramaswamy and Swaroop Kishen
Debuts: India — K. Srikkanth

India

*S.M. Gavaskar	c Taylor b Botham	55	c Taylor b Botham	14
K. Srikkanth	c Fletcher b Willis	0	run out	13
D.B. Vengsarkar	c Tavaré b Dilley	17	c Tavaré b Botham	5
G.R. Viswanath	c Boycott b Botham	8	c Taylor b Botham	37
S.M. Patil	lbw b Botham	17	lbw b Botham	13
K. Azad	c sub (M.W. Gatting) b Underwood	14	(7) lbw b Emburey	17
Kapil Dev	c Taylor b Botham	38	(8) lbw b Willis	46
†S.M.H. Kirmani	lbw b Dilley	12	(9) c Taylor b Emburey	0
Madan Lal	c Taylor b Dilley	0	(10) not out	17
R.J. Shastri	not out	3	(6) lbw b Dilley	33
D.R. Doshi	c Taylor b Dilley	0	b Botham	7
Extras	(lb 5, nb 10)	15	(b 8, lb 8, nb 9)	25
Total		**179**		**227**

England

G.A. Gooch	b Madan Lal	2	c Kirmani b Kapil Dev	1
G. Boycott	c Srikkanth b Azad	60	lbw b Madan Lal	3
C.J. Tavaré	c Shastri b Doshi	56	c Gavaskar b Kapil Dev	0
D.I. Gower	run out	5	lbw b Kapil Dev	20
*K.W.R. Fletcher	lbw b Doshi	15	lbw b Madan Lal	3
I.T. Botham	c Gavaskar b Doshi	7	c Azad b Kapil Dev	29
J.E. Emburey	lbw b Doshi	0	c Gavaskar b Madan Lal	1
G.R. Dilley	b Shastri	0	b Madan Lal	9
†R.W. Taylor	not out	9	b Madan Lal	1
D.L. Underwood	c Kirmani b Kapil Dev	8	not out	13
R.G.D. Willis	c Gavaskar b Doshi	1	c Kirmani b Kapil Dev	13
Extras	(b 1, lb 2)	3	(b 4, lb 3, nb 2)	9
Total		**166**		**102**

England	O	M	R	W	O	M	R	W
Willis	12	5	33	1	13	4	31	1
Botham	28	6	72	4	22.3	3	61	5
Dilley	13	1	47	4	18	5	61	1
Underwood	4	2	12	1	11	4	14	0
Emburey					13	2	35	2

India	O	M	R	W	O	M	R	W
Kapil Dev	22	10	29	1	13.2	0	70	5
Madan Lal	12	2	24	1	12	6	23	5
Doshi	29.1	12	39	5	1	1	0	0
Shastri	19	6	27	1				
Patil	3	0	9	0				
Azad	15	4	35	1				

Fall of Wickets

Wkt	I 1st	E 1st	I 2nd	E 2nd
1st	1	3	19	2
2nd	40	95	24	4
3rd	70	105	43	28
4th	104	131	72	29
5th	112	143	90	42
6th	164	146	138	50
7th	164	147	154	73
8th	168	147	157	74
9th	179	163	203	75
10th	179	166	227	102

*Captain   † Wicket-keeper

India v England 1981–82 2nd Test
Match drawn
Played at K.S.C.A. Stadium, Bangalore, December 9, 10, 12, 13, 14
Toss: England. Umpires: M.V. Gothoskar and P.R. Punjabi.
Debuts: Nil

England

G.A. Gooch	c Gavaskar b Shastri	58	lbw b Kapil Dev	40
G. Boycott	c Gavaskar b Kapil Dev	36	b Doshi	50
C.J. Tavaré	lbw b Madan Lal	22	c Patil b Shastri	31
D.I. Gower	lbw b Shastri	82	not out	34
J.K. Lever	lbw b Kapil Dev	1		
*K.W.R. Fletcher	c Kirmani b Shastri	25	(5) not out	12
I.T. Botham	c Madan Lal b Doshi	55		
M.W. Gatting	lbw b Kapil Dev	29		
G.R. Dilley	c Gavaskar b Shastri	52		
†R.W. Taylor	c Kapil Dev b Doshi	33		
D.L. Underwood	not out	2		
Extras	(lb 2, nb 3)	5	(lb 6, nb 1)	7
Total		**400**	(3 wickets declared)	**174**

India

*S.M. Gavaskar	c and b Underwood	172
K. Srikkanth	c Gooch b Botham	65
D.B. Vengsarkar	c Taylor b Lever	43
G.R. Viswanath	lbw b Lever	3
R.J. Shastri	lbw b Lever	1
S.M. Patil	lbw b Lever	17
K. Azad	c Fletcher b Underwood	24
Kapil Dev	c Taylor b Lever	59
†S.M.H. Kirmani	lbw b Botham	9
Madan Lal	not out	7
D.R. Doshi	c Boycott b Underwood	0
Extras	(b 2, lb 15, w 3, nb 8)	28
Total		**428**

India	O	M	R	W	O	M	R	W
Kapil Dev	40	3	136	3	12	2	49	1
Madan Lal	24	7	46	1	4	2	14	0
Doshi	39	15	83	2	21	8	37	1
Azad	12	1	47	0	12	3	36	0
Shastri	43	14	83	4	20	7	31	1

England	O	M	R	W
Botham	47	9	137	2
Dilley	24	4	75	0
Lever	36	9	100	5
Underwood	43	21	88	3

Fall of Wickets

Wkt	E 1st	L 1st	E 2nd
1st	88	102	59
2nd	96	195	105
3rd	180	208	152
4th	181	214	—
5th	223	242	—
6th	230	284	—
7th	278	376	—
8th	324	412	—
9th	393	428	—
10th	400	428	—

*Captain † Wicket-keeper

India v England 1981-82 3rd Test
Match drawn
Played at Feroz Shah Kotla, Delhi, December 23, 24, 26, 27, 28
Toss: England. Umpires: S.N. Hanumantha Rao and Swaroop Kishen
Debuts: Nil

England

G.A. Gooch	c Kapil Dev b Doshi	71	not out	20
G. Boycott	c Madan Lal b Doshi	105	not out	34
C.J. Tavaré	b Madan Lal	149		
D.I. Gower	lbw b Madan Lal	0		
*K.W.R. Fletcher	b Patil	51		
I.T. Botham	c Azad b Madan Lal	66		
M.W. Gatting	b Madan Lal	5		
†R.W. Taylor	lbw b Madan Lal	0		
J.K. Lever	b Kapil Dev	2		
D.L. Underwood	not out	2		
R.G.D. Willis	did not bat			
Extras	(lb 15, nb 10)	25	(b 9, nb 5)	14
Total	(9 wickets declared)	**476**	(0 wickets declared)	**68**

India

*S.M. Gavaskar	c Taylor b Lever	46
K. Srikkanth	b Willis	6
D.B. Vengsarkar	c Fletcher b Underwood	8
G.R. Viswanath	b Botham	107
S.M. Patil	b Willis	31
K. Azad	st Taylor b Underwood	16
Kapil Dev	c Gooch b Botham	16
R.J. Shastri	lbw b Gooch	93
†S.M.H. Kirmani	lbw b Lever	67
Madan Lal	b Gooch	44
D.R. Doshi	not out	0
Extras	(b 20, lb 8, w 4, nb 21)	53
Total		**487**

India	O	M	R	W	O	M	R	W
Kapil Dev	40.4	5	126	1	4	1	18	0
Madan Lal	32	4	85	5	3	1	4	0
Doshi	40	15	68	2				
Shastri	27	3	109	0				
Azad	9	2	35	0				
Patil	8	1	28	1	3	1	10	0
Srikkanth					6	1	10	0
Gavaskar					3	0	12	0

England

	O	M	R	W
Willis	26	3	99	2
Lever	37	7	104	2
Underwood	48	18	97	2
Botham	41	6	122	2
Gooch	8.1	1	12	2

Fall of Wickets

	E	I	E
Wkt	1st	1st	2nd
1st	132	11	—
2nd	248	41	—
3rd	248	89	—
4th	368	174	—
5th	459	213	—
6th	465	237	—
7th	465	254	—
8th	474	382	—
9th	476	486	—
10th	—	487	—

* Captain   † Wicket-keeper

D.B. Vengsarkar kept wicket during England's second innings.

India v England 1981-82 4th Test
Match drawn
Played at Eden Gardens, Calcutta, January 1, 2, 3, 5, 6
Toss: England. Umpires: M.V. Gothoskar and Swaroop Kishen
Debuts: Nil

England

G.A. Gooch	*c* Viswanath *b* Doshi	47	*b* Doshi	63
G. Boycott	*c* Kirmani *b* Kapil Dev	18	*lbw b* Madan Lal	6
C.J. Tavaré	*c* Kirmani *b* Kapil Dev	7	*run out*	25
D.I. Gower	*c* Kirmani *b* Shastri	11	*run out*	74
*K.W.R. Fletcher	*lbw b* Madan Lal	69	(6) *not out*	60
I.T. Botham	*c* Gavaskar *b* Kapil Dev	58	(5) *c* Yadav *b* Doshi	31
D.L. Underwood	*c* Patil *b* Kapil Dev	13		
M.W. Gatting	*c* Kirmani *b* Kapil Dev	0	(7) *not out*	2
J.E. Emburey	*lbw b* Kapil Dev	1		
†R.W. Taylor	*c* Vengsarkar *b* Doshi	6		
R.G.D. Willis	*not out*	11		
Extra	(*lb* 3, *nb* 4)	7	(*lb* 4)	4
Total		**248**	(5 wickets declared)	**265**

India

*S.M. Gavaskar	*b* Underwood	42	*not out*	83
K. Srikkanth	*b* Underwood	10	*c* Botham *b* Emburey	25
D.B. Vengsarkar	*c* Taylor *b* Botham	70	*c* Tavaré *b* Fletcher	32
G.R. Viswanath	*c* and *b* Emburey	15	*c* Gooch *b* Emburey	0
S.M. Patil	*c* Fletcher *b* Emburey	0	*not out*	17
Kapil Dev	*c* Tavaré *b* Underwood	22		
R.J. Shastri	*run out*	8		
†S.M.H. Kirmani	*b* Botham	10		
Madan Lal	*c* Gooch *b* Willis	1		
N.S. Yadav	*c* Taylor *b* Willis	5		
D.R. Doshi	*not out*	7		
Extras	(*b* 2, *lb* 4, *w* 1, *nb* 11)	18	(*lb* 2, *nb* 11)	13
Total		**208**	(3 wickets)	**170**

India	O	M	R	W	O	M	R	W
Kapil Dev	31	6	91	6	21	3	81	0
Madan Lal	20	4	58	1	19	3	58	1
Doshi	19.2	8	28	2	27	5	63	2
Yadav	17	7	42	0	3	0	11	0
Shastri	21	10	22	1	17	4	35	0
Patil					3	0	13	0

England	O	M	R	W	O	M	R	W
Willis	14	3	28	2	6	0	21	0
Botham	27	8	63	2	11	3	26	0
Underwood	29	13	45	3	31	18	38	0
Emburey	24	11	44	2	30	11	62	2
Gooch	6	1	10	0	2	0	4	0
Fletcher					3	1	6	1

Fall of Wickets

Wkt	E 1st	I 1st	E 2nd	I 2nd
1st	25	33	24	48
2nd	39	83	88	117
3rd	68	117	107	120
4th	95	117	154	—
5th	188	143	259	—
6th	216	180	—	—
7th	218	184	—	—
8th	224	187	—	—
9th	230	196	—	—
10th	248	208	—	—

* Captain   † Wicket-keeper

India v England 1981–82 5th Test
Match drawn
Played at Chidambaram Stadium, Chepauk, Madras, January 13, 14, 15, 17, 18
Toss: England. Umpires: B. Ganguli and S.N. Hanumantha Rao
Debuts: India — A. Malhotra, P. Roy

India

*S.M. Gavaskar	c Taylor b Willis	25		c Botham b Willis	11
P. Roy	c Taylor b Dilley	6		not out	60
D.B. Vengsarkar	retired hurt	71			
G.R. Viswanath	b Willis	222			
Yashpal Sharma	c Tavaré b Botham	140	(4)	c Botham b Underwood	25
Kapil Dev	not out	6	(5)	not out	15
A. Malhotra			(3)	run out	31
†S.M.H. Kirmani					
R.J. Shastri	did not bat				
Madan Lal					
D.R. Doshi					
Extras	(lb 1, w 1, nb 9)	11		(b 12, lb 1, nb 5)	18
Total	(4 wickets declared)	**481**		(3 wickets declared)	**160**

India	O	M	R	W
Kapil Dev	25.5	7	88	3
Madan Lal	9	1	41	0
Shastri	63	23	104	3
Doshi	57	31	69	4
Gavaskar	1	0	2	0

England

G.A. Gooch	c and b Shastri	127
C.J. Tavaré	c Gavaskar b Doshi	35
*K.W.R. Fletcher	b Doshi	3
D.I. Gower	lbw b Shastri	64
I.T. Botham	c Kirmani b Shastri	52
M.W. Gatting	c Viswanath b Doshi	0
G.R. Dilley	c and b Kapil Dev	8
†R.W. Taylor	b Doshi	8
D.L. Underwood	c Kirmani b Kapil Dev	0
P.J.W. Allott	c Roy b Kapil Dev	6
R.G.D. Willis	not out	1
Extras	(b 1, lb 11, nb 12)	24
Total		**328**

* Captain † Wicket-keeper

England	O	M	R	W	O	M	R	W
Willis	28.1	7	79	2	7	2	15	1
Botham	31	10	83	1	8	1	29	0
Dilley	31	4	87	1	5	1	13	0
Allott	31	4	135	0				
Underwood	22	7	59	0	15	8	30	1
Gooch	9	2	27	0	8	2	24	0
Fletcher					1	0	9	0
Taylor					2	0	6	0
Tavare					2	0	11	0
Gower					1	0	1	0
Gatting					1	0	4	0

Fall of Wickets

Wkt	I 1st	E 1st	I 2nd
1st	19	155	19
2nd	51	164	69
3rd	466	195	122
4th	481	279	—
5th	—	283	—
6th	—	307	—
7th	—	307	—
8th	—	311	—
9th	—	320	—
10th	—	328	—

D.B. Vengsarkar retired hurt at 150–2. S.M.H. Kirmani kept wicket without conceding a bye since the 1st Test at Bombay, during which 1964 runs were scored. G.A. Gooch kept wicket during the last 12 overs of India's second innings.

India v England 1981–82 6th Test
Match drawn
Played at Green Park, Kanpur, January 30, 31, February 1, 3, 4
Toss: England. Umpires D.N. Dotiwalla and M.V. Gothoskar
Debuts: Nil

England

G.A. Gooch	*b* Doshi	58
C.J. Tavaré	*b* Doshi	24
*K.W.R. Fletcher	*b* Kapil Dev	14
D.I. Gower	*lbw b* Kapil Dev	85
I.T. Botham	*st* Kirmani *b* Doshi	142
M.W. Gatting	*c* Madan Lal *b* Doshi	32
G.R. Dilley	*lbw b* Shastri	1
†R.W. Taylor	*b* Shastri	0
J.E. Emburey	*run out*	2
D.L. Underwood	*not out*	0
R.G.D. Willis	*did not bat*	
Extras	(*b* 2, *lb* 5, *w* 6, *nb* 7)	20
Total	(9 wickets declared)	**378**

India

*S.M. Gavaskar	run out	52
P. Roy	*b* Botham	5
D.B. Vengsarkar	*b* Fletcher *b* Dilley	46
G.R. Viswanath	*c* Gower *b* Willis	74
Yashpal Sharma	*not out*	55
A. Malhotra	*lbw b* Willis	0
R.J. Shastri	*c* Taylor *b* Willis	2
Kapil Dev	*c* Dilley *b* Gower	116
†S.M.H. Kirmani	*not out*	1
Madan Lal	⎱ *did not bat*	
D.R. Doshi	⎰	
Extras	(*b* 1, *lb* 7, *w* 2, *nb* 16)	26
Total	(7 wickets declared)	**377**

India	O	M	R	W
Kapil Dev	34	3	147	2
Madan Lal	24	4	79	0
Doshi	34.2	8	81	4
Shastri	23	6	51	2

England	O	M	R	W
Willis	23	5	75	3
Botham	25	6	67	1
Dilley	14	2	67	1
Underwood	25	8	55	0
Emburey	32	7	81	0
Fletcher	2	1	5	0
Gower	1	0	1	1

Fall of Wickets

	E	I
Wkt	1st	1st
1st	82	12
2nd	89	79
3rd	121	166
4th	248	197
5th	349	197
6th	354	207
7th	354	376
8th	360	—
9th	378	—
10th	—	—

*Captain   † Wicket-keeper

Test Match Averages — India v England 1981-82

Ind.—Batting/Fielding	M	I	NO	Runs	HS	Avge	100	50	Ct	St
Yashpal Sharma	2	3	1	220	140	110.00	1	1	—	—
S.M. Gavaskar	6	9	1	500	172	62.50	1	3	9	—
G.R. Viswanath	6	8	0	466	222	58.25	2	1	2	—
Kapil Dev	6	8	2	318	116	53.00	1	1	3	—
D.B. Vengsarkar	6	8	1	292	71*	41.71	—	2	1	—
P. Roy	2	3	1	71	60*	35.50	—	1	1	—
R.J. Shastri	6	6	1	140	93	28.00	—	1	2	—
Madan Lal	6	5	2	69	44	23.00	—	—	3	—
K. Srikkanth	4	6	0	119	65	19.83	—	1	1	—
S.M.H. Kirmani	6	6	1	99	67	19.80	—	1	10	1
S.M. Patil	4	6	1	95	31	19.00	—	—	2	—
K. Azad	3	4	0	71	24	17.75	—	—	2	—
A. Malhotra	2	2	0	31	31	15.50	—	—	—	—
D.R. Doshi	6	5	2	14	7*	4.66	—	—	—	—

Played in one Test: N.S. Yadav 5 (1 ct).

India — Bowling	O	M	R	W	Avge	BB	5w/I	10w/M
Doshi	267.5	103	468	22	21.27	5-39	1	—
Madan Lal	159	34	432	14	30.85	5-23	2	—
Kapil Dev	243.5	40	835	22	37.95	6-91	2	—
Shastri	233	73	462	12	38.50	4-83	—	—

Also bowled: Azad 48-10-153-1; Gavaskar 4-0-14-0; Patil 17-2-60-1; Srikkanth 6-1-10-0; Yadav 20-7-53-0.

Eng.—Batting/Fielding	M	I	NO	Runs	HS	Avge	100	50	Ct	St
I.T. Botham	6	8	0	440	142	55.00	1	4	3	—
G.A. Gooch	6	10	1	487	127	54.11	1	4	4	—
D.I. Gower	6	9	1	375	85	46.87	—	4	1	—
G. Boycott	4	8	1	312	105	44.57	1	2	2	—
C.J. Tavaré	6	9	0	349	149	38.77	1	1	5	—
K.W.R. Fletcher	6	9	2	252	69	36.00	—	3	5	—
G.R. Dilley	4	5	0	70	52	14.00	—	1	1	—
M.W. Gatting	5	6	1	68	32	13.60	—	—	—	—
R.G.D. Willis	5	4	2	26	13	13.00	—	—	—	—
D.L. Underwood	6	7	4	38	13*	12.66	—	—	1	—
R.W. Taylor	6	7	1	57	33	9.50	—	—	15	1
J.K. Lever	2	2	0	3	2	1.50	—	—	—	—
J.E. Emburey	3	4	0	4	2	1.00	—	—	1	—

Played in one Test: P.J.W. Allott 6.

England — Bowling	O	M	R	W	Avge	BB	5w/I	10w/M
Lever	73	16	204	7	29.14	5-100	1	—
Willis	129.1	29	381	12	31.75	3-75	—	—
Emburey	99	31	222	6	37.00	2-35	—	—
Botham	240.3	52	660	17	38.82	5-61	1	—
Underwood	228	99	438	10	43.80	3-45	—	—
Dilley	105	17	350	7	50.00	4-47	—	—

Also bowled: Allott 31-4-135-0; Fletcher 6-2-20-1; Gatting 1-0-4-0; Gooch 33.1-6-77-2; Gower 2-0-2-1; Tavaré 2-0-11-0; Taylor 2-0-6-0.

* Not out.

First one-day international: Ahmedabad, November 25.
England won by 5 wickets.
Before a crowd of 40,000, England won the opening one-day international with 13 deliveries in hand, thanks largely to an intelligent innings by Gatting. England had to come to terms with playing conditions that were new to them: all but two fielders inside 30-yard circles and at least two in 'catching positions' for the first 15 overs. With a 9.30 a.m. start there was also a 3½-hour morning session, in the hope of bowling the maximum 50 overs. The latter, predictably, was not achieved, but England had few problems with the former, putting India in on a damp, two-paced pitch that would have demanded attacking fields in any case.

On it, India made uneven progress against good bowling by Willis, Botham, and Underwood. England, in turn, had more than one early mishap before Gatting and Fletcher doubled the total together, leaving Botham to finish the match with two successive sixes.

Second one-day international: Jullundur, December 20.
India won by 6 wickets.
After seven years and five attempts, India at last registered a one-day triumph over England, winning with three balls to spare, thanks to Vengsarkar who made an unbeaten 88 with a brilliance that mostly eluded him in the Test series.

Morning mist delayed play for an hour, reducing the match to a 36-over affair. England owed much to a partnership of 110 in 17 overs between Gower and Gatting, which dug them out of trouble after they had been put in on a pitch that resembled baked, rolled mud.

The high spot of this was Gatting's 26 in an over from Shastri. It included four sixes. England's total, however, rarely appeared adequate, and Vengsarkar and Yashpal saw India to their historic win.

Third one-day international: Cuttack, January 27.
India won by 5 wickets.
India, needing 231 at 5 an over, made them with much enterprise and vigour to win the third and most stirring one-day international with 4 overs in hand. Thus they won the series by 2–1, their first success in limited-over cricket.

Ironically, from England's viewpoint, they produced their most dashing batting of the tour. Gower, Botham, and especially Fletcher played their parts in a formidable revival after being put in on a damp pitch. At one stage in Fletcher's brilliant innings, he progressed from 11 to 50 in less than 3 overs, and he and Botham added 80 in only 10.

India, however, took up the challenge with new-found confidence in their one-day expertise, and Gavaskar, dropped at 6, and Patil paved the way for victory against increasingly ragged bowling.

India v England 1st One-Day International
England won by 5 wickets
Played at Sardar Patel Stadium, Ahmedabad, November 25
Toss: England. Umpires: M.V. Gothoskar and S.N. Hanumantha Rao

India

*S.M. Gavaskar	c Gooch b Willis	0
K. Srikkanth	b Botham	0
D.B. Vengsarkar	c and b Underwood	46
G.R. Viswanath	c Cook b Gooch	8
K. Azad	b Botham	30
Madan Lal	c Lever b Underwood	6
†S.M.H. Kirmani	not out	18
R.J. Shastri	run out	19
R.M. Binny	not out	2
Randhir Singh	did not bat	
D.R. Doshi		
Extras	(b 4, lb 13, w 7, nb 3)	27
Total	(46 overs; 210 minutes)	**156-7**

England

G.A. Gooch	c Kirmani b Binny	23
G. Boycott	lbw b Madan Lal	5
G. Cook	c Viswanath b Binny	13
D.I. Gower	c and b Binny	8
*K.W.R. Fletcher	b Doshi	26
M.W. Gatting	not out	47
I.T. Botham	not out	25
†C.J. Richards		
J.K. Lever	did not bat	
D.L. Underwood		
R.G.D. Willis		
Extras	(lb 7, w 2, nb 4)	13
Total	(43.5 overs; 193 minutes)	**160-5**

England	O	M	R	W
Willis	9	3	17	1
Botham	10	4	20	2
Lever	10	0	46	3
Gooch	7	0	28	1
Underwood	10	3	18	2

India	O	M	R	W
Madan Lal	10	2	30	1
Randhir	6	0	18	0
Binny	7.5	3	35	3
Shastri	10	1	24	0
Doshi	10	1	40	1

Fall of Wickets

Wkt	I	E
1st	2	15
2nd	8	43
3rd	39	46
4th	91	61
5th	113	126
6th	119	—
7th	154	—
8th	—	—
9th	—	—
10th	—	—

* Captain   † Wicket-keeper

India v England 2nd One-Day International
India won by 6 wickets
Played at Burlton Park, Jullundur, December 20
Toss: India. Umpires: J.D. Ghosh and Swaroop Kishen

England

G.A. Gooch	*b* Madan Lal	12
G. Boycott	*run out*	6
I.T. Botham	*lbw b* Madan Lal	5
*K.W.R. Fletcher	*c* Azad *b* Patil	5
D.I. Gower	*run out*	53
M.W. Gatting	*not out*	71
G. Cook	*b* Kapil Dev	1
†C.J. Richards	*lbw b* Kapil Dev	0
J.K. Lever		
D.L. Underwood	*did not bat*	
R.G.D. Willis		
Extras	(*b* 2, *lb* 4, *w* 1, *nb* 1)	8
Total	(36 overs; 173 minutes)	**161-7**

India

K. Srikkanth	*lbw b* Botham	17
D.B. Vengsarkar	*not out*	88
Kirti Azad	*c* Gower *b* Gooch	14
S.M. Patil	*b* Gooch	3
Kapil Dev	*c* Willis *b* Underwood	6
Yashpal Sharma	*not out*	28
*S.M. Gavaskar		
S.V. Nayak		
Madan Lal	*did not bat*	
†S.M.H. Kirmani		
R.J. Shastri		
Extras	(*b* 3, *lb* 3, *nb* 2)	8
Total	(35.3 overs; 188 minutes)	**164-4**

India	O	M	R	W
Kapil Dev	8	1	26	2
Madan Lal	7	0	33	2
Nayak	7	2	25	0
Patil	7	0	16	1
Shastri	7	0	53	0

England	O	M	R	W
Willis	7.3	2	41	0
Lever	7	0	31	0
Gooch	7	0	25	2
Botham	7	0	33	1
Underwood	7	1	26	1

Fall of Wickets

Wkt	E	I
1st	18	41
2nd	22	69
3rd	25	78
4th	48	89
5th	158	—
6th	161	—
7th	161	—
8th	—	—
9th	—	—
10th	—	—

*Captain † Wicket-keeper

India v England 3rd One-Day International
India won by 5 wickets
Played at Barabati Stadium, Cuttack, January 27
Toss: India. Umpires: P.R. Punjabi and K.B. Ramaswamy

England

G.A. Gooch	c Arun Lal b Madan Lal	3
G. Cook	c Nayak b Patil	30
C.J. Tavaré	c Madan Lal b Shastri	11
D.I. Gower	c and b Patil	42
I.T. Botham	b Nayak	52
*K.W.R. Fletcher	b Madan Lal	69
M.W. Gatting	not out	8
†R.W. Taylor	not out	2
D.L. Underwood		
J.K. Lever	did not bat	
R.G.D. Willis		
Extras	(lb 9, w 1, nb 3)	13
Total	(46 overs; 210 minutes)	**230-6**

India

*S.M. Gavaskar	st Taylor b Underwood	71
Arun Lal	c Gooch b Botham	9
D.B. Vengsarkar	c Willis b Gooch	13
S.M. Patil	b Underwood	64
Yashpal Sharma	not out	34
Kapil Dev	c Gooch b Underwood	0
A. Malhotra	not out	28
†S.M.H. Kirmani		
Madan Lal	did not bat	
R.J. Shastri		
S.V. Nayak		
Extras	(lb 7, w 2, nb 3)	12
Total	(42 overs; 201 minutes)	**231-5**

India	O	M	R	W
Kapil Dev	8	3	23	0
Madan Lal	8	0	56	2
Nayak	10	1	51	1
Shastri	10	1	34	1
Patil	10	0	53	2

England	O	M	R	W
Willis	6	1	29	0
Botham	8	0	48	1
Lever	10	0	55	0
Gooch	8	0	39	1
Underwood	10	0	48	3

Fall of Wickets

Wkt	I	E
1st	13	16
2nd	33	59
3rd	86	135
4th	101	184
5th	181	184
6th	228	—
7th	—	—
8th	—	—
9th	—	—
10th	—	—

* Captain † Wicket-keeper

England in Sri Lanka

The England party left India for Sri Lanka having almost forgotten what winning was like. They had, indeed, not beaten anyone since November 25. In Colombo, the one-day series against Sri Lanka was halved. But the inaugural Test, an event the entire island had been awaiting for years, at last gave Fletcher victory in what, ironically, was to be his final Test match.

Inaugural Test: Colombo, February 17, 18, 20, 21.
England won by 7 wickets.
England triumphed in Sri Lanka's inaugural Test match, though not before the newest full members of the International Cricket Conference had given an excellent account of themselves. Even before the start, they endeared themselves to many people by choosing not only a leg-spinner, D.S. de Silva, but a 17-year-old student, Arjuna Ranatunga.

There was more than one moment when the game looked like slipping from England's grasp. Yet in the end, after Emburey had induced a Sri Lankan collapse on the fourth morning, they made the 171 they needed with more comfort than probably expected against three spinners who did not make the most of the conditions.

The crowds for this historic match at the Saravanamuttu Stadium were smaller than expected, perhaps because it followed close on the heels of the two one-day internationals. They saw Sri Lanka enjoy their share of supremacy, notably on the first day, when they reduced England to 40 for 3 after being bowled out themselves for 218 on a pitch already responsive to spin.

This would have been 44 for 4 if Fletcher had been caught soon afterwards. Using his expertise against the turning ball, the captain avoided further mishaps, and Gower's 89, an innings of judicious discipline and well-timed strokes, ensured a slender first-innings lead.

By the end of the third day, however, Sri Lanka were 147 ahead with 7 wickets standing after a splendid 77 by Roy Dias. With England uneasy about needing to make many more than 200 in the fourth innings, a tense finish seemed likely.

Next morning, however, Emburey found more turn and bounce than previously and, helped by good close catching, took 5 wickets for 5 runs in 33 deliveries. He emerged with 6 for 33, his best performance in Test cricket. Sri Lanka, betrayed perhaps by their lack of experience, lost their last 7 wickets for only 8 runs.

England were thus left with a less demanding task and with time enough to spare. Even so, there might have been complications against more accurate spin bowling. But Tavaré, playing with great fluency and sharing in partnerships of 81 and 83 with Gooch and Gower, enabled England to win with more than a day to spare.

Sri Lanka v England 1981–82 only Test
England won by 7 wickets
Played at the Saravanamuttu Stadium, Colombo, February 17, 18, 20, 21
Toss: Sri Lanka. Umpires: H.C. Felsinger and K.T. Francis
Debuts: England — G. Cook; Sri Lanka — all

Sri Lanka

*B. Warnapura	c Gower b Willis	2	c Gooch b Emburey	38
S. Wettimuny	c Taylor b Botham	6	b Willis	9
R.L. Dias	c Cook b Willis	0	c Taylor b Underwood	77
L.R.D. Mendis	lbw b Botham	17	c Willis b Emburey	27
R.S. Madugalle	c Gower b Underwood	65	c Cook b Emburey	3
A. Ranatunga	b Underwood	54	c Fletcher b Emburey	2
D.S. de Silva	c Gower b Underwood	3	c Fletcher b Underwood	1
A.L.F. De Mel	c Fletcher b Underwood	19	c Gower b Emburey	2
L.W. Kaluperuma	c Cook b Underwood	1	c Taylor b Emburey	0
†H.M. Goonatillake	not out	22	not out	2
G.R.A. de Silva	c Emburey b Botham	12	c Willis b Underwood	0
Extras	(b 2, lb 4, w 2, nb 9)	17	(lb 6, nb 8)	14
Total		**218**		**175**

England

G.A. Gooch	lbw b De Mel	22	b G.R.A. de Silva	31
G. Cook	c Kaluperuma b De Mel	11	lbw b De Mel	0
C.J. Tavaré	b De Mel	0	st Goonatillake b G.R.A. de Silva	85
D.I. Gower	c Goonatillake b D.S. de Silva	89	not out	42
*K.W.R. Fletcher	c Warnapura b G.R.A. de Silva	45	not out	0
I.T. Botham	b De Mel	13		
†R.W. Taylor	not out	31		
J.E. Emburey	lbw b G.R.A. de Silva	0		
P.J.W. Allott	c Kaluperuma b D.S. de Silva	3		
D.L. Underwood	c Mendis b D.S. de Silva	0		
R.G.D. Willis	run out	0		
Extras	(lb 3, nb 6)	9	(b 7, lb 5, nb 1)	13
Total		**223**	(3 wickets)	**171**

England	O	M	R	W	O	M	R	W
Willis	19	7	46	2	9	3	24	1
Botham	12.5	1	28	3	12	1	37	0
Allott	13	4	44	0				
Emburey	19	3	55	0	25	9	33	6
Underwood	18	6	28	5	37.5	15	67	3

Sri Lanka	O	M	R	W	O	M	R	W
De Mel	17	2	70	4	13.1	4	33	1
Warnapura	3	1	9	0	1	0	1	0
D.S. de Silva	27.5	11	54	3	15	5	38	0
Kaluperuma	9	1	29	0	12	3	40	0
G.R.A. de Silva	30	12	52	2	17	6	46	2

Fall of Wickets

Wkt	SL 1st	E 1st	SL 2nd	E 2nd
1st	9	34	30	3
2nd	11	34	113	84
3rd	29	40	140	167
4th	34	120	167	—
5th	133	151	169	—
6th	149	200	170	—
7th	181	207	172	—
8th	183	216	173	—
9th	190	216	174	—
10th	218	223	175	—

*Captain † Wicket-keeper

First one-day international: Colombo, February 13.
England won by 5 runs.
England were run much closer than seemed likely in the opening one-day international at the Sinhalese Sports Club ground, largely because they failed to capitalize on a good start after being put in on a pitch that was never entirely straightforward.

At one stage, with Botham making 60 from 52 balls, they seemed capable of putting the game out of their opponents' reach. But starting with Fletcher, their last 7 wickets went down in only 24 balls while 20 runs were scored.

Sri Lanka, however, also batted unevenly. Although there was a threat when Madugalle and Ranasinghe added 68 in 8 overs, England latterly bowled too accurately for lower-order batsmen required to take risks, and the task of making 21 from the last 2 overs proved beyond them.

Second one-day international: Colombo, February 14.
Sri Lanka won by 3 runs.
Against all expectations, England were the losers in another close finish, notably after a remarkable piece of mismanagement, even by one-day standards, that resulted in 4 run-outs in 9 balls during a hectic finish.

Sri Lanka were put in on a variable pitch. With Wettimuny playing the role of anchorman and the 17-year-old Ranatunga playing with remarkable panache, they overcame early problems and ensured that England had plenty to do.

It seemed straightforward when Gooch and Cook put on 109 in 26 overs. And even though wickets then fell cheaply, there appeared only one winner with 14 required from 2 overs and the experienced Fletcher and Gatting together. Fletcher then refused Gatting's call, precipitating a chapter of accidents, and to the delight of a crowd of 20,000 Sri Lanka pulled off an improbable victory.

Sri Lanka v England 1st One-Day International
England won by 5 runs
Played at Sinhalese Sports Club Ground, Colombo, February 13
Toss: Sri Lanka. Umpires: E.C.B. Anthony and H.C. Felsinger

England

G.A. Gooch	*b* G.R.A. de Silva	64
G. Cook	*c* G.R.A. de Silva *b* Kaluperuma	28
D.I. Gower	*run out*	15
I.T. Botham	*b* De Mel	60
*K.W.R. Fletcher	*b* D.S. de Silva	12
M.W. Gatting	*c* Mendis *b* De Mel	3
†C.J. Richards	*b* G.R.A. de Silva	3
J.E. Emburey	*lbw b* De Mel	0
P.J.W. Allott	*run out*	0
D.L. Underwood	*b* De Mel	4
R.G.D. Willis	*not out*	2
Extras	(*b* 6, *lb* 11, *w* 2, *nb* 1)	20
Total	(44.4 overs, 200 minutes)	**211**

Sri Lanka

*B. Warnapura	*c* Gower *b* Allott	10
S. Wettimuny	*c* Richards *b* Allott	46
†R.S.A. Jayasekera	*c* Gooch *b* Willis	17
R.L. Dias	*c and b* Underwood	4
L.R.D. Mendis	*c* Gower *b* Underwood	2
R.S. Madugalle	*b* Willis	22
A.N. Ranasinghe	*c* Cook *b* Botham	51
D.S. de Silva	*b* Botham	8
A.L.F. de Mel	*not out*	13
L.W. Kaluperuma	*not out*	14
G.R.A. de Silva	*did not bat*	—
Extras	(*b* 5, *lb* 10, *w* 2, *nb* 2)	19
Total	(45 overs, 225 minutes)	**206-8**

Sri Lanka	O	M	R	W
De Mel	8.4	1	34	4
Ranasinghe	8	2	20	0
Kaluperuma	7	0	35	1
D.S. de Silva	9	0	31	1
G.R.A. de Silva	9	0	56	2
Wettimuny	3	0	15	0

England	O	M	R	W
Willis	9	1	32	2
Botham	9	0	45	2
Emburey	5	0	18	0
Allott	9	0	40	2
Gooch	6	1	18	0
Underwood	7	0	34	2

Fall of Wickets

Wkt	E	SL
1st	55	34
2nd	83	75
3rd	152	84
4th	191	92
5th	197	92
6th	202	160
7th	205	175
8th	205	182
9th	205	—
10th	211	—

* Captain † Wicket-keeper

Sri Lanka v England 2nd One-Day International
Sri Lanka won by 3 runs
Played at Sinhalese Sports Club Ground, Colombo, February 14
Toss: England. Umpires: K.T. Francis and P.W. Vidanagamage

Sri Lanka

*B. Warnapura	c Taylor b Botham	4
S. Wettimuny	not out	86
L.R.D. Mendis	c and b Botham	0
R.L. Dias	hit wkt b Lever	26
A. Ranatunga	run out	42
A.N. Ranasinghe	c Gooch b Underwood	0
R.S. Madugalle	c Taylor b Lever	12
A.L.F. de Mel	run out	14
D.S. de Silva	not out	9
†H.M. Goonatillake	did not bat	
G.R.A. de Silva	did not bat	
Extras	(b 2, lb 16, w 1, nb 3)	22
Total	(45 overs, 230 minutes)	**215-7**

England

G.A. Gooch	st Goonatillake b G.R.A. de Silva	74
G. Cook	st Goonatillake b G.R.A. de Silva	32
D.I. Gower	lbw b De Mel	6
I.T. Botham	c and b Warnapura	13
*K.W.R. Fletcher	run out	38
C.J. Tavaré	b D.S. de Silva	5
M.W. Gatting	run out	17
†R.W. Taylor	run out	3
J.K. Lever	not out	2
D.L. Underwood	run out	0
R.G.D. Willis	c Madugalle b De Mel	0
Extras	(lb 20, w 1, nb 1)	22
Total	(44.5 overs, 195 minutes)	**212**

England	O	M	R	W
Willis	9	1	26	0
Botham	9	4	29	2
Lever	9	0	51	2
Gooch	9	0	50	0
Underwood	9	0	37	1

Sri Lanka	O	M	R	W
De Mel	8.5	4	14	2
Ranasinghe	9	0	36	0
Warnapura	9	0	42	1
D.S. de Silva	9	0	54	1
G.R.A. de Silva	9	1	44	2

Fall of Wickets

Wkt	SL	E
1st	5	109
2nd	5	122
3rd	43	122
4th	130	147
5th	130	170
6th	158	203
7th	186	206
8th	—	211
9th	—	211
10th	—	212

* Captain   † Wicket-keeper

Tour Summary

England in India and Sri Lanka
First-Class Match Statistics
Results: Played 15 Won 3 Lost 1 Drew 11

Batting/Fielding	M	I	NO	Runs	HS	Avge	100	50	Ct	St
G. Boycott	8	14	5	701	105	77.88	2	6	3	—
I.T. Botham	11	15	1	760	142	54.28	2	5	7	—
G.A. Gooch	13	21	3	967	127	53.72	2	6	10	—
D.I. Gower	13	18	3	755	94	50.33	—	7	7	—
C.J. Richards	6	6	4	97	46	48.50	—	—	11	1
K.W.R. Fletcher	13	18	6	581	108	48.41	1	4	9	—
G. Cook	7	10	1	372	104*	41.33	2	—	5	—
C.J. Tavare—	13	19	0	761	149	40.05	1	6	10	—
M.W. Gatting	12	14	1	509	127	39.15	2	2	5	—
G.R. Dilley	10	11	2	204	52	22.66	—	2	3	—
R.W. Taylor	11	10	2	132	40	16.50	—	—	27	1
D.L. Underwood	11	10	5	74	22*	14.80	—	—	3	—
R.G.D. Willis	10	6	3	26	13	8.66	—	—	3	—
J.E. Emburey	12	12	2	79	33	7.90	—	—	6	—
J.K. Lever	8	6	1	36	16	7.20	—	—	2	—
P.J.W. Allott	7	5	1	22	9*	5.50	—	—	3	—

Bowling	O	M	R	W	Avge	BB	5w/I	10w/M
Underwood	385.3	150	784	34	23.05	6–64	3	1
Emburey	380.1	96	1063	42	25.30	6–33	1	—
Willis	242.1	62	687	24	28.62	4–35	—	—
Lever	214	45	664	20	33.20	5–100	1	—
Botham	317.2	64	928	25	37.12	5–61	1	—
Allott	181.4	40	601	15	40.06	5–54	2	—
Dilley	210.2	29	767	15	51.13	4–47	—	—

Also bowled: Cook 6.5–1–21–2; Fletcher 29–2–121–2; Gatting 11–1–40–1;
Gooch 58.1–14–150–2; Gower 5–2–6–1; Richards 2–0–5–0; Tavaré 4–0–18–0;
Taylor 2–0–6–0.

* Not out.

Overseas cricket
1981-82

Australia v Pakistan

Australia's previous two series against Pakistan had been riddled with controversy and acrimony, and were intensely competitive. This three-match series, in the first half of the 1981-82 Australian summer, set new standards of bitterness and ill-feeling, but the match results were surprisingly conclusive both ways. Australia won by 286 runs in Perth and by 10 wickets in Brisbane; Pakistan were successful by an innings and 82 runs in Melbourne — on a pitch that Greg Chappell, the Australian captain, described as 'a disgrace to Australian cricket'.

Sadly, but with reason, it will be remembered as the series of 'The Kick'. This distasteful and regrettable incident occurred in Perth on the fourth day of the first Test, when Pakistan captain Javed Miandad pushed a ball from Dennis Lillee to mid-wicket and ran for what was a comfortable single. As he passed half-way along the pitch, Lillee moved towards him in what seemed a deliberate attempt to block him. He appeared to check Miandad with his right shoulder. Miandad, who had been looking towards the ball until the last moment, then pushed him away with his bat, held horizontally in both hands. It seemed a reflex, almost protective action, although the Australian players later were adamant that it was a surprisingly strong push and not quite as reflex an action as it had appeared. Lillee spun round and swung his right arm back towards Miandad without connecting with him. Miandad ran on past umpire Tony Crafter. Lillee moved towards Miandad and Crafter promptly moved between them. Lillee threw out his left leg and connected behind Miandad's left knee. Miandad raised his bat above his head threateningly as Crafter remained between him and Lillee. Chappell yelled 'Dennis' and ran up the pitch from his position at first slip. Tempers cooled and play resumed, although there looked to be considerable animosity between the two combatants.

Umpires Crafter and Mel Johnson lodged complaints against Lillee and Miandad and, that night, Lillee was fined $A200 (one fifth of his basic match fee) by his team-mates, who, through Chappell, said he had 'acted under extreme provocation', and they sought (in vain) an apology from Miandad. Two nights later, after the umpires had appealed against the leniency of the penalty, Lillee was suspended by the Australian Cricket Board for two one-day internationals, losing at least $A1,150 in fees, sponsorships, and prize money, but the $A200 fine was quashed.

Chappell's memorable double century in the second Test was the individual jewel of the series, which also produced fighting hundreds from Australia's vice-captain Kim Hughes and left-hand opener Graeme Wood in the first and third Tests, respectively.

Australian Bruce Yardley, a much-improved off-spinner, was the surprise leading wicket-taker (18) on either side. Lillee took 15 wickets, one fewer than Pakistan's big-hearted fast-bowling all-rounder Imran Khan, a comfortable winner of the Player of the Series award. If all the Pakistanis had displayed Imran's courage, stamina, and commitment to duty, they would not have surrendered the first two Tests so meekly.

Australia v Pakistan 1981-82 1st Test
Australia won by 286 runs
Played at WACA Ground, Perth, November 13, 14, 15, 16, 17
Toss: Pakistan. Umpires: A.R. Crafter and M.W. Johnson
Debuts: Pakistan — Rizwanuz Zaman

Australia

B.M. Laird	c Wasim Bari b Imran	27	(2) c Wasim Bari b Imran	85
G.M. Wood	lbw b Sikander	33	(1) b Qasim	49
*G.S. Chappell	lbw b Imran	22	b Imran	6
K.J. Hughes	b Sarfraz	14	c Majid b Imran	106
G.N. Yallop	c and b Qasim	20	c Imran b Sikander	38
A.R. Border	c Wasim Bari b Sarfraz	3	c Mudassar b Sikander	37
†R.W. Marsh	c Qasim b Sikander	16	c Mansoor b Wasim Raja	47
B. Yardley	c Wasim Bari b Imran	9	st Wasim Bari b Qasim	22
D.K. Lillee	c Wasim Bari b Wasim Raja	16	not out	4
J.R. Thomson	b Imran	2	not out	5
T.M. Alderman	not out	0		
Extras	(lb 5, w 1, nb 12)	18	(b 1, lb 9, w 1, nb 14)	25
Total		**180**	(8 wickets declared)	**424**

Pakistan

Mudassar Nazar	c Marsh b Lillee	0	lbw b Alderman	5
Rizwanuz Zaman	lbw b Alderman	0	c Marsh b Alderman	8
Mansoor Akhtar	c Marsh b Alderman	6	c Hughes b Thomson	36
*Javed Miandad	c Hughes b Alderman	6	b Yardley	79
Majid Khan	c Marsh b Lillee	3	c Marsh b Yardley	0
Wasim Raja	c Thomson b Lillee	4	c Hughes b Yardley	48
Imran Khan	c Yardley b Lillee	4	c Alderman b Yardley	31
Sarfraz Nawaz	c Marsh b Alderman	26	c and b Yardley	9
†Wasim Bari	c Marsh b Lillee	1	c Border b Yardley	20
Iqbal Qasim	c Alderman b Thomson	5	c Alderman b Lillee	4
Sikander Bakht	not out	3	not out	0
Extras	(nb 4)	4	(lb 1, nb 15)	16
Total		**62**		**256**

Pakistan	O	M	R	W	O	M	R	W
Imran	31.4	8	66	4	39	12	90	3
Sarfraz	27	10	43	2	27	5	88	0
Sikander	21	4	47	2	23	3	79	2
Qasim	3	1	6	1	26	4	81	2
Wasim Raja	11	1	0	1	20	3	58	1
Miandad					1	0	2	0
Mudassar					2	1	1	0

Australia	O	M	R	W	O	M	R	W
Lillee	9	3	18	5	20	3	78	1
Alderman	10.3	2	36	4	16	4	43	2
Thomson	2	1	4	1	12	4	35	1
Yardley					25.5	5	84	6

Fall of Wickets

Wkt	A 1st	P 1st	A 2nd	P 2nd
1st	45	1	92	8
2nd	81	1	105	27
3rd	89	14	192	96
4th	113	17	262	99
5th	119	21	327	174
6th	136	25	380	198
7th	154	25	412	229
8th	165	26	416	236
9th	180	57	—	254
10th	180	62	—	256

* Captain   † Wicket-keeper

Australia v Pakistan 1981-82 2nd Test
Australia won by 10 wickets
Played at Woolloongabba, Brisbane, November 27, 28, 29, 30, December 1
Toss: Australia. Umpires: A.R. Crafter and M.W. Johnson
Debuts: Nil

Pakistan

Mudassar Nazar	*c* Marsh *b* Lillee	36	*c* Laird *b* Lillee		33
Mohsin Khan	*c* Border *b* Chappell	11	*c* Marsh *b* Lillee		43
Majid Khan	*c* Chappell *b* Lillee	29	*c* Chappell *b* Yardley		15
*Javed Miandad	*b* Lillee	20	*lbw b* Lillee		38
Zaheer Abbas	*b* Lillee	80	*lbw b* Yardley		0
Wasim Raja	*c* Laird *b* Lillee	43	*b* Lillee		36
Imran Khan	*c* Marsh *b* Alderman	0	*c* Wellham *b* Yardley		3
Ijaz Faqih	*b* Yardley	34	*c* Chappell *b* Thomson		21
Sarfraz Nawaz	*c* Border *b* Alderman	4	*c* Alderman *b* Yardley		13
†Wasim Bari	*c* Marsh *b* Thomson	7	*not out*		4
Sikander Bakht	*not out*	1	*b* Thomson		2
Extras	(*b* 12, *lb* 1, *w* 1, *nb* 12)	26	(*b* 2, *lb* 3, *w* 1, *nb* 9)		15
Total		**291**			**223**

Australia

B.M. Laird	*c* Zaheer *b* Ejaz	44	(2) *not out*		3
G.M. Wood	*c* Mudassar *b* Wasim Raja	72	(1) *not out*		0
*G.S. Chappell	*c* Zaheer *b* Sikander	201			
A.R. Border	*b* Imran	36			
K.J. Hughes	*b* Imran	28			
D.M. Wellham	*b* Imran	36			
†R.W. Marsh	*c* Zaheer *b* Imran	27			
B. Yardley	*b* Sarfraz	2			
D.W. Lillee	*b* Sarfraz	14			
J.R. Thomson	*not out*	22			
T.M. Alderman	*not out*	5			
Extras	(*b* 1, *lb* 5, *w* 2, *nb* 17)	25			
Total	(9 wickets declared)	**512**	(0 wickets)		**3**

Australia	O	M	R	W	O	M	R	W
Lillee	20	3	81	5	19	4	51	4
Alderman	25	6	74	2	15	3	37	0
Thomson	15	2	52	1	15	3	43	2
Chappell	3	1	6	1				
Yardley	15	1	51	1	24	4	77	4
Border	1	0	1	0				

Pakistan	O	M	R	W	O	M	R	W
Imran	40	6	92	4	1.2	1	2	0
Sikander	24	2	81	1	1	0	1	0
Sarfraz	35	4	121	2				
Ejaz	22	1	76	1				
Wasim Raja	17	0	68	1				
Mudassar	2	0	10	0				
Miandad	3	0	18	0				
Majid	9	1	21	0				

Fall of Wickets

Wkt	P 1st	A 1st	P 2nd	A 2nd
1st	40	109	72	—
2nd	60	149	90	—
3rd	105	219	115	—
4th	111	298	115	—
5th	236	429	177	—
6th	237	448	178	—
7th	245	469	189	—
8th	263	470	216	—
9th	285	492	219	—
10th	291	—	223	—

* Captain   † Wicket-keeper

Australia v Pakistan 1981-82 3rd Test
Pakistan won by an innings and 82 runs
Played at Melbourne Cricket Ground, December 11, 12, 13, 14, 15
Toss: Pakistan.Umpires: R.C. Bailhache and R.A. French
Debuts: Nil

Pakistan

Mudassar Nazar	c Lillee b Yardley	95
Mohsin Khan	c Thomson b Yardley	17
Majid Khan	c Wood b Yardley	74
*Javed Miandad	lbw b Yardley	62
Zaheer Abbas	c and b Yardley	90
Wasim Raja	c Laird b Yardley	50
Imran Khan	not out	70
Sarfraz Nawaz	c Yardley b Chappell	0
†Wasim Bari	b Yardley	8
Iqbal Qasim	not out	16
Sikander Bakht	did not bat	
Extras	(b 1, lb 5, nb 12)	18
Total	(8 wickets declared)	**500**

Australia

B.M. Laird	lbw b Qasim	35	(2) c Sarfraz b Qasim	52
G.M. Wood	c Mohsin b Sarfraz	100	(1) c Wasim Bari b Sarfraz	1
G.S. Chappell	c Wasim Bari b Wasim Raja	22	c Miandad b Sarfraz	0
A.R. Border	run out	7	run out	1
K.J. Hughes	c and b Qasim	34	c Majid b Qasim	11
D.M. Wellham	c Mudassar b Sarfraz	26	b Sarfraz	13
†R.W. Marsh	c Mudassar b Imran	31	c Mohsin b Qasim	21
B. Yardley	b Qasim	20	b Imran	0
D.K. Lillee	lbw b Imran	1	c Wasim Bari b Qasim	4
J.R. Thomson	not out	3	b Imran	17
T.M. Alderman	lbw b Imran	1	not out	4
Extras	(b 4, lb 6, nb 3)	13	(b 1)	1
Total		**293**		**125**

Australia	O	M	R	W
Lillee	36.3	9	104	0
Alderman	27	8	62	0
Thomson	25	2	85	0
Yardley	66	16	187	7
Border	4	1	16	0
Chappell	9	2	17	1
Hughes	3	1	2	0
Laird	1	0	9	0

Pakistan	O	M	R	W	O	M	R	W
Imran	24.1	7	41	3	14.1	5	21	2
Sarfraz	14	2	43	2	15	10	11	3
Wasim Raja	37	7	73	1	13	2	34	0
Qasim	55	17	104	3	24	11	44	4
Sikander	2	0	9	0				
Majid	2	0	10	0	4	1	5	0
Miandad					2	0	9	0

Fall of Wickets

Wkt	P 1st	A 1st	A 2nd
1st	40	75	1
2nd	181	118	9
3rd	201	127	13
4th	329	173	29
5th	363	232	77
6th	443	235	78
7th	444	286	79
8th	457	288	92
9th	—	289	121
10th	—	293	125

* Captain   † Wicket-keeper

Test Match Averages: Australia v Pakistan 1981-82

Australia — Batting/Fielding	M	I	NO	HS	R	Avge	100	50	Ct	St
G.M. Wood	3	6	1	100	255	51.00	1	1	1	—
G.S. Chappell	3	5	0	201	251	50.20	1	—	3	—
B.M. Laird	3	6	1	85	246	49.20	—	2	3	—
K.J. Hughes	3	5	0	106	193	38.60	1	—	3	—
R.W. Marsh	3	5	0	47	142	28.40	—	—	11	—
D.M. Wellham	2	3	0	36	75	25.00	—	—	1	—
J.R. Thomson	3	5	3	22*	49	24.50	—	—	2	—
A.R. Border	3	5	0	37	84	16.80	—	—	3	—
B. Yardley	3	5	0	22	53	10.60	—	—	4	—
T.M. Alderman	3	4	3	5*	10	10.00	—	—	4	—
D.K. Lillee	3	5	1	16	39	9.75	—	—	1	—

Played in one Test: G.N. Yallop 20, 38.

Australia — Bowling	O	M	R	W	Avge	Best	5w/I	10/wM
Lillee	104.3	22	332	15	22.13	5-18	2	—
Yardley	130.5	26	399	18	22.16	7-187	2	—
Alderman	93.3	23	252	8	31.50	4-36	—	—
Thomson	69	12	219	5	43.80	2-43	—	—

Also bowled: Border 5-1-17-0; Chappell 12-3-23-2; Hughes 3-1-2-0; Laird 1-0-9-0.

Pakistan — Batting/Fielding	M	I	NO	HS	R	Avge	100	50	Ct	St
Zaheer Abbas	2	3	0	90	170	56.66	—	2	3	—
Javed Miandad	3	5	0	79	205	41.00	—	2	1	—
Wasim Raja	3	5	0	50	181	36.20	—	1	—	—
Mudassar Nazar	3	5	0	95	169	33.80	—	1	4	—
Imran Khan	3	5	1	70*	108	27.00	—	1	1	—
Majid Khan	3	5	0	74	121	24.20	—	1	2	—
Mohsin Khan	2	3	0	43	71	23.66	—	—	2	—
Iqbal Qasim	2	3	1	16*	25	12.50	—	—	3	—
Sarfraz Nawaz	3	5	0	26	52	10.40	—	—	1	—
Wasim Bari	3	5	1	20	40	10.00	—	—	8	1
Sikander Bakht	3	4	3	3*	6	6.00	—	—	—	—

Played in one Test: Ijaz Faqih 34, 21; Mansoor Akhtar 6, 36 (1 ct); Rizwanus Zaman 0, 8.

Pakistan/Bowling	O	M	R	W	Avge	Best	5w/I	10/wM
Imran Khan	150.2	39	312	16	19.50	4-66	—	—
Iqbal Qasim	108	33	235	10	23.50	4-44	—	—
Sarfraz Nawaz	118	31	306	9	34.00	3-11	—	—
Sikander Bakht	71	9	217	5	43.40	2-47	—	—

Also bowled: Ijaz Faqih 22-1-76-1; Javed Miandad 6-0-29-0; Majid Khan 15-2-36-0; Mudassar Nazar 4-1-11-0; Wasim Raja 88-13-233-4.

Pakistan Tour of Australia
First-Class Match Statistics
Results: Played 8 Won 2 Lost 2 Drawn 4

Batting and Fielding	M	I	NO	HS	R	Avge	100	50	Ct	St
Javed Miandad	7	11	2	158*	682	75.77	2	4	6	—
Zaheer Abbas	7	9	1	117	461	57.62	1	3	5	—
Mansoor Akhtar	4	7	0	86	345	49.28	—	3	1	—
Imran Khan	6	7	2	93*	244	48.80	—	2	1	—
Rizwanus Zaman	6	10	0	126	431	43.10	2	1	1	—
Ijaz Faqih	4	6	2	61*	164	41.00	—	1	3	—
Salim Malik	3	5	1	62	159	39.75	—	2	1	—
Mudassar Nazar	6	9	1	95	295	36.87	—	2	5	—
Majid Khan	6	9	0	110	264	29.33	1	1	5	—
Mohsin Khan	3	5	1	43	99	24.75	—	—	2	—
Wasim Raja	7	10	0	50	239	23.90	—	1	2	—
Tahir Naqqash	4	3	1	25*	39	19.50	—	—	—	—
Ashraf Ali	2	4	2	17	35	17.50	—	—	5	—
Wasim Bari	6	8	1	26	68	9.71	—	—	12	3
Sarfraz Nawaz	6	7	0	26	63	9.00	—	—	1	—
Iqbal Qasim	5	4	1	16*	25	8.33	—	—	5	—
Sikander Bakht	6	7	4	11	21	7.00	—	—	—	—

Bowling	O	M	R	W	Avge	Best	5w/I	10w/M
Iqbal Qasim	214.4	56	532	23	23.13	5-31	2	—
Imran Khan	281.2	66	686	28	24.50	5-89	1	—
Ijaz Faqih	124.4	20	324	9	36.00	3-32	—	—
Tahir Naqqash	81	15	272	6	45.33	4-60	—	—
Sikander Bakht	146.3	26	454	10	45.40	3-93	—	—
Sarfraz Nawaz	208	51	590	12	49.16	3-11	—	—
Wasim Raja	163	30	480	7	68.57	3-49	—	—

Also bowled: Javed Miandad 38-4-137-1; Majid Khan 56-13-137-2; Mansoor Akhtar 2-1-3-0; Mudassar Nazar 22-6-78-0; Rizwanuz Zaman 6-1-15-0; Salim Malik 7-1-33-0; Wasim Bari 2-1-1-0.

Australia v West Indies

On December 27, Dennis Lillee had West Indian left-hander Larry Gomes caught at first slip by Australian captain Greg Chappell, and a wildly excited Melbourne crowd of 44,894 stood to salute Australia's champion fast bowler, who had just taken his 310th wicket in his 58th Test to become the greatest wicket-taker in Test history.

Lillee's annexing of West Indies off-spinner Lance Gibbs's world record on the second day of the first Test was a fitting introduction to a magnificent mini-series, which was drawn 1-1. In the final Test, at Adelaide, West Indies captain Clive Lloyd hit the winning run with just 17 balls to spare. It gave him a fine match double of 53 and 77 not out, and enabled his team to retain the Sir Frank Worrell Trophy. It was Lloyd's 84th Test, and his 49th as captain (a West Indies record). In the same match, Rod Marsh made his 80th Test appearance, passing Neil Harvey's previous Australian record.

The first Test, in Melbourne, ended early on the fifth day with the West Indies rueing their first defeat in 16 Tests, since their one-wicket loss to New Zealand in Dunedin in February, 1980. On an inadequate pitch, belatedly condemned to be dug up a month later, Australian vice-captain Kim Hughes played probably the most valuable innings of the series — a resolute, unbeaten 100 which steered Australia from 59 for 5 to 198 all out.

Lillee had a match bag of 10 wickets, and his West Indian counterpart Holding claimed 11. A superb athlete and, at his peak, the fastest bowler in the world, Holding went on to take 5 wickets in Australia's first innings of the second Test and 8 in the third Test. With 24 wickets at 14.33 apiece, he walked away with the Player of the Series award.

Gomes confirmed his reputation as a batsman of genuine Test quality by scoring important centuries in Sydney and Adelaide and heading the aggregates and averages for both teams. Newcomer Jeffrey Dujon, from Jamaica, chosen for the tour mainly as second wicket-keeper to David Murray, matched his captain Lloyd for consistency, with scores of 41, 43, 44, 48, 51, and 0 not out.

Left-hander Allan Border made amends for his unhappy series against Pakistan by topping Australia's aggregate and averages. Patient opener John Dyson resurrected his Test career with a stubborn, unconquered century in the second innings in Sydney, where he also grabbed, at deep mid-wicket just inside the fence in front of the Hill, one of the most spectacular catches in Test history.

The great Viv Richards never exploded with the bat as expected (2, 0, 44, 22, 42, 50), and Chappell had a miserable time, save for his first innings of 61 in the third Test. His other scores were 0, 6, 12, 0, 7. Chappell's inexplicably bad trot (he said later he had not been studying the ball properly as it left the bowler's hand) had continued in the triangular series of one-day matches for the Benson and Hedges World Series Cup. In all, he failed to score seven times — four in Cup games, three in Tests.

Australia v West Indies 1981-82 1st Test
Australia won by 58 runs
Played at Melbourne Cricket Ground, December 26, 27, 28, 29, 30
Toss: Australia. Umpires: R.C. Bailhache and A.R. Crafter
Debuts: West Indies — P.J. Dujon

Australia

B.M. Laird	c Murray b Holding	4	(2)	lbw b Croft	64
G.M. Wood	c Murray b Roberts	3	(1)	c Murray b Garner	46
*G.S. Chappell	c Murray b Holding	0		c Murray b Garner	6
A.R. Border	c Murray b Holding	4		b Holding	66
K.J. Hughes	not out	100		b Holding	8
D.M. Wellham	c sub (A.L. Logie) b Croft	17		lbw b Holding	2
†R.W. Marsh	c Richards b Garner	21		c Murray b Holding	2
B. Yardley	b Garner	21		b Garner	13
D.K. Lillee	c Gomes b Holding	1		c Murray b Holding	0
G.F. Lawson	b Holding	2		not out	0
T.M. Alderman	c Murray b Croft	10		b Holding	1
Extras	(b 1, lb 6, nb 8)	15		(b 5, lb 4, w 1, nb 4)	14
Total		**198**			**222**

West Indies

D.L. Haynes	c Border b Lillee	1		c Lillee b Yardley	28
S.F.A.F. Bacchus	c Wood b Alderman	1		lbw b Alderman	0
C.E.H. Croft	lbw b Lillee	0	(11)	not out	0
I.V.A. Richards	b Lillee	2	(3)	b Alderman	0
*C.H. Lloyd	c Alderman b Yardley	29	(4)	c Border b Lawson	19
H.A. Gomes	c Chappell b Lillee	55	(5)	b Yardley	24
P.J. Dujon	c Hughes b Lillee	41	(6)	c Marsh b Yardley	43
†D.A. Murray	not out	32	(7)	c Marsh b Yardley	10
A.M.E. Roberts	c Marsh b Lillee	18	(8)	lbw b Lillee	10
M.A. Holding	c and b Alderman	2	(9)	lbw b Lillee	7
J. Garner	c Laird b Lillee	7	(10)	lbw b Lillee	0
Extras	(b 1, lb 3, nb 9)	13		(b 1, lb 10, nb 9)	20
Total		**201**			**161**

West Indies	O	M	R	W	O	M	R	W
Holding	17	3	45	5	21.3	5	62	6
Roberts	15	6	40	1	18	4	31	0
Garner	20	6	59	2	18	5	37	3
Croft	16.1	3	39	2	20	2	61	1
Richards					5	0	17	0

Australia	O	M	R	W	O	M	R	W
Lillee	26.3	3	83	7	27.1	8	44	3
Alderman	18	3	54	2	9	3	23	2
Lawson	9	2	28	0	17	3	36	1
Yardley	7	2	23	1	21	7	38	4
Chappell	2	2	0	0				

Fall of Wickets

	A	WI	A	WI
Wkt	1st	1st	2nd	2nd
1st	4	3	82	4
2nd	4	5	106	4
3rd	8	6	139	38
4th	26	10	184	80
5th	59	62	190	88
6th	115	134	199	116
7th	149	147	215	150
8th	153	174	218	154
9th	155	183	220	154
10th	198	201	222	161

* Captain † Wicket-keeper

Australia v West Indies 1981-82 2nd Test
Match Drawn
Played at Sydney Cricket Ground, January 2, 3, 4, 5, 6
Toss: West Indies. Umpires: A.R. Crafter and R.A. French
Debuts: Nil

West Indies

C.G. Greenidge	c Laird b Lillee	66	c Yardley b Lillee	8
D.L. Haynes	lbw b Thomson	15	lbw b Lillee	51
I.V.A. Richards	c Marsh b Lillee	44	c Border b Alderman	22
H.A. Gomes	c Chappell b Yardley	126	c Border b Yardley	43
*C.H. Lloyd	c Marsh b Thomson	40	c Hughes b Yardley	57
P.J. Dujon	c and b Thomson	44	c and b Yardley	48
†D.A. Murray	b Yardley	13	c Laird b Yardley	1
M.A. Holding	lbw b Lillee	9	c Dyson b Yardley	5
S.T. Clarke	b Yardley	14	c Dyson b Yardley	5
J. Garner	c Marsh b Lillee	1	(11) b Yardley	0
C.E.H. Croft	not out	0	(10) not out	4
Extras	(lb 3, nb 9)	12	(lb 1, w 5, nb 5)	11
Total		**384**		**255**

Australia

B.M. Laird	c Dujon b Garner	14	c Murray b Croft	38
G.M. Wood	c Murray b Holding	63	(6) not out	7
J. Dyson	lbw b Holding	28	(2) not out	127
*G.S. Chappell	c Dujon b Holding	12	(3) c Murray b Croft	0
T.M. Alderman	b Clarke	0		
K.J. Hughes	b Garner	16	(4) lbw b Gomes	13
A.R. Border	not out	53	(5) b Gomes	9
†R.W. Marsh	c Holding b Gomes	17		
B. Yardley	b Holding	45		
D.K. Lillee	c Garner b Holding	4		
J.R. Thomson	run out	8		
Extras	(b 1, lb 2, w 2, nb 2)	7	(b 2, lb 1, nb 3)	6
Total		**267**	(4 wickets)	**200**

Australia	O	M	R	W	O	M	R	W
Lillee	39	6	119	4	20	6	50	2
Alderman	30	9	73	0	12	2	46	1
Thomson	20	1	93	3	15	3	50	0
Yardley	26.2	3	87	3	31.4	6	98	7
Border	1	1	0	0				

West Indies	O	M	R	W	O	M	R	W
Holding	29	9	64	5	19	6	31	0
Clarke	16	4	51	1	16	9	25	0
Garner	20	4	52	2	12	3	27	0
Croft	20	7	53	0	27	6	58	2
Richards	13	7	21	0	13	3	33	0
Gomes	9	1	19	1	15	7	20	2

Fall of Wickets

Wkt	WI 1st	A 1st	WI 2nd	A 2nd
1st	37	38	29	104
2nd	128	108	52	104
3rd	133	111	112	149
4th	229	112	179	169
5th	325	128	208	—
6th	346	141	225	—
7th	363	172	231	—
8th	379	242	246	—
9th	380	246	255	—
10th	384	267	255	—

* Captain   † Wicket-keeper

Australia v West Indies 1981-82 3rd Test
West Indies won by 5 wickets
Played at Adelaide Oval, January 30, 31, February 1, 2, 3
Toss: West Indies. Umpires: R.C. Bailhache and M.W. Johnson
Debuts: Nil

Australia

B.M. Laird	*c* Dujon *b* Roberts	2	(2)	*c* Dujon *b* Croft	78
G.M. Wood	*c* Garner *b* Roberts	5	(1)	*c* and *b* Holding	6
J. Dyson	*c* Dujon *b* Holding	1		*c* Lloyd *b* Garner	10
K.J. Hughes	*c* Greenidge *b* Holding	5	(5)	*c* Bacchus *b* Garner	84
*G.S. Chappell	*c* Garner *b* Holding	61	(7)	*lbw b* Holding	7
A.R. Border	*c* Dujon *b* Roberts	78	(4)	*c* Dujon *b* Roberts	126
†R.W. Marsh	*c* Dujon *b* Holding	39	(6)	*c* Haynes *b* Holding	38
B. Yardley	*b* Croft	8		*b* Garner	6
D.K. Lillee	*b* Roberts	2		*c* Dujon *b* Garner	1
J.R. Thomson	*not out*	18		*c* Bacchus *b* Garner	0
L.S. Pascoe	*b* Holding	10		*not out*	0
Extras	(*b* 1, *lb* 2, *w* 1, *nb* 5)	9		(*b* 7, *lb* 10, *nb* 13)	30
Total		**238**			**386**

West Indies

C.G. Greenidge	*c* Border *b* Thomson	8		*c* Marsh *b* Thomson	52
D.L. Haynes	*c* Marsh *b* Thomson	26		*c* Marsh *b* Thomson	4
I.V.A. Richards	*c* Laird *b* Yardley	42		*b* Pascoe	50
H.A. Gomes	*not out*	124		*b* Pascoe	21
S.F.A.F. Bacchus	*c* Laird *b* Pascoe	0	(6)	*c* Lillee *b* Pascoe	27
*C.H. Lloyd	*c* Marsh *b* Thomson	53	(5)	*not out*	77
C.E.H. Croft	*b* Thomson	0			
†P.J. Dujon	*c* Thomson *b* Yardley	51	(7)	*not out*	0
A.M.E. Roberts	*c* sub (D.W. Hookes) *b* Yardley	42			
M.A. Holding	*b* Yardley	3			
J. Garner	*c* Wood *b* Yardley	12			
Extras	(*b* 4, *lb* 7, *w* 3, *nb* 14)	28		(*lb* 2, *w* 1, *nb* 5)	8
Total		**389**		(5 wickets)	**239**

West Indies	O	M	R	W	O	M	R	W
Holding	25	5	72	5	29	9	70	3
Roberts	19	7	43	4	24	7	64	1
Croft	23	4	60	1	32	4	90	1
Garner	17	4	44	0	35	15	56	5
Gomes	7	3	10	0	14	1	38	0
Richards					18	3	38	0

Australia	O	M	R	W	O	M	R	W
Lillee	4.5	3	4	0	4	0	17	0
Thomson	29	1	112	4	19.1	4	62	2
Pascoe	30	3	94	1	22	3	84	3
Yardley	40.5	10	132	5	16	0	68	0
Border	5	0	19	0				

Fall of Wickets

	A	WI	A	WI
Wkt	1st	1st	2nd	2nd
1st	3	12	10	7
2nd	8	72	35	107
3rd	8	85	201	114
4th	17	92	267	176
5th	122	194	362	235
6th	193	194	373	—
7th	206	283	383	—
8th	209	365	383	—
9th	210	369	383	—
10th	238	389	386	—

* Captain   † Wicket-keeper

Test Match Averages: Australia v West Indies 1981-82

Australia —
Batting/Fielding

	M	I	NO	HS	R	Avge	100	50	Ct	St
A.R. Border	3	6	1	126	336	67.20	1	3	5	—
J. Dyson	2	4	1	127*	166	55.33	1	—	2	—
K.J. Hughes	3	6	1	100*	226	45.20	1	1	2	—
B.M. Laird	3	6	0	78	200	33.33	—	2	5	—
G.M. Wood	3	6	1	63	130	26.00	—	1	2	—
R.W. Marsh	3	5	0	39	117	23.40	—	—	10	—
B. Yardley	3	5	0	45	93	18.60	—	—	2	—
G.S. Chappell	3	6	0	61	86	14.33	—	1	2	—
J.R. Thomson	2	3	1	18*	26	13.00	—	—	2	—
T.M. Alderman	2	3	0	10	11	3.66	—	—	2	—
D.K. Lillee	3	5	0	4	8	1.60	—	—	2	—

Played in one Test: G.F. Lawson 2, 0*; L.S. Pascoe 10, 0*; D.M. Wellham 17, 2.

Australia — Bowling

	O	M	R	W	Avge	Best	5w/I	10/wM
D.K. Lillee	121.3	26	317	16	19.81	7-83	1	1
B. Yardley	142.5	28	446	20	22.30	7-98	2	1
J.R. Thomson	83.1	9	317	9	35.22	4-112	—	—
T.M. Alderman	69	17	196	5	39.20	2-23	—	—

Also bowled: A.R. Border 6-1-19-0; G.S. Chappell 2-2-0-0; G.F. Lawson 26-5-64-1;
L.S. Pascoe 52-6-178-4.

West Indies —
Batting/Fielding

	M	I	NO	HS	R	Avge	100	50	Ct	St
H.A. Gomes	3	6	1	126	393	78.60	2	1	1	—
C.H. Lloyd	3	6	1	77*	275	55.00	—	3	1	—
P.J. Dujon	3	6	1	51	227	45.40	—	1	9	—
C.G. Greenidge	2	4	0	66	134	33.50	—	2	1	—
I.V.A. Richards	3	6	0	50	160	26.66	—	1	1	—
A.M.E. Roberts	2	3	0	42	70	23.33	—	—	—	—
D.L. Haynes	3	6	0	51	125	20.83	—	1	1	—
D.A. Murray	2	4	1	32*	56	18.66	—	—	12	—
S.F.A.F. Bacchus	2	4	0	27	28	7.00	—	—	2	—
M.A. Holding	3	5	0	9	26	5.20	—	—	2	—
J. Garner	3	5	0	12	20	4.00	—	—	3	—
C.E.H. Croft	3	5	3	4*	4	2.00	—	—	—	—

Played in one Test: S.T. Clarke 14, 5.

West Indies — Bowling

	O	M	R	W	Avge	Best	5w/I	10w/M
M.A. Holding	140.3	37	344	24	14.33	6-62	4	1
J. Garner	122	37	275	12	22.91	5-56	1	—
A.M.E. Roberts	76	24	178	6	29.66	4-43	—	—
C.E.H. Croft	138.1	26	361	7	51.57	2-39	—	—

Also bowled: S.T. Clarke 32-13-76-1; H.A. Gomes 45-12-87-3; I.V.A. Richards 49-13-109-0.

West Indies Tour of Australia
First-Class Match Statistics
Results: Played 7 Won 4 Lost 1 Drawn 2

Batting and Fielding	M	I	NO	HS	R	Avge	100	50	Ct	St
H.A. Gomes	7	10	2	200*	712	89.00	3	2	1	—
C.H. Lloyd	5	8	1	77*	394	56.28	—	5	3	—
P.J. Dujon	5	8	2	104*	332	55.33	1	1	16	—
I.V.A. Richards	7	11	1	121	436	43.60	1	3	4	—
S.F.A.F. Bacchus	6	10	2	85	319	39.87	—	4	4	—
D.L. Haynes	6	11	0	139	383	34.81	1	2	3	—
D.A. Murray	4	6	2	72	139	34.75	—	1	20	—
M.D. Marshall	2	2	0	66	66	33.00	—	1	—	—
A.M.E. Roberts	4	5	1	42	103	25.75	—	—	1	—
C.G. Greenidge	5	8	0	66	179	22.37	—	2	3	—
A.L. Logie	3	4	0	43	81	20.25	—	—	—	—
C.E.H. Croft	6	8	4	34	48	12.00	—	—	3	—
M.A. Holding	6	7	0	24	56	8.00	—	—	3	—
J. Garner	5	7	0	18	50	7.14	—	—	4	—
S.T. Clarke	4	3	0	14	19	6.33	—	—	—	—
H. Joseph	2	2	0	7	11	5.50	—	—	1	—

Bowling	O	M	R	W	Avge	Best	5w/I	10/wM
M.D. Marshall	46	14	105	11	9.54	5-31	1	—
J. Garner	165.3	51	372	23	16.17	5-45	2	—
M.A. Holding	214.3	49	535	32	16.71	6-62	4	1
A.M.E. Roberts	147	44	318	13	24.46	4-43	—	—
S.T. Clarke	89	18	261	9	29.00	3-28	—	—
H.A. Gomes	72	13	169	5	33.80	2-20	—	—
C.E.H. Croft	251.5	43	673	18	37.38	3-78	—	—
H. Joseph	91	25	217	5	43.40	3-45	—	—
I.V.A. Richards	120.5	28	304	6	50.66	5-88	1	—

New Zealand v Australia

Any review of Australia's six-week tour of New Zealand in February and March, 1982, should start and finish with two words — Greg Chappell. This was to be the tour in which New Zealanders vented their anger at Chappell's directive role in the infamous under-arm incident in Melbourne a year earlier. The Australian captain steeled himself for the inevitable, like a man waiting to be pushed into shark-infested waters.

At Auckland's Eden Park on February 13, the banners and T-shirts shrieked: 'Aussies have an under-arm problem.' At Christchurch's Lancaster Park on March 21, a sign on the fence read: 'Chappell, you're okay.' On both days, Chappell scored majestic centuries — 108 out of 194 in the first of the three one-day internationals; 176 out of 353 in the first innings of the last Test. In between, he was a master diplomat: courteous, obliging, tactful, uncomplaining, and always a willing signer of youngsters' autograph books.

Chappell went to New Zealand with easily his worst Australian season behind him. Always insisting that he preferred to let his bat do the talking, his 'voice' was loud and clear in New Zealand. And it was indicative of New Zealanders' interest in Chappell's tour that the Australians set ground records in their first four matches — 43,000 in Auckland, 7,000 in Hamilton, 15,000 in Dunedin, and 20,000 in Wellington.

In Auckland, New Zealand's biggest-ever cricket crowd saw the first of the three one-day internationals (for the Rothmans Cup) and, appropriately, the home team won by 46 runs, despite Chappell's Man of the Match century. Australia still took the series 2–1; winning by 6 wickets in Dunedin and by 8 wickets in Wellington.

'Windy' Wellington's Basin Reserve also hosted the drawn first Test, a rain-ruined affair that offered not quite 10 hours' play out of a possible 30.

Auckland's Eden Park then was the scene of one of New Zealand's most historic triumphs — a 5-wicket win, only their second in 14 Tests against Australia and 13th in 147 Tests against all countries. Bruce Edgar's dour 161 paved the way for New Zealand's first-innings lead of 177. Then pacemen Richard Hadlee and Lance Cairns shared eight wickets to leave them a second-innings target of 104. Hadlee scored the winning runs with a six.

In Christchurch, Australia surged back for an emphatic 8-wicket win in a match that belonged mostly to Chappell. But it was the dynamic Hadlee who won the Man of the Series award (a motor-car), and there was a satisfying touch of irony about Chappell's winning of the Sportsman of the Series award.

The Australians flew home anxious for a winter's rest. In 17 busy months, they had played 37 one-day internationals and 21 Tests.

A lasting impression of the tour was that no one would dare to underrate New Zealand cricket any more, however much it retained a streak of inconsistency. The Kiwis are not alone in that regard.

New Zealand v Australia 1981-82 1st Test
Match Drawn
Played at Basin Reserve, Wellington, February 25, 26, 27, March 1, 2
Toss: Australia. Umpires: F.R. Goodall and S.J. Woodward
Debuts: New Zealand — M.D. Crowe

New Zealand

B.A. Edgar	*lbw b* Alderman	55
J.G. Wright	*c* Chappell *b* Yardley	38
J.F.M. Morrison	*b* Thomson	15
*G.P. Howarth	*not out*	58
J.V. Coney	*lbw b* Yardley	1
M.D. Crowe	*run out*	9
R.J. Hadlee	*b* Thomson	21
†I.D.S. Smith	*c* Chappell *b* Yardley	11
B.L. Cairns	*not out*	19
M.C. Snedden	*did not bat*	
E.J. Chatfield		
Extras	(*b* 5, *lb* 19, *w* 4, *nb* 11)	39
Total	(7 wickets declared)	**266**

Australia

G.M. Wood	*b* Cairns	41
B.M. Laird	*not out*	27
J. Dyson	*not out*	12
*G.S. Chappell		
K.J. Hughes		
A.R. Border		
†R.W. Marsh	*did not bat*	
B. Yardley		
J.R. Thomson		
D.K. Lillee		
T.M. Alderman		
Extras	(*lb* 2, *nb* 3)	5
Total	(1 wicket)	**85**

Australia	O	M	R	W
Thomson	26	13	35	2
Alderman	44	20	93	1
Lillee	15	5	32	0
Chappell	8	2	18	0
Yardley	23	10	49	3

New Zealand	O	M	R	W
Hadlee	7	2	15	0
Snedden	8	1	24	0
Cairns	11	4	20	1
Chatfield	8	5	7	0
Crowe	4	1	14	0

Fall of Wickets

Wkt	NZ 1st	A 1st
1st	86	65
2nd	120	—
3rd	149	—
4th	162	—
5th	186	—
6th	212	—
7th	246	—
8th	—	—
9th	—	—
10th	—	—

* Captain   † Wicket-keeper

New Zealand v Australia 1981-82 2nd Test
New Zealand won by 5 wickets
Played at Eden Park, Auckland, March 12, 13, 14, 15, 16
Toss: New Zealand. Umpires: B.A. Bricknell and S.J. Woodward
Debuts: Nil

Australia

B.M. Laird	c Smith b Troup	38	lbw b Hadlee	39
G.M. Wood	c Smith b Cairns	9	c Snedden b Cairns	100
J. Dyson	b Snedden	33	b Cairns	33
K.J. Hughes	c Smith b Troup	0	b Cairns	17
*G.S. Chappell	run out	32	c Edgar b Hadlee	24
A.R. Border	run out	0	c Howarth b Morrison	38
†R.W. Marsh	b Troup	33	c Crowe b Hadlee	3
B. Yardley	b Hadlee	25	c Coney b Hadlee	0
J.R. Thomson	lbw b Hadlee	13	lbw b Hadlee	4
D.K. Lillee	c Crowe b Troup	9	c Smith b Morrison	5
T.M. Alderman	not out	0	not out	0
Extras	(lb 2, nb 16)	18	(b4, lb 5, nb 8)	17
Total		**210**		**280**

New Zealand

B.A. Edgar	c and b Yardley	161	c Lillee b Yardley	29
J.G. Wright	c Yardley b Lillee	4	c Laird b Alderman	4
J.F.M. Morrison	b Lillee	11	c Marsh b Lillee	8
*G.P. Howarth	run out	56	c Chappell b Yardley	19
J.V. Coney	b Yardley	73	(6) not out	5
M.D. Crowe	c Wood b Lillee	2		
R.J. Hadlee	c Chappell b Yardley	25	(7) not out	6
†I.D.S. Smith	lbw b Yardley	5		
B.L. Cairns	c Lillee b Alderman	14	(5) b Border	34
M.C. Snedden	not out	18		
G.B. Troup	c Border b Alderman	4		
Extras	(b 4, lb 7, w 1, nb 2)	14	(lb 4)	4
Total		**387**	(5 wickets)	**109**

New Zealand	O	M	R	W	O	M	R	W
Hadlee	20	7	38	2	28	9	63	5
Troup	18.3	3	82	4	15	4	31	0
Cairns	17	7	38	1	42	10	85	3
Snedden	12	5	26	1	8	2	22	0
Howarth	1	0	8	0	4	2	4	0
Coney					4	1	6	0
Morrison					34.5	15	52	2

Australia	O	M	R	W	O	M	R	W
Thomson	23	8	52	0				
Alderman	24.3	5	59	2	7	0	30	1
Lillee	39	7	106	3	13	5	32	1
Yardley	56	22	142	4	7.4	2	40	2
Border	3	2	11	0	2	1	3	1
Chappell	5	2	3	0				

Fall of Wickets

Wkt	A 1st	NZ 1st	A 2nd	NZ 2nd
1st	19	15	106	4
2nd	75	35	167	17
3rd	76	122	196	44
4th	120	276	202	97
5th	120	291	241	103
6th	131	326	254	—
7th	173	345	254	—
8th	187	352	260	—
9th	203	366	277	—
10th	210	387	280	—

* Captain † Wicket-keeper

New Zealand v Australia 1981-82 3rd Test
Australia won by 8 wickets
Played at Lancaster Park, Christchurch, March 19, 20, 21, 22
Toss: New Zealand. Umpires: F.R. Goodall and D.A. Kinsella
Debuts: Nil

Australia

B.M. Laird	c Smith b Troup	12	c Coney b Hadlee		15
G.M. Wood	c Crowe b Hadlee	64	c Edgar b Snedden		31
J. Dyson	c Hadlee b Snedden	1	not out		14
*G.S. Chappell	c Smith b Coney	176	not out		3
K.J. Hughes	b Hadlee	12			
A.R. Border	b Snedden	6			
†R.W. Marsh	c Cairns b Hadlee	23			
B. Yardley	c Cairns b Hadlee	8			
J.R. Thomson	b Hadlee	25			
D.K. Lillee	c and b Hadlee	7			
T.M. Alderman	not out	1			
Extras	(b 2, lb 8, nb 8)	18	(b 2, lb 2, nb 2)		6
Total		**353**	(2 wickets)		**69**

New Zealand

B.A. Edgar	c Dyson b Alderman	22	c Marsh b Alderman		11
J.G. Wright	c Marsh b Lillee	13	b Alderman		141
J.F.M. Morrison	lbw b Thomson	8	lbw b Chappell		4
*G.P. Howarth	c Alderman b Thomson	9	c Wood b Border		41
J.V. Coney	b Lillee	0	b Border		0
M.D. Crowe	c Marsh b Lillee	0	b Yardley		9
R.J. Hadlee	c Marsh b Thomson	40	c Alderman b Yardley		0
†I.D.S. Smith	b Thomson	0	c Wood b Yardley		0
B.L. Cairns	run out	3	lbw b Yardley		16
M.C. Snedden	b Alderman	32	b Border		20
G.B. Troup	not out	0	not out		8
Extras	(b 8, lb 2, w 1, nb 11)	22	(b 4, lb 7, w 1, nb 10)		22
Total		**149**			**272**

New Zealand	O	M	R	W	O	M	R	W
Hadlee	28.5	5	100	6	8	2	10	1
Troup	11	1	53	1				
Snedden	18	2	89	2	4	0	15	1
Cairns	21	3	74	0	9	1	28	0
Coney	8	2	15	1	1	0	2	0
Morrison	3	0	4	0	2	1	6	0
Wright					1	0	2	0
Crowe					0.3	0	0	0

Australia	O	M	R	W	O	M	R	W
Thomson	21	5	51	4	19	5	54	0
Alderman	19.2	3	63	2	23	5	66	2
Lillee	12	6	13	3				
Chappell					18	5	30	1
Yardley					27	7	80	4
Border					10.3	4	20	3

Fall of Wickets

Wkt	A 1st	NZ 1st	A 2nd	NZ 2nd
1st	50	33	24	21
2nd	57	57	60	36
3rd	82	57	—	129
4th	125	57	—	133
5th	145	67	—	162
6th	237	82	—	166
7th	256	82	—	166
8th	340	87	—	215
9th	352	149	—	249
10th	353	149	—	272

* Captain   † Wicket-keeper

Test Match Averages: New Zealand v Australia 1981-82

New Zealand —

Batting/Fielding	M	I	NO	HS	R	Avge	100	50	Ct	St
B.A. Edgar	3	5	0	161	278	55.60	1	1	2	—
G.P. Howarth	3	5	1	58*	183	45.75	—	2	1	—
J.G. Wright	3	5	0	141	200	40.00	1	—	—	—
M.C. Snedden	3	3	1	32	70	35.00	—	—	1	—
R.J. Hadlee	3	5	1	40	92	23.00	—	—	2	—
B.L. Cairns	3	5	1	34	86	21.50	—	—	2	—
J.V. Coney	3	5	1	73	79	19.75	—	1	2	—
G.B. Troup	2	3	2	8*	12	12.00	—	—	—	—
J.F.M. Morrison	3	5	0	15	46	9.20	—	—	—	—
M.D. Crowe	3	4	0	9	20	5.00	—	—	3	—
I.D.S. Smith	3	4	0	11	16	4.00	—	—	6	—

Played in one Test: E.J. Chatfield (did not bat).

New Zealand — Bowling	O	M	R	W	Avge	Best	5w/I	10/wM
R.J. Hadlee	91.5	25	226	14	16.14	6-100	2	—
G.B. Troup	44.3	8	166	5	33.20	4-82	—	—
B.L. Cairns	100	25	245	5	49.00	3-85	—	—

Also bowled: E.J. Chatfield 8-5-7-0; J.V. Coney 13-3-23-1; M.D. Crowe 4.3-1-14-0; G.P. Howarth 5-2-12-0; J.F.M. Morrison 39.5-16-62-2; M.C. Snedden 50-10-176-4; J.G. Wright 1-0-2-0.

Australia —

Batting and Fielding	M	I	NO	HS	R	Avge	100	50	Ct	St
G.S. Chappell	3	4	1	176	235	78.33	1	—	4	—
G.M. Wood	3	5	0	100	229	45.80	1	1	3	—
B.M. Laird	3	5	1	39	147	36.75	—	—	1	—
J. Dyson	3	5	2	33	93	31.00	—	—	1	—
R.W. Marsh	3	3	0	33	59	19.66	—	—	5	—
A.R. Border	3	3	0	38	48	16.00	—	—	1	—
J.R. Thomson	3	3	0	25	42	14.00	—	—	—	—
B. Yardley	3	3	0	25	33	11.00	—	—	2	—
K.J. Hughes	3	3	0	17	29	9.66	—	—	—	—
D.K. Lillee	3	3	0	9	17	5.66	—	—	2	—
T.M. Alderman	3	3	3	1*	1	—	—	—	2	—

Australia — Bowling	O	M	R	W	Avge	Best	5w/I	10/wM
B. Yardley	113.4	41	311	13	23.92	4-80	—	—
D.K. Lillee	79	23	183	7	26.14	3-13	—	—
J.R. Thomson	89	31	192	6	32.00	4-51	—	—
T.M. Alderman	117.5	33	311	8	38.87	2-59	—	—

Also bowled: A.R. Border 15.3-7-34-4; G.S. Chappell 31-9-51-1.

Australian Tour of New Zealand

First-Class Match Statistics

Results: Played 5 Won 1 Lost 1 Drawn 3

Batting and Fielding	M	I	NO	HS	R	Avge	100	50	Ct	St
G.S. Chappell	5	6	2	176	317	79.25	1	1	4	—
G.M. Wood	5	7	0	100	388	55.42	1	3	4	—
B.M. Laird	4	6	1	39	155	31.00	—	—	1	—
J. Dyson	4	6	2	33	124	31.00	—	—	1	—
K.J. Hughes	5	5	0	66	115	23.00	—	1	3	—
R.W. Marsh	5	4	1	33	59	19.66	—	—	7	—
A.R. Border	5	5	0	38	95	19.00	—	—	2	—
J.R. Thomson	5	4	0	25	51	12.75	—	—	—	—
B. Yardley	5	4	0	25	42	10.50	—	—	3	—
D.K. Lillee	4	3	0	9	17	5.66	—	—	2	—
T.M. Alderman	5	4	4	5*	6	—	—	—	2	—

Also batted: R.J. Bright (2 matches) 27 (1ct); L.S. Pascoe (1 match) 1.

Bowling	O	M	R	W	Avge	Best	5wI	10wM
D.K. Lillee	79	23	183	7	26.14	3-13	—	—
B. Yardley	150.2	50	462	17	27.17	4-80	—	—
J.R. Thomson	109	39	238	8	29.75	4-51	—	—
T.M. Alderman	136.5	37	362	12	30.16	3-35	—	—

Also bowled: A.R. Border 20.3-7-52-4; R.J. Bright 42-10-156-2; G.S. Chappell 35-10-58-1; J. Dyson 3-0-18-1; K.J. Hughes 2-1-3-1; L.S. Pascoe 29-3-110-3.

One-Day Internationals

13 February at Eden Park, Auckland. NEW ZEALAND won by 46 runs. New Zealand 240-6 (50 overs) (B.A. Edgar 79). Australia 194 (44.5 overs) (G.S. Chappell 108, G.B. Troup 10-1-44-4). Toss: Australia. Man of the Match: G.S. Chappell.

17 February at Carisbrook, Dunedin. AUSTRALIA won by 6 wickets. New Zealand 159-9 (49 overs) (J.V. Coney 54). Australia 160-4 (45 overs) (B.M. Laird 71*, A.R. Border 53*). Toss: Australia. Man of the Match: A.R. Border.

20 February at Basin Reserve, Wellington. AUSTRALIA won by 8 wickets. New Zealand 74 (29 overs) (T.M. Alderman 10-2-17-5). Australia 75-2 (20.3 overs). Toss: Australia. Man of the Match: T.M. Alderman.

Pakistan v Sri Lanka

Pakistan cricket suffered one of its severest crises in memory, when the players, comprising the cream of Pakistan cricket, expressed their unavailability for the tour of England if Miandad were retained as captain. The Board of Control for Cricket in Pakistan adopted a hard line to begin with, but in the face of mounting public pressure and dismal crowds at the first Test, in Karachi, they eventually adopted a compromising stance. Miandad voluntarily stepped down from the captaincy, and a full-strength Pakistan team played against the Sri Lankans in the last Test at Lahore. This was just as well, particularly for the visitors, who needed to play against a true Pakistan side to get the right experience of big-time cricket.

The Sri Lanka team arrived in Pakistan full of expectations and understandable apprehensions, this being their first ever tour as a Test-playing country. They had indeed received their baptism in Test cricket only a few days before, when England played a match against them in Colombo on their way home from India.

Statistically, the Sri Lankans did not fare well, losing two Tests, drawing one, and winning only one of the three one-day internationals. But the tour was, all things considered, a very useful testing time for them. Dias and Wettimuny excelled with the bat, the latter achieving the supreme distinction of being the first Sri Lankan to score a century for his country in Test cricket. Dias became the second, with a scorching 109 in the last Test. Dias was by far the most attractive player and scored a 50 in each match, except for the last one-day international in which he missed by one run. But the two most experienced batsmen, Mendis and Warnapura, fell far below expectations.

The spinning duo of the De Silvas — D.S. with his leg-spin and G.R.A. with his slow left-arm spin — did most of the bowling for Sri Lanka. Ratnayake and De Mel, both medium-pacers, gained in experience with long spells, and De Mel particularly showed fine promise, swinging the ball both ways. The fielding was led by Dias and Ranasinghe. Wicket-keeper Goonatillake kept efficiently and had eight victims in the Tests, six of them in the first match.

The series obviously did not have the same importance or significance for Pakistan. The absence of the regular players in the first two Tests gave an opportunity to youngsters such as Salim Malik, and he made the most of it, scoring a century on his Test debut. Zaheer Abbas scored two fluent hundreds at Lahore, one in the last Test and one in the one-day international. Haroon Rashid and Mohsin Khan also chipped in with centuries in the first and third Tests, respectively.

Imran Khan played in only one Test, and it was a personal triumph for this great fast bowler. He sliced his way through the Sri Lankans in Lahore and finished with 14 wickets, a record for Pakistan.

Although the Sri Lankans were not great crowd-pullers, they nevertheless had occasion to sound a warning to the rest of the cricket-playing countries that in future years they would be a side to reckon with.

Pakistan v Sri Lanka 1981-82 1st Test

Pakistan won by 204 runs
Played at National Stadium, Karachi, March 5, 6, 7, 9, 10
Toss: Pakistan. Umpires: Amanullah Khan and Mahboob Shah
Debuts: Pakistan — Rashid Khan, Salim Malik, Salim Yousuf, Tahir Naqqash; Sri Lanka — J.R. Ratnayeke

Pakistan

Mansoor Akhtar	c Goonatillake b De Mel	6	c Mendis b D.S. de Silva	23
Rizwanuz Zaman	c Goonatillake b Ratnayeke	42	c Goonatillake b De Mel	10
Salim Malik	b D.S. de Silva	12	(4) not out	100
*Javed Miandad	c Goonatillake b De Mel	4	(5) st Goonatillake b D.S. de Silva	92
Wasim Raja	c Dias b De Mel	31	(6) not out	12
Haroon Rashid	run out	153		
†Salim Yousuf	st Goonatillake b D.S. de Silva	4		
Tahir Naqqash	c Mendis b D.S. de Silva	57		
Iqbal Qasim	lbw b D.S. de Silva	1	(3) c sub (R.G.C.E. Wijesuriya) b D.S. de Silva	56
Rashid Khan	c Madugalle b G.R.A. de Silva	59		
Tausif Ahmed	not out	5		
Extras	(lb 9, w 4, nb 9)	22	(b 5, lb 1, w 1, nb 1)	8
Total		**396**	(4 wickets declared)	**301**

Sri Lanka

*B. Warnafura	lbw b Tahir	13	b Tahir	0
S. Wettimuny	c Mansoor b Rashid	71	c Yousuf b Rashid	14
R.L. Dias	lbw b Qasim	53	lbw b Tahir	19
R.S. Madugalle	c Yousuf b Rashid	29	c Tausif b Qasim	18
J.R. Ratnayeke	c Rizwanuz b Qasim	24	(10) c Malik b Wasim Raja	0
L.R.D. Mendis	c Rashid b Tahir	54	(5) c Yousuf b Qasim	15
A. Ranatunga	st Yousuf b Tausif	13	(6) c Yousuf b Tausif	33
D.S. de Silva	b Tausif	26	(7) st Yousuf b Qasim	12
†H.M. Goonatillake	c Yousuf b Tahir	14	c Haroon b Wasim Raja	3
A.L.F. de Mel	run out	9	(8) c Miandad b Qasim	2
G.R.A. de Silva	not out	10	not out	0
Extras	(b 1, lb 12, w 3, nb 12)	28	(b 9, lb 11, w 1, nb 2)	23
Total		**344**		**149**

Sri Lanka	O	M	R	W	O	M	R	W
De Mel	28	2	124	3	23.2	3	100	1
Ratnayeke	16	6	49	1	5.4	2	20	0
D.S. de Silva	38	8	102	4	26	3	99	3
G.R.A. de Silva	17.2	2	69	1	35	5	74	0
Warnapura	2	0	9	0				
Wettimuny	2	0	21	0				

Pakistan	O	M	R	W	O	M	R	W
Tahir	32	11	83	3	9	1	34	2
Rashid	26	7	53	2	8	3	25	1
Qasim	28	7	88	2	15.1	8	27	4
Tausif	21.4	6	64	2	12	1	39	1
Wasim Raja	5	1	28	0	3	2	1	2

Fall of Wickets

Wkt	P 1st	SL 1st	P 2nd	SL 2nd
1st	6	24	16	1
2nd	46	120	53	27
3rd	53	152	107	41
4th	72	199	269	68
5th	113	221	—	91
6th	126	242	—	121
7th	230	285	—	125
8th	232	308	—	139
9th	359	322	—	149
10th	396	344	—	149

* Captain † Wicket-keeper

Pakistan v Sri Lanka 1981-82 2nd Test
Match drawn
Played at Iqbal Stadium, Faisalabad, March 14, 15, 16, 18, 19
Toss: Sri Lanka. Umpires: Javed Akhtar and Khizer Hayat
Debuts: Pakistan — Ashraf Ali; Sri Lanka — A.N. Ranasinghe
Sri Lanka

S. Wettimuny	*b* Wasim Raja	157	*c* Ashraf *b* Tahir	13
†H.M. Goonatillake	*c* Malik *b* Qasim	27	*b* Qasim	56
R.L. Dias	*c* Malik *b* Qasim	98	*c* Mohsin *b* Tahir	7
R.S. Madugalle	*not out*	91	*lbw b* Qasim	12
*L.R.D. Mendis	*b* Qasim	16	*run out*	0
A. Ranatunga	*b* Qasim	0	*c* Ashraf *b* Tausif	2
A.N. Ranasinghe	*c* Miandad *b* Qasim	6	*c* Miandad *b* Tausif	5
A.L.F. de Mel	*c* Malik *b* Qasim	4	(9) *not out*	25
D.S. de Silva	*lbw b* Rizwanuz	25	(8) *st* Ashraf *b* Tausif	8
L.W. Kaluperuma	*b* Rizwanuz	0	*not out*	11
G.R.A. de Silva	*lbw b* Rizwanuz	5		
Extras	(*lb* 11, *w* 2, *nb* 12)	25	(*lb* 9, *w* 1, *nb* 5)	15
Total		**454**	(8 wickets declared)	**154**

Pakistan

Rizwanuz Zaman	*b* G.R.A. de Silva	36	*b* De Mel	16
Mohsin Khan	*c* Wettimuny *b* De Mel	12	*c* De Mel *b* D.S. de Silva	74
Salim Malik	*b* De Mel	23	*lbw b* De Mel	4
*Javed Miandad	*c* Ranatunga *b* D.S. de Silva	18	*c* Madugalle *b* D.S. de Silva	36
Wasim Raja	*c* Madugalle *b* D.S. de Silva	22	*c* Wettimuny *b* D.S. de Silva	0
Haroon Rashid	*c* De Mel *b* D.S. de Silva	25	*b* D.S. de Silva	0
†Ashraf Ali	*b* Ranasinghe	58	*not out*	29
Tahir Naqqash	*c* De Mel *b* G.R.A. de Silva	1	*c* sub (J.B.N. Perera) *b* D.S. de Silva	13
Iqbal Qasim	*run out*	5		
Rashid Khan	*not out*	43	(9) *not out*	3
Tausif Ahmed	*c* Madugalle *b* D.S. de Silva	18		
Extras	(*lb* 1, *nb* 8)	9	(*b* 3, *lb* 7, *nb* 1)	11
Total		**270**	(7 wickets)	**186**

Pakistan	O	M	R	W	O	M	R	W
Tahir	26	4	108	0	13	3	53	2
Rashid	13	3	52	0	1	0	4	0
Qasim	65	18	141	6	30	9	51	2
Tausif	12	3	35	0	14	4	18	3
Wasim Raja	26	6	66	1				
Miandad	1	0	1	0				
Rizwanuz	12	3	26	3	5	2	13	0
Sri Lanka	O	M	R	W	O	M	R	W
De Mel	23	4	73	2	17	2	71	2
Ranasinghe	7	1	23	1	5	0	17	0
D.S. de Silva	32	3	103	4	18	2	59	5
G.R.A. de Silva	24	10	38	2	19	4	28	0
Kaluperuma	6	0	24	0				

Fall of Wickets

	SL	P	SL	P
Wkt	1st	1st	2nd	2nd
1st	77	19	19	24
2nd	294	54	44	40
3rd	304	83	82	132
4th	341	116	82	132
5th	341	124	86	132
6th	355	154	104	137
7th	385	156	114	174
8th	446	185	114	—
9th	448	222	—	—
10th	454	270	—	—

* Captain   † Wicket-keeper

Pakistan v Sri Lanka 1981-82 3rd Test
Pakistan won by an innings and 102 runs
Played at Gaddafi Stadium, Lahore, March 22, 23, 24, 25, 26, 27
Toss: Pakistan. Umpires: Khizer Hayat and Shakoor Rana
Debuts: Sri Lanka — R.S.A. Jayasekera, R.G.C.E. Wijesuriya

Sri Lanka

*B. Warnapura	c Mohsin b Imran	7		c Miandad b Tausif	26
S. Wettimuny	c Qasim b Imran	20		c Majid b Imran	41
R.S.A. Jayasekera	b Imran	0	(6)	b Imran	2
R.L. Dias	c Tausif b Imran	109	(3)	c Wasim Raja b Tausif	9
R.S. Madugalle	c Ashraf b Imran	0	(4)	b Tausif	5
L.R.D. Mendis	c and b Tausif	26	(5)	c Mudassar b Tausif	5
D.S. de Silva	b Imran	7		not out	36
A.L.F. de Mel	st Ashraf b Qasim	34		lbw b Imran	0
†H.M. Goonatillake	b Imran	15		c and b Imran	21
J.R. Ratnayeke	not out	1		b Imran	0
R.G.C.E. Wijesuriya	lbw b Imran	0		b Imran	3
Extras	(lb 11, w 6, nb 4)	21		(b 4, lb 2, w 1, nb 3)	10
Total		**240**			**158**

Pakistan

Mudassar Nazar	c Madugalle b D.S. de Silva	37
Mohsin Khan	b Ratnayeke	129
Majid Khan	c sub (A.N. Ranasinghe) b Ratnayeke	63
*Javed Miandad	c Goonatillake b De Mel	26
Zaheer Abbas	b Ratnayeke	134
Wasim Raja	c Goonatillake b De Mel	1
Imran Khan	c Mendis b De Mel	39
†Ashraf Ali	not out	45
Tahir Naqqash	not out	1
Iqbal Qasim ⎤ Tausif Ahmed ⎦	did not bat	
Extras	(b 5, lb 5, w 5, nb 10)	25
Total	(7 wickets declared)	**500**

Pakistan	O	M	R	W	O	M	R	W
Imran	29.3	8	58	8	22.5	3	58	6
Tahir	10	0	54	0	6	0	22	0
Qasim	12	4	21	0	1	0	1	0
Mudassar	8	1	23	0				
Tausif	12	1	50	1	25	7	58	4
Wasim Raja	5	1	13	0	6	4	9	0
Majid					1	1	0	0

Sri Lanka	O	M	R	W
De Mel	28	3	120	3
Ratnayeke	28	3	121	3
D.S. de Silva	39	4	129	1
Wijesuriya	24	2	105	0

Fall of Wickets

Wkt	SL 1st	P 1st	SL 2nd
1st	17	79	56
2nd	17	230	78
3rd	79	247	84
4th	83	297	90
5th	141	306	93
6th	171	406	95
7th	209	494	96
8th	231	—	142
9th	239	—	142
10th	240	—	158

* Captain   † Wicket-keeper

Test Match Averages: Pakistan v Sri Lanka 1981-82

Pakistan — Batting/Fielding	M	I	NO	HS	R	Avge	100	50	Ct	St
Ashraf Ali	2	3	2	58	132	132.00	—	1	3	2
Rashid Khan	2	3	2	59	105	105.00	—	1	1	—
Mohsin Khan	2	3	0	129	215	71.66	1	1	2	—
Haroon Rashid	2	3	0	153	178	59.33	1	—	1	—
Salim Malik	2	4	1	100*	139	46.33	1	—	4	—
Javed Miandad	3	5	0	92	176	35.20	—	1	4	—
Rizwanuz Zaman	2	4	0	42	104	26.00	—	—	1	—
Tahir Naqqash	3	4	1	57	72	24.00	—	1	—	—
Tausif Ahmed	3	2	1	18	23	23.00	—	—	3	—
Iqbal Qasim	3	3	0	56	62	20.66	—	1	1	—
Wasim Raja	3	5	1	31	66	16.50	—	—	1	—

Played in one Test: Imran Khan 39 (1 ct); Majid Khan 63 (1 ct); Mansoor Akhtar 6, 23 (1 ct); Mudassar Nazar 37 (1 ct); Salim Yousuf 4 (5 ct, 2 st); Zaheer Abbas 134.

Pakistan — Bowling	O	M	R	W	Avge	Best	5w/I10/wM	
Imran Khan	52.2	11	116	14	8.28	8-58	2	1
Iqbal Qasim	151.1	46	329	15	21.93	6-141	1	—
Tausif Ahmed	96.4	22	264	11	24.00	4-58	—	—
Tahir Naqqash	96	19	354	7	50.57	3-83	—	—

Also bowled: Javed Miandad 1-0-1-0; Majid Khan 1-1-0-0; Mudassar Nazar 8-1-23-0; Rashid Khan 48-13-134-3; Rizwanuz Zaman 17-5-39-3; Wasim Raja 45-14-117-3.

Sri Lanka — Batting/Fielding	M	I	NO	HS	R	Avge	100	50	Ct	St
S. Wettimuny	3	6	0	157	316	52.66	1	1	2	—
R.L. Dias	3	6	0	109	295	49.16	1	2	1	—
R.S. Madugalle	3	6	1	91*	155	31.00	—	1	5	—
H.M. Goonatillake	3	6	0	56	147	24.50	—	1	6	2
D.S. de Silva	3	6	1	35*	113	22.60	—	—	—	—
L.R.D. Mendis	3	6	0	54	116	19.33	—	1	3	—
G.R.A. de Silva	2	3	2	10*	15	15.00	—	—	—	—
A.L.F. de Mel	3	6	1	34	74	14.80	—	—	3	—
A. Ranatunga	2	4	0	33	48	12.00	—	—	1	—
B. Warnapura	2	4	0	26	46	11.50	—	—	—	—
J.R. Ratnayeke	2	4	1	24	25	8.33	—	—	—	—

Played in one Test: R.S.A. Jayasekera 0, 2; L.W. Kaluperuma 0, 11*; A.N. Ranasinghe 6, 5; R.G.C.E. Wijesuriya 0, 3.

Sri Lanka — Bowling	O	M	R	W	Avge	Best	5w/I10/wM	
D.S. de Silva	153	20	492	17	28.94	5-59	1	—
A.L.F. de Mel	119.2	14	488	11	44.36	3-120	—	—

Also bowled: G.R.A. de Silva 95.2-21-209-3; L.W. Kaluperuma 6-0-24-0; A.N. Ranasinghe 12-1-40-1; J.R. Ratnayeke 49.4-11-190-4; B. Warnapura 2-0-9-0; S. Wettimuny 2-0-21-0; R.G.C.E. Wijesuriya 24-2-105-0.

(contd at bottom of page 65)

Benson & Hedges World Series Cup

The Benson & Hedges World Series Cup was played in Australia between 21 November and 27 January. Each country met its opponents in five 50-overs matches to determine which two sides should contest the finals.

	P	W	L	Points	
WEST INDIES	10	7	3	14	
AUSTRALIA	10	4	6	8	Australia qualified for the finals because of
Pakistan	10	4	6	8	a higher scoring rate than Pakistan.

Final Round Results

23 January at Melbourne. WEST INDIES won by 86 runs. West Indies 216-8 (49 overs) (I.V.A. Richards 78, C.G. Greenidge 59). Australia 130 (37.4 overs).

24 January at Melbourne. WEST INDIES won by 128 runs. West Indies 235-9 (50 overs) (I.V.A. Richards 60, D.L. Haynes 52; L.S. Pascoe 10-1-39-4). Australia 107 (32.2 overs) (H.A. Gomes 6-1-31-4).

26 January at Sydney. AUSTRALIA won by 46 runs. Australia 214-8 (50 overs) (A.R. Border 69*). West Indies 168 (42.5 overs) (C.H. Lloyd 63*).

27 January at Sydney. WEST INDIES won by 18 runs. West Indies 234-6 (50 overs) (I.V.A. Richards 70, C.G. Greenidge 64). Australia 216-9 (50 overs) (G.M. Wood 69).

WEST INDIES won the WSC Finals by three matches to one, the fifth Final being unnecessary. Player of the Series: I.V.A. Richards.

Leading Averages

Batting	Team	M	I	NO	HS	R	Avge
C.H. Lloyd	WI	13	13	5	80*	462	57.75
I.V.A. Richards	WI	14	14	1	72*	536	41.23
Zaheer Abbas	P	9	9	0	108	343	38.11
C.G. Greenidge	WI	12	12	0	103	438	36.50
A.R. Border	A	14	14	4	75*	352	35.20
Imran Khan	P	10	9	3	62*	211	35.16
K.J. Hughes	A	11	11	2	67	300	33.33
G.M. Wood	A	14	13	1	69	384	32.00
Mudassar Nazar	P	9	9	0	51	285	31.66
Javed Miandad	P	10	10	0	74	282	28.20
B.M. Laird	A	11	11	1	117*	275	27.50
D.L. Haynes	WI	14	14	1	84	343	26.38
W.M. Darling	A	9	9	0	74	235	26.11

Bowling	Team	O	M	R	W	Avge	Best
Mudassar Nazar	P	43	5	160	12	13.33	3-20
H.A. Gomes	WI	29.4	2	140	10	14.00	4-31
L.S. Pascoe	A	45.5	4	183	12	15.25	4-39
J. Garner	WI	121	13	373	24	15.54	4-45
S.T. Clarke	WI	64.2	11	177	10	17.70	3-22
M.D. Marshall	WI	73.4	2	242	12	20.16	3-31
Imran Khan	P	96.1	9	305	15	20.33	3-19
M.A. Holding	WI	118	15	390	19	20.52	4-32
A.M.E. Roberts	WI	119	14	411	18	22.83	3-15
Sarfraz Nawaz	P	81	4	326	13	25.07	4-37
J.R. Thomson	A	114.2	6	523	19	27.52	3-55
Sikander Bakht	P	76.5	2	343	12	28.58	4-34
D.K. Lillee	A	110.3	17	427	12	35.58	2-18

Cricket in Australia

South Australia won the Sheffield Shield for the 11th time in the 1981–82 season. It was one of Australian cricket's most improbable rags-to-riches stories.

South Australia had finished bottom of the six-State competition the previous season, winning only one of their nine matches. Now they won four, including the last three, to 'steal' the Shield by two points from New South Wales. Western Australia, the titleholders, missed their many Test representatives in several matches and were third.

Tasmania played only five matches, and their points total was multiplied by 1.8. They will compete for the first time on an unrestricted basis in the 1982-83 season when, also for the first time, the Shield will be decided by a five-day play-off match between the top two teams (from March 4 to 8).

The young South Australian team, which did not provide a player for Australia's Test team all season, thrived under the leadership of former Test batsman David Hookes, in his first experience of captaincy at first-class level. Hookes's appointment initially was greeted with some derision by inter-state critics — and even a few players. He had lost his place in the South Australian team during the previous season, and doubts were expressed about his maturity, at the age of 26, and his rather flamboyant, adventurous ways. But he approached his task with a grim resolve to prove his detractors wrong. And how he succeeded! He was immensely popular with his players, one of whom was former Test batsman John Inverarity, Western Australia's longest-serving captain, now living in Adelaide. Inverarity had given up the South Australian captaincy after the 1980-81 season. At 38, he was the oldest state player in Australia, and he proved a guiding, steadying influence on Hookes and the other players, much in the manner of a senior pro.

Hookes let his behavioural guard slip only once. In the match against New South Wales in Sydney, the umpires stopped play because of rain during the second session on the last day, with South Australia only 11 runs short of what would have been their first outright win of the season. Hookes kicked the stumps down, threw his bat to the ground, and stayed at the wicket while ground staff applied the covers. Under the players' code of behaviour, umpires Michael Jay and Ian Jones charged Hookes with showing resentment at their decision. The South Australian players rejected the charge, but the umpires appealed and Hookes was subsequently fined his match fee of $A130.

South Australia's attack had its limitations at times in the pace bowling department, but the batting strength and consistency of Rick Darling, Wayne Phillips, New Zealander Jeff Crowe, Hookes, Peter Sleep, Inverarity, and wicket-keeper Kevin Wright proved decisive.

Queensland's prolific left-handed opening batsman, South African-born Kepler Wessels, won the Sheffield Shield Player of the Year award, topping the umpires' poll. New South Wales captain and opening batsman Rick McCosker was second.

Sheffield Shield

South Australia, winning the Sheffield Shield for the first time since 1975-76, did so by only two points — the narrowest margin possible under the current system. They gained the title by defeating Victoria on the last day of the season. Scores:

26, 27, 28 February, 1 March at Adelaide Oval. South Australia (16 points) beat Victoria (0) by 9 wickets. Victoria 297 (J.M. Wiener 116, J.W. Scholes 64, D.A. Sincock 4-85) and 286 (J.W. Scholes 71, P.J. Davies 57). South Australia 423-8 declared (J.J. Crowe 126, D.W. Hookes 63, P.R. Sleep 53, I.W. Callen 4-98) and 161-1 (W.B. Phillips 84*).

Final Table	P	W	L	D	1st Inns Points	Total Points
SOUTH AUSTRALIA	9	4	1	4	26	74
New South Wales	9	4	1	4	24	72
Western Australia	9	3	1	5	18	54
Tasmania	5	1	3	1	8	36
Queensland	9	1	2	6	8	20
Victoria	9	0	5	4	16	16

Points scoring: Win — 12 points; 1st innings lead (retained regardless of final result) — 4 points; undecided draw — 2 points. Tasmania, whose 20 points were multiplied by 1.8, have been admitted on a full basis for 1982-83, when they will play each opponent state twice.

Notable Record

J.M. Weiner (221*) and J.K. Moss (200*) added 390 runs in an unbroken record Australian third-wicket partnership for Victoria against Western Australia at Junction Oval, St Kilda, Melbourne, on 27 and 28 November, 1981. The previous Australian third-wicket record was 389 by W.H. Ponsford and S.J. McCabe for W.M. Woodfull's 1934 Australians against the MCC at Lord's.

Shield Wins:

36	New South Wales	8	Western Australia
24	Victoria	0	Queensland, Tasmania
12	South Australia		

(continued on page 66)

Sri Lankan Tour of Pakistan 1981-82 (contd from page 62)
Results of Other Matches
First-Class

28 February, 1, 2 March v BCCP Patron's XI at Rawalpindi. Match abandoned without a ball being bowled (rain).

One-Day Internationals

12 March at National Stadium, Karachi. PAKISTAN won by 8 wickets — match reduced to 33 overs per innings because of crowd disturbances. Sri Lanka 171-3 (33 overs) (B. Warnapura 77, R.L. Dias 57). Pakistan 174-2 (29.2 overs) (Mohsin Khan 85, Javed Miandad 56*). Toss: Pakistan. Man of the Match: Mohsin Khan.

29 March at Gaddafi Stadium, Lahore. SRI LANKA won on faster scoring rate when bad light caused play to be abandoned. Pakistan 239-4 (40 overs) (Zaheer Abbas 123, Haroon Rashid 63*). Sri Lanka 227-4 (33 overs) (R.L. Dias 81, L.R.D. Mendis 52). Toss: Sri Lanka. Man of the Match: R.L. Dias.

31 March at National Stadium, Karachi. PAKISTAN won by 5 wickets. Sri Lanka 218 (38.3 overs). Pakistan 222-5 (38.1 overs) (Mudassar Nazar 79). Toss: Pakistan. Man of the Match: Mudassar Nazar.

McDonald's Cup

Final: 7 March at Sydney. QUEENSLAND beat NEW SOUTH WALES by 27 runs. Queensland 224-8 (47 overs) (W.R. Broad 85). NSW 197 (44.4 overs) (P.M. Toohey 66; G. Dymock 8.4-1-27-5). Man of the Match: W.R. Broad.

Leading Averages (All first-class matches)

Batting	State	M	I	NO	HS	R	Avge	100	50
W.M. Darling	SA	9	17	3	134	1011	72.21	3	6
R.B. McCosker	NSW	9	15	3	146*	796	66.33	4	2
K.C. Wessels	Q	11	18	0	220	1094	60.77	5	3
G.M. Ritchie	Q	10	16	2	136*	833	59.50	3	3
M.F. Kent	Q	3	4	1	91	167	55.66	—	1
J. Dyson	NSW	8	14	1	127*	709	54.53	3	3
G.R. Marsh	WA	5	10	0	176	545	54.50	2	3
J.M. Weiner	V	9	17	1	221*	847	52.93	3	3
K.J. Hughes	WA	9	15	1	113	706	50.42	3	3
J.J. Crowe	SA	10	18	4	157	704	50.28	3	2
W.B. Phillips	SA	10	19	1	260	857	47.61	2	4
R.B. Kerr	Q	8	14	1	158	613	47.15	3	1
B.M. Laird	WA	9	16	2	110*	659	47.07	1	4
P.M. Toohey	NSW	8	13	2	137	511	46.45	1	2
J.K. Moss	V	5	9	1	200*	358	44.75	1	1

Qualification: 4 innings.

Bowling	State	O	M	R	W	Avge	Best	5w/I	10w/M
T.M. Alderman	WA	240.5	60	627	37	16.94	7-28	3	2
F.D. Stephenson	T	229.5	57	630	36	17.50	6-19	3	1
R.J. Inverarity	SA	343.2	117	639	30	21.30	5-40	1	—
P.M. Clough	T	148.3	42	390	18	21.66	4-57	—	—
D.K. Lillee	WA	301	66	819	37	22.13	7-83	3	1
G.F. Lawson	NSW	200.4	48	533	24	22.20	6-70	1	—
B. Yardley	WA	360.4	73	1105	49	22.55	7-98	4	1
R.G. Holland	NSW	332.4	128	661	27	24.48	6-64	1	—
I.W. Callen	V	265.1	45	789	31	25.45	4-76	—	—
G.J. Winter	SA	318.4	97	773	29	26.65	7-65	2	—
S.D.H. Parkinson	SA	310.5	79	851	28	30.39	4-50	—	—
M.G. Hughes	V	192.4	37	567	18	31.50	4-59	—	—
L.S. Pascoe	NSW	234.3	45	760	23	33.04	8-41	1	1
P.R. Sleep	SA	343.3	103	878	26	33.76	5-117	1	—
G.R. Beard	NSW	355	116	747	22	33.95	5-67	1	—

Qualification: 15 wickets.

Cricket in South Africa

From the season's start in October 1981, with the shock announcement that West Indian Alvin Kallicharran had signed to play for Transvaal, to its delayed climax in the rugby-playing days of mid-April 1982, surprise followed surprise in South African cricket. But nothing could match the sensational news that a tour by an English team was on.

Gooch's team showed that South African cricket, in its 12-year isolation, had lost touch with reality when it came to appreciating its own strength at international level alongside that of West Indies, England, Australia, and even New Zealand. Ageing super-stars of the calibre of Procter, Pollock, Richards, Van der Bijl, and Clive Rice, and rising stars of the likes of Kirsten, Ray Jennings (wicket-keeper-batsman), and Stephen Jefferies (left-arm fast-medium) will still be plus factors indeed. But was there sufficient all-round depth to a current Springbok team to take on and beat Test-hardened campaigners from England or West Indies in a full series?

The resounding impact of the tour was such that it totally overshadowed the domestic Currie Cup scene and the rather pertinent fact that the balance of power in one season had swung dramatically from Natal (Currie Cup champions) and Transvaal (Datsun Shield holders) to Newlands. Captained by Peter Kirsten, taking over from Eddie Barlow, a young Western Province side won both the Currie Cup and the one-day knock-out competition for the Datsun Shield. Their success came from the consistent batting form of Kirsten, Allan Lamb, Lawrence Seeff, and Ken McEwan, and the penetrative bowling of Garth le Roux, Stephen Jefferies, and Denys Hobson with his leg-spin. The two giants, Transvaal and Natal, were completely upstaged.

The 1981-82 season also marked the arrival of 'comic cricket' in South Africa — the gimmicky, inter-provincial Benson and Hedges 50-over night game, with its garish coloured gear, white balls, black sightscreens, and pop-style commentaries during the match. Like it or not, it is due for a stay of at least two more summers, after which, many hope, the novelty will have worn off.

Currie Cup

Final Table	P	W	L	D	Points
WESTERN PROVINCE	8	5	2	1	116
Transvaal	8	4	3	1	107
Natal	8	4	2	2	88
Northern Transvaal	8	1	3	4	52
Eastern Province	8	0	2	6	37

Currie Cup Wins: 19 Transvaal
18 Natal
12 Western Province
1 Kimberley (now
Griqualand West)

Shared Titles: 4 Transvaal
3 Natal
2 Western Province

Leading Currie Cup Averages

Batting	Prov	M	I	NO	HS	R	Avge	100	50
R.G. Pollock	T	6	9	3	124	486	81.00	1	4
P.N. Kirsten	WP	8	12	1	151	624	56.72	3	1
C.E.B. Rice	T	8	12	3	108	500	55.55	2	2

In all first-class matches Peter Kirsten scored 948 runs, average 59.25, with 4 hundreds.

Bowling	Prov	O	M	R	W	Avge	Best	5w/I
G.S. le Roux	WP	239.3	65	524	43	12.18	6-44	5
V.A.P. van der Bijl	N	359.3	103	804	57	14.10	8-47	7

Vincent van der Bijl set a new Currie Cup record with 57 wickets and also exceeded his own record for a South African in a home season by taking 75 wickets, average 14.92.

Section 'B' (Sab Bowl) Winners
Final: 24, 25, 26, 27 March at Oude Libertas, Stellenbosch. BOLAND beat WESTERN PROVINCE 'B' by 149 runs. Boland 237 and 291 (P.D. Swart 89; J.L. Louw 7-57). W. Province 'B' 115 and 264 (E. Muntingh 67, M.D. Mellor 60; P. Anker 5-73).
Boland thus won their first title in only their second season of first-class cricket.

Datsun Shield
Final: At the Wanderers, Johannesburg. WESTERN PROVINCE beat NATAL by 2 runs (55 overs match).

Cricket in the West Indies

The 1982 first-class season in the West Indies fell disappointingly short of the great expectations held out for it. There was no international home series, so that the Shell Shield held the public's undivided attention. With the separation of the Combined Islands team into the Leeward Islands and the Windward Islands, it was the most intense itinerary ever planned for a domestic season; 15 first-class and 15 limited-over matches were packed into six weeks between March 4 and April 15. Moreover, the West Indies team returned from Australia well in time and, it was felt, all of its members would be involved for their various territories.

As it turned out, both the Shield and the Geddes Grant/Harrison Line limited-over competition were seriously affected by Guyana's fickle equatorial weather, which completely washed out five of the six matches scheduled there and restricted the other to a few hours. In addition, several of those back from Australia were troubled by injury at some stage. Gordon Greenidge, Joel Garner, Sylvester Clarke, Augustine Logie, and David Murray were all forced to miss matches, while Michael Holding (with a cartilage knee operation) and Malcolm Marshall (injured back) played no Shield cricket at all.

For the tenth time in its 16 years, the Shell Shield was won by Barbados, although it was not a particularly convincing triumph. It included two hard-fought victories over Trinidad & Tobago and the Leewards and a humiliating defeat, at home at Kensington Oval, against the Windwards.

The Windwards, without a single current Test player and given little chance at the start, proved the team of the season. They beat not only Barbados but Trinidad & Tobago and Jamaica as well, to be runners-up in the Shield. Their success was based on enormous team spirit, steady batting, led by Middlesex's Wilf Slack, who averaged 41 an innings in his first appearance back home since emigrating to England, and a lively new-ball combination of the experienced Norbert Phillip, the Essex all-rounder, and the hostile young Winston Davis.

On the whole, the established players were the dominant individuals. But Franklyn Stephenson, a 23-year-old Barbadian dynamo with a vitality reminiscent of Keith Boyce's, returned from an outstanding season with Tasmania in the Sheffield Shield to stroke a scintillating 165, batting as nightwatchman, against the Leewards. He also bowled with speed and enthusiasm and fielded and threw as Boyce used to. He is, decidedly, one to watch.

Jamaica, disappointingly beaten in their three away matches after two convincing victories at home at Sabina Park, included two tall teenagers who made an immediate impression. Courtenay Walsh, 19, replacing Holding, took 15 wickets in four matches at 25 each. Richard Haynes used his 6ft 4in to bounce his leg-breaks off the hard Sabina pitch and take 20 wickets in the two matches there. He had only 3 wickets after that, but is undoubtedly an exciting prospect at a time when the emphasis in the West Indies remains heavily on speed.

In the limited-over tournament, the Leewards comfortably beat Barbados in a low-scoring final after a hat-trick by Kent's Eldine Baptiste and remarkable figures of 10-6-5-4 by the former Test off-spinner Derek Parry.

Shell Shield

Final Table	P	W	L	D	Points
Barbados	5	3	1	1	57
Windward Islands	4	3	1	0	52
Jamaica	5	2	2	1	36
Guyana	3	0	1	2	25
Leeward Islands	4	1	2	1	24
Trinidad and Tobago	5	0	2	3	20

Guyana played neither the Leeward nor Windward Islands.

Shell Shield Winners: 9 Barbados   *Shared Titles:* 1 Barbados, Trinidad
2 Guyana, Trinidad
1 Combined Islands, Jamaica

Leading Shell Shield Averages

Batting	Team	M	I	NO	HS	R	Avge	100	50
S.F.A.F. Bacchus	G	3	5	1	126	326	81.50	1	3
F.D. Stephenson	B	3	3	0	165	187	62.33	1	—
I.V.A. Richards	LI	4	7	0	167	433	61.85	1	3

Franklyn Stephenson went in as 'nightwatchman' and scored 165 against Leeward Islands in his first first-class match for Barbados (having represented Tasmania earlier in the season).

Bowling	Team	O	M	R	W	Avge	Best	5w/I
J. Garner	B	91.4	23	251	16	15.68	6-73	2
N. Phillip	WI	121	24	342	21	16.28	7-33	2
A.M.E. Roberts	LI	133.4	37	398	24	16.58	6-84	1

Geddes Grant Harrison Line Trophy

Final: At Recreation Ground, Antigua. LEEWARD ISLANDS beat BARBADOS by 5 wickets. Barbados 94 (47.5 overs) (D.R. Parry 4-5 in 10 overs, E.A. Baptiste did the hat-trick). Leeward Islands 95-5.

Cricket in New Zealand

Seldom has a team dominated New Zealand's domestic cricket so completely as did Wellington last summer. In the three-day Shell Trophy matches they scored six wins in seven games, and in the other were untroubled to draw with Northern Districts, who alone ever looked like challenging John Morrison's compact, highly efficient side. The other five sides managed only nine wins among them.

Wellington were equally dominant in the one-day Shell Cup series, winning all five and finishing off with a clear-cut victory over Canterbury in the final between the two leading sides.

Morrison, in the autumn of a career that was to have him recalled to Test duty, led his side coolly and well. His simple plan, amid the proliferation of bonus points and first-innings limitations of 100 overs, was to disregard these distractions and plan his matches as three-day exercises.

He had two trump cards, Bruce Edgar, the left-hand opening batsman, and Ewen Chatfield, the indefatigable right-arm medium-fast bowler. Edgar made 513 runs in 13 Shell Trophy innings. He scored only one century, but he invariably provided a solid start. Edgar also performed with Bradman-like consistency in the one-day matches — scores of 96, 97, 147 not out, 106 not out, 3, and 79 not out, in innings limited to 50 overs.

Chatfield hewed away steadily, 47 wickets in 14 innings, only twice taking fewer than three wickets in an innings. Towards the end, he had substantial support from an itinerant West Indian, Junior Williams, perhaps the fastest bowler on show in New Zealand last season. Although Jeremy Coney, the Test batsman, had a modest season, Wellington had a very solid middle to their batting — Morrison 498 runs, Evan Gray 495 and two centuries, Ross Ormiston 382. Gray also gained stature as an all-rounder, taking 22 wickets with his left-arm spin.

Northern Districts had their moments, especially with the batting of John Wright, 672 runs, and John Parker, who had a golden summer — 618 runs, including two hundreds in one match. Canterbury were half a team — short on runs, but with Richard Hadlee quite dominant as a bowler, taking 45 wickets at bargain rates. Auckland, who won both competitions the previous summer, worked fitfully, for they could score runs but, like Northern Districts, could not bowl sides out. Otago and Central Districts had disappointing seasons.

But from the first ball to the last, Wellington were the dominant, outstanding team. They had few spectacular patches, but under Morrison's canny leadership they also had few crises — simply a consistent, effective effort that won matches.

Shell Trophy

Final Table	P	W	L	D	Batting Points	Bowling Points	Total Points
WELLINGTON	7	6	0	1	19	26	116*
Northern Districts	7	4	1	2	17	27	92
Auckland	7	3	2	2	15	28	78*
Canterbury	7	1	5	1	15	24	51
Otago	7	1	2	4	8	22	47*
Central Districts	7	0	5	2	9	19	33*

* Total after being penalized one point

Points Scoring: Win — 12 points. Bonus Points — awarded for performances in the first 100 overs of each first innings on a scale similar to that used in the Schweppes Championship. Otago and Central Districts were awarded 6 points each for their rain-affected match at Invercargill on 23, 24, 25 January.

Leading First-Class Averages

Batting	Team	M	I	NO	HS	R	Avge	100	50
J.M. Parker	ND	7	13	7	117	618	103.00	2	2
B.A. Edgar	W	11	19	1	161	934	51.88	3	4
J.G. Wright	ND	11	18	0	141	872	48.44	4	2

Bowling	Team	O	M	R	W	Avge	Best	5w/I
R.J. Hadlee	C	425.1	130	870	59	14.74	6-26	7
E.J. Chatfield	W	396.2	135	868	51	17.01	5-29	2
B.L. Cairns	ND	373.3	110	816	41	19.90	6-19	3

Shell Cup

Final: 6 February at Lancaster Park, Christchurch. WELLINGTON beat CANTER-BURY by 8 wickets. WELLINGTON became the third North Island team in successive seasons to achieve the Shell Series double. Northern Districts won both the three-day first-class Trophy and the one-day 50-overs Cup in 1979-80, and Auckland emulated them in 1980-81.

Cricket in India

The 1981-82 season was eventful for the visit of the England team, but the domestic tournaments, principally the Duleep Trophy and the one-match Irani Trophy, provided invaluable opportunities for players aspiring to Test cricket.

Bengal's opening batsman Pronob Roy made his mark in the Duleep Trophy with carefully compiled scores in the semi-final against South Zone and in the final against West Zone. Sterling performances, with the bat in the Duleep Trophy final and with the ball in the Irani Trophy, contributed substantially to the victories of West Zone and Bombay, respectively. In the latter tournament, at Indore, hard-hitting Sandeep Patil made an untypically combative and tight century.

In the National Championship for the Ranji Trophy, the holders, Bombay, succumbed to Karnataka in a controversial semi-final interrupted by crowd violence and marred by hesitant umpiring. Patil made a century, which helped him gain a place in the touring side, but Bombay's strong batting (Gavaskar had scored 340 and put on 421 for the first wicket with Parkar in the quarter-final against Bengal) fell to pieces against Karnataka's duo of slow left-arm spin bowlers. Bank clerk Raghuram Bhatt took 13 wickets in the match, including a hat-trick in the important first innings.

In the final between Delhi (who edged Tamil Nadu in a violence-marred quarter-final) and Karnataka, over 1,400 runs were scored with just 18 wickets lost, the match extending into an unprecedented sixth day. (The statistical report of the final, below, is by Bill Frindall.)

Duleep Trophy
Final: 5, 6, 7, 8 November at Brabourne Stadium, Bombay. WEST ZONE beat EAST ZONE on first innings. East Zone 327 (Arun Lal 109, P. Roy 90, B.S. Sandhu 4-50; R.J. Shastri 4-103) and 138-5. West Zone 431 (R.J. Shastri 134, D.B. Vengsarkar 108; D.R. Doshi 4-131, Randhir Singh 4-147).

Ranji Trophy Final
When overnight rain seeped under the covers to delay the start by $2\frac{1}{2}$ hours and the most experienced batsman on either side, Gundappa Viswanath, was dismissed for nought, it would have required a formidable talent to predict the epic outcome of the Ranji Trophy final. Even on the fourth morning when Karnataka (formerly Mysore) finally ended their innings in its 16th hour for the highest Ranji Trophy final total for 35 years, only the heartiest supporters of Delhi and Districts could have considered the possibility of a first innings lead.

Delhi's batsmen adopted a belligerent approach from the outset. Only a first innings lead could gain their third Ranji Trophy championship in four seasons. Raman Lamba (61 off 62 balls) and Gursharan Singh, who reached his maiden Ranji Trophy century off 170 balls in 200 minutes, paved the way for a heroic innings by Mohinder Amarnath. His 185 off 370 balls was his third hundred in these finals, and carried the total to 548 for 7. But Karnataka must have considered the game theirs when the Delhi captain was dismissed early on the unscheduled sixth morning; surely the Delhi tail could not muster 158 runs before three wickets fell. The last experienced all-rounder, Madan Lal, was bowled by a shooter with 117 still wanted. His departure heralded the bravest partnership of the match, with Rakesh Shukla and Rajesh Peter scoring 118 runs in 125 minutes. With seven minutes left before the sixth tea interval of the match, Peter clipped a legside boundary to create a flurry of records.

The match produced the highest first-innings aggregate (1,412) in all first-class cricket. For the first time ever, a side scoring 700 had been led on first innings. There is only one previous instance of a side scoring 600 being passed on first innings (Queensland 613 v New South Wales 661 at Brisbane in October 1963). One Indian bowling record emerged as well, with Raghuram Bhatt's 94 overs just beating the 92.3 delivered by Ghulam Ahmed for Hyderabad against Holkar at Indore in 1950-51.

Spare a thought for Karnataka's wicket-keeper, Syed Kirmani. After batting superbly for his century, he had to be constantly active throughout the 14 hours 47 minutes of Delhi's reply. At Arundel a few weeks later, I asked him how he had felt when Karnataka made that winning hit. 'Very, very tired, Mister Bill!'

Delhi v Karnataka 1982 Ranji Trophy Final
Delhi won Ranji Trophy by leading on first innings
Played at Feroz Shah Kotla, Delhi, March 24, 25, 26, 27, 28, 29
Toss: Karnataka. Umpires: D.N. Dotiwala and P.G. Pandit

Karnataka First innings

R.M. Binny	lbw b Shukla	115
M.R.S. Prasad	lbw b Shukla	35
A.V. Jayaprakesh	b Shukla	6
*G.R. Viswanath	lbw b Maninder	0
B.P. Patel	c Peter b Madan Lal	124
R. Sudhakar Rao	c Azad b Madan Lal	71
†S.M.H. Kirmani	c Shukla b Maninder	116
R. Kanvilkar	c and b Chauhan	113
J. Abhiram	not out	75
B. Vijayakrishna	b Chauhan	0
A.R. Bhatt	b Maninder	15
Extras	(b 15, lb 16, w 3, nb 1)	35
Total	(255.5 overs; 948 min)	705

Delhi First innings

C.P.S. Chauhan	c Viswanath b Vijaya-krishna	36
R. Lamba	b Kanvilkar	61
Gursharan Singh	c Sudhakar Rao b Binny	101
S. Amarnath	lbw b Binny	22
*M. Amarnath	b Binny	185
K.B.J. Azad	b Kanvilkar	50
†S.C. Khanna	c Kanvilkar b Vijaya-krishna	31
Madan Lal	b Bhatt	48
R. Shukla	not out	69
R. Peter	not out	67
Maninder Singh	did not bat	
Extras	(b 18, lb 16, nb 3)	37
Total	(252.5 overs; 887 min)	707-8

Delhi	O	M	R	W
Madan Lal	40	8	112	2
M. Amarnath	23	3	62	0
Maninder	87.5	18	204	3
Peter	15	4	38	0
Shukla	63	10	158	3
Azad	18	2	62	0
Chauhan	7	0	24	2
Gursharan	2	0	10	0

Karnataka	O	M	R	W
Binny	28	0	134	3
Abhiram	8	0	28	0
Kanvilkar	33.5	4	138	2
Vijayakrishna	71	19	141	2
Bhatt	94	26	180	1
Viswanath	6	1	18	0
Prasad	9	1	24	0
Sudhakar Rao	3	1	7	0

Fall of Wickets
Karnataka: 1-109, 2-123, 3-124, 4-215, 5-332, 6-412, 7-568, 8-659, 9-659, 10-705
Delhi: 1-95, 2-137, 3-302, 4-308, 5-406, 6-466, 7-548, 8-589

* Captain   † Wicket-keeper

Close of play scores: 1st day: Karnataka 172-3 (Binny 103*, Patel 15*). 2nd day: Karnataka 405-5 (Sudhakar Rao 66*, Kirmani 33*). 3rd day: Karnataka 670-9 (Abhiram 51*, Bhatt 4*). 4th day: Delhi 302-3 (M. Amarnath 64*). 5th day: Delhi 543-6 (M. Amarnath 181*, Madan Lal 29*).
Note: S. Amarnath retired ill at tea (172-2) when 18* and resumed at the start of the 5th day (302-3).

Cricket in Pakistan

National Bank achieved most victories in the Quaid-e-Azam tournament, but acquired fewer bonus points than the next two teams. Their one defeat was inflicted by last year's champions, United Bank, who were themselves uniquely unbeaten.

The 45-match competition embraced the period when Pakistan's leading players were touring Australia. Their absence provided opportunities for several young players to experience competition just one stage removed from the Test match arena. Indeed, it explains why Salim Malik, Tahir Naqqash, Rashid Khan, Salim Yousuf, and Ashraf Ali were able to give such a good account of themselves in March when they were selected as replacements for the senior players who rebelled against Javed Miandad's leadership.

Shoaib Mohammad (PIA), who headed the Q-e-A batting averages, is the son of Hanif, and was a surprising omission from the side that toured England. Spin bowlers dominated the championship. Off-spinner Mohammad Nazir (Railways) led the averages, and the beguiling Abdul Qadir's variations on a leg-spinner's theme claimed most victims (58). Iqbal Sikander recorded the outstanding innings and match figures of 9-81 and 14-199 in PIA's encounter with Lahore.

Habib Bank won the Paco Cup, the second of Pakistan's major first-class competitions. Sponsored by Pakistan Automobile Corporation, it is played on a league basis between the five leading (available) sides in the Quaid-e-Azam Trophy tournament. PIA won the limited-over Wills Cup, beating Lahore by 7 wickets in the final.

Leading First-Class Averages 1981-82

Batting and Fielding	Team	M	I	NO	HS	R	Avge	100	50
Shoaib Mohammad	PIA	7	12	4	177*	711	88.87	4	1
Nasir Valika	UB	13	22	8	109	931	66.50	3	5
Mudassar Nazar	UB	7	11	1	241	624	62.40	2	2
Mohsin Khan	HB	12	20	1	129	1160	61.05	4	6
Agha Zahid	HB	13	24	3	136	1218	58.00	3	6
Gulfraz Khan	Rwy	7	12	5	74*	405	57.85	—	3
Arshad Pervez	HB	13	24	4	164	1102	55.10	4	4
Salim Taj	L	7	13	2	92	598	54.36	—	6
Javed Miandad	HB	6	10	1	177	517	51.70	2	2
Shafiq Ahmed	NB	13	26	3	161	1058	46.00	4	3

Bowling	Team	O	M	R	W	Avge	Best	5w/I	10w/M
Mohammad Nazir	Rwy	504	171	822	56	14.67	7-35	5	1
Abdur Raqib	HB	449.3	113	1123	62	18.11	7-40	3	2
Ehtesham Uddin	NB	436.5	88	1400	77	18.18	7-90	5	2
Tausif Ahmed	UB	715.1	195	1586	87	18.22	7-28	8	1
Iqbal Qasim	PAK	315.3	86	752	41	18.34	9-80	3	1
Abdul Qadir	HB	596.4	132	1609	87	18.49	7-44	9	2

Teams: Habib Bank (HB), Lahore (L), National Bank (NB), Pakistan (PAK), Pakistan International Airlines (PIA), Railways (Rwy), and United Bank (UB).

Quaid-e-Azam Trophy — Final Table on page 77.

Women's World Cup

New Zealand hosted the third Women's Cricket World Cup in January and February 1982. The six-week competition culminated in a thrilling, skilful final at Lancaster Park, Christchurch, Australia beating England by 3 wickets, with just one over remaining.

The first World Cup competition was staged in England in 1973. It was the brainchild of British-born, Bahamas-based millionaire Jack Hayward, who has been a great benefactor to women's cricket for more than a decade. England beat Australia to win the inaugural competition at Edgbaston, but in 1978 Australia gained revenge, beating England in the final in India.

The build-up to the 1982 final was a triumph of organization by the New Zealand Women's Cricket Council. The five teams (Australia, England, New Zealand, India, and an International XI captained by Lynne Thomas, the former England opener) played each other three times in 60-over matches on first-class grounds throughout North and South Island. The finalists were the top two teams in the resultant league. In their three meetings prior to the final, Australia had beaten England twice and the other game had ended in a pulsating tie — the only point taken off Australia in the preliminary-round matches.

The final itself was played in glorious sunshine with temperatures in the eighties. The crowd of 3,000 were enthralled by the excellent cricket and fluctuating fortunes — which made the match worthy of the live television coverage throughout the day's play.

England, electing to bat, put on 42 in the first 20 overs. Janette Brittin (Surrey), who in an earlier match against the International XI had scored a World Cup record 138 not out, was the first wicket to fall — caught and bowled by the diminutive off-spinner Marie Cornish, who plays in men's grade cricket up-country in Western Australia. With tight bowling and sharp fielding, Australia kept a rein on England's scoring. But when they went in, needing 152 to win, they slumped to 28 for 3 in 20 overs, thanks largely to two superb catches by England captain Sue Goatman (Kent) off the economical seam bowling of Avril Starling (Lancs & Cheshire).

Australia's middle-order batsmen hit out boldly, and, though wickets were lost, there were still three left when, at the end of the 59th over, the winning run was scored and the Jack Hayward Trophy retained.

It was evident from the preliminary-round matches that both New Zealand and India are sides with a great future. New Zealand have a pool of young talented players being groomed for the national side. India are fast improving in world cricket — they caused the major shock of the tournament by beating an off-key England in Wanganui by 47 runs. Their players are, in effect, professionals who are taken away from their homes and jobs to be trained and coached for the national side — they were even given spending money while in New Zealand, and the entire cost of their participation was funded by the Indian government.

Each of the England team contributed £250 towards their own travel costs, but the squad of 17, including manager Audrey Disbury (Kent), assistant manager Pam Crain (East Anglia), and physiotherapist 'Pip' Vyvyan, had marvellous support from British sports-goods firms and manufacturers who donated £5,500 worth of clothing and equipment.

The next World Cup is scheduled for Australia in 1986, and the comments of Dickie Bird who umpired in this World Cup should make it an event worthy of even greater recognition:

'Umpiring the Women's World Cup was something very special for me. I was most impressed by the overall standard — the batting, fielding, and slow bowling stood out. It was very refreshing to umpire women's matches — it's no tea party! They play very, very hard, but are always fair. And there was far less appealing than in the men's game. One game at New Plymouth (England v Australia) was one of the best games I have ever seen in any form of cricket. If people at home could have seen it, they would watch more women's cricket. The girls deserve a breakthrough — it only needs one major sponsor to get them recognized.'

Preliminary Matches, Results Table

	P	W	T	L	Points
AUSTRALIA	12	11	1	0	46
ENGLAND	12	7	2	3	32
New Zealand	12	6	1	5	26
India	12	4	0	8	16
International XI	12	0	0	12	0

(Scorecard of the final is on page 78.)

Pakistan (contd from page 75)

Quaid-e-Azam Trophy

Final Table	P	W	L	D	Bonus Pts Bat	Bonus Pts Ball	Total Pts
1 NATIONAL BANK (5)	9	7	1	1	27	31	128
2 United Bank (1)	9	6	0	3	34	31	125
3 Habib Bank (3)	9	5	2	2	35	37	122
4 PIA (2)	9	5	2	2	25	27	102
5 Muslim Commercial Bank (6)	9	2	5	2	29	30	79
6 Railways (4)	9	5	2	2	11	18	79
7 Rawalpindi	9	2	6	1	25	28	73
8 IDBP (7)	9	2	5	2	20	28	68
9 Lahore (8)	9	3	5	1	18	18	66
10 Karachi (10)	9	0	9	0	11	27	38

1980-81 final positions are shown in brackets — Rawalpindi were promoted to this championship as winners of last season's BCCP Patron's Trophy.

The totals include an additional 10 points awarded to both Habib Bank and Muslim Commercial Bank, and exclude 21 bonus points deducted from Railways (players' qualification regulations infringements).

Australia v England Women's World Cup Final
Australia won by 3 wickets
Played at Lancaster Park, Christchurch, February 7
Toss: England. Umpires: H.D. Bird and F.R. Goodall

England

*S. Goatman	*b* Fullston	29
J. Brittin	*c* and *b* Cornish	17
C. Watmough	*c* Kennare *b* Fullston	9
J. Southgate	*c* Hill *b* Tredrea	53
R. Heyhoe Flint	*c* Fullston *b* Tredrea	29
G. Hullah	*not out*	1
C. Hodges		
E. Bakewell		
J. Tedstone	*did not bat*	
A. Starling		
†S. Hodges		
Extras	(*b* 5, *lb* 7, *w* 1)	13
Total	(60 overs)	**151-5**

Australia

P. Vercoe	*c* Goatman *b* Starling	7
S. Hill	*c* Goatman *b* Starling	12
J. Kennare	*run out*	4
K. Read	*c* Southgate *b* Tedstone	32
*S. Tredrea	*c* S. Hodges *b* C. Hodges	25
J. Jacobs	*run out*	37
M. Cornish	*not out*	24
R. Thompson	*run out*	3
L. Fullston	*not out*	0
†T. Russell	*did not bat*	
D. Martin		
Extras	(*b* 2, *lb* 3, *w* 1, *nb* 2)	8
Total	(59 overs)	**152-7**

Australia	O	M	R	W
Tredrea	12	2	36	2
Martin	12	2	31	0
Cornish	12	6	17	1
Thompson	12	2	34	0
Fullston	12	3	20	2

England	O	M	R	W
Tedstone	12	4	24	1
Starling	11	3	21	2
Hullah	11	0	35	0
Bakewell	12	3	26	0
C. Hodges	12	1	33	1
Watmough	1	0	5	0

Fall of Wickets

Wkt	E	A
1st	42	18
2nd	54	22
3rd	63	28
4th	150	82
5th	151	97
6th	—	134
7th	—	145
8th	—	—
9th	—	—
10th	—	—

* Captain   † Wicket-keeper

Tours to England
1982

India in England

With a new captain in Bob Willis, a sprinkling of new faces, and a virtually new panel of selectors, England successfully put aside memories of their struggles the previous winter and overcame India by 1–0 in their three-match Cornhill Test series in June and July.

Even when they were losing the decisive Jubilee Test at Lord's, however, Sunil Gavaskar's team performed with great spirit. And although the series as a whole was some £100,000 down on the Test and County Cricket Board's estimated receipts, the tourists went home having won many friends if not too many matches.

Why were India, to borrow Willis's apt phrase, an unfashionable side? After all, they have world-class performers in the captain, his brother-in-law Gundappa Viswanath, and the all-rounder Kapil Dev, plus many other players of emerging talents. It is hard to escape the conclusion that many people, having followed last winter's dreary series in India from afar, decided the first part of this summer was not for them. There was competition, too, from Wimbledon and the World Cup, and the weather, as ever, played its part.

The discerning spectator, too, may have examined India's resources and decided, correctly, that they lacked the bowling to make a genuine challenge. Others may have stayed away because of the Test and County Cricket Board's ban on the players who unofficially toured South Africa. Yet those who went saw a Test series that frequently exploded into life. Rarely a day passed without a contribution from Ian Botham on the one side or Kapil Dev on the other. There were batting collapses and recoveries, but, in the end, perhaps not enough penetrative bowling on either side, especially on pitches that were mostly of the mildest type.

Even before the series began, it was clear that India's attack would have problems. They had difficulty in bowling out county sides (even though, nowadays, these are rarely at full strength), and Kapil Dev, their only strike bowler, had to be carefully used.

For the most part, the county games passed without incident — or outright result. But there was an echo of the umpiring difficulties that preoccupied England on their winter tour, when the tourists lodged an official objection against David Constant, who was to have stood in the Tests.

Constant, who had officiated in more Tests than any other English umpire since 1971, had umpired in two of the Indians' matches — against Yorkshire at Bradford and in the one-day international at Headingley.

It was probably because of their interpretation of events during these games — rather than any vendetta carried over from the previous winter — that India made their complaint. Ironically, however, Constant's replacement, Barrie Meyer, was to have an unhappy match in the Jubilee Test at Lord's.

There, the reshaped England side included, for the first time, Northamptonshire's Allan Lamb, born in South Africa but qualified because of his English parentage and residence. Also in the England side was the Cambridge University captain and all-rounder Derek Pringle, only the thirteenth player this century to be chosen while still an undergraduate.

England went into this match with four seam bowlers and only one spinner, a formula that worked on this occasion though not later in the series. Recovering from a poor start, thanks to Randall's century and a revival that saw the last 4 wickets add 267, they forced India to follow on. They eventually triumphed early on the last day, despite being highly discomforted at a late stage by Kapil Dev with both bat and ball.

At Old Trafford, in the second match, disappointingly small crowds saw England again put an uneasy start behind them, thanks to Botham's century on his 50th Test appearance, and Miller's 98. But this time Patil's thrilling innings of 129 not out saw to it that there was no follow-on.

Both there and at Lord's there had been more than 300 runs in a day, a luxury indeed in modern Test cricket. Despite this, there was another modest crowd at the Oval, where Ian Botham's epic double century was the highlight of a drawn match.

An injury to Gavaskar brought a premature end for him to what had been a moderate series. But adversity brought the best out of his team, and another spirited innings by Kapil Dev enabled them to end the series with honour.

The three-match series also indicated that, in England anyway, a decent over rate is possible. The agreement to bowl 16 overs an hour — or 96 a day — was appreciated by both sides, and was a definite factor in the matches being played at a more acceptable tempo.

First Test: Lord's, June 10, 11, 12, 14, 15.
England won by 7 wickets.
England had their share of awkward moments in the Jubilee Test, which started 50 years almost to the day after India's first Test at Lord's. But they played with growing conviction, and on the final morning achieved the victory that was to decide the series.

Umpire David Constant had been stood down following an objection by India. And it fell to his replacement, Barrie Meyer, to give two close lbw decisions on the first morning, which rewarded Kapil Dev's lively bowling and put England under considerable pressure.

They counter-attacked boldly, however, Botham showing the right mixture of restraint and aggression before falling to Malhotra's tumbling catch at square leg. By the end of the first day, they had reached 278 for 6. Next morning, Randall and Edmonds, both recalled to the side, took their seventh-wicket partnership to 125, beating the previous highest against India, 103 by Knott and R.A. Hutton at Old Trafford in 1971.

Randall went on to his third Test century before being caught at cover after 350 minutes. In all, the last four wickets added 267. Allott and Willis put on 70 for the last wicket, beating the previous record, 57 by Murray and Hobbs at Edgbaston in 1967. And for good measure, Willis also reached his highest Test score on his first appearance as captain.

This was followed by penetrative bowling by Willis and Botham and by Pringle on his Test debut. All found the new ball would occasionally bounce disconcertingly and India's earlier batsmen, opting to play back rather than forward, disappeared in a rush of undisputed lbw decisions. By the close they were 92 for 5.

Saturday, like so many in recent years at Lord's, was ruined by rain, which allowed time only for 36 of the day's agreed minimum 94 overs. The frequent stoppages kept England's bowlers fresh, and India's first innings was quickly wrapped up. The sixth-wicket stand of 67 between Gavaskar and Kapil Dev produced over half India's total. Following on 305 behind, they soon lost two more wickets, including the vital one of Gavaskar.

Under these dispiriting circumstances, previous Indian sides might have capitulated. But on the fourth day, despite two more early blows, this one fought back with much character and skill, especially Vengsarkar, who overcame an indifferent start to bat with considerable application and spasmodic outbreaks of brilliance for the best part of six hours.

He was in luck when, at 65, Taylor, diving to his right in front of first slip, clearly thought he had caught him off Pringle, though this appeal was turned down. Vengsarkar went on to his sixth Test century before Allott held a good catch on the long leg boundary when he mishooked Willis.

Not long afterwards, Taylor's diving one-handed catch removed Malhotra, and India found themselves still needing 30 to avoid an innings defeat with only two wickets left: one of them, however, was Kapil Dev's, and, encouraged by an escape in the slips at 5, he launched a memorable onslaught on bowling that became increasingly short and ragged.

Hooking, driving and forcing, mostly with great power and little sign of fallibility, he raced to 50 out of 67 from 35 balls. Two sixes in one over from Edmonds maintained the tempo, and he seemed quite capable of beating the fastest Test century (Roy Fredericks' hundred from 71 balls against Australia) when he was caught off Botham for 89. He had received only 55 balls, and had struck 3 sixes and 13 fours.

Even then Kapil Dev was not done. When England embarked on the task of making 65 to win, he removed Tavaré, Cook, and Taylor, the nightwatchman, in four overs while 18 runs were scored. England were left profoundly relieved that their target was no stiffer.

There was a good deal of tension on the last morning, even though England needed only another 42. Doshi, pitching in the rough outside the left-hander's off stump, gave Gower more than one awkward moment. But Lamb saw England home with some forthright strokes. Nevertheless, Kapil Dev was an undisputed winner of the Man of the Match award.

ENGLAND 1ST INNINGS v. INDIA at LORD'S, LONDON on 10,11,12,14,15 JUNE, 1982. 1ST TEST. TOSS: ENGLAND

IN	OUT	MINS	No.	BATSMAN	HOW OUT	BOWLER	RUNS	WKT	TOTAL	6s	4s	BALLS	NOTES ON DISMISSAL
11.00	11.10	10	1	G. COOK	LBW	KAPIL DEV	4	1	5	·	1	11	Beaten by late inswinger/breakback. Half forward.
11.00	12.04	64	2	C.J. TAVARÉ	C VISWANATH	KAPIL DEV	4	3	37	·	·	31	Edged low to 1st slip. Flushed half-forward. KAPIL DEV'S 150th WICKET
11.12	11.35	23	3	A.J. LAMB	LBW	KAPIL DEV	9	2	18	·	2	21	Scored 4 off first ball in Tests. Beaten by breakback half forward.
11.37	2.00	103	4	D.I. GOWER	C VISWANATH	KAPIL DEV	37	4	96	·	2	83	Followed away-seamer - edged low to 1st slip's left.
12.06	2.48	123	5	I.T. BOTHAM	C MALHOTRA	MADAN LAL	67	5	149	1	8	105	Diving disputed catch at mid-wicket.
2.02	1.53	353	6	D.W. RANDALL	C PARKAR	KAPIL DEV	126	9	363	1	11	290	(3rd in TESTS - 1st in ENGLAND). Drove low to cover.
2.50	3.14	24	7	D.R. PRINGLE	C GAVASKAR	DOSHI	7	6	166	·	·	26	Edged leg-break via pad to silly-point.
3.16	11.13	159	8	P.H. EDMONDS	C KIRMANI	MADAN LAL	64	7	291	·	6	136	Edged leg-glance - 'walked'. Its in TESTS.
11.15	1.50	115	9	R.W. TAYLOR †	C VISWANATH	DOSHI	31	8	363	·	2	96	Down wicket. changed mind - gentle cut to slip.
1.52	(2.59)	67	10	P.J.W. ALLOTT	NOT OUT		41	·	·	1	2	51	-
1.55	2.59	64	11	R.G.D. WILLIS *	BOWLED	MADAN LAL	28	10	433	·	2	54	HS in TESTS. Missed steer - straight, good length ball.
				EXTRAS	b 1 lb 5 w - nb 9		15						

TOTAL (off 148.1 overs in 561 min.) **433** all out at 2.59 pm on 2nd DAY.

6s 3   4s 36   904 balls (inc. 15 no balls)

* CAPTAIN   † WICKET-KEEPER

© BILL FRINDALL

BOWLER	O	M	R	W	nb	wb	HRS	OVERS	RUNS
KAPIL DEV	43	8	125	5	10	-	1	14	37
MADAN LAL	28.1	6	99	3	-	-	2	15	55
SHASTRI	34	10	73	0	3	-	3	16	45
DOSHI	40	7	120	2	2	-	4	16	42
YASHPAL	3	2	1	0	-	-	5	19	54
		15					6	16	45
	148.1	33	433	10			7	14	35
							8	17	40
							9	16	56

2ND NEW BALL taken at 5:22 pm 1ST DAY - ENGLAND 242-6 after 86.2 overs

LUNCH: 92-3	GOWER 34* (83 min.) BOTHAM 39* (54 min.) OFF 29 OVERS IN 120 MINUTES
TEA: 179-6	RANDALL 40* (98 min.) EDMONDS 4* (24 min.) OFF 61 OVERS IN 240 MINUTES
STUMPS: 278-6 (1ST DAY)	RANDALL 84* (220 min.) EDMONDS 55* (146 min.) OFF 96 OVERS IN 362 MINUTES
LUNCH: 354-7	RANDALL 122* (341 min.) TAYLOR 26* (106 min.) OFF 128 OVERS IN 483 MINUTES

ENGLAND'S LAST 4 WICKETS ADDED 267.
KAPIL DEV took 5 wkts for 11th TIME IN 38 TESTS
† ENGLAND RECORD PARTNERSHIP v. INDIA

RUNS	MINS	OVERS	LAST 50 (in mins)
50	86	19.1	86
100	132	35.1	46
150	192	46.5	60
200	266	68.3	74
250	332	88.2	66
300	405	106	73
350	475	125.3	70
400	532	140.3	57

WKT	PARTNERSHIP		RUNS	MINS
1st	Cook	Tavaré	5	10
2nd	Tavaré	Lamb	13	23
3rd	Tavaré	Gower	19	27
4th	Gower	Botham	59	74
5th	Botham	Randall	53	46
6th	Randall	Pringle	17	24
7th	Randall	Edmonds	125†	159
8th	Randall	Taylor	72	115
9th	Randall	Allott	0	1
10th	Allott	Willis	70†	64

15 OVERS 5 BALLS/HOUR
2.92 RUNS/OVER
48 RUNS/100 BALLS

INDIA — 1st INNINGS

In reply to ENGLAND'S 433 all out

IN	OUT	MINS	No.	BATSMAN	HOW OUT	BOWLER	RUNS	WKT	TOTAL	6s	4s	BALLS	NOTES ON DISMISSAL
3·10	1·58	191	1	S.M. GAVASKAR*	BOWLED	BOTHAM	48	8	116	·	·	133	Missed drive at ball that hit middle stump. slight breakback.
3·10	3·38	28	2	G.A. PARKAR	LBW	BOTHAM	6	1	17	·	·	33	Pushed half-forward to ball of full length. Front leg.
4·02	4·14	12	3	D.B. VENGSARKAR	LBW	WILLIS	2	2	21	·	·	9	Played back - tried to force overpitched ball.
4·16	4·26	10	4	G.R. VISWANATH	BOWLED	BOTHAM	1	3	22	·	·	7	Off stump - ball kept low - played back - late.
4·28	4·50	22	5	YASHPAL SHARMA	LBW	PRINGLE	4	4	31	·	·	18	Misjudged line of full-length ball - half forward. PRINGLE'S 1st BALL in TEST
4·52	5·05	13	6	A. MALHOTRA	LBW	PRINGLE	5	5	45	·	1	10	Beaten by shortish ball which kept low and came back.
5·07	1·51	91	7	KAPIL DEV	C' COOK	WILLIS	41	6	112	·	4	69	Fended lifting ball one-handed to gully.
1·53	1·55	2	8	R.J. SHASTRI	C' COOK	WILLIS	4	7	116	·	1	3	Reflex jab to backward short-leg.
1·57	(2·18)	21	9	S.M.H. KIRMANI†	NOT OUT		6			·	·	14	
2·00	2·15	15	10	MADAN LAL	C' TAVARÉ	BOTHAM	6	9	128	·	1	9	His first f-c dismissal on tour (115 runs). Edged low to 2nd slip.
2·17	2·18	1	11	D.R. DOSHI	C' TAYLOR	BOTHAM	0	10	128	·	·	3	Lifter took inside edge - caught falling to right.

EXTRAS: b - lb 1 w - nb 4 = 5 of 9* 308 balls (inc 4 no balls)

TOTAL: 128 all out at 2·18 pm on 3rd day (OFF 50·4 OVERS IN 211 MIN)

* CAPTAIN † WICKET-KEEPER

© BILL FRINDALL

14 OVERS 2 BALLS/HOUR
2·53 RUNS/OVER
42 RUNS/100 BALLS

WKT	PARTNERSHIP		RUNS	MINS
1st	Gavaskar	Parkar	17	28
2nd	Gavaskar	Vengsarkar	4	12
3rd	Gavaskar	Viswanath	1	10
4th	Gavaskar	Yashpal	9	22
5th	Gavaskar	Malhotra	14	13
6th	Gavaskar	Kapil Dev	67	91
7th	Gavaskar	Shastri	4	2
8th	Gavaskar	Kirmani	0	1
9th	Kirmani	Madanlal	12	15
10th	Kirmani	Doshi	0	1
			128	

TEA: 17-1 GAVASKAR 9* (28 min.) OFF 6·5 OVERS IN 28 MIN.

STUMPS: 92-5 (2nd DAY) GAVASKAR 41* (166 min.) KAPIL DEV 28* (73 min.) OFF 41 OVERS IN 166 MIN. [341 BEHIND - 142 to avoid follow on]

3RD DAY: RAIN at 11·00 a.m. STARTED 12·15 pm. 75mm LOST

LUNCH: 99-5 at 12·45pm GAVASKAR 45* (172 min.) KAPIL DEV 31* (79 min.) (7 balls in 6 min.) 334 BEHIND - 135 to avoid f-on

INDIA all out in 39 minutes after resumption off 8·3 overs - 29 runs added for last 5 wickets

INDIA asked to follow on - 305 BEHIND

BOTHAM 5 WICKETS FOR 19th TIME IN 49 TESTS

BOWLER	O	M	R	W	nb
BOTHAM	19·4	3	46	5	·
WILLIS	16	2	41	3	4
PRINGLE	9	4	16	2	·
EDMONDS	2	1	5	0	·
ALLOTT	4	1	15	0	·
	50·4	11	128	10	5

HRS	OVERS	RUNS
1	14	25
2	16	30
3	14	53

RUNS	MINS	OVERS	LAST 50
50	104	25·1	104
100	173	42·5	69

INDIA 2nd INNINGS   Following on 305 runs behind on first innings

IN	OUT	MINS	No.	BATSMAN	HOW OUT	BOWLER	RUNS	WKT	TOTAL	6s	4s	BALLS	NOTES ON DISMISSAL
2:30	5:59	84	1	S.M.GAVASKAR*	C' COOK	WILLIS	24	2	47	.	1	73	Fended lifting ball to backward short leg - off glove.
2:30	2:54	24	2	G.A.PARKAR	BOWLED	WILLIS	1	1	6	.	.	12	Misjudged line - played no stroke to ball angled in to him.
2:56	4:03	334	3	D.B.VENGSARKAR	C' ALLOTT	WILLIS	157	5	252	.	21	263	Top-edged hook at bouncer - skier to long-leg. (6th in TESTS)
6:01	12:08	94	4	R.J.SHASTRI	BOWLED	ALLOTT	23	3	107	.	.	71	Off stump out - beaten by breakback.
12:10	12:14	6	5	G.R.VISWANATH	C' TAYLOR	PRINGLE	3	4	110	.	.	6	Legside catch off attempted leg-glance at short-ish ball.
12:16	4:10	179	6	YASHPAL SHARMA	BOWLED	WILLIS	37	6	252	.	.	146	Beaten by breakdown - late on stroke.
4:05	4:16	11	7	A.MALHOTRA	C' TAYLOR	WILLIS	0	7	254	.	.	7	Fenced at ball outside off stump - caught in front of 1st slip. WILLS from WKT
4:13	5:31	78	8	KAPIL DEV	C' COOK	BOTHAM	89	10	369	3	13	55	Pulled long hop to mid-on.
4:18	4:37	19	9	S.M.H.KIRMANI †	C' GOWER	WILLIS	3	8	275	.	.	14	Edged low to 4th slip.
4:39	5:12	33	10	MADAN LAL	LBW	PRINGLE	15	9	341	.	3	21	Played back - ball kept low.
5:14	(5:13)	17	11	D.R.DOSHI	NOT OUT		4			.	.	14	
				EXTRAS	b -	lb 2	13			3ᵇ	3⁹	682 balls (inc. 11 no balls).	

TOTAL   b - lb 2   w - nb 11   **369** all out at 5.31 pm on 4th day.

(OFF 111.5 OVERS IN 448 MIN)

* CAPTAIN   † WICKET-KEEPER

© BILL FRINDALL

BOWLER	O	M	R	W	nb
BOTHAM	31.5	7	103	1	-
WILLIS	28	3	101	6	9
PRINGLE	19	4	58	2	-
ALLOTT	17	3	51	1	1
EDMONDS	15	6	39	0	-
COOK	1	0	4	0	-
TOTAL	111.5	23	369	10	

NEW BALL taken at 3.08pm 4th day.
INDIA 209.4 after 85 overs.

nb	HRS	OVERS	RUNS
.	1	14	32
9	2	14	35
	3	15	40
1	4	16	26
	5	20	54
.	6	15	65
	7	12	75

RUNS	MINS	OVERS	LAST 50 (in mins)
50	94	21.5	94
100	168	39.5	74
150	260	66	92
200	309	81	49
250	360	93.3	51
300	412	103.5	52
350	434	108.3	22

TEA: 15-1 [29.0 BEHIND]

STUMPS: 61-2 (3RD DAY) [244 BEHIND]   157 MIN PLAY (85.4 OVERS)

LUNCH: 132-4 [173 BEHIND]

TEA: 246-4 [59 BEHIND]

GAVASKAR 12" (39 min.)
VENGSARKAR 2" (13 min.)
OFF 9 OVERS IN 39 MINUTES
RESP: 3.09-5.14 pm (inc TEA)   28 OVERS LOST

VENGSARKAR 30ᵈ (86 min.)
SHASTRI 6" (26 min.)
OFF 26 OVERS IN 112 MINUTES

VENGSARKAR 65" (208 min.)
YASHPAL 14ᵈ (46 min.)
OFF 58 OVERS IN 234 MINUTES

VENGSARKAR 151" (331 min.)
YASHPAL 37ᵈ (169 min.)
OFF 93 OVERS IN 357 MINUTES

15 OVERS 0 BALLS/HOUR
3.30 RUNS/OVER
54 RUNS/100 BALLS

WKT	PARTNERSHIP		RUNS	MINS
1st	Gavaskar	Parkar	6	24
2nd	Gavaskar	Vengsarkar	41	58
3rd	Vengsarkar	Shastri	60	94
4th	Vengsarkar	Viswanath	3	4
5th	Vengsarkar	Yashpal	142	172
6th	Yashpal	Malhotra	0	5
7th	Malhotra	Kapil Dev	2	3
8th	Kapil Dev	Kirmani	21	19
9th	Kapil Dev	Madanlal	66	33
10th	Kapil Dev	Doshi	28	17

369

ENGLAND 2ND INNINGS — Requiring 65 runs to win.

IN	OUT	MINS	No.	BATSMAN	HOW OUT	BOWLER	RUNS	WKT	TOTAL	6s	4s	BALLS	NOTES ON DISMISSAL
5.41	6.07	26	1	G. COOK	LBW	KAPIL DEV	10	3	18	.	.	24	Hit on back leg by ball that came back and kept low.
5.41	5.57	16	2	C.J. TAVARÉ	BOWLED	KAPIL DEV	3	1	11	.	.	6	Played back to good length ball - lost off stump.
5.59	6.01	2	3	R.W.TAYLOR †	C⁷MALHOTRA	KAPIL DEV	1	2	13	.	.	2	Bat/pad catch to short-leg.
6.02	(11.40)	52	4	A.J. LAMB	NOT OUT		37			.	5	53	
6.09	(11.40)	45	5	D.I. GOWER	NOT OUT		14			.	.	30	
			6	I.T. BOTHAM	⎫								
			7	D.W. RANDALL	⎪								
			8	D.R. PRINGLE	⎬ Did not bat								
			9	P.H. EDMONDS	⎪								
			10	P.J.W. ALLOTT	⎪								
			11	R.G.D WILLIS*	⎭								
				EXTRAS	b - lb 2 w - nb -		2			0⁶	5⁴	115 balls (inc 1 no ball)	

TOTAL (off 19 OVERS in 73 MIN) = 67-3

* CAPTAIN   † WICKET-KEEPER

© BILL FRINDALL

15 OVERS 3 BALLS/HOUR
3.53 RUNS/OVER
58 RUNS/100 BALLS

WKT	PARTNERSHIP		RUNS	MINS
1st	Cook	Tavaré	11	16
2nd	Cook	Taylor	2	2
3rd	Cook	Lamb	5	5
4th	Lamb	Gower	49*	45
			67	

STUMPS: 23-3   LAMB 6* (12 min)
(4th DAY)   (42 REQUIRED)   GOWER 2* (5 min)
OFF 8 OVERS IN 33 MIN.

5TH DAY: ENGLAND SCORED 44 RUNS
IN 40 MINUTES OFF 11 OVERS

ENGLAND beat INDIA
by 7 wickets at 11.40 am on 5th day.

MAN OF THE MATCH : KAPIL DEV
(Adjudicator: F.S.TRUEMAN)

TOTAL TIME LOST : 58 OVERS on 3RD DAY (92·1 NET)

BOWLER	O	M	R	W	nb	HRS	OVERS	RUNS	RUNS	MINS	OVERS	LAST 50 (in mins)
KAPIL DEV	10	1	43	3	.	1	15	49	50	59	15·1	59
MADAN LAL	2	1	2	0	.							
DOSHI	5	3	11	0	.							
SHASTRI	2	0	9	0	.							
			2									
	19	5	67	3								

Second Test: Old Trafford, June 24, 25, 26, 27, 28.
Drawn.

Cruelly treated by the weather and spurned by the public though it was, the second Test match had its share of memorable moments before it was abandoned as a draw without a ball being bowled on the final day.

These included centuries by Ian Botham and Sandeep Patil, another near miss by Geoff Miller, and more hostile bowling by Bob Willis, who during the course of the match overtook Brian Statham's 252 wickets for England. This put him third behind Fred Trueman (307) and Derek Underwood (297).

The light was poor when England batted after winning the toss, having left Allott (who was unfit) and Jarvis out of their 13 and opted for two spinners. Cook and Tavaré figured in their first century opening partnership, though not without difficulty and some luck on a pitch that helped the quicker bowlers and also took some spin.

Another semi-crisis followed, however, when Lamb fell driving at a late outswinger and Gower was caught off a firm stroke. Botham, in his fiftieth Test match, found this an ideal occasion to demonstrate his more disciplined approach, and with Miller added 169 for the sixth wicket.

Initially, Botham batted so vigorously that he made 50 from 46 balls, with 10 fours. He adopted a more sober approach with the advent of the second new ball, and on the third morning moved to three figures with much brilliance, despite being struck on the boot at 67 by a full toss from the otherwise highly inoffensive Nayak.

With Gower as a runner, Botham made his next 33 from 4 overs, with 7 fours, before playing-on to a ball from Shastri that spun back just enough to dislodge a bail. Miller, in his first Test innings since Port of Spain in February 1981, had not been entirely inactive while batting in Botham's giant shadow. And, but for rain washing out the rest of the day, he might well have gone on to three figures.

England were eventually able to declare late on the third day, in time to give India a testing hour, in moderate light, in which they were reduced to 35 for 3.

On the Sunday, both Viswanath and Kirmani, the nightwatchman, played well in their vastly different styles. But India still had some way to go when Patil appeared and, with Kapil Dev, avoided the possibility of following on for the second successive Test.

By now England's bowlers were some way below their best, and Patil, having dealt severely with the spinners, turned his attention to Willis. Hitting 6 fours off an over that included a no-ball, he equalled the Test record for the number of runs from the bat off a six-ball over.

This onslaught took him from 80 to beyond 100, his second 50 needing only 51 deliveries. India had also scored 344 runs in the day, effectively saving the match, although, as it happened, the weather had the last word.

ENGLAND 1ST INNINGS v INDIA 2ND TEST at OLD TRAFFORD, MANCHESTER, on 24,25,26,27,28 (no play) JUNE, 1982. TOSS: ENGLAND

IN	OUT	MINS	No.	BATSMAN	HOW OUT	BOWLER	RUNS	WKT	TOTAL	6s	4s	BALLS	NOTES ON DISMISSAL
11.00	3.16	192	1	G. COOK	BOWLED	DOSHI	66	1	106	.	9	173	Pushed forward - leg-spin took off stump. HS in TESTS.
11.00	4.32	249	2	C.J. TAVARÉ	BOWLED	DOSHI	57	4	161	.	7	176	Down wicket - attempted drive - misjudged flight.
3.18	3.30	12	3	A.J. LAMB	C VISWANATH	MADAN LAL	9	2	117	.	1	9	Edged drive at widish half-volley to 1st slip (via 2nd slip)
3.32	4.14	23	4	D.I. GOWER	C SHASTRI	MADAN LAL	9	3	141	.	.	21	Turned in-swinger firmly to backward short leg.
4.16	12.43	199	5	I.T. BOTHAM	BOWLED	SHASTRI	128	6	330	2	19	169	(C in TESTS. Down wicket, drove, played on.
4.34	4.35	1	6	D.W. RANDALL	C KIRMANI	DOSHI	0	5	161	.	.	3	Edged attempted off-glide to 'keeper.
4.37	3.31	324	7	G. MILLER	C VENGSARKAR	DOSHI	98	9	419	.	13	244	Pushed half-forward - edged to silly-point via foot.
12.45	1.47	82	8	D.R. PRINGLE	ST KIRMANI	DOSHI	23	7	382	.	1	74	Down wicket - aimed drive - beaten by leg-break.
1.49	3.25	54	9	P.H. EDMONDS	C KIRMANI	MADAN LAL	12	8	413	.	.	53	Edged off-drive to keeper.
3.27	(4.56)	10	10	R.W. TAYLOR †	NOT OUT		1			.	.	5	
4.50	4.56	6	11	R.G.D. WILLIS *	C GAVASKAR	DOSHI	6	10	425	.	1	5	Skied slog to 2nd slip position (caught by gully).

EXTRAS b 2 lb 5 w - nb 9 | 16 | 2s 4 5s 2 | 932 balls (inc 13 no balls)

TOTAL (off 153.1 overs in 585 min.) 425 all out at 4.56 pm on 3rd day.

* CAPTAIN † WICKET-KEEPER

15 OVERS 4 BALLS/HOUR
2.77 RUNS/OVER
46 RUNS/100 BALLS

WKT	PARTNERSHIP		RUNS	MINS
1st	Cook	Tavaré	106†	192
2nd	Tavaré	Lamb	11	12
3rd	Tavaré	Gower	24	23
4th	Tavaré	Botham	20	16
5th	Botham	Randall	0	1
6th	Botham	Miller	169‡	178
7th	Miller	Pringle	52	82
8th	Miller	Edmonds	31	54
9th	Miller	Taylor	6	4
10th	Taylor	Willis	6	6

† England record for 1st wkt v India at Manchester.
‡ England record for 6th v India in England.
© BILL FRINDALL 1982

BOWLER	O	M	R	W	nb		HRS	OVERS	RUNS
KAPIL DEV	36	5	109	0	2		1	15	30
MADAN LAL	35	9	104	3	-		2	16	38
NAYAK	12	1	50	0	-		3	17	30
DOSHI	47.1	17	102	6	11		4	15	48
SHASTRI	23	8	44	1	-		5	14	78
							6	17	24
			16				7	15	57
	153.1	40	425	10			8	17	55
							9	16	36

2nd NEW BALL taken at 5.55 pm 1st day.
- ENGLAND 236-5 after 87.2 overs

RUNS	MINS	OVERS	LAST 50 (in mins)
50	90	22.4	90
100	184	49.1	94
150	245	64.1	61
200	285	72.5	40
250	366	96	81
300	412	107	46
350	462	121.4	50
400	553	145	91

LUNCH: 68-0
BLSP 2.11 - 2.35 pm (24 minutes - 6 overs - lost)
TEA: 126-2   COOK 38* (97 balls) TAVARÉ 27* (92 balls)
OFF 31 OVERS IN 120 MINUTES
TAVARÉ 45* (217 min.) GOWER 1* (9 min.)
OFF 57 OVERS IN 217 MINUTES
STUMPS: 239-5 (1st DAY) BOTHAM 60* (109 min.) MILLER 26* (88 min.)
OFF 90 OVERS IN 342 MINUTES
LUNCH: 340-6 (STUMPS 2nd DAY) MILLER 53* (195 min.) PRINGLE 3* (15 min.)
OFF 118 OVERS IN 449 MINUTES
PLAY ABANDONED AT 4.15pm - 4 HR 15 MIN LOST 2nd DAY.
3rd DAY: DRYING OPERATIONS DELAYED START BY ONE HOUR
LUNCH: 373-6 MILLER 75* (250 min.) 13rd OVERS PRINGLE 14* (76 min.) 510 MIN.
RSP 2.25-3.10 pm and again at 3.34 pm
TEA: 419-9 TAYLOR 2* (4 min.)
OFF 151.5 OVERS IN 579 MIN.

INDIA 1ST INNINGS — In reply to ENGLAND'S 425 all out

IN	OUT	MINS	No.	BATSMAN	HOW OUT	BOWLER	RUNS	WKT	TOTAL	6s	4s	BALLS	NOTES ON DISMISSAL
5·08	5·27	19	1	S.M.GAVASKAR*	Cᵗ TAVARÉ	WILLIS	2	2	8	·	·	20	Edged lifting ball low to 2nd slip.
5·08	5·20	12	2	R.J.SHASTRI	Cᵗ COOK	WILLIS	0	1	5	·	·	7	Fended lifting ball to backward short leg.
5·22	6·08	26	3	D.B.VENGSARKAR	Cᵗ RANDALL	PRINGLE	12	3	25	·	1	17	Edged square-drive to 4th slip - hard, fast catch.
5·29	1·54	110	4	G.R.VISWANATH	Cᵗ TAYLOR	BOTHAM	54	4	112	·	8	91	Top-edged cut at off-side long hop (away-steamer).
6·10	3·42	159	5	S.M.H.KIRMANI†	BOWLED	EDMONDS	58	6	173	·	8	135	Played back - beaten by leg-spin - quicker ball.
1·56	3·09	35	6	YASHPAL SHARMA	BOWLED	EDMONDS	10	5	136	·	1	34	Beaten by ball that kept low - played back.
3·11	(1·00)	210	7	S.M.PATIL	NOT OUT		129			2	18	196	2nd [HIT by Indian in O.T.Test] HIT 44④ 0 444 (2x) off willis 17thover.
3·44	5·19	77	8	KAPIL DEV	Cᵗ TAYLOR	MILLER	65	7	269	1	9	55	Top-edged square-cut at top-spinner. 50 off 33 balls.
5·21	6·37	76	9	MADAN LAL	BOWLED	EDMONDS	26	8	366	·	4	64	Tried to cut quicker 'arm' ball.
6·39	(1·00)	21	10	S.V.NAYAK	NOT OUT		2			·	·	19	
			11	D.R.DOSHI	DID NOT BAT								
				EXTRAS	b 6 lb 2 w 3 nb 10		21			3⁶ 4⁹		638 balls (inc. 14 no balls)	

TOTAL (off 104 overs in 380 minutes) **379-8**

* CAPTAIN   † WICKET-KEEPER

16 OVERS 2 BALLS/HOUR
3·64 RUNS/OVER
59 RUNS/100 BALLS

WKT	PARTNERSHIP		RUNS	MINS
1st	Gavaskar	Shastri	5	12
2nd	Gavaskar	Vengsarkar	3	5
3rd	Vengsarkar	Viswanath	17	19
4th	Viswanath	Kirmani	87	89
5th	Kirmani	Yashpal	24	35
6th	Kirmani	Patil	37	30
7th	Patil	Kapil Dev	96	77
8th	Patil	Madanlal	97	76
9th	Patil	Nayak	13*	21
			379	

PATIL: Hit 24 runs off Willis's 17th over (2nd new ball) - TEST RECORD IN ENGLAND (MOST RUNS off over) - WORLD TEST RECORD (SIX BOUNDARIES off AN OVER)

BOWLER	O	M	R	W
WILLIS	17	2	94	2
PRINGLE	15	4	33	1
EDMONDS	37	12	94	3
BOTHAM	19	4	86	1
MILLER	16	4	51	1
			21	
	104	26	379	8

HRS	OVERS	RUNS
1	14	42
2	15	62
3	17	45
4	17	79
5	19	58
6	16	80
	104	

2ND NEW BALL TAKEN at 5·52pm on 4th day
- INDIA 301-7 after 86 overs

RUNS	MINS	OVERS	LAST 50 (in mins)
50	68	16	68
100	117	28·1	49
150	179	46·2	62
200	225	60	46
250	251	65·5	26
300	311	86	60
350	332	90·4	21

BLSP 5·42-6·02 pm - (20 min. lost)
STUMPS: 35-3 (3rd DAY) [390 BEHIND]
VISWANATH 15* (27 min.)
KIRMANI 0* (6 min.)

BLSP 12·47-1·02 pm (15 min/4 over lost); OFF 11 OVERS IN 48 MIN.
LUNCH: 113-4
KIRMANI 33* (97 min.); YASHPAL 0* (6 min.) OFF 35 OVERS IN 139 MIN.

TEA: 255-6
PATIL 42* (90 min.); KAPIL DEV 60* (57 min.) OFF 69 OVERS IN 260 MIN

STUMPS: 379-8 (4th DAY) [46 BEHIND]
PATIL 129* (210 min.); NAYAK 2* (21 min.) OFF 104 OVERS IN 380 MIN.

NO PLAY POSSIBLE ON FIFTH DAY - ABANDONED at 3·35pm; TOTAL TIME LOST: 13hr 52min (220 OVERS)
MATCH DRAWN
MAN OF THE MATCH: S.M. PATIL (adjudicator: A.E.R.Gilligan)

Third Test: the Oval, July 8, 9, 10, 12, 13.
Drawn.
Like both its predecessors, the third and final Test had moments of high excitement and great quality, though it was also a disappointment for India, whose captain Sunil Gavaskar took no further part after being injured on the first day. Despite his absence and in the face of a huge total, India batted with much character to avoid the follow-on, albeit with 7 wickets down.

Allan Lamb made the maiden century that had been easy to predict since his debut. But more than anything this was Ian Botham's match: his 208, made from only 226 deliveries, ranks as one of the great Test match exhibitions of batting.

On the first morning, however, England were again indebted to Cook and Tavaré. In a manner not dissimilar to Old Trafford, they prevailed against the moving ball and eccentric bounce to put on 96 and, equally importantly, allow the stroke-players the benefit of easing conditions later.

How well they showed their appreciation! Lamb, after a lengthy examination of the bowling, batted with growing fluency. Nevertheless, cutting at Nayak, who returned to the attack bowling leg-spin, he could have been out off the stroke that took him to 50.

Botham struck the ball with great power, off front and back foot. Early in his innings, going back to force Shastri, he hit the unfortunate Gavaskar, fielding at silly point, a fearsome blow on his left shin. Gavaskar limped off, but a broken bone was diagnosed soon after close of play, and with England already at 329 for 3 it was a gloomy evening for India.

Botham and Lamb had already added 144 from 28 overs and English mouths watered at the thought of what India's bowlers might suffer if both became re-established. As it happened, Lamb was run out soon after reaching three figures, when he set off somewhat hesitantly for a second for Botham's stroke to mid-wicket.

By then Botham had reached his 11th century in Test matches — curiously only his 19th in all — and he enriched the rest of the day with a marvellous piece of batting. Driving straight with ferocious power, cutting and forcing off the back foot, he never lost his self-discipline, and, as a result, gave the bowlers little hope.

One straight six off Doshi left its mark for posterity in the shape of a hole on the pavilion roof. When he reached 200 from 220 balls in 268 minutes, it was the fastest double century by an English batsman since Denis Compton's innings against Pakistan in 1954. In terms of balls received, it may well have been the fastest of all time.

When he was caught soon afterwards, playing a reverse sweep at Doshi, he had hit 19 fours and 4 sixes. The entire ground rose to applaud a memorable innings and inevitably there was a sense of anticlimax afterwards.

The Indian spinners, indeed, posed problems for the rest of England's middle order, and Randall was not at his best as he worked his way towards what appeared to be a certain hundred. By now England's progress was so limited that they would probably have declared, but for the fact that increasingly poor light might well have restricted their opportunity of bowling at India.

So the innings meandered on until Randall was stumped five short of three figures. Next day, with Vengsarkar opening in place of Gavaskar, India batted with much spirit. Shastri, Viswanath, and Patil all made half-centuries. With only four effective wickets left, however, they still needed 111 to avoid the follow-on, and could not have been sorry when bad light delayed Monday's start until 2.20 p.m., with a resulting loss of 42 overs.

Kapil Dev then played another important, vigorous innings, in company with Kirmani, while England laboured on an increasingly mild pitch. The all-rounder made 97 from 93 balls before falling to a stroke intended to take him to three figures, and India avoided the prospect of batting again with two effective wickets left.

Cook was then dismissed in a lively spell of new-ball bowling by Kapil Dev, but the game died a predictable, lingering death on the last day, with Willis delaying his declaration until the match was out of India's reach. Though some spectators in a small crowd voiced their displeasure, no other sensible course was open to him.

ENGLAND 1ST INNINGS v. INDIA 3RD TEST at KENNINGTON OVAL, LONDON, on 8,9,10,12,13 JULY, 1982.

TOSS: ENGLAND

IN	OUT	MINS	No.	BATSMAN	HOW OUT	BOWLER	RUNS	WKT	TOTAL	6s	4s	BALLS	NOTES ON DISMISSAL
11·00	2·05	146	1	G. COOK	c SHASTRI	PATIL	50	1	96	·	4	98	Simple catch to mid-off. (checked stroke - ball 'stopped'.
11·00	2·10	151	2	C.J. TAVARÉ	BOWLED	KAPIL DEV	39	2	96	·	4	123	KAPIL DEV'S 50th WKT v. ENGLAND (4th Indian). Aimed on-drive - missing, took edge and pad.
2·07	11·35	200	3	A.J. LAMB	RUN OUT [SHASTRI→ KAPIL DEV]		107	4	361	1	8	202	Called late by Botham for second run to mid-wicket.
2·12	4·21	108	4	D.I. GOWER	c KIRMANI	SHASTRI	47	3	185	·	3	90	Edged dab-cut to 'keeper. 'Walked'.
4·23	2·26	276	5	I.T. BOTHAM	c VISWANATH	DOSHI	208	5	512	4	19	226	Hit reverse sweep to slip - anticipated catch. HS in TESTS (11th)
11·36	5·54	247	6	D.W. RANDALL	st KIRMANI	SHASTRI	95	10	594	·	5	212	Down wicket - beaten by leg-break.
2·28	3·00	32	7	D.R. PRINGLE	st KIRMANI	DOSHI	9	6	534	·	2	26	Down wicket - missed big drive at leg-break. (ct out Taylor)
3·02	3·36	34	8	P.H. EDMONDS	c SUB (PARKAR)	DOSHI	14	7	562	·	1	25	Top-edged sweep to backward square-leg.
3·38	5·31	22	9	R.W. TAYLOR†	LBW	SHASTRI	3	8	569	·	·	31	Played back - beaten by top-spinner.
5·33	5·43	10	10	P.J.W. ALLOTT	c YASHPAL	DOSHI	3	9	582	·	·	12	Pushed forward - lobbed catch to short extra-cover.
5·45	(5·54)	9	11	R.G.D. WILLIS	NOT OUT		1		-	·	·	8	-
				EXTRAS	b 3 lb 5 w - nb 10		18			5⁵	4⁶	1053 balls (inc 12 no balls)	
				TOTAL	(off 173·3 overs in 656 min)		594						all out at 5·54 pm on 2nd day (STUMPS)

* CAPTAIN   † WICKET-KEEPER

© BILL FRINDALL

BOWLER	O	M	R	W	nb	HRS	OVERS	RUNS
KAPIL DEV	25	4	109	1	3	1	14	41
MADAN LAL	26	8	69	0	2	2	15	42
NAYAK	21	5	66	0	·	3	15	39
PATIL	14	1	48	1	·	4	16	44
DOSHI	46	6	175	4	4	5	18	64
SHASTRI	41·3	8	109	3	2	6	14	79
					18	7	14	63
	173·3	32	594	10		8	15	63
						9	18	77
						10	18	45

2nd NEW BALL TAKEN at 5·39pm 1st day
- ENGLAND 269-3 after 85·3 overs

RUNS	MINS	OVERS	LAST 50 (in mins)
50	90	21	90
100	161	38·5	71
150	220	53·3	59
200	276	70·5	56
250	311	80·1	35
300	349	89·5	38
350	401	102·3	52
400	446	112·2	45
450	488	123·4	42
500	531	136·2	43
550	593	155·1	62

LUNCH: 83-0

TEA: 169-2

STUMPS: 329-3 (1st DAY)

LUNCH: 452-4

TEA: 562-7

RAIN 4·00-4·06pm (6 min lost). RAIN 4·10-5·15pm (65 min lost).
71 MINUTES LOST ON SECOND DAY.

COOK 42* (83 balls)   TAVARÉ 36* (94 balls)
OFF 29 OVERS IN 121 MIN

LAMB 31* (96 min)
GOWER 40* (91 min)
OFF 61 OVERS IN 244 MIN

LAMB 96* (225 min)
BOTHAM 82* (110 min)
OFF 96 OVERS IN 373 MIN

BOTHAM 162* (230 min)
RANDALL 29* (84 min)
OFF 125 OVERS IN 493 MIN

RANDALL 70* (204 min)
TAYLOR 0* (2 min)
OFF 161 OVERS IN 612 MIN

15 OVERS 5 BALLS/HOUR
3·42 RUNS/OVER
56 RUNS/100 BALLS

WKT	PARTNERSHIP		RUNS	MINS
1st	COOK	TAVARÉ	96	146
2nd	TAVARÉ	LAMB	0	3
3rd	LAMB	GOWER	89	108
4th	LAMB	BOTHAM	176	145
5th	BOTHAM	RANDALL	151	130
6th	RANDALL	PRINGLE	22	32
7th	RANDALL	EDMONDS	28	34
8th	RANDALL	TAYLOR	7	22
9th	RANDALL	ALLOTT	13	10
10th	RANDALL	WILLIS	12	9
			594	

INDIA — 1st INNINGS — In reply to ENGLAND'S 594 all out

IN	OUT	MINS	No.	BATSMAN	HOW OUT	BOWLER	RUNS	WKT	TOTAL	6s	4s	BALLS	NOTES ON DISMISSAL
11.00	2.57	197	1	R.J. SHASTRI	c BOTHAM	WILLIS	66	3	135	-	4	175	Brilliant 3rd slip catch - played downwards - fast ball.
11.00	11.35	35	2	D.B. VENGSARKAR	c EDMONDS	BOTHAM	6	1	21	-	1	24	Fended bouncer to short leg (square) - fine forward to take catch.
11.37	2.51	154	3	G.R. VISWANATH	LBW	WILLIS	56	2	134	-	3	119	Beaten by inswing - in delivery that kept low (low after 'tea'.)
2.53	5.42	149	4	YASHPAL SHARMA	c GOWER	WILLIS	38	5	248	-	4	118	Edged lifting ball to 3rd slip.
2.59	5.21	122	5	S.M. PATIL	c SUB (N.R.TAYLOR)	BOTHAM	62	4	232	-	9	102	Top-edged hook as bounces to fine leg - superb running, diving catch.
5.23	4.33	158	6	S.M.H. KIRMANI†	BOWLED	ALLOTT	43	8	396	-	5	113	Off stump out - missed backfoot square cut.
5.44	4.01	105	7	KAPIL DEV	c ALLOTT	EDMONDS	97	6	378	2	14	93	Mistimed drive - backward point catch.
4.03	4.25	22	8	MADAN LAL	c TAYLOR	EDMONDS	5	7	394	-	-	18	Edged leg-break to 'keeper'.
4.27	4.53	26	9	S.V. NAYAK	BOWLED	EDMONDS	11	9	410	-	2	18	Played on - attempted cut at off-break (to left-hander)
4.35	(4.53)	18	10	D.R. DOSHI	NOT OUT		5					13	
			11	S.M. GAVASKAR *	ABSENT HURT		-						Fractured left fibula - hit by Botham while at silly point - 1st day.
				EXTRAS	b 3 lb 5 w - nb 13		21						2b 41* 793 balls (inc. 17 no balls)

TOTAL (off 129.2 overs in 501 MINUTES)

410 all out at 4.53 pm on 4th Aug. [84 BEHIND]

15 OVERS 3 BALLS/HOUR
3.17 RUNS/OVER
52 RUNS/100 BALLS

* CAPTAIN † WICKET-KEEPER

© BILL FRINDALL

BOWLER	O	M	R	W	nb
WILLIS	23	4	78	3	
BOTHAM	19	4	73	2	
ALLOTT	24	4	69	1	
PRINGLE	28	5	80	0	
EDMONDS	35.2	11	89	3	21
	129.2	26	410	9	

HRS	OVERS	RUNS
1	13	43
2	18	29
3	18	58
4	14	39
5	17	49
6	14	55
7	15	62
8	15	60

2nd NEW BALL taken at 5.19 pm on 3rd day - INDIA 231-3 after 85 overs.

RUNS	MINS	OVERS	LAST 50 (in mins)
50	71	15.5	71
100	155	41.1	84
150	212	55.3	57
200	282	74.5	70
250	348	91.1	66
300	388	100.2	40
350	429	110.4	41
400	484	125.1	55

LUNCH: 72-1

TEA: 169-3 SHASTRI 30* (120 min.) VISWANATH 51* (83 min.) OFF 31 OVERS IN 120 MIN.

YASHPAL 13* (47 min) PATIL 19* (41 min) OFF 63 OVERS IN 240 MIN.

STUMPS: 284-5 (3RD DAY) KIRMANI 12* (96 min.) KAPIL DEV 28* (35 min.) OFF 96 OVERS IN 369 MIN

BAD LIGHT PREVENTED 4TH DAY'S START UNTIL 2.22 pm. (162 min - 42 OVERS LOST)

TEA: 374-5 KIRMANI 34* (115 min.) KAPIL DEV 93* (104 min.) OFF 117 OVERS IN 443 MIN.

ADDED 90 off 21 overs in 73 min. (395-7)

FOLLOW ON AVOIDED at 4.30 pm 4th day (395-7)

WKT	PARTNERSHIP		RUNS	MINS
1st	Shastri	Vengsarkar	21	35
2nd	Shastri	Viswanath	113	154
3rd	Shastri	Yashpal	1	4
4th	Yashpal	Patil	97	122
5th	Yashpal	Kirmani	16	19
6th	Kirmani	Kapil Dev	130†	105
7th	Kirmani	Madan Lal	16	22
8th	Kirmani	Nayak	2	6
9th	Nayak	Doshi	14	18

† Record India 6th wkt pair v England 410

ENGLAND 2ND INNINGS   184 runs ahead on first innings

IN	OUT	MINS	No.	BATSMAN	HOW OUT	BOWLER	RUNS	WKT	TOTAL	6s	4s	BALLS	NOTES ON DISMISSAL
5·05	5·30	25	1	G. COOK	c' YASHPAL	KAPIL DEV	8	1	12	·	1	19	Fended faster, lifting ball to short square-leg.
5·05	(2·50)	255	2	C. J. TAVARÉ	NOT OUT		75			·	6	207	
5·32	12·21	118	3	A. J. LAMB	BOWLED	DOSHI	45	2	94	·	5	93	Down wicket - played over well-flighted slower ball.
12·23	2·50	108	4	D. I. GOWER	c' and BOWLED	NAYAK	45	3	191	·	4	108	Simple return catch. Nayak's first Test wicket.
			5	I. T. BOTHAM									
			6	D. W. RANDALL									
			7	D. R. PRINGLE	DID NOT BAT								
			8	P. H. EDMONDS									
			9	R. W. TAYLOR †									
			10	P. J. W. ALLOTT									
			11	R. G. D. WILLIS *									
				EXTRAS	b 6 lb 8 w - nb 4		18			0	16	427 balls (inc. 4 no balls)	

TOTAL (OFF 70·3 OVERS IN 255 MINUTES)   191 - 3 DECLARED at 2·50pm on 5th day. [375 AHEAD]

* CAPTAIN   † WICKET-KEEPER

© BILL FRINDALL

BOWLER	O	M	R	W	nb
KAPIL DEV	19	3	53	1	3
MADAN LAL	11	6	17	0	1
DOSHI	19	5	47	1	·
SHASTRI	16	3	40	0	·
NAYAK	5·3	0	16	1	·
				8	
	70·3	17	191	3	

HRS	OVERS	RUNS
1	15	25
2	16	49
3	18	64
4	18	40

	RUNS	MINS	OVERS	LAST 50 (in mins)
	50	88	23	88
	100	152	41·2	64
	150	198	54·2	46

16 OVERS 3 BALLS/HOUR
2·71 RUNS/OVER
45 RUNS/100 BALLS

WKT	PARTNERSHIP		RUNS	MINS
1st	Cook	Tavaré	12	25
2nd	Tavaré	Lamb	82	118
3rd	Tavaré	Gower	97	108
			191	

STUMPS: 30 - 1   TAVARÉ 5* (64 min)
(4th DAY) [314 AHEAD]   LAMB 16* (37 min)
OFF 17 OVERS IN 64 MINUTES

LUNCH: 140 - 2   TAVARÉ 51* (185 min)
[324 AHEAD]   GOWER 25* (38 min)
OFF 51 OVERS IN 185 MINUTES

ENGLAND declared at 2·50 pm leaving INDIA a minimum of 160 minutes to score 376 runs to win and level series.

INDIA 2ND INNINGS

Needing 376 runs to win in a minimum of 160 minutes.

IN	OUT	MINS	No	BATSMAN	HOW OUT	BOWLER	RUNS	WKT	TOTAL	6s	4s	BALLS	NOTES ON DISMISSAL
3·02	3·03	1	1	R.J. SHASTRI	c' TAYLOR	WILLIS	0	1	0	·	·	3	Fenced at offside ball.
3·02	3·20	18	2	S.V. NAYAK	c' TAYLOR	PRINGLE	6	2	18	·	1	12	Low left-handed catch in front of slip. Edged offside push.
3·05	4·03	39	3	D.B. VENGSARKAR	c' TAYLOR	PRINGLE	16	3	43	·	1	29	Edged hook at bouncer—leg-side catch.
3·21	(5·30)	110	4	G.R. VISWANATH	NOT OUT		75			·	9	116	
4·05	(5·30)	85	5	YASHPAL SHARMA	NOT OUT		9			·	·	59	
			6	S.M. PATIL									
			7	KAPIL DEV									
			8	S.M.H. KIRMANI †	⎤								
			9	MADAN LAL	⎟ DID NOT BAT								
			10	D.R. DOSHI	⎟								
			11	S.M. GAVASKAR *	⎦								

* CAPTAIN † WICKET-KEEPER

EXTRAS b - lb 3 w - nb 2 5 0b 11 4s 219 balls (inc. 3 no balls)

TOTAL (OFF 36 OVERS IN 129 MINUTES) **111 - 3**

16 OVERS 4 BALLS/HOUR
3·08 RUNS/OVER
51 RUNS/100 BALLS

BOWLER	O	M	R	W	nb	HRS	OVERS	RUNS	RUNS	MINS	OVERS	LAST 50 (in mins)
WILLIS	4	0	16	1	3	1	15	47	50	59	15·1	59
PRINGLE	11	5	32	2	-	2	18	53	100	118	32·1	59
EDMONDS	13	5	34	0	·							
ALLOTT	4	1	12	0	·							
BOTHAM	4	0	12	0	·							
			5									
	36	11	111	3								

TEA : 42 - 2 VENGSARKAR 16* (36 min.)
VISWANATH 18* (20 min.)
OFF 9 OVERS IN 35 MINUTES

MATCH DRAWN ENGLAND WIN SERIES 1-0.

MAN OF THE MATCH : I.T. BOTHAM
MAN OF THE SERIES : KAPIL DEV
Adjudicator J.C. LAKER.

TOTAL TIME LOST : 3 hours 53 min (60 overs)

WKT	PARTNERSHIP		RUNS	MINS
1st	Shastri	Nayak	0	1
2nd	Nayak	Vengsarkar	18	18
3rd	Vengsarkar	Viswanath	25	23
4th	Viswanath	Yashpal	68*	85
			111	

© BILL FRINDALL

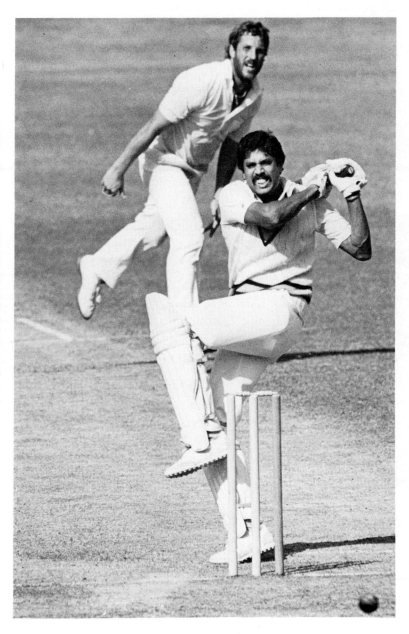

One of many duels between Kapil Dev and Ian Botham.

Middlesex (above), 1982 Schweppes County Champions. Standing: H. Sharp (scorer), D. Bennett (coach), C.R. Cook, W.N. Slack, N.J. Kemp, W.G. Merry, A.J. Smith, N.G. Cowans, K.D. James, N. Williams, P.R. Downton, R.O. Butcher, J. Miller (physiotherapist); seated: W.W. Daniel, G.D. Barlow, M.W.W. Selvey, M.W. Gatting, J.M. Brearley (captain), P.H. Edmonds, C.T. Radley, J.E. Emburey; front row: G. Ritchie, R.J. Maru, S.P. Hughes, C.P. Metson, K.P. Tomlins.

Sussex (below), 1982 John Player League Winners. Standing: L.V. Chandler (scorer), I.J. Gould, C.M. Wells, C.P. Phillipson, G.S. le Roux, A.P. Wells, I.A. Greig, S.J. Storey (senior coach); seated: A.C.S. Pigott, Imran Khan, J.R.T. Barclay (captain), P.W.G. Parker, C.E. Waller, G.D. Mendis.

Winners of the Daily Telegraph 'Twin Hundreds'
awards (see page 15). Malcolm Marshall (left), the only
bowler to reach 100 wickets in the season, did so on
August 25. Ian Botham (above) played the extraordinary innings that brought him the season's fastest
hundred for Somerset against Warwickshire at
Taunton on September 3.

Above: Mohsin Khan, the first batsman to make 200 in a Lord's Test since Martin Donnelly in 1949, departs momentarily from the effortless elegance that contributed so much to the attraction of the Pakistan touring side.

Left: Derek Randall hooks Imran Khan during the remarkable innings of 105 that enabled England to beat Pakistan in the first Test, on an unpredictable Edgbaston pitch, which baffled most batsmen in a low-scoring match.

A tale of two Illingworths. The saga of Yorkshire's captaincy took an unexpected turn when Chris Old resigned in mid-season and was succeeded by the manager, Ray Illingworth (left), at the age of 50. He had last played first-class cricket, for Leicestershire, in 1978. Richard Illingworth (above), no relation but also Yorkshire-born, is a left-arm spinner who took a lot of wickets for Young England in the Agatha Christie series against West Indies, and also made a promising start for Worcestershire.

Right: Sidath Wettimuny scored the first Test hundred by a Sri Lankan, against Pakistan at Faisalabad in March. His 157 and second-wicket stand of 217 with Dias gave Sri Lanka the better of a drawn match.

Right: 'Eight of the Best'. The Daily Telegraph Cricketers of the Year (see page 16).

1 Ian Botham (England)
2 Bruce Yardley (Australia)
3 Peter Kirsten (S. Africa)
4 Larry Gomes (W. Indies)
5 Richard Hadlee (NZ)
6 Kapil Dev (India)
7 Imran Khan (Pakistan)
8 D.S. de Silva (Sri Lanka)

Left: Abdul Qadir in the first Test, at Edgbaston. The return to Test cricket of a top-class leg-spinner, capable of mesmerizing young batsmen to whom his art was almost unknown, was one of the season's great joys.

Geoffrey Boycott and Graham Gooch go out to bat on the Wanderers Ground, in Johannesburg, during the tour of the South African Breweries team that earned them and 13 others a three-year ban from Test cricket.

ree newcomers to England sides for
om selection for the tour of Australia
uld have been no more than a wild
am at the start of the 1982 season: all-
nder Derek Pringle (right) of
mbridge University and Essex, wicket-
per Ian Gould (below) of Sussex, and
ce-man Norman Cowans (below right)
Middlesex.

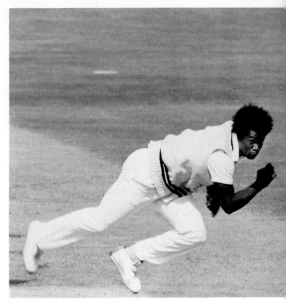

Roger Knight, one of the most respected county captains in the country, holds the NatWest Trophy aloft after Surrey had easily ended their run of three losing Lord's finals in three seasons by beating Warwickshire by nine wickets.

New Zealanders headed both the batting and bowling first-class averages in England in 1982. Glenn Turner (above left) marked his last season for Worcestershire by scoring his 100th hundred. Richard Hadlee (above) was mainly responsible for Nottinghamshire's first appearance in a Lord's final. The leading player available for England in both batting and bowling averages was Mike Gatting (left), but in one of the most widely criticized omissions of its type for years, he was left out of the England party to tour Australia.

Mike Brearley: end of a captain's innings.

Statistical Survey: England v India 1982

England — Batting/Fielding	M	I	NO	HS	R	Avge	100	50	Sixes	Fours	Mins.	Balls	R/H	Ct	St
I.T. Botham	3	3	0	208	405	134.33	2	1	7	46	598	500	81	1	—
D.W. Randall	3	3	0	126	221	73.66	1	1	1	16	601	505	44	1	—
A.J. Lamb	3	5	1	107	207	51.75	1	—	1	21	465	378	55	—	—
C.J. Tavaré	3	5	1	75*	178	44.50	—	2	—	17	735	543	33	2	—
P.J.W. Allott	2	2	1	41*	44	44.00	—	—	1	2	77	63	70	2	—
D.I. Gower	3	5	1	47	152	38.00	—	—	—	9	387	332	46	2	—
P.H. Edmonds	3	3	0	64	90	30.00	—	1	—	8	247	214	42	1	—
G. Cook	3	5	0	66	138	27.60	—	2	—	15	399	325	42	5	—
R.G.D. Willis	3	3	1	28	35	17.50	—	—	—	3	79	67	52	—	—
D.R. Pringle	3	3	0	23	39	13.00	—	—	—	3	138	126	31	1	—
R.W. Taylor	3	4	1	31	36	12.00	—	—	—	2	149	134	27	9	—
Also batted:															
G. Miller	1	1	0	98	98	98.00	—	1	—	13	324	244	40	—	—
Totals	33	42	6	(208)	1641	45.58	4	8	10	155	4199	3431	48	23†	—

England — Bowling	O	M	R	W	Avge	Best	5w/I	10w/M	B/W	R/H	NB	Wides
Willis	88	11	330	15	22.00	6-101	1	—	35	63	39	—
Pringle	82	22	219	7	31.28	2-16	—	—	70	45	2	1
Botham	93.3	16	320	9	35.55	5-46	1	—	62	57	2	3
Edmonds	102.2	35	261	6	43.50	3-89	—	—	102	43	5	—
Allott	49	9	147	2	73.50	1-51	—	—	147	50	1	—
Also bowled:												
Miller	16	4	51	1	51.00	1-51	—	—	96	53	—	—
Cook	1	0	4	0	—	—	—	—	—	67	—	—
Totals	431.5	97	1332	40	33.30	(6-101)	2	—	65	51	49	3

* Not out. = Plus one 'ct substitute'. R/H = runs per 100 balls. B/W = balls per wicket.

Statistical Survey: England v India 1982/continued

India — Batting/Fielding	M	I	NO	HS	R	Avge	100	50	Sixes	Fours	Minutes	Balls	R/H	Ct	St
S.M. Patil	2	2	1	129*	191	191.00	1	1	2	27	332	298	64	—	—
Kapil Dev	3	4	0	97	292	73.00	—	3	6	40	351	272	107	—	—
G.R. Viswanath	3	5	1	75*	189	47.25	—	3	—	20	388	339	56	5	—
D.B. Vengsarkar	3	5	0	157	193	38.60	1	—	—	23	446	342	56	1	—
S.M.H. Kirmani	3	4	1	58	110	36.66	—	1	—	13	357	276	40	4	3
S.M. Gavaskar	3	3	0	48	74	24.66	—	—	—	2	294	226	33	2	—
Yashpal Sharma	3	5	1	38	98	24.50	—	—	—	6	470	375	26	2	—
R.J. Shastri	3	5	0	66	93	18.60	—	1	—	5	306	259	36	2	—
Madan Lal	3	4	0	26	52	13.00	—	—	—	8	146	112	46	—	—
S.V. Nayak	2	3	1	11	19	9.50	—	—	—	3	65	49	39	1	—
D.R. Doshi	3	3	2	5*	9	9.00	—	—	—	—	36	30	30	—	—
Also batted:															
G.A. Parkar	1	2	0	6	7	3.50	—	—	—	1	52	45	16	1	—
A. Malhotra	1	2	0	5	5	2.50	—	—	—	1	24	17	29	2	—
Totals	33	47	7	(157)	1332	33.30	2	9	8	149	3267	2640	50	20†	3

India — Bowling	O	M	R	W	Avge	Best	5w/I	10w/M	B/W	R/H	NB	Wides
Doshi	157.1	38	455	13	35.00	6-102	1	—	73	48	17	—
Kapil Dev	133	21	439	10	43.90	5-125	1	—	80	55	19	—
Madan Lal	102.1	30	291	6	48.50	3-99	—	—	102	47	3	—
Shastri	116.3	29	275	4	68.75	3-109	—	—	175	39	5	—
Also bowled:												
Patil	14	1	48	1	48.00	1-48	—	—	84	57	—	—
Nayak	38.3	6	132	1	132.00	1-16	—	—	231	57	1	—
Yashpal	3	2	1	0	—	—	—	—	—	6	—	—
Totals	564.2	127	1641	35	46.88	(6-102)	2	—	97	48	45	—

* Not out † Plus one 'ct substitute'. R/H = runs per hundred. B/W = Balls per wicket.

First one-day international: Headingley, June 2.
England won by 9 wickets.
England enjoyed a comfortable win, with almost 5 overs in hand, after Willis had won a crucial toss on his first appearance as captain. The ball moved about on a sultry morning, and the pitch was damp after heavy thunderstorms the previous day had got under the covers.

At 114 for 7, they seemed entirely without hope. But with conditions improving, Kapil Dev made 60 from 37 balls, with 3 sixes and 5 fours, and his partnership of 40 in 8 overs with Kirmani restored some respectability.

A total of 193, however, never looked like seriously testing England. And Wood, recalled at the age of 39, shared in an opening partnership of 133 with Tavaré that put the issue beyond doubt and earned the Derbyshire captain the Man of the Match award.

Second one-day international: the Oval, June 4.
England won by 114 runs.
England took the Prudential Trophy with another convincing win, this time after Gavaskar had put them in on a slow pitch, slightly uneven in bounce, but offering few problems to the careful batsman.

England's innings was built around a partnership of 159 in 27 overs between Gower and Lamb, who sacrificed a century as he tried to push on with the overs ebbing away. The innings subsided quietly, with four run-outs.

India were never able to reach the necessary tempo, and the regular loss of early wickets soon made theirs a lost cause. When Gavaskar was fifth out at 42, the match was effectively over. And although Kapil Dev and Madan Lal played some good strokes, their 65-run stand for the eighth wicket was merely a face-saving operation.

England v India 1st Prudential Trophy Match
England won by 9 wickets
Played at Headingley, Leeds, June 2
Toss: England. Umpires: D.J. Constant and D.O. Oslear
Man of the Match B. Wood

India		Runs	Mins	Balls	6s	4s
S.M. Gavaskar*	c Botham b Allott	38	82	61	—	4
G.A. Parkar	c Tavaré b Willis	10	42	33	—	1
D.B. Vengsarkar	c Taylor b Botham	5	35	26	—	—
G.R. Viswanath	b Botham	9	16	14	—	2
S.M. Patil	c Taylor b Botham	0	4	6	—	—
Yashpal Sharma	c Taylor b Allott	20	69	59	1	1
R.J. Shastri	run out (Wood)	18	56	56	—	1
Kapil Dev	run out (Willis/Botham)	60	51	37	3	5
S.M.H. Kirmani†	c Taylor b Botham	11	27	24	—	—
S.V. Nayak	c Tavaré b Willis	3	25	19	—	—
Madan Lal	not out	1	5	1	—	—
Extras	(b 4, lb 9, w 2, nb 3)	18				
Total	(55 overs; 214 minutes)	**193**				

England		Runs	Mins	Balls	6s	4s
B. Wood	not out	78	186	137	—	4
C.J. Tavaré	lbw b Madan Lal	66	134	120	—	5
A.J. Lamb	not out	35	51	50	—	4
D.I. Gower						
I.T. Botham						
D.W. Randall						
G. Miller	did not bat					
G.R. Dilley						
R.W. Taylor†						
P.J.W. Allott						
R.G.D. Willis*						
Extras	(lb 8, w 2, nb 5)	15				
Total	(50.1 overs; 186 minutes)	**194-1**				

England	O	M	R	W
Willis	11	0	32	2
Dilley	5	1	20	0
Allott	11	4	21	2
Botham	11	0	56	4
Wood	7	2	17	0
Miller	10	0	29	0

India	O	M	R	W
Kapil Dev	9	2	21	0
Madan Lal	9	3	21	1
Nayak	9	0	37	0
Patil	7	0	29	0
Shastri	11	0	37	0
Yashpal	5.1	0	34	0

Fall of Wickets

Wkt	I	E
1st	30	133
2nd	54	—
3rd	58	—
4th	59	—
5th	68	—
6th	113	—
7th	114	—
8th	154	—
9th	192	—
10th	193	—

* Captain   † Wicket-keeper

England v India 2nd Prudential Trophy Match
England won by 114 runs
Played at the Oval, June 4
Toss: India. Umpires: D.G.L. Evans and B.J. Meyer
Man of the Match: A.J.Lamb
Men of the Series: A.J. Lamb and Kapil Dev

England		Runs	Mins	Balls	6s	4s
B. Wood	*b* Patil	15	60	39	—	—
C.J. Tavaré	*b* Patil	27	70	53	—	1
A.J. Lamb	*c* and *b* Madan Lal	99	156	109	—	5
D.I. Gower	*c* Vengsarkar *b* Yashpal	76	109	90	1	2
I.T. Botham	*run out* (Parkar)	4	5	7	—	1
D.W. Randall	*run out* (Parkar)	24	34	25	—	—
G. Miller	*run out* (Malhotra)	0	2	0	—	—
G.R. Dilley	*c* Yashpal *b* Madan Lal	1	7	3	—	—
R.W. Taylor†	*not out*	3	11	8	—	—
P.J.W. Allott	*run out* (Kapil Dev)	5	7	4	—	1
R.G.D. Willis*	*did not bat*					
Extras	(*b* 3, *lb* 10, *w* 5, *nb* 4)	22				
Total	(55 overs; 239 minutes)	**276–9**				

India		Runs	Mins	Balls	6s	4s
S.M. Gavaskar*	*c* Willis *b* Miller	15	90	54	—	—
G.A. Parkar	*c* Botham *b* Willis	2	18	14	—	—
D.B. Vengsarkar	*c* Taylor *b* Dilley	15	29	27	—	1
Yashpal Sharma	*lbw b* Allott	2	23	21	—	—
A. Malhotra	*b* Botham	4	13	14	—	—
S.M. Patil	*b* Miller	1	7	5	—	—
Kapil Dev	*c* Gower *b* Wood	47	73	62	1	4
S.M.H. Kirmani†	*c* Botham *b* Miller	8	21	29	—	1
Madan Lal	*not out*	53	73	75	1	4
R.J. Shastri	*not out*	9	27	30	—	—
S.V. Nayak	*did not bat*					
Extras	(*b* 1, *lb* 3, *w* 2)	6				
Total	(55 overs; 194 minutes)	**162–8**				

India	O	M	R	W
Kapil Dev	11	1	39	0
Madan Lal	11	0	50	2
Nayak	11	1	48	0
Patil	11	0	37	2
Shastri	8	0	53	0
Yashpal	3	0	27	1

England	O	M	R	W
Willis	7	2	10	1
Dilley	7	1	19	1
Botham	9	2	22	1
Allott	8	3	24	1
Miller	11	3	27	3
Wood	11	0	51	1
Tavaré	2	0	3	0

Fall of Wickets

Wkt	E	I
1st	43	5
2nd	53	28
3rd	212	36
4th	218	42
5th	260	42
6th	264	43
7th	267	66
8th	268	131
9th	276	—
10th	—	—

* Captain   † Wicket-keeper

India in England 1982
First-Class Averages

Batting/fielding	M	I	NO	HS	R	Avge	100	50	Ct	St
G.R. Viswanath	9	12	3	106*	561	62.33	2	4	8	—
Madan Lal	9	15	10	58*	309	61.80	—	2	1	—
D.B. Vengsarkar	9	13	2	157	610	55.45	1	4	9	—
S.M. Gavaskar	8	10	0	172	438	43.80	1	1	3	—
Yashpal Sharma	9	15	5	77*	418	41.80	—	3	6	—
Kapil Dev	8	11	0	97	438	39.81	—	3	5	—
S.V. Nayak	10	13	6	67*	253	36.14	—	1	3	—
G.A. Parkar	7	14	2	146	433	36.08	1	2	7	1
A. Malhotra	8	15	1	154*	462	33.00	1	2	5	—
S.M.H. Kirmani	9	12	3	65	265	29.44	—	2	11	4
R.J. Shastri	9	15	2	74	359	27.61	—	3	6	—
S.M. Patil	9	16	1	129*	390	26.00	1	1	1	—
P. Roy	7	12	0	51	174	14.50	—	1	1	—
D.R. Doshi	9	4	2	5*	11	5.50	—	—	—	—
N.S. Yadav	7	2	1	1*	1	1.00	—	—	—	—
Randhir Singh	5	3	0	0	0	0.00	—	—	—	—

Bowling	O	M	R	W	Avge	Best	5w/I	10w/M
Madan Lal	246.1	49	763	22	34.68	4–28	—	—
Patil	60	9	155	4	38.75	2–26	—	—
Doshi	345.3	78	1003	25	40.12	6–102	1	—
Kapil Dev	255.4	45	810	20	40.50	5–39	2	—
Shastri	269.5	69	634	15	42.26	3–109	—	—
Nayak	205.3	39	645	14	46.07	5–54	1	—
Randhir	131	24	418	7	59.71	2–50	—	—
Yadav	195	33	604	7	86.28	3–77	—	—

Also bowled: Gavaskar 5–0–23–0; Malhotra 9–1–37–1; Roy 1–0–14–0; Vengsarkar 0.2–0–2–0; Yashpal 10–2–32–0.

Results: Played 12 Won 1 Lost 1 Drawn 10
* Not out.

Hundreds (7)
2 G.R. Viswanath: 100 v Hants, Southampton; 106* v Northants, Northampton.
1 S.M. Gavaskar: 172 v Warwicks, Birmingham.
  A. Malhotra: 154* v Kent, Canterbury.
  G.A. Parkar: 146 v Yorks, Bradford.
  S.M. Patil: 129* v England (second Test), Manchester.
  D.B. Vengsarkar: 157 v England (first Test), Lord's.

Pakistan in England

A stirring series caught and held the imagination of the public as it see-sawed its way from Edgbaston to Lord's and to Leeds, with scarcely a dull moment on the way. It was eventually won 2-1 by England, when they triumphed at Headingley, though even there nothing was straightforward, with drama and unpredictability to the end.

England, under Bob Willis's leadership in all but one Test, when David Gower deputized, thus won both Cornhill series against India and Pakistan in a summer when their resources had been considerably weakened by the suspension of 15 players who had toured South Africa unofficially. Unfortunately, whereas the first series had been presaged by Indian objections to England's senior umpire, David Constant, who was stood down from those games, the second ended with unmitigated criticism of the umpiring by Pakistan's captain, Imran Khan.

Imran, whose sterling efforts with both bat and ball earned him the man-of-the-series award in what was probably his last appearance in England at Test level, went so far as to single out Constant as having had 'a disappointing match' in the Headingley Test. He argued that one dismissal — that of Sikander in Pakistan's second innings — may well have cost Pakistan the match, and followed this with the now-familiar pleas for neutral umpires and for a panel of assessors sitting in judgment at every Test match.

Public criticism of an umpire cannot be condoned (India, remember, had made their objections privately and in advance). But it was recognized by all concerned — including, it is said, the umpires — that there had been errors affecting the fortunes of both sides during the series. The crux of the matter is that, while umpires have always been prone to human error — just as players are — the game today is played in a blaze of publicity at international level: decisions that have to be made on the spur of the moment can be seen over and over again on television, often in slow motion. Add to that the extra pressure put on umpires by appeals that at best can be termed as frivolous and at worst something more sinister, and it can be seen that the only solution probably lies in more flexible attitudes and understanding among the playing fraternity.

As for neutral officials, Test umpires are usually the best available in any country. To 'import' others would hardly be an incentive to home-produced umpires. And it is hard to imagine, for instance, an English batsman being any more satisfied at suffering what he regarded as a dubious decision from an Indian or Pakistani in Melbourne than from an Australian.

Fortunately, this series will probably be remembered more for the absorbing, fluctuating nature of the cricket than for anything else. Certainly, it was reflected in increased attendances that resulted in receipts some £100,000 more than the Test and County Cricket Board had expected over the entire summer.

Pakistan themselves had contributed to this before the series began. Although disappointed at being confronted by below-strength county sides, they — unlike India — adopted a positive attitude to these matches. They outplayed many opponents and introduced, in Qadir, the leg-spinner, a player whom the public took to their hearts as the season progressed. County players, unfamiliar these days with the art of leg-breaks, googlies, top-spinners, and the like, succumbed to him in great numbers. He made less of an impact in the Tests, where the pitches lacked bounce, though he will not be quickly forgotten by one or two England batsmen, especially perhaps Randall and Marks.

The trend for the entire series was set at Edgbaston, where, contrary to wide expectation, wickets fell with great regularity on a pitch that was slow, low, and slightly variable. Both sides mostly bowled rather better than they batted on it. Ian Greig, brother of the former England captain, took four wickets on his first appearance — a deceptive performance as events turned out — and Randall, pressed into service as a somewhat reluctant opener, made England's only century of the series. Even so, England were hugely indebted to a record last-wicket partnership of 79 between Willis and Bob Taylor, which enabled them to set Pakistan the highest total of a low-scoring match, and they went on to win with more than a day to spare.

At Lord's, Pakistan made history, achieving only their second win against England in 35 Tests. Mohsin Khan, benefiting from England's fielding lapses, made only the eighth double century seen in a Test there, while the mantle of Fazal Mahmood, Pakistan's bowling hero of their only other win in 1954, fell on the unlikely shoulders of Mudassar Nazar, their opening batsman. After England had followed on, he took three quick wickets without cost, and finished with 6 for 32. Tavaré came into his own with an innings of monumental patience and discipline, which was not far short of the slowest Test 50 ever, but it was not enough to save England.

And so the series went all square to Headingley, where Willis returned after injury and the 37-year-old Jackman surpassed himself. There was also an innings of 86 by Fowler on his Test debut, and the match lived up to all the expectations of drama and tension before England finally got home early on the fifth day.

First Test: At Edgbaston, July 29, 30, 31, August 1.
England won by 113 runs.
England achieved a remarkable win with more than a day to spare in a game that had been widely forecast as a high-scoring draw. As it happened, the pitch, with a low and variable bounce, was not as perfect as expected, and the bowlers on both sides had the better of things. The Pakistan batsmen, especially, paid the price for their lack of discipline.

Before the start, England took the rare and possibly unprecedented step of calling in two players already involved in county matches — Geoff Cook of Northants and Gladstone Small of Warwickshire — as a precaution because of injuries to Derek Pringle and David Gower. Neither was called upon, although Pringle was unfit and Ian Greig of Sussex made his Test debut in his place.

Against erratic use of the new ball, England made 27 from four overs after winning the toss. But this proved deceptive, and after Randall had been bowled offering no stroke, England lost wickets regularly. The chief wicket-taker was Imran Khan, who in a sustained, accurate and sometimes hostile piece of bowling took 7 for 52, his best figures against England.

Gower played with more assurance and fluency than most, sharing in a third-wicket partnership of 127 with the ever-patient Tavaré. And towards the end of the innings, Miller batted with controlled aggression before discovering that this was not the pitch on which to play the pull.

The low bounce also contributed to the downfall of Mudassar in the only over Pakistan were required to negotiate at the end of the first day. He took evasive action against a short ball from Botham that failed to lift and he was adjudged leg before.

On the second day, Pakistan contributed lavishly to their own downfall, starting when Mohsin, apparently in a fit of pique after the ball had been changed, was caught trying to hook. The slide continued when Miandad paid the penalty for trying to hit Hemmings over the top in his first over in Test cricket.

Zaheer, suffering from the after-effects of an upset stomach, was not at his most commanding. But he stayed for two hours before becoming, by some way, the most distinguished of Greig's four victims. From that point, Pakistan lost their last 5 wickets for 53 runs, giving England a modest but psychologically valuable first innings lead, which they increased with a little luck to 72 before the close.

The third day brought even more fascinating cricket, with wickets falling regularly at one end while Randall went on to a century at the other. Curiously, England were undone not by Imran, nor by the skilful and frequently unlucky Qadir, but by Tahir, who moved the ball about at medium pace and dismissed the England middle order in a way that made it hard to believe that he had previously taken only 7 Test wickets at 50 runs apiece.

Although often bemused by Qadir, Randall played some fine strokes against the other bowlers, making 103 out of 175. But when he was disappointingly and perhaps unnecessarily eighth out, England were only 209 ahead. And their lead was a mere 233 when Taylor and Willis joined forces in a last-wicket partnership that was not only a record against Pakistan, but in retrospect could be seen to have contributed substantially to England's win. Taylor, making his second Test 50, and Willis, achieving his highest Test score for the second time in the season, added 79, surpassing the 55 scored by Underwood and Pocock at Hyderabad in 1972-73. This ensured that Pakistan would need to make the highest score of the match, 313, for victory.

With two days at their disposal, Pakistan were not entirely without hope — even if history was against them — but after a delay for bad light, Botham, overcoming the problem of an injured hand, removed Mudassar and Mansoor in his first over without a run scored, a setback from which they never recovered. Gatting, brilliantly running out Miandad from short leg, contributed to Pakistan's problems, and when Zaheer was fifth out to a reckless stroke during a hostile spell by Willis, only one result looked likely. Imran, whose bowling won him the man-of-the-match award, played a bold captain's innings towards the end, but it was soon all over, with 24 of the fourth day's scheduled 81 overs to spare.

ENGLAND 1ST INNINGS v. PAKISTAN 1ST TEST at EDGBASTON. BIRMINGHAM on 29, 30, 31 JULY, 1, 2 AUGUST, 1982. TOSS: ENGLAND

IN	OUT	MINS	No.	BATSMAN	HOW OUT	BOWLER	RUNS	WKT	TOTAL	6s	4s	BALLS	NOTES ON DISMISSAL
11·03	11·35	32	1	D.W.RANDALL	BOWLED	IMRAN	17	1	29	.	3	23	Deceived by ball angled in from wide of the crease - off stump - No stroke.
11·03	3·54	252	2	C.J.TAVARÉ	C⁵ MIANDAD	QADIR	54	5	179	.	8	179	Edged googly to silly point via pad. Last ball before tea.
11·37	11·49	12	3	A.J.LAMB	C⁵ WASIM BARI	SIKANDER	6	2	37	.	1	10	Edged firm-footed drive at outswinger - low catch in front of 1st slip.
11·51	3·14	164	4	D.I.GOWER	C⁵ WASIM BARI	IMRAN	74	3	164	.	12	143	Edged ball angled across him - low catch. Firm-footed stroke.
3·16	3·31	15	5	I.T.BOTHAM	BOWLED	IMRAN	2	4	172	.	.	6	Off stump out - late on fast ball.
3·33	5·00	68	6	M.W.GATTING	BOWLED	TAHIR	17	6	228	.	2	54	Played on via pad - edged drive.
4·13	5·50	97	7	G.MILLER	BOWLED	IMRAN	47	7	263	.	6	92	Missed pull - terrible firm-footed stroke - off stump hit.
5·01	6·18	77	8	I.A.GREIG	C⁵ SUB (HAROON RASHID)	IMRAN	14	10	272	.	2	55	Fended bouncer - skied off glove to short-leg - ran forward.
5·52	5·55	3	9	E.E.HEMMINGS	LBW	IMRAN	2	8	265	.	.	5	Late on break back.
5·57	6·07	10	10	R.W.TAYLOR †	LBW	IMRAN	1	9	271	.	.	4	Played back to breakback that kept low. Plumb.
6·09	(6·18)	9	11	R.G.D.WILLIS *	NOT OUT		0	.		.	.	8	4* "not out" - extending his world Test record.
				EXTRAS	b4 lb10 w6 nb18		38			0	6 34*	579 balls (inc. 24 no balls)	

TOTAL **272** all out at 6·18 pm on 1st day. (off 92·3 overs in 377 min)

14 OVERS 4 BALLS/HOUR
2·94 RUNS/OVER
47 RUNS/100 BALLS

DEBUTS: I.A.GREIG (s), E.E.HEMMINGS (M)

* CAPTAIN † WICKET-KEEPER

BOWLER	O	M	R	W	Ws	HRS	OVERS	RUNS
IMRAN	25·3	11	52	7	-3	1	12	38
TAHIR	15	4	46	1	1¼	2	17	33
SIKANDER	18	5	58	1	¼	3	15	57
MUDASSAR	5	2	8	0	2¼	4	13	46
QADIR	29	7	70	1	4½	5	16	47
			38			6	15	45
TOTAL	92·3	29	272	10				

© BILL FRINDALL

RUNS	MINS	OVERS	LAST 50 (in mins)
50	83	17.5	83
100	157	33.6	74
150	196	47.5	39
200	264	64.1	68
250	332	81.2	68

LUNCH: 71-2
TEA: 179-5

TAVARÉ 21* (118 min.)
GOWER 13* (70 min.)
28 OVERS · 113 MINUTES
GATTING 0* (21 min.)
61 OVERS · 252 MINUTES

IMRAN KHAN'S 7-52 ESTABLISHED A RECORD ANALYSIS FOR PAKISTAN AGAINST ENGLAND IN EITHER COUNTRY.

WKT	PARTNERSHIP		RUNS	MINS
1st	Randall	Tavaré	29	32
2nd	Tavaré	Lamb	8	12
3rd	Tavaré	Gower	127	164
4th	Tavaré	Botham	8	15
5th	Tavaré	Gatting	7	21
6th	Gatting	Miller	49	47
7th	Miller	Greig	35	49
8th	Greig	Hemmings	2	3
9th	Greig	Taylor	6	10
10th	Greig	Willis	1	9

272

PAKISTAN 1st INNINGS

In reply to ENGLAND's 272 all out

IN	OUT	MINS	No.	BATSMAN	HOW OUT	BOWLER	RUNS	WKT	TOTAL	6s	4s	BALLS	NOTES ON DISMISSAL
6·27	6·28	1	1	MUDASSAR NAZAR	LBW	BOTHAM	0	1	0	·	·	2	Turned back on short ball that kept low.
6·27	11·43	48	2	MOHSIN KHAN	C' WILLIS	BOTHAM	26	3	53	·	5	35	Mistimed pull at long hop after ball change - Falling catch at mid-on
6·30	11·15	17	3	TAHIR NAQQASH	C' TAYLOR	GREIG	12	2	29	·	2	17	Edged drive at shortish ball - right-handed catch. GREIG 14th ball
11·17	2·50	176	4	MANSOOR AKHTAR	C' MILLER	HEMMINGS	58	5	164	·	7	151	HS in TESTS Swept half volley to backward square-leg.
11·45	12·44	59	5	JAVED MIANDAD	C' WILLIS	HEMMINGS	30	4	110	·	3	40	Mistimed lofted on-drive - skier behind bowler held by mid-off. HEMMINGS 4th ball
12·45	3·27	124	6	ZAHEER ABBAS	LBW	GREIG	40	6	198	·	4	93	Missed on-drive - front leg. Slight breakback
2·52	4·12	62	7	WASIM RAJA	C' TAVARÉ	WILLIS	26	7	217	·	3	55	Fenced at ball that lifted and left him - edged low to 2nd slip
3·29	4·30	43	8	IMRAN KHAN *	C' TAYLOR	WILLIS	22	8	227	1	2	35	Top-edged fierce pull - very high skier near square-leg.
4·13 (5·03)		50	9	WASIM BARI †	NOT OUT		16			·	2	25	
4·32	4·54	22	10	ABDUL QADIR	LBW	GREIG	7	9	248	·	·	20	Missed ball - played back - 'plumb'
4·55	5·03	8	11	SIKANDER BAKHT	C' HEMMINGS	GREIG	13	10	251	·	·	8	Drove full-toss to mid-on - low, tumbling catch.
				EXTRAS		b 5 lb 2 w 1 nb 5	13			1 6	2s 4s	481 balls (inc. 5 no balls)	

TOTAL (off 79·2 overs in 312 min.)

251 all out at 5·03 pm 2nd DAY. (21 BEHIND)

* CAPTAIN † WICKET-KEEPER

BOWLER	O	M	R	W
BOTHAM	24	1	86	2
GREIG	14·2	3	53	4
WILLIS	15	3	42	2
HEMMINGS	24	5	56	2
MILLER	2	1	1	0
	79·2	13	251	10

W	HRS	OVERS	RUNS
2/	1	14	63
2/	2	14	54
2	3	18	35
-	4	16	46
1	5	14	42

RUNS	MINS	OVERS	LAST 50 (in mins)
50	50	45	11	45
100	100	23·2	55
150	174	43·3	74
200	245	63·3	71
250	310	78·4	65

STUMPS: 4-0 (1st DAY) — Mohsin 0* (6 min), Tahir 0* (2 min), 1 over, 5 min

LUNCH: 119-4 (153 BEHIND) — Mansoor 39* (105 min), Zaheer 2* (17 min), off 31 overs in 127 min

TEA: 210-6 — Wasim Raja 23* (50 min), Imran 10* (13 min), off 65 overs in 249 min

15 OVERS 1 BALLS/HOUR
3·16 RUNS/OVER
52 RUNS/100 BALLS

WKT	PARTNERSHIP		RUNS	MINS
1st	Mudassar	Mohsin	0	1
2nd	Mohsin	Tahir	29	17
3rd	Mohsin	Mansoor	24	26
4th	Mansoor	Miandad	57	59
5th	Mansoor	Zaheer	54	87
6th	Zaheer	Wasim Raja	34	34
7th	Wasim Raja	Imran	19	25
8th	Imran	Wasim Bari	10	17
9th	Wasim Bari	Qadir	21	22
10th	Wasim Bari	Sikander	3	8
				251

© BILL FRINDALL

ENGLAND 2ND INNINGS   21 RUNS AHEAD ON FIRST INNINGS

IN	OUT	MINS	No.	BATSMAN	HOW OUT	BOWLER	RUNS	TOTAL	WKT	6s	4s	BALLS	NOTES ON DISMISSAL
5.14	2.43	249	1	D.W.RANDALL	BOWLED	IMRAN	105	188	8		11	156	4th in Tests. Played on. 55-85% of total whilst at wicket.
5.14	11.25	88	2	C.J.TAVARÉ	c' MOHSIN	IMRAN	17	62	1		2	70	Fended bouncer (angled in) - during catch at short square leg. 'Puns'.
11.27	12.12	45	3	A.J.LAMB	LBW	TAHIR	5	98	2		1	27	Played back - missed breakback. 'Puns'.
12.14	12.35	21	4	D.I.GOWER	c' MUDASSAR	TAHIR	13	127	3		2	19	Forced at ball leaving him - edged to 2nd slip.
12.37	12.49	12	5	M.W.GATTING	c' WASIM BARI	TAHIR	5	137	4		1	14	Edged drive at widish off side ball.
12.51	12.52	1	6	I.T.BOTHAM	LBW	TAHIR	0	137	5			1	1st ball - played half-cock - beaten by breakback. 'Puns'.
12.53	1.50	19	7	G.MILLER	BOWLED	TAHIR	5	146	6			21	Break back - kept low - through 'gate' - leg stump out.
1.52	2.20	28	8	I.A.GREIG	BOWLED	QADIR	7	170	7			27	Mistimed drive - misread googly - through 'gate'.
2.22	3.26	64	9	E.E.HEMMINGS	c' MANSOOR	QADIR	19	212	9		2	52	Mistimed off-drive - extra-cover - simple catch.
2.45	5.57	172	10	R.W.TAYLOR†	c' QADIR	WASIM RAJA	54	291	10		4	149	Edged leg-break to slip.
3.28	(5.57)	129	11	R.G.D.WILLIS*	NOT OUT		28				3	103	HS in TESTS (1st specialist fast bowler to play 100 Test inns. 45th natural)
				EXTRAS	b 10 lb 11 w 7 nb 5		33			0	26	639 balls (inc. 6 no balls)	

TOTAL 291. All out in 422 MIN. (OFF 105.3 OVERS IN 422 MIN.) 291. all out at 5.57 pm on 3rd DAY

*CAPTAIN   †WICKET-KEEPER

© BILL FRINDALL

BOWLER	O	M	R	W	
IMRAN	32	5	84	2	.1/4
SIKANDER	13	5	34	0	-1/3
QADIR	40	10	100	2	.
TAHIR	18	7	40	5	5/-
WASIM RAJA	2.3	2	0	1	.
		.	33		
	105.3	29	291	10	

HRS	OVERS	RUNS
1	14	50
2	15	37
3	13	54
4	14	35
5	15	43
6	18	38
7	16	34

RUNS	MINS	OVERS	LAST 50 (in mins)
50	58	13.4	58
100	138	32.4	80
150	202	47.3	64
200	270	63.5	68
250	353	86.4	83

2ND NEW BALL taken at 5.13 pm on 3rd DAY
- ENGLAND 266-9 after 94 overs

STUMPS (2ND DAY) 51-0 (LEAD: 72 RUNS)
RANDALL 30* 15'
TAVARÉ 15'
16 OVERS 63 MIN

LUNCH: 143-5 (LEAD: 164 RUNS)
RANDALL 85* (185 min)
MILLER 2* (9 min)
43 OVERS 185 MIN

TEA: 235-9 (LEAD: 256 RUNS)
TAYLOR 20* (86 min)
WILLIS 7* (43 min)
81 OVERS 336 MIN

PAKISTAN NEED 313 RUNS TO WIN

TAHIR NAQQASH took 5 for 20 in 45 BALLS
(W:2-|:2-:@:41:|:21:W|:....:|:.|:.WW|O....|......|:W)
† RECORD 10th WICKET PARTNERSHIP in E v P TESTS

15 OVERS 0 BALLS/HOUR
2.76 RUNS/OVER
46 RUNS/100 BALLS

WKT	PARTNERSHIP		RUNS	MINS
1st	Randall	Tavaré	62	88
2nd	Randall	Lamb	36	45
3rd	Randall	Gower	29	21
4th	Randall	Gatting	10	12
5th	Randall	Botham	0	1
6th	Randall	Miller	9	19
7th	Randall	Greig	24	28
8th	Randall	Hemmings	18	21
9th	Hemmings	Taylor	24	41
10th	Taylor	Willis	79†	129
			291	

PAKISTAN 2ND INNINGS — NEEDING 313 RUNS TO WIN IN A MINIMUM OF 195 OVERS.

IN	OUT	MINS	No.	BATSMAN	HOW OUT	BOWLER	RUNS	WKT	TOTAL	6s	4s	BALLS	NOTES ON DISMISSAL
12 42	12 43	1	1	MUDASSAR NAZAR	LBW	BOTHAM	0	1	0	·	·	2	'PAIR' - played across straight ball that kept low.
12 42	2 57	77	2	MOHSIN KHAN	LBW	BOTHAM	35	4	54	·	5	55	Played no stroke - shuffled across stumps - misjudged line
12 44	12 46	2	3	MANSOOR AKHTAR	c' TAYLOR	BOTHAM	0	2	0	·	·	4	Edged outswinger.
12 47	1 55	50	4	JAVED MIANDAD	RUN OUT (BATTING)		10	3	38	·	·	29	Brilliant stop and throw by short square leg.
1 57	3 12	35	5	ZAHEER ABBAS	c' TAYLOR	WILLIS	4	5	66	·	·	26	Top-edged square-cut at fast short ball - shoulder high cut.
2 59	3 20	21	6	WASIM RAJA	c' GOWER	WILLIS	16	6	77	·	1	12	Edged low to 5th slip.
3 14	5 52	137	7	IMRAN KHAN *	BOWLED	MILLER	65	10	199	2	6	103	Made room to square cut - missed.
3 22	4 08	46	8	WASIM BARI †	c' TAYLOR	BOTHAM	12	7	98	·	2	35	Edged low to keeper's right.
3 10	4 52	42	9	TAHIR NAQQASH	c AND BOWLED	HEMMINGS	39	8	151	1	6	44	Checked on-side push - left-handed leaping catch.
4 53	5 43	29	10	ABDUL QADIR	c' RANDALL	MILLER	9	9	178	·	2	34	Silly point dived across pitch to hold bat/pad catch.
5 44	(5 52)	8	11	SIKANDER BAKHT	NOT OUT		1			·	·	2	-
				EXTRAS	b - lb 3 w - nb 5		8			2ᵇ	23	346 balls (inc 6 no balls)	

TOTAL (off 56.4 overs in 231 min.) **199** all out at 5·52 pm on 4th DAY.

* CAPTAIN † WICKET-KEEPER

14 OVERS 4 BALLS/HOUR
3.51 RUNS/OVER
58 RUNS/100 BALLS

WKT	PARTNERSHIP		RUNS	MINS
1st	Mudassar	Mohsin	0	1
2nd	Mohsin	Mansoor	0	2
3rd	Mohsin	Miandad	38	50
4th	Mohsin	Zaheer	16	20
5th	Zaheer	Wasim Raja	12	13
6th	Wasim Raja	Imran	11	6
7th	Imran	Wasim Bari	21	46
8th	Imran	Tahir	53	42
9th	Imran	Qadir	27	29
10th	Imran	Sikander	21	8
			199	

3ʳᵈ DAY: RAIN at 6pm prevented start of innings - 3 OVERS LOST
4ᵗʰ DAY: BAD LIGHT DELAYED START - 42 MIN (10 overs) LOST
BLSP: 1.12 to 1.30 - 18 MIN (5 OVERS) LOST (21-2)
LUNCH: 40-3 13 OVERS MOHSIN 22* (40 min) ZAHEER 2* (3 min) 80 MIN
TEA: 157-8 IMRAN 33* (47 min) QADIR 0* (8 min) 46 OVERS 201 MIN

ENGLAND beat PAKISTAN by 113 RUNS at 5.52 pm on fourth day

MAN OF THE MATCH: IMRAN KHAN Adjudicator: M.J.K. SMITH

TOTAL TIME LOST: 63 minutes (18 overs)

BOWLER	O	M	R	W		HRS	OVERS	RUNS
BOTHAM	21	7	70	4		1	13	40
WILLIS	14	2	49	2		2	12	42
GREIG	4	1	19	0		3	15	54
HEMMINGS	10	4	27	1				
MILLER	7.4	1	26	2				
	56.4	15	199	10				

RUNS	MINS	OVERS	LAST 50 (in mins)
50	74	15.5	74
100	151	32.3	77
150	190	45.4	39

© BILL FRINDALL

Second Test: At Lord's, August 12, 13, 14, 15, 16.
Pakistan won by 10 wickets.

Pakistan gained a richly deserved and historic win in a match in which England, performing moderately with both bat and ball, were dominated virtually from start to finish. It was Pakistan's first Test triumph at Lord's, only their second in 35 meetings between the countries, and it threw up an unlikely hero in Mudassar Nazar, the opening batsman, to whose medium-paced bowling England succumbed after following on. He took three wickets in six balls without cost, finishing with 6 for 32, although Mohsin Khan's double century earned him the man-of-the-match award.

England were without Bob Willis, who had an injured neck. Robin Jackman replaced him, making his first appearance in a home Test, which coincided with his 37th birthday. And to David Gower fell the dubious distinction of leading England to such a comprehensive defeat in his first match as captain. He was, however, scarcely helped either by an attack painfully lacking in variety or by a series of lapses in the field on the first day.

On a good pitch, perhaps the best produced for any Test at that stage of the season, and without Willis's extra penetration, England could not afford to miss the chances and half-chances, the most costly of which allowed Mohsin to escape at slip off Botham at 72. He went on to beat the previous highest score by a Pakistani at Lord's, Hanif Mohammad's 186, and then became only the eighth batsman to make a Test double hundred there, and the first since New Zealand's Martin Donnelly hit 206 in 1949. Because of a stoppage for the weather on the second afternoon, he was obliged to spend some four hours waiting in the pavilion on 199. The interruption also helped England to check Pakistan's progress, three wickets falling cheaply in the last hour, including Mohsin's after 491 minutes.

But Imran declared promptly the next morning, and from the moment that Tavaré played on, fending off a short-pitched ball from Sarfraz, England's innings ran a depressing and uneven course. With Imran and Sarfraz both moving the ball about and the mystical Qadir again perplexing the middle order, they had been reduced to 226 for 9, still needing 3 to avoid the follow-on, when Gatting and Jackman took the option of going off for bad light on the Saturday evening. Imran was not then in action, but with the last ball of his first over the next morning — the first time Sunday play had been seen in a Lord's Test — he won a close lbw decision against Jackman, and England had to follow on.

Mudassar then struck. He probably would not have bowled had not Tahir been temporarily absent with an injury, and as he removed Randall, Lamb, and Gower within six balls, researchers discovered that as a professional in the Bolton League he was rarely invited to bowl for his club, and the previous year he figured among the 'also bowled' when playing for Cheshire.

Disciplined batting by Tavaré and Botham saw England through to 95 for 3 when bad light ended play on a day in which only 46 overs had been possible. The next morning they took their partnership to 121 and, with the pitch still playing well, it looked as though Pakistan would have to work much harder than previously for their rewards.

Mudassar, however, then reappeared, not having bowled since his earlier success, and Botham, forcing off the back foot, was caught at gully. Soon afterwards, Mudassar persuaded Gatting to play at a very wide delivery, and England were quickly in the throes of another struggle. Not until Hemmings joined Tavaré, with seven wickets down, were the arrears cleared in mid-afternoon.

Tavaré, having come within five minutes of depriving T.E. Bailey of the slowest 50 in Test history (357 minutes at Brisbane in 1958), was then eighth out after batting for 407 minutes, and when Hemmings went England were only 34 ahead. Taylor and Jackman, however, played so sensibly for the last wicket that Pakistan showed increasing signs of anxiety, and by the time Jackman, for the second time in the match, failed to get the benefit of a hairline decision, Pakistan were left to make 76 from 18 overs.

This was accomplished by Mohsin and Miandad with 29 deliveries to spare, mostly against highly undemanding bowling, but with the weather threatening to intrude on Pakistan's moment of triumph. It was the first time this century that each side had gained a win in the first two matches of a three-match series. And not even a suggestion, presumably emanating from the England dressing-room, that Pakistan were using an illegal substance on the ball to make it swing could detract from their performance. This allegation was said to be without foundation by the umpires, after inspection, and also by TCCB officials.

PAKISTAN 1ST INNINGS v. ENGLAND   2ND TEST at LORD'S, LONDON on 12,13,14,15,16 AUGUST, 1982.   TOSS: PAKISTAN

IN	OUT	MINS	No.	BATSMAN	HOW OUT	BOWLER	RUNS	WKT	TOTAL	6s	4s	BALLS	NOTES ON DISMISSAL
11.01	6.11	496	1	MOHSIN KHAN	c Tavaré	JACKMAN	200	6	380	·	23	386	Only 8th 200 in 74 Lord's Tests. Turned half-volley to backward square-leg.
11.01	11.53	52	2	MUDASSAR NAZAR	c Taylor	JACKMAN	20	1	53	·	1	42	Edged off-side steer. Low, wide. Judged catch. 'Walked'.
11.55	3.27	173	3	MANSOOR AKHTAR	c Lamb	BOTHAM	57	2	197	·	7	143	Mishooked long-hop (loosener) to mid-on – gentle skier.
3.30	4.03	13	4	JAVED MIANDAD	Run out (Tavaré/Hemmings)		6	3	208	·	·	17	Attempted reckless second run to cover – shot back.
4.05	12.44	203	5	ZAHEER ABBAS	Bowled	JACKMAN	75	4	361	·	8	156	off stump. ? played on via inside edge.
12.46	12.53	7	6	HAROON RASHID	LBW	BOTHAM	1	5	364	·	·	5	Played across line.
12.55	6.37	62	7	IMRAN KHAN*	c Taylor	BOTHAM	12	8	401	·	1	33	Edged cover drive to 'keeper – walked'.
6.13	6.15	2	8	TAHIR NAQQASH	c Gatting	JACKMAN	2	7	382	·	·	3	Mishit slower ball – skier behind bowler to mid-off.
6.17	(7.02)	45	9	WASIM BARI†	NOT OUT		24			·	2	28	
6.39	(7.02)	23	10	ABDUL QADIR	NOT OUT		18			·	3	23	
			11	SARFRAZ NAWAZ	DID NOT BAT		·						

EXTRAS   b 3 lb 8 w – nb 2   = 13   0 6s 4s 5   836 balls (inc. 2 no balls)

TOTAL   (off 139 overs in 547 min)   = 428 – 8 DECLARED

* CAPTAIN   † WICKET-KEEPER

© BILL FRINDALL

BOWLER	O	M	R	W	nb
BOTHAM	44	8	148	3	
JACKMAN	36	5	110	4	
PRINGLE	26	9	62	0	-
GREIG	13	2	42	0	
HEMMINGS	20	3	53	0	1
			13	1	
	139	27	428	8	

2ND NEW BALL taken at 5.25 pm 1st DAY
PAKISTAN 272-3 after 88 overs.

HRS	OVERS	RUNS
1	14	58
2	18	49
3	16	45
4	18	48
5	18	45
6	14	45
7	15	53
8	14	23
9	12	41

RUNS	MINS	OVERS	LAST 50 (in mins)
50	50	12.4	50
100	114	29.4	64
150	174	47.2	60
200	237	63.1	63
250	299	81.5	62
300	374	100	75
350	423	112	49
400	520	133.1	97

LUNCH: 107-1   120 MINUTES; 32 OVERS   MOHSIN 64* (120'/104') MANSOOR 19* (66')

TEA: 206-2   242 MINUTES   MOHSIN 116* (243', 154") MIANDAD 5* (21')   65 OVERS

STUMPS: 295-3 (1st DAY)   360 MINUTES   MOHSIN 159* (360') ZAHEER 44* (115')   96 OVERS

2nd DAY: RSP 11.24½-11.51 am   16'5 MINS – 4 overs – LBP   MOHSIN 183* (464 min.)

LUNCH: 364-5   464 MINUTES   IMRAN 0* (5 min.)   121 OVERS

RSP at 2.01 pm   371-5 MOHSIN 199*, IMRAN 1* (445 min.)

STUMPS: 428-8   WASIM BARI 24* (45 min.) ABDUL QADIR 18* (23 min.)
2nd DAY   547 MINUTES   139 OVERS
[75 mins (53 overs) LOST]

PAKISTAN DECLARED BEFORE START OF 3RD DAY

15 OVERS 1 BALLS/HOUR
3.08 RUNS/OVER
51 RUNS/100 BALLS

WKT	PARTNERSHIP		RUNS	MINS
1st	Mohsin	Mudassar	53	52
2nd	Mohsin	Mansoor	144	173
3rd	Mohsin	Miandad	11	13
4th	Mohsin	Zaheer	153†	203
5th	Mohsin	Haroon	3	7
6th	Mohsin	Imran	16	36
7th	Imran	Tahir	2	2
8th	Imran	Bari	19	20
9th	Bari	Qadir	27*	23

† Equalled Pakistan 4th-wicket record v. England 428

ENGLAND 1ST INNINGS — IN REPLY TO PAKISTAN'S 428 FOR 8 DECLARED

IN	OUT	MINS	No.	BATSMAN	HOW OUT	BOWLER	RUNS	WKT	TOTAL	6s	4s	BALLS	NOTES ON DISMISSAL
11.01	12.28	87	1	D.W.RANDALL	BOWLED	SARFRAZ	29	2	69	.	2	53	Played back - misjudged line - off stump out
11.01	11.18	17	2	C.J.TAVARÉ	BOWLED	SARFRAZ	8	1	16	.	1	15	Played on - short ball - defensive dead bat - ball rolled on.
11.20	2.00	122	3	A.J.LAMB	C' HAROON	TAHIR	33	3	89	.	3	77	Deceived by bounce - edged via pad to short leg - fine catch.
12.30	4.57	204	4	D.I.GOWER *	C' MANSOOR	IMRAN	29	5	173	.	1	147	Mistimed hook - skier to mid-wicket
2.02	4.06	124	5	I.T.BOTHAM	C' MOHSIN	QADIR	31	4	157	.	4	81	Swept low to deep square leg - tumbling catch (Qadir's 1st...)
4.08	(2.06)	125	6	M.W.GATTING	NOT OUT		32			.	3	75	
4.59	5.31	32	7	D.R.PRINGLE	C' HAROON	QADIR	5	6	187	.	.	29	Edged googly via pad to short leg.
5.33	5.50	17	8	I.A.GREIG	LBW	QADIR	3	7	197	.	.	12	Deceived by quicker ball (Flipper) - yorked - back leg
5.52	6.13	21	9	E.E.HEMMINGS	BOWLED	SARFRAZ	6	8	217	.	1	19	Drove across yorker.
6.15	6.28	13	10	R.W.TAYLOR †	LBW	QADIR	5	9	226	.	.	15	Played half-cock - beaten by top-spinner. Plumb
6.30	12.06	8	11	R.D.JACKMAN	LBW	IMRAN	0	10	227	.	.	5	Missed fast half-volley.
				EXTRAS	b 11 lb 12 w 13 nb 10		46			8	15⁴	528 balls (inc 12 no balls)	

TOTAL ... 227 ALL OUT at 12.06pm 4th DAY.

(OFF 86 OVERS in 394 MIN.)

13 OVERS O BALLS/HOUR
2.64 RUNS/OVER
43 RUNS/100 BALLS

* CAPTAIN   † WICKET-KEEPER
† MOST WIDES IN ANY TEST INNINGS (932nd TEST MATCH)   EXTRAS TOP-SCORER FOR 5th TIME IN TESTS.

BOWLER	O	M	R	W		HRS	OVERS	RUNS
IMRAN	23	4	55	2	²/₁₀	1	12	58
SARFRAZ	23	4	56	3	³/₄	2	12	22
TAHIR	12	4	25	1	¹/₃	3	12	34
QADIR	24	9	39	4	⁴/₇	4	14	22
MUDASSAR	4	1	6	0	-/₄	5	14	38
	86	22	227	10	46	6	15	34

RUNS	MINS	OVERS	LAST 50 (m.mns)
50	49	9.4	49
100	170	33.5	121
150	258	54.2	88
200	355	78	97

LUNCH: 80 - 2
  LAMB 27* (103 min)
  GOWER 2 (33 min)
  24 OVERS 122 MINUTES

TEA: 166 - 4 (SESSION: 2hrs 44 min)
  GOWER 29* (49 min)
  GATTING 2* (17 min)
  61 OVERS 286 MINUTES

STUMPS: 226 - 9 (3rd DAY)
  GATTING 31* (115)
  JACKMAN 0* (2 min)
  85 OVERS 388 MINUTES
(11 OVERS LOST 3rd DAY) NEEDING 3 RUNS TO AVOID FOLLOW ON.

WKT	PARTNERSHIP		RUNS	MINS
1st	Randall	Tavaré	16	17
2nd	Randall	Lamb	53	68
3rd	Lamb	Gower	20	52
4th	Gower	Botham	68	124
5th	Gower	Gatting	16	24
6th	Gatting	Pringle	14	32
7th	Gatting	Greig	10	17
8th	Gatting	Hemmings	20	21
9th	Gatting	Taylor	9	13
10th	Gatting	Jackman	1	8
			227	

© BILL FRINDALL

ENGLAND 2ND INNINGS 201 RUNS BEHIND ON FIRST INNINGS (FOLLOWING ON FOR 2ND TIME IN 35 TESTS AGAINST PAKISTAN)

IN	OUT	MINS	No	BATSMAN	HOW OUT	BOWLER	RUNS	WKT	TOTAL	6s	4s	BALLS	NOTES ON DISMISSAL
12·18	1·04	46	1	D.W. RANDALL	BOWLED	MUDASSAR	9	1	9	·	1	33	Played inside ball which removed off-stump (4" bounced in string)
12·18	3·21	404	2	C.J. TAVARÉ	C MIANDAD	IMRAN	82	8	224	·	6	277	67 min in O. 5o in 350 min. Edged drive to 2nd slip (chest high)
1·06	1·07	1	3	A.J. LAMB	LBW	MUDASSAR	0	2	9	·	·	2	Hit on front pad playing half-cock defensive push.
1·09	1·14	5	4	D.I. GOWER *	C WASIM BARI	MUDASSAR	0	3	9	·	·	3	Edged offside length ball angled across him.
1·16	12·15	199	5	I.T. BOTHAM	C SARFRAZ	MUDASSAR	69	4	121	·	9	156	Square cut hard to gully.
12·17	12·40	23	6	M.W. GATTING	C WASIM BARI	MUDASSAR	7	5	132	·	1	18	Top-edged square cut at widish ball - caught in front of 2nd slip
12·42	2·34	72	7	D.R. PRINGLE	C MIANDAD	QADIR	14	6	171	·	1	62	Pushed leg-break to silly point.
2·36	2·43	7	8	I.A. GREIG	LBW	MUDASSAR	2	7	180	·	·	8	Played back - beaten by break back
2·45	4·03	58	9	E.E. HEMMINGS	C WASIM BARI	IMRAN	14	9	235	·	·	38	Edged wild at fast offside ball - 'walked'.
3·23	(5·06)	83	10	R.W. TAYLOR †	NOT OUT		24			·	2	68	
4·05	5·06	61	11	R.D. JACKMAN	C HAROON	QADIR	17	10	276	·	1	58	Edged wide pad to forward short-leg

EXTRAS   b 10 lb 19 w 5 nb 4 = 38

TOTAL   276 ALL OUT at 5·06pm 5TH DAY.   (OFF 119.5 OVERS IN 488 MINUTES)

0b 21 4   723 balls (inc 4 no balls)

* CAPTAIN   † WICKET-KEEPER

14 OVERS 4 BALLS/HOUR
2·30 RUNS/OVER
38 RUNS/100 BALLS

WKT	PARTNERSHIP		RUNS	MINS
1st	Randall	Tavaré	9	46
2nd	Tavaré	Lamb	0	1
3rd	Tavaré	Gower	0	5
4th	Tavaré	Botham	112	199
5th	Tavaré	Gatting	11	23
6th	Tavaré	Pringle	39	72
7th	Tavaré	Greig	9	7
8th	Tavaré	Hemmings	44	36
9th	Hemmings	Taylor	11	20
10th	Taylor	Jackman	41	61
			276	

	RUNS	MINS	OVERS	LAST 50 (in mins)
	50	93	21.5	93
	100	215	51.2	122
	150	317	74.2	102
	200	382	91.5	65
	250	448	108	66

LUNCH: 54-3   147 BEHIND
BAD LIGHT AND RAIN PREVENTED PLAY 2·40p - 5·40p (1hr) 40 min LOST (4th DAY)
STUMPS: 95-3   106 BEHIND   47 OVERS 196 MINUTES
BLSP 11:16 to 11:39p 13 MIN (2 OVERS) LOST
LUNCH: 140-5   61 BEHIND   65 WERE LEFT
TEA: 235-8

TAVARÉ 8" (02 min) BOTHAM 35" (44 min)   24 OVERS 102 MIN
TAVARÉ 24" (196°); BOTHAM 55" (152°)   (46 OVERS 146 MIN - LOST)
TAVARÉ 97-5 (2 HOURS MISSED)
TAVARÉ 32" (302 min) PRINGLE 5" (18 min)   71 OVERS 302 MIN
HEMMINGS 14" (57"); TAYLOR 7" (19")   off 101-1 OVERS in 424 MIN (+34)

BOWLER	O	M	R	W		HRS	OVERS	RUNS
IMRAN	42	13	84	2	½	1	12	9
SARFRAZ	14	5	22	0	-	2	16	49
QADIR	37.5	15	94	2		3	15	33
MUDASSAR	19	7	32	6	¼	4	4	21
TAHIR	7	5	6	0		5	13	28
			38			6	16	33
	119.5	45	276	10		7	14	58
						8	17	41

2ND NEW BALL TAKEN at 4.53 pm 5TH DAY - ENGLAND 269-9 after 116.1 OVERS

PAKISTAN 2ND INNINGS   REQUIRING 76 RUNS OFF 18 OVERS (4.2 runs/over)

IN	OUT	MINS	No.	BATSMAN	HOW OUT	RUNS	WKT TOTAL	6s	4s	BALLS	NOTES
5.17	(6.15)	58	1	MOHSIN KHAN	NOT OUT	39		.	3	43	
5.17	(6.15)	58	2	JAVED MIANDAD	NOT OUT	26		.	3	36	made winning hit - cover drive to boundary off Hemmings
			3	MANSOOR AKHTAR							
			4	JAVED MIANDAD							
			5	ZAHEER ABBAS							
			6	HAROON RASHID							
			7	IMRAN KHAN *	DID NOT BAT						
			8	TAHIR NAQQASH							
			9	WASIM BARI †							
			10	ABDUL QADIR							
			11	SARFRAZ NAWAZ							

* CAPTAIN   † WICKET-KEEPER

EXTRAS   b 1   lb 10   w 1   nb -   12   0s 6+   79 balls (0 no ball)

TOTAL   (OFF 13.1 OVERS IN 58 MINUTES)   **77-0**

13 OVERS 4 BALLS/HOUR
5.85 RUNS/OVER
97 RUNS/100 BALLS

WKT	PARTNERSHIP		RUNS	MINS
1*	Mohsin	Miandad	77*	58

BOWLER	O	M	R	W	HRS	OVERS	RUNS	RUNS	MINS	OVERS	LAST 50 (in mins)
BOTHAM	7	0	30	0		1		50	38	8.5	38
JACKMAN	4	0	22	0		.					
HEMMINGS	2.1	0	13	0		.					
			12								
	13.1	0	77	0							

PAKISTAN beat ENGLAND
BY 10 WICKETS at 6.15pm on 5TH day
(4.5 overs to spare)   2ND VICTORY IN 35 TESTS v ENG

MAN OF THE MATCH: MOHSIN KHAN
(Adjudicator: T.E.BAILEY)

TOTAL TIME LOST: 113 OVERS (REPRESENTING 424 MINUTES)

© BILL FRINDALL

Third Test: At Headingley, August 26, 27, 28, 30, 31.
England won by 7 wickets.
England duly won the final Test against Pakistan, and with it the Cornhill Trophy, after a match that in its absorbing uncertainty proved a fitting climax to a compelling series. Even when England appeared to have the game won comfortably inside four days, they contrived to lose 5 wickets for 21 runs and were obliged to live on their nerves till the end.

Even the recrimination about the umpiring could not detract from the merits of a contest that was played mostly in gratifyingly perfect weather and which ended with Imran Khan, the Pakistan captain, taking the awards for both man-of-the match and man-of-the-series.

Not the least remarkable aspect of England's performance was that it was achieved with virtually a three-man attack. Although 13 players were available, one of them, Pringle, was declared unfit with an injured back (said to have been sustained during a spell of letter-writing on the eve of the match) and Hemmings was omitted. Fowler of Lancashire and Marks of Somerset both won their first caps.

Whether Jackman would have played if Pringle had been fit was unclear. But he sustained England's attack after Willis had lost the toss, bowling 35 overs unchanged on the first day in a spell of 4 hours 40 minutes broken by lunch and tea. He regularly beat the bat, and by his unflagging accuracy induced frustration among batsmen who were finding it hard to come to terms with a slow pitch.

Pakistan started indifferently, both Mohsin and Mansoor falling to short-pitched deliveries. Mudassar and Miandad, however, added 100 together in a disciplined way that suggested that England, with only four recognized bowlers, would have to work hard on this pitch. Botham, however, prised out Mudassar, and with Jackman now established into his accurate groove, even Miandad had to bat in a sober way that had eluded him earlier in the series. Eventually he fell to Fowler's athletic catch, and Imran was left unbeaten with 67 — only his sixth half-century in 65 Test innings — when Pakistan were all out early on the second day.

Fowler's first Test innings was then ended by a good ball from Ehtesham Uddin, a portly medium-pacer who was a professional with Daisy Hill CC in the Bolton League and had been pressed into service because of Sarfraz's unfitness. This presaged another piece of uneven batting by England during which Imran, bowling with great fire, removed Gatting, Lamb, and Tavaré in successive overs.

Botham's answer to this was to counter-attack in typical fashion. Oddly enough, Imran did not bowl at this stage, putting his trust in Qadir and no doubt feeling that Botham might lapse into error against him. As it happened, the leg-spinner was below his best, and Botham drove him out of the attack before falling to a brilliant catch in the deep by Haroon, the substitute, after making 57 out of 69 from 15 overs. Randall then immediately ran himself out, Marks was bowled playing no stroke to Qadir's googly, and it needed a restrained innings by Gower, who overcame an indifferent start to make 74 in some four hours, to keep England in contention. First Taylor and then Jackman supported him well, but England still fell 19 behind on first innings.

Instead of building quietly on this advantage, Pakistan began their second innings in a manner that was barely credible. Willis achieved the rare distinction of removing both openers, Mohsin and Mudassar, first ball in his opening two overs. Miandad followed this by batting with much brilliance until Botham persuaded him to drive at a wide outswinger during the course of a controlled, inventive, and profitable spell of bowling in mid-afternoon.

With Jackman again giving little away, Pakistan were reduced to 128 for 7, whereupon Imran and Sikander stood firm in a partnership that left England, for the first time, wondering where to turn. In a display of exaggerated cat-and-mouse tactics, Imran protected his partner while both Willis and Botham operated off short run-ups, until Marks finally had Sikander adjudged caught off bat and pad at short leg, a decision not without controversy.

Soon afterwards, Tavaré and Fowler embarked on the task of making 219 for victory with more than two days at England's disposal, and on the fourth day they took their partnership to 103 before Tavaré was caught at slip. Not long before this, Miandad, having had an appeal for a slip catch from the same batsman turned down had been involved in an exchange of words with the umpires as the teams left the field at lunch.

Fowler, meanwhile, had commended himself by batting with rare composure in only his second Test innings. Playing very straight, he missed little that could be driven, especially off the back foot, while Gatting, despite knowing little about his first ball from Imran, stayed with him while the target was whittled away.

With 64 needed, the batsmen opted to stay on when offered the light by the umpires, and soon afterwards Fowler, needing 14 to become the first opening batsman to make a debut Test century since Arthur Milton in 1958, was caught behind after some four hours. The bowler was Mudassar, who then had Lamb lbw as he played across the line and Gower caught behind, thus taking 3 for 11 in 16 balls. In the gloom, Imran now bowled with great hostility. In one over he won lbw appeals against Gatting and Randall, and both Marks and Botham lived dangerously before bad light ended play.

On the last morning, Mudassar produced a ball that bounced and moved away to have Botham caught at slip when England still needed 20 runs for victory. But Imran, striving to bowl at his fastest, was not at his most accurate, and Qadir was not used at all. Taylor and Marks eventually saw England home after another tense 40 minutes, though not without a few alarms as far as the Somerset player was concerned.

PAKISTAN 1st INNINGS v. ENGLAND 3RD TEST at HEADINGLEY, LEEDS — TOSS: PAKISTAN

IN	OUT	MINS	No.	BATSMAN	HOW OUT	BOWLER	RUNS	WKT	TOTAL	6s	4s	BALLS	NOTES ON DISMISSAL
11·00	11·22	22	1	MOHSIN KHAN	c TAYLOR	BOTHAM	10	1	16	·	2	23	Mishooked bouncer - lobbed catch off glove and mouth.
11·00	2·23	164	2	MUDASSAR NAZAR	BOWLED	BOTHAM	65	3	119	·	8	118	Beaten by inswinging yorker - leg stump hit.
11·24	11·27	3	3	MANSOOR AKHTAR	c GATTING	WILLIS	0	2	19	·	·	2	Fended bouncer to short square-leg.
11·29	4·27	238	4	JAVED MIANDAD	c FOWLER	WILLIS	54	6	168	·	3	183	Edged legside stroke - low, swirling catch. diving at cover.
2·25	2·29	4	5	ZAHEER ABBAS	c TAYLOR	JACKMAN	8	4	128	·	2	5	Top edged cut at wide outswinger.
2·31	3·37	66	6	MAJID KHAN	LBW	JACKMAN	21	5	160	·	4	50	Played back to break back. Broke HANIF'S PAK RECORD (8315)
3·39 (11·22)		172	7	IMRAN KHAN *	NOT OUT		67			2	9	131	6th FIFTY in 64 TEST INNINGS.
4·29	5·09	40	8	WASIM BARI †	BOWLED	JACKMAN	23	7	207	·	4	29	Missed appalling slog at straight ball.
5·11	5·45	34	9	ABDUL QADIR	c WILLIS	BOTHAM	5	8	224	·	·	30	Miscued hook at long-hop - gentle catch to mid-on.
5·47	11·16	59	10	SIKANDER BAKHT	c TAVARÉ	WILLIS	7	9	274	·	·	34	Edged low to 2nd slip.
11·18	11·22	4	11	EHTESHAM UDDIN	BOWLED	BOTHAM	0	10	275	·	·	3	Hit on side of helmet by short ball that fell on stumps.

EXTRAS: b 1 lb 7 w 4 nb 3 = 15

TOTAL 275 all out at 11·22 am on second day. (off 100·5 OVERS ≈ 412 MIN.)

2 (6s) 32 (4s) 608 balls (inc 3 no balls)

* CAPTAIN † WICKET-KEEPER

© BILL FRINDALL

BOWLER	O	M	R	W	nb/w
WILLIS	26	6	76	3	2/4
BOTHAM	24·5	9	70	4	1/3
JACKMAN	37	14	74	3	3/·
MARKS	5	0	23	0	·
GATTING	8	2	17	0	·
			15		
	100·5	31	275	10	

HRS	OVERS	RUNS
1	14	46
2	18	45
3	13	37
4	15	36
5	14	33
6	14	35

2ND NEW BALL taken at 5·43 pm on 1st day - PAKISTAN 223-7 after 85 overs.

	RUNS	MINS	OVERS	LAST 50 (mins)
	50	62	14·5	62
	100	139	36·2	77
	150	229	57·4	90
	200	303	74·2	74
	250	380	94	77

LUNCH: 91-2
MUDASSAR 47* (121 min), MIANDAD 31* (57 min)
121 MINUTES - 32 OVERS

TEA: 164-5
MIANDAD 50* (216 min), IMRAN 4* (6 min)
245 MINUTES - 61 OVERS

STUMPS: 255-8 (1st DAY)
IMRAN 49* (150 min), SIKANDER 6* (43 min)
390 MINUTES - 96 OVERS

PAKISTAN added 20 runs off 4·5 overs in 22 minutes for loss of last 2 wickets on second morning.

14 OVERS 4 BALLS/HOUR
2·73 RUNS/OVER
45 RUNS/100 BALLS

WKT	PARTNERSHIP		RUNS	MINS
1st	Mohsin	Mudassar	16	22
2nd	Mudassar	Mansoor	3	3
3rd	Mudassar	Miandad	100	136
4th	Miandad	Zaheer	9	4
5th	Miandad	Majid	32	66
6th	Miandad	Imran	8	27
7th	Imran	Bari	39	40
8th	Imran	Qadir	17	34
9th	Imran	Sikander	50	59
10th	Imran	Ehtesham	1	4

275.

ENGLAND 1st INNINGS   IN REPLY TO PAKISTAN'S 275 ALL OUT

IN	OUT	MINS	No.	BATSMAN	HOW OUT	BOWLER	RUNS	WKT	TOTAL	6s	4s	BALLS	NOTES ON DISMISSAL
11:33	2:19	127	1	C.J.TAVARÉ	c sub (Haroon)	IMRAN	22	4	77	·	3	90	Fended fast short ball to short leg's (diving) right
11:33	11:59	26	2	G.FOWLER	BOWLED	EHTESHAM	9	1	15	·	1	19	Pushed outside break-back that hit off stump
12:01	2:02	82	3	M.W.GATTING	LBW	IMRAN	25	2	67	·	4	61	Played back to inswinging break-back. Late on stroke
2:04	2:10	6	4	A.J.LAMB	c Mohsin	IMRAN	0	3	69	·	·	3	Late on hook - square-leg - spooned catch
2:12	6:25	233	5	D.I.GOWER	c sub (Haroon)	SIKANDER	74	9	255	·	8	169	Cut short ball to gully
2:21	3:20	59	6	I.T.BOTHAM	c sub (Haroon)	SIKANDER	57	5	146	·	8	59	Diving catch off skier at deep backward square leg
3:22	3:43	21	7	D.W.RANDALL	run out (Sikander)		8	6	159	·	1	20	Attempted quick single on off side - sent back - bowler threw at wkt
3:45	3:55	10	8	V.J.MARKS	BOWLED	QADIR	7	7	170	·	1	14	Last ball before tea - played no stroke to googly - off stump
4:15	5:07	52	9	R.W.TAYLOR†	c Miandad	IMRAN	18	8	209	·	2	47	Edged low to second slip
5:09	11:01	90	10	R.D.JACKMAN	c Mohsin	IMRAN	11	10	256	·	1	51	Turned second ball of 3rd day to backward short-leg
6:27	(11:01)	12	11	R.G.D.WILLIS*	NOT OUT		1	·	·			13	Extended his record number of 'not outs' to 46
				EXTRAS	b 4 lb 10 w 2 nb 8		24				- 29	546 balls (inc. 10 no balls)	

TOTAL (off 89.2 overs in 367 min.)   256 all out at 11:01 on third day

* CAPTAIN   † WICKET-KEEPER

© BILL FRINDALL

BOWLER	O	M	R	W
IMRAN	25.2	7	49	5
EHTESHAM	14	4	46	1
SIKANDER	24	5	47	2
QADIR	22	5	87	1
MUDASSAR	4	1	3	0
			24	
	·7	22	256	10

HRS	OVERS	RUNS
1	13	28
2	14	40
3	15	76
4	16	34
5	14	44
6	15	34

RUNS	MINS	OVERS	LAST 50
50	86	20	86
100	148	34	62
150	203	48.1	55
200	258	63	55
250	344	83.4	86

LUNCH: 52-1   TAVARÉ 17* (45 min) (61 min)   GATTING 17*   21 OVERS - 89 MINUTES

TEA: 170-7   GOWER 28* (103 min)   54 OVERS - 223 MIN.

STUMPS: 256-9 (2nd DAY) (19 BEHIND)   JACKMAN 11* (45 min)   WILLIS 1* (11 min)   89 OVERS - 366 MIN.

WKT	PARTNERSHIP		RUNS	MINS
1st	Tavaré	Fowler	15	26
2nd	Tavaré	Gatting	52	82
3rd	Tavaré	Lamb	2	6
4th	Tavaré	Gower	8	7
5th	Gower	Botham	69	59
6th	Gower	Randall	13	21
7th	Gower	Marks	11	10
8th	Gower	Taylor	39	52
9th	Gower	Jackman	46	76
10th	Jackman	Willis	1	12
			256	

14 OVERS 3 BALLS/HOUR
2·87 RUNS/OVER
47 RUNS/100 BALLS

PAKISTAN 2ND INNINGS — 19 RUNS AHEAD ON FIRST INNINGS

IN	OUT	MINS	No.	BATSMAN	HOW OUT	BOWLER	RUNS	WKT	TOTAL	6s	4s	BALLS	NOTES ON DISMISSAL
11.09	11.10	1	1	MOHSIN KHAN	c TAYLOR	WILLIS	0	1	0	.	.	1	Drove outside first ball of the innings - inside edge.
11.09	11.15	6	2	MUDASSAR NAZAR	c BOTHAM	WILLIS	0	2	3	.	.	1	Pushed fast, short, off side ball to 3rd slip.
11.12	2.07	137	3	MANSOOR AKHTAR	c RANDALL	BOTHAM	39	5	108	.	5	108	Edged push at outswinger to 3rd slip - widish ball.
11.17	12.47	90	4	JAVED MIANDAD	c TAYLOR	BOTHAM	52	3	81	.	9	57	Magnificent driving. Low, right-handed catch - drive at ½ volley.
12.49	12.52	3	5	ZAHEER ABBAS	LBW	BOTHAM	4	4	85	.	1	5	Turned round and beaten by breakback.
12.54	2.23	51	6	MAJID KHAN	c GOWER	BOTHAM	10	6	115	.	1	33	Edged lifting off side ball to 1st slip.
2.09	6.02	213	7	IMRAN KHAN*	c RANDALL	WILLIS	46	10	199	.	7	158	Pulled short ball to short mid-wicket - low catch.
2.25	2.34	9	8	WASIM BARI †	c TAYLOR	WILLIS	7	7	128	.	.	47	Edged fast away-seamer low to 'keeper's right.
2.36	4.48	52	9	ABDUL QADIR	BOWLED	JACKMAN	17	8	169	.	3	38	Played on via inside edge.
4.50	5.55	65	10	SIKANDER BAKHT	c GATTING	MARKS	7	9	199	.	.	47	Edged off break via pad to short square leg (high, right-handed)
5.57	(6.02)	5	11	EHTESHAM UDDIN	NOT OUT		0			.	.	2	Batted with Miandad as runner (pulled hamstring)
				EXTRAS	b - lb 6	w 4 nb 7	17			0	25	497 balls (inc. 11 no balls)	
				TOTAL	(off 81 overs in 355 minutes)		199					199 all out at 6·02 pm on third day.	

13 OVERS 4 BALLS/HOUR
2.46 RUNS/OVER
40 RUNS/100 BALLS

* CAPTAIN † WICKET-KEEPER
© BILL FRINDALL

LUNCH: 89-4 — 108 AHEAD
TEA: 159-7 — 178 AHEAD

MANSOOR 25* (110 min), MAJID 3* (8 min) — 25 OVERS - 113 MIN.
IMRAN 21* (117 min), QADIR 14* (30 min) — 58 OVERS - 259 MIN.

BOWLER	O	M	R	W
WILLIS	19	3	55	3
BOTHAM	30	8	74	5
JACKMAN	28	11	41	1
MARKS	2	1	8	1
GATTING	2	1	4	0
	81	24	199	10

HRS	OVERS	RUNS	RUNS	MINS	OVERS	LAST 50 (in mins)
1	12	33	50	72	15.1	72
2	14	59	100	129	28.3	57
3	13	26	150	254	56.5	125
4	14	21				
5	14	39				
	81					

WKT	PARTNERSHIP		RUNS	MINS
1st	Mohsin	Mudassar	0	1
2nd	Mudassar	Mansoor	3	3
3rd	Mansoor	Miandad	78	90
4th	Mansoor	Zaheer	4	3
5th	Mansoor	Majid	23	35
6th	Majid	Imran	7	14
7th	Imran	Bari	13	69
8th	Imran	Qadir	41	52
9th	Imran	Sikander	30	65
10th	Imran	Ehtesham	0	5
			199	

ENGLAND 2ND INNINGS — NEEDING 219 RUNS TO WIN OFF A MINIMUM OF 201 OVERS (1.09 runs/over)

IN	OUT	MINS	No.	BATSMAN	HOW OUT	BOWLER	RUNS	WKT	TOTAL	6s	4s	BALLS	NOTES ON DISMISSAL
6.13	2.21	138	1	C.J.TAVARÉ	c MAJID	IMRAN	33	1	103	.	4	103	Edged firm-footed push at rising ball to first slip (low catch)
6.13	5.14	261	2	G.FOWLER	c WASIM BARI	MUDASSAR	86	2	168	.	11	204	Edged drive at outswinger to 'keeper's left.
2.23	5.47	155	3	M.W.GATTING	LBW	IMRAN	25	5	189	.	2	96	Played back to fast ball that kept low.
5.16	5.23	7	4	A.J.LAMB	LBW	MUDASSAR	4	3	172	.	1	4	Missed late outswinger that kept low - played back.
5.25	5.37	12	5	D.I.GOWER	c WASIM BARI	MUDASSAR	15	4	187	.	1	11	Edged outswinger to keeper's left.
5.38	11.08	27	6	I.T.BOTHAM	c MAJID	MUDASSAR	4	7	199	.	1	19	Edged steer to first slip - ball popped and left him.
5.48	5.49	1	7	D.W.RANDALL	LBW	IMRAN	0	6	189	.	.	2	Hit on front foot by inswinger - half-cock stroke
5.51	(11.39)	45	8	V.J.MARKS	NOT OUT		12			.	1	38	
11.09	(11.39)	30	9	R.W.TAYLOR†	NOT OUT		6			.	.	12	Made winning hit
			10	R.D.JACKMAN	} did not bat								
			11	R.G.D.WILLIS*	}								
				EXTRAS	b 19 lb 16 w 1 nb 6		42			0	20	489 balls (inc 7 no balls)	

TOTAL (off 80.2 overs in 343 minutes) **219-7**

ENGLAND won by 3 wickets at 11.39 am on fifth day and won series 2-1.

*M CAPTAIN † WICKET-KEEPER

BOWLER	O	M	R	W
SIKANDER	20	4	40	0
IMRAN	30²	8	66	3
QADIR	8	2	16	0
MUDASSAR	22	7	55	4
			42	
	80.2	21	229	7

HRS	OVERS	RUNS	RUNS	MINS	OVERS	LAST 50 (in mins)
1	14	38	50	69	16.1	69
2	16	53	100	157	34.1	68
3	14	35	150	216	52.5	79
4	14	30	200	315	74	99
5	13	34				

14 OVERS 0 BALLS/HOUR
2.73 RUNS/OVER
45 RUNS/100 BALLS

WKT	PARTNERSHIP		RUNS	MINS
1st	Tavaré	Fowler	103	138
2nd	Fowler	Gatting	65	122
3rd	Gatting	Lamb	4	7
4th	Gatting	Gower	15	12
5th	Gatting	Botham	2	9
6th	Botham	Randall	0	1
7th	Botham	Marks	10	14
8th	Marks	Taylor	20*	30
			219	

B.I.SP 6.26 to 6.44 pm - 18 minutes (4 overs) lost
STUMPS (3RD DAY): 15-0 Tavaré 8* Fowler 3* off 5 overs in 21 min.

R.S.P 12.14 to 12.47pm - 33 minutes (8 overs) lost 77-0
LUNCH: 86-0 Tavaré 22* Fowler 45* off 27 overs in 110 min
NEEDING 133 TO WIN
- RESTARTED 14 MIN LATE (4 overs lost). R.S.P 2.44pm-3.14pm 111-1
- R.S.P 30 MIN (7 overs lost) - EXTRA HOUR AVAILABLE

TEA: 150-1 Fowler 75* Gatting 13* (78m) off 53 overs in 217 minutes.

B.I.SP 5.57pm
STUMPS: 190-6 Botham 0* (9 min) Marks 1* (6 min)
(4TH DAY) 72 OVERS - 304 MIN

MAN OF THE MATCH: IMRAN KHAN (Adjudicator: T.W.Graveney)
MAN OF THE SERIES: IMRAN KHAN
TOTAL TIME LOST: 33 OVERS (98 MINUTES)

BILL FRINDALL

Statistical Survey: England v Pakistan 1982 — England

England — Batting/Fielding	M	I	NO	HS	R	Avge	100	50	Sixes	Fours	Min.	Balls	R/H	Ct	St
C.J. Tavaré	3	6	0	82	216	36.00	—	2	—	24	1026	734	29	3	—
D.I. Gower	3	6	0	74	197	32.83	—	2	—	24	639	492	40	2	—
D.W. Randall	3	6	0	105	168	28.00	1	—	—	18	436	287	59	3	—
I.T. Botham	3	6	0	69	163	27.16	—	2	—	21	425	322	51	1	—
R.W. Taylor	3	6	2	54	108	27.00	—	1	—	8	360	295	37	12	—
M.W. Gatting	3	6	1	32*	111	22.20	—	—	—	13	465	318	35	3	—
E.E. Hemmings	2	4	0	19	41	10.25	—	—	—	3	146	114	36	3	—
R.D. Jackman	2	3	0	17	28	9.33	—	—	—	2	159	114	25	2	—
A.J. Lamb	3	6	0	33	48	8.00	—	—	—	6	193	123	39	1	—
I.A. Greig	2	4	0	14	26	6.50	—	—	—	2	129	102	25	—	—
Also batted:															
R.G.D. Willis	2	3	3	28*	29	—	—	—	—	3	150	124	23	3	—
G. Fowler	1	2	0	86	95	47.50	—	1	—	12	287	223	43	1	—
G. Miller	1	2	0	47	52	26.00	—	—	—	6	116	113	46	1	—
V.J. Marks	1	2	1	12*	19	19.00	—	—	—	2	55	52	37	—	—
D.R. Pringle	1	2	0	14	19	9.50	—	—	—	1	104	91	21	—	—
Totals	33	64	7	(105)	1320	23.15	1	8	—	145	4690	3504	38	32	—

England — Bowling	O	M	R	W	Avge	Best	5w/I	10w/M	B/W	R/H	NB	Wides
Willis	74	14	222	10	22.20	3-55	—	—	44	50	23	2
Botham	150.5	33	478	18	26.55	5-74	1	—	50	53	2	7
Greig	31.2	6	114	4	28.50	4-53	—	—	47	61	—	—
Jackman	105	30	247	8	30.87	4-110	—	—	79	39	2	—
Hemmings	56.1	12	149	3	49.66	2-56	—	—	112	44	—	—
Also bowled:												
Miller	9.4	2	27	2	13.50	2-26	—	—	29	47	—	—
Marks	7	1	31	1	31.00	1-8	—	—	42	74	—	—
Gatting	10	3	21	0	—	—	—	—	—	35	—	1
Pringle	26	9	62	0	—	—	—	—	—	40	—	—
Totals	470	110	1351	46	29.36	(5-74)	1	—	61	48	27	10

* Not out   R/H = runs per 100 balls. B/W = balls per wicket.

Statistical Survey: England v Pakistan 1982 — Pakistan

Pakistan — Batting/Fielding	M	I	NO	HS	R	Avge	100	50	Sixes	Fours	Min.	Balls	R/H	Ct	St
Mohsin Khan	3	6	1	200	310	62.00	1	—	—	38	702	543	57	4	—
Imran Khan	3	5	1	67*	212	53.00	—	2	5	25	627	460	46	—	—
Javed Miandad	3	6	1	54	178	35.60	—	2	—	19	508	362	49	4	—
Mansoor Akhtar	3	5	0	58	154	30.80	—	2	—	19	491	408	38	2	—
Wasim Bari	3	5	2	24*	82	27.33	—	—	—	10	250	164	50	8	—
Zaheer Abbas	3	5	0	75	131	26.20	—	1	—	15	369	285	46	—	—
Tahir Naqqash	2	3	0	39	53	17.66	—	—	—	8	61	64	83	—	—
Mudassar Nazar	3	5	0	65	85	17.00	—	1	—	9	224	165	52	1	—
Abdul Qadir	3	5	1	18*	56	14.00	—	—	—	8	160	145	39	1	—
Sikander Bakht	2	4	1	7	16	5.33	—	—	—	—	140	91	18	—	—
Also batted/played:															
Wasim Raja	1	2	0	26	42	21.00	—	—	—	4	83	67	63	—	—
Majid Khan	1	2	0	21	31	15.50	—	—	—	4	117	83	37	2	—
Haroon Rashid	1	1	0	1	1	1.00	—	—	—	—	7	5	20	3	—
Ehtesham Uddin	1	2	1	0*	0	0.00	—	—	—	—	9	5	0	—	—
Sarfraz Nawaz	1	—	—	—	—	—	—	—	—	—	—	—	—	1	—
Totals	33	56	8	(200)	1351	28.14	1	8	5	159	3748	2847	47	†26	—

* Not out. † Plus four 'ct substitute' — all by Haroon Rashid. R/H = runs per 100 balls. B/W = balls per wicket.

Pakistan — Bowling	O	M	R	W	Avge	Best	5w/I	10w/M	B/W	R/H	NB	Wides
Mudassar Nazar	54	18	104	10	10.40	6-32	1	—	32	32	4	6
Tahir Naqqash	52	20	117	7	16.71	5-40	1	—	45	38	24	1
Imran Khan	178.1	48	390	21	18.57	7-52	2	—	51	36	2	21
Sarfraz Nawaz	37	9	78	3	26.00	3-56	—	—	74	35	7	1
Abdul Qadir	160.5	48	406	10	40.60	4-39	—	—	97	42	9	1
Sikander Bakht	75	19	179	3	59.60	2-47	—	—	150	40	13	4
Also bowled:												
Wasim Raja	2.3	2	0	1	0.00	1-0	—	—	15	0	—	—
Ehtesham Uddin	14	4	46	1	46.00	1-46	—	—	84	55	4	—
Totals	573.3	168	1320	56	23.57	(7-52)	4	—	61	38	63	34

First one-day international: Trent Bridge, July 17.
England won by 7 wickets.
An accomplished innings by Allan Lamb enabled England to win with 47 balls to spare. Yet such a comfortable victory had seemed unlikely earlier when Pakistan's opening pair, Mudassar and Mohsin, put on 102 in 26 overs.

As they made the most of a variable England attack on a mild pitch, Pakistan seemed capable of making at least 300. Mudassar's run-out, quickly followed by the departure of Mohsin, however, enabled England to gain more control and, helped by steady spin bowling, to keep Pakistan within bounds.

When he had made only one, Lamb survived an appeal for a catch at the wicket. Afterwards, he played strokes of great quality, and Pakistan, handicapped by an injury to Sarfraz, lacked the bowling resources to change the pattern of the game.

Second one-day international: Old Trafford, July 19.
England won by 73 runs.
After being put in, England amassed 295 for 8, though even that total fell short of what seemed possible during an onslaught by Gatting and Botham. It was, however, well beyond Pakistan's capabilities, and England finished as 2-0 winners of the series and took the Prudential Trophy.

Botham's 49 was made off only 29 balls, with 4 sixes and 2 fours. And with Gatting driving almost as powerfully, the pair took Pakistan's attack to pieces, adding 84 in 11 overs.

Progress was more sober after that, with Gatting run out after making 76 from 82 balls. Pakistan were never allowed to perform with the vigour that was necessary to make a challenge. And although Wasim Raja played some bold strokes in his 60, it was too late to change the course of the match.

England v Pakistan 1st Prudential Trophy Match
England won by 7 wickets
Played at Trent Bridge, Nottingham, July 17
Toss: Pakistan. Umpires: D.G.L. Evans and A.G.T. Whitehead
Man of the Match: A.J. Lamb

Pakistan		Runs	Mins	Balls	6s	4s
Mudassar Nazar	*run out* (Hemmings)	51	92	86	—	5
Mohsin Khan	*b* Botham	47	95	74	1	4
Zaheer Abbas	*lbw b* Pringle	53	78	72	—	5
Javed Miandad	*c* Willis *b* Pringle	28	56	49	—	1
Majid Khan	*c* Willis *b* Botham	23	30	20	—	2
Wasim Raja	*c* Hemmings *b* Botham	14	21	19	—	1
Imran Khan*	*not out*	16	16	10	—	1
Sarfraz Nawaz	*not out*	2	6	3	—	—
Wasim Bari†						
Iqbal Qasim	*did not bat*					
Sikander Bakht						
Extras	(*b* 4, *lb* 4, *w* 6, *nb* 2)	16				
Total	(55 overs; 202 minutes)	**250–6**				

England		Runs	Mins	Balls	6s	4s
D.I. Gower	*c* Wasim Bari *b* Sikander	17	41	32	—	2
C.J. Tavaré	*b* Imran	48	126	83	—	4
A.J. Lamb	*c* Wasim Bari *b* Imran	118	149	121	—	14
M.W. Gatting	*not out*	37	81	46	—	4
I.T. Botham	*not out*	10	15	9	—	1
D.W. Randall						
G. Miller						
D.R. Pringle	*did not bat*					
E.E. Hemmings						
R.W. Taylor†						
R.G.D. Willis*						
Extras	(*lb* 11, *w* 5, *nb* 6)	22				
Total	(47.1 overs; 209 minutes)	**252–3**				

England	O	M	R	W
Willis	11	1	46	0
Botham	11	0	57	3
Pringle	11	1	50	2
Miller	11	1	36	0
Hemmings	11	1	45	0

Pakistan	O	M	R	W
Imran	11	2	35	2
Sarfraz	11	3	43	0
Sikander	7	0	34	1
Qasim	7	0	49	0
Mudassar	5.1	0	26	0
Majid	4	0	25	0
Wasim Raja	2	0	18	0

Fall of Wickets

Wkt	P	E
1st	102	25
2nd	103	132
3rd	175	234
4th	208	—
5th	222	—
6th	238	—
7th	—	—
8th	—	—
9th	—	—
10th	—	—

* Captain   † Wicket-keeper

England v Pakistan 2nd Prudential Trophy Match
England won by 73 runs
Played at Old Trafford, Manchester, July 19
Toss: Pakistan. Umpires: D.J. Constant and H.D. Bird
Man of the Match: M.W. Gatting
Men of the Series: A.J. Lamb; Mudassar Nazar

England		Runs	Mins	Balls	6s	4s
D.I. Gower	c Wasim Bari b Mudassar	33	67	50	—	4
C.J. Tavaré	run out (Wasim Bari/ Wasim Raja)	16	42	31	—	1
A.J. Lamb	c Wasim Bari b Qasim	27	59	41	—	4
M.W. Gatting	run out (Sikander)	76	105	81	1	8
I.T. Botham	c Wasim Raja b Imran	49	27	28	4	2
D.W. Randall	run out (Mudassar/Sikander)	6	22	11	—	—
G. Miller	b Imran	26	51	33	—	3
D.R. Pringle	not out	34	59	45	—	3
E.E. Hemmings	c Qasim b Tahir	1	6	7	—	—
R.W. Taylor†	not out	1	6	3	—	—
R.G.D. Willis*	did not bat					
Extras	(lb 16, w 10)	26				
Total	(55 overs; 235 minutes)	**295-8**				

Pakistan		Runs	Mins	Balls	6s	4s
Mudassar Nazar	run out (Taylor)	31	54	50	—	3
Mohsin Khan	b Pringle	17	58	40	—	—
Zaheer Abbas	c Randall b Pringle	13	15	14	—	1
Mansoor Akhtar	run out (Botham/Miller)	28	53	37	—	3
Majid Khan	b Miller	5	13	19	—	—
Wasim Raja	c Botham b Willis	60	65	61	2	6
Imran Khan*	c Gower b Miller	31	50	45	—	5
Tahir Naqqash	run out (Hemmings/Miller)	1	12	3	—	—
Wasim Bari†	b Hemmings	4	13	10	—	—
Iqbal Qasim	lbw b Botham	13	16	18	—	2
Sikander Bakht	not out	2	4	3	—	—
Extras	(lb 14, w 2, nb 1)	17				
Total	(49.5 overs; 184 minutes)	**222**				

Pakistan	O	M	R	W
Imran	11	1	48	2
Tahir	10	0	37	1
Sikander	11	0	42	0
Mudassar	11	0	50	1
Qasim	8	0	76	1
Majid	4	1	16	0

England	O	M	R	W
Willis	8	0	36	1
Botham	8.5	0	40	1
Miller	11	1	56	2
Pringle	11	0	43	2
Hemmings	11	3	30	1

Fall of Wickets

Wkt	E	P
1st	32	52
2nd	54	55
3rd	101	82
4th	185	97
5th	217	123
6th	226	183
7th	280	200
8th	284	201
9th	—	213
10th	—	222

* Captain   † Wicket-keeper

Pakistan in England 1982
First-Class Averages

Batting and Fielding	M	I	NO	HS	R	Avge	100	50	Ct	St
Mudassar Nazar	11	16	6	211*	825	82.50	4	2	4	—
Zaheer Abbas	9	12	3	148*	664	73.77	2	4	2	—
Mohsin Khan	13	20	3	203*	1248	73.41	4	4	5	—
Imran Khan	9	8	4	67*	291	72.75	—	2	—	—
Javed Miandad	10	13	6	105*	450	64.28	1	3	14	—
Mansoor Akhtar	11	17	2	153	595	39.66	1	5	5	—
Haroon Rashid	10	13	3	90	331	33.10	—	2	8	—
Wasim Bari	11	7	2	45	162	32.40	—	—	22	7
Majid Khan	11	17	3	88	403	28.78	—	1	8	—
Wasim Raja	12	12	2	50*	247	24.70	—	1	5	—
Tahir Naqqash	6	4	0	39	65	16.25	—	—	3	—
Abdul Qadir	12	9	3	21*	93	15.50	—	—	3	—
Salim Yousuf	4	4	1	15*	38	12.66	—	—	5	2
Salim Malik	5	7	1	25*	68	11.33	—	—	4	—
Sikander Bakht	12	7	2	9	29	5.80	—	—	3	—
Iqbal Qasim	7	4	1	5	9	3.00	—	—	2	—

Also batted: Ehtesham Uddin (2 matches) 0, 0*; Intikhab Alam (1 match) 0, 4; Jalal Uddin (3 matches) 10, 0; Sarfraz Nawaz (6 matches) 7 (1 ct).

* not out

Bowling	O	M	R	W	Avge	Best	5w/I	10w/M
Mudassar Nazar	139	35	368	21	17.52	6-32	1	—
Imran Khan	290.3	76	621	35	17.74	7-52	2	—
Abdul Qadir	452.4	123	1187	57	20.82	7-44	4	1
Sarfraz Nawaz	127	24	351	16	21.93	6-92	1	—
Sikander Bakht	326	86	959	27	35.51	4-68	—	—
Tahir Naqqash	160	44	537	15	35.80	5-40	1	—
Wasim Raja	117.4	30	346	9	38.44	3-34	—	—
Iqbal Qasim	161.1	36	434	12	36.16	5-52	1	—

Also bowled: Ehtesham Uddin 28-9-81-1; Intikhab Alam 6-0-17-1; Jalal Uddin 56-19-123-4; Javed Miandad 3-0-16-0; Majid Khan 22-9-57-2; Mansoor Akhtar 16.3-6-43-1; Mohsin Khan 5-0-32-1; Salim Malik 1-0-5-0; Zaheer Abbas 0.1-0-0-0.

Hundreds

4 **Mohsin Khan:** 151 v Sussex (Hove); 165* v Worcestershire (Worcester); 203* v Leicestershire (Leicester); 200 v England (Lord's).

Mudassar Nazar: 211* v Sussex (Hove); 163* v Glamorgan (Swansea); 100* v Derbyshire (Chesterfield); 163* v England B (Leicester).

2 **Zaheer Abbas:** 147 v Worcestershire (Worcester); 148* v Derbyshire (Chesterfield).

1 **Javed Miandad:** 105* v Somerset (Taunton).

Mansoor Akhtar: 153 v Somerset (Taunton)

Results: Played 15 Won 5 Lost 4 Drawn 6

Notes: Mohsin Khan's aggregate of 1,248 runs is the third-highest by a batsman on a shared tour of Britain and has been exceeded only by Zaheer Abbas (1,508 in 1971) and Glenn Turner (1,380 in 1973). Shared tours began in 1965. Only three bowlers on shared tours have exceeded Abdul Qadir's total of 57 wickets: Intikhab Alam (72), S. Venkataraghavan (63), and Bishan Bedi (58) — all in 1971.

English season
1982

Schweppes County Championship

Middlesex, outright champions for the third time in seven seasons, came under serious pressure only once — when Leicestershire drew up to within two points of them with two matches to play — but in the second half of the season, when they had Mike Gatting available less often, they were clearly more vulnerable than in the first half.

That they had the most varied and probably the strongest bowling was not in much doubt, but, strangely, it was also a season of transition for them. They had their full share of injuries and losses of form in senior players, but every time they gave a less convincing performance than usual they hit back decisively in some way and drew away again from their pursuers. They led from the end of May.

They hit back mainly through positive captaincy and strong reserves. Mike Brearley, ending his tenure of office in a felicitous way, would be the first to admit that it is easier to be enterprising if you have penetrative bowlers of different types. But the whole side is more effective if they believe that their captain is a bit of a wizard who will do the right thing at the right time — hence successes such as the one against Surrey at Lord's in August, when on the last day of an important match reduced by rain Brearley made a declaration asking for only 161 in 135 minutes. Middlesex themselves had just made 157 for 2, but the pitch was wearing enough for Surrey to run into trouble as they went for the runs. They were bowled out in two hours, and the pressure on Middlesex eased again. Mike Brearley's thinking leadership has been eulogized often enough, and no further words are needed here save that it seemed entirely fitting that he should finish by winning again the most prized domestic trophy of all.

Because the Schweppes Championship involves so many more days' cricket, and better cricket, than the other competitions, and because it is more affected by injuries and Test claims, it probes the counties' strength in depth. Middlesex used no fewer than 22 players in championship matches, an extraordinary number for a winning side, and few did not make a useful contribution at some point. When everyone was fit, they were leaving out players whom many other counties would have welcomed. In North London they have huge resources, which are probably becoming greater as that part of the population which is of West Indian descent produces the young cricketers of talent long expected. However, the larger the resources, the more they need sifting, and Middlesex have been lucky to have as wise, energetic, and far-seeing a provider of future talent as Don Bennett.

At the start of the season, there was a strong feeling that this might be the year when Sussex won their first championship, though obviously much would depend on how they fared when Imran Khan departed in late June to captain Pakistan. Together, Imran and Le Roux might have done for Sussex what Clive Rice and Richard Hadlee had done for Notts a year before.

But Parker could not match for Sussex the large number of runs that

Gatting was making for Middlesex, and if one stopped to consider Sussex's all-round bowling strength for all pitches, it scarcely approached Middlesex's potential.

By mid-season, it became clear that another county, Leicestershire, might have what was needed. Les Taylor looked a fitter and better fast bowler than in other years. When Andy Roberts came down from the league to partner him in mid-week matches, Leicestershire had a good bowling side, the better for the return to form of a top-class left-arm spinner in Nick Cook. The batting was equally strong. Balderstone and Davison were as consistent as ever, David Gower, when available, was having his best season in the championship, and there was nothing wrong with a middle order containing Tolchard and Steele.

All this was emphasized at Uxbridge in early July when Middlesex and Leicestershire met. Leicestershire were as yet not serious rivals, still only in ninth place 61 points behind. But for a few days two months later it seemed that this match might in retrospect become the one that determined the Championship.

Leicestershire scored 400 in quick time, made Middlesex follow on, bowled them out again, and won handsomely by six wickets. With an engagingly human show of fallibility Brearley had put Leicestershire in. They proved to have been given the best of what started as a superb batting pitch with lightning fast outfield. Though still a good one, the pitch was not quite as true subsequently, and Leicestershire bowled better on it.

When Middlesex, with only a two-point lead, returned to Uxbridge in September to play Hampshire, they found by a happy chance a bare pitch on which a result was assured and on which their advantage in spin was likely to be decisive. This coincided with Leicestershire's losing of an important toss at Trent Bridge. In three days, the championship was settled save for four points, which Middlesex soon acquired the next day at Worcester.

The Schweppes Championship of 1982 probably contained more weak bowling sides than for some years. They are to be found at the bottom of the table, whence Hampshire rose to make the season's most spectacular improvement. Early on they were without their captain, Nick Pocock, and they went to the Oval on June 5 plumb bottom. Surrey were near the top. In an unusual match of low scores but high last-wicket stands, on a fiery, unpredictable pitch, Marshall and Emery announced themselves as one of the most formidable pairs of fast bowlers in the country. Though Surrey needed only 105 in the last innings, Marshall added seven wickets to his three in the first innings, his captain held two vital slip catches, and Hampshire scrambled home by three runs. From that moment they were away, gaining confidence all the time until they finished an honourable third, their highest place since 1975 — a remarkable achievement considering that only two seasons previously they had actually finished bottom.

Schweppes County Championship 1982 — Final Table

		P	W	L	D	First Innings Points		Total Points
						Batting	Bowling	
1	MIDDLESEX (4)	22	12	2	8	59	74	325
2	Leicestershire (8)	22	10	4	8	57	69	286
3	Hampshire (7)	22	8	6	8	48	74	250
4	Nottinghamshire (1)	21	7	7	7	44	65	221
5	Surrey (6)	22	6	6	10	56	62	214
6	Somerset (3)	22	6	6	10	51	66	213
7	Essex (5)	22	5	5	12	57	75	212
8	Sussex (2)	22	6	7	9	43	68	207
9	Northamptonshire (15)	22	5	3	14	61	54	195
10	Yorkshire (10)	21	5	1	15	48	51	179
11	Derbyshire (12)	22	4	3	15	45	64	173
12	Lancashire (16)	22	4	3	15	48	55	167
13	Kent (9)	22	3	4	15	55	63	166
14	Worcestershire (11)	22	3	5	14	43	54	141
15	Gloucestershire (13)	22	2	9	11	46	55	133
16	Glamorgan (14)	22	1	8	13	43	60	119
17	Warwickshire (17)	22	0	8	14	58	53	111

1981 final positions are shown in brackets. Worcestershire's total includes 12 points for winning a match reduced to one innings. The match between Yorkshire and Nottinghamshire at Harrogate on 26, 28, 29 June was abandoned without a ball being bowled and is excluded from the above table.

Points

For a win: 16 points, plus any first innings points. For winning a match reduced to a single innings because it started with less than eight hours of playing time remaining: 12 points. First innings points (awarded during the first 100 overs of each first innings and retained whatever the result of the match):

Batting		*Bowling*	
150 to 199 runs	1	3 or 4 wickets	1
200 to 249 runs	2	5 or 6 wickets	2
250 to 299 runs	3	7 or 8 wickets	3
300 runs and over	4	9 or 10 wickets	4

Final Positions 1890–1982

	D	E	Gm	Gs	H	K	La	Le	M	Nh	Nt	Sm	Sy	Sx	Wa	Wo	Y
1890	—	—	—	6	—	3	2	—	7	—	5	—	1	8	—	—	3
1891	—	—	—	9	—	5	2	—	3	—	4	5	1	7	—	—	8
1892	—	—	—	7	—	7	4	—	5	—	2	3	1	9	—	—	6
1893	—	—	—	9	—	4	2	—	3	—	6	8	5	7	—	—	1
1894	—	—	—	9	—	4	4	—	3	—	7	6	1	8	—	—	2
1895	5	9	—	4	10	14	2	12	6	—	12	8	1	11	6	—	3
1896	7	5	—	10	8	9	2	13	3	—	6	11	4	14	12	—	1
1897	14	3	—	5	9	12	1	13	8	—	10	11	2	6	7	—	4
1898	9	5	—	3	12	7	6	13	2	—	8	13	4	9	9	—	1
1899	15	6	—	9	10	8	4	13	2	—	10	13	1	5	7	12	3
1900	13	10	—	7	15	3	2	14	7	—	5	11	7	3	6	12	1
1901	15	10	—	14	7	7	3	12	2	—	9	12	6	4	5	11	1
1902	10	13	—	14	15	7	5	11	12	—	3	7	4	2	6	9	1
1903	12	8	—	13	14	8	4	14	1	—	5	10	11	2	7	6	3
1904	10	14	—	9	15	3	1	7	4	—	5	12	11	6	7	13	2
1905	14	12	—	8	16	6	2	5	11	13	10	15	4	3	7	8	1
1906	16	7	—	9	8	1	4	15	11	11	5	11	3	10	6	14	2
1907	16	7	—	10	12	8	6	11	5	15	1	14	4	13	9	2	2

	D	E	Gm	Gs	H	K	La	Le	M	Nh	Nt	Sm	Sy	Sx	Wa	Wo	Y
1908	14	11	—	10	9	2	7	13	4	15	8	16	3	5	12	6	1
1909	15	14	—	16	8	1	2	13	6	7	10	11	5	4	12	8	3
1910	15	11	—	12	6	1	4	10	3	9	5	16	2	7	14	13	8
1911	14	6	—	12	11	2	4	15	3	10	8	16	5	13	1	9	7
1912	12	15	—	11	6	3	4	13	5	2	8	14	7	10	9	16	1
1913	13	15	—	9	10	1	8	14	6	4	5	16	3	7	11	12	2
1914	12	8	—	16	5	3	11	13	2	9	10	15	1	6	7	14	4
1919	9	14	—	8	7	2	5	9	13	12	3	5	4	11	15	—	1
1920	16	9	—	8	11	5	2	13	1	14	7	10	3	6	12	15	4
1921	12	15	17	7	6	4	5	11	1	13	8	10	2	9	16	14	3
1922	11	8	16	13	6	4	5	14	7	15	2	10	3	9	12	17	1
1923	10	13	16	11	7	5	3	14	8	17	2	9	4	6	12	15	1
1924	17	15	13	6	12	5	4	11	2	16	6	8	3	10	9	14	1
1925	14	7	17	10	9	5	3	12	6	11	4	15	2	13	8	16	1
1926	11	9	8	15	7	3	1	13	6	16	4	14	5	10	12	17	2
1927	5	8	15	12	13	4	1	7	9	16	2	14	6	10	11	17	3
1928	10	16	15	5	12	2	1	9	8	13	3	14	6	7	11	17	4
1929	7	12	17	4	11	8	2	9	6	13	1	15	10	4	14	16	2
1930	9	6	11	2	13	5	1	12	16	17	4	13	8	7	15	10	3
1931	7	10	15	2	12	3	6	16	11	17	5	13	8	4	9	14	1
1932	10	14	15	13	8	3	6	12	10	16	4	7	5	2	9	17	1
1933	6	4	16	10	14	3	5	17	12	13	8	11	9	2	7	15	1
1934	3	8	13	7	14	5	1	12	10	17	9	15	11	2	4	16	5
1935	2	9	13	15	16	10	4	6	3	17	5	14	11	7	8	12	1
1936	1	9	16	4	10	8	11	15	2	17	5	7	6	14	13	12	3
1937	3	6	7	4	14	12	9	16	2	17	10	13	8	5	11	15	1
1938	5	6	16	10	14	9	4	15	2	17	12	7	3	8	13	11	1
1939	9	4	13	3	15	5	6	17	2	16	12	14	8	10	11	7	1
1946	15	8	6	5	10	6	3	11	2	16	13	4	11	17	14	8	1
1947	5	11	9	2	16	4	3	14	1	17	11	11	6	9	15	7	7
1948	6	13	1	8	9	15	5	11	3	17	14	12	2	16	7	10	4
1949	15	9	8	7	16	13	11	17	1	6	11	9	5	13	4	3	1
1950	5	17	11	7	12	9	1	16	14	10	15	7	1	13	4	6	3
1951	11	8	5	12	9	16	3	15	7	13	17	14	6	10	1	4	2
1952	4	10	7	9	12	15	3	6	5	8	16	17	1	13	10	14	2
1953	6	12	10	6	14	16	3	3	5	11	8	17	1	2	9	15	12
1954	3	15	4	13	14	11	10	16	7	7	5	17	1	9	6	11	2
1955	8	14	16	12	3	13	9	6	5	7	11	17	1	4	9	15	2
1956	12	11	13	3	6	16	2	17	5	4	8	15	1	9	14	9	7
1957	4	5	9	12	13	14	6	17	7	2	15	8	1	9	11	16	3
1958	5	6	15	14	2	8	7	12	10	4	17	3	1	13	16	9	11
1959	7	9	6	2	8	13	5	16	10	11	17	12	3	15	4	14	1
1960	5	6	11	8	12	10	2	17	3	9	16	14	7	4	15	13	1
1961	7	6	14	5	1	11	13	9	3	16	17	10	15	8	12	4	2
1962	7	9	14	4	10	11	16	17	13	8	15	6	5	12	3	2	1
1963	17	12	2	8	10	13	15	16	6	7	9	3	11	4	4	14	1
1964	12	10	11	17	12	7	14	16	6	3	15	8	4	9	2	1	5
1965	9	15	3	10	12	5	13	14	6	2	17	7	8	16	11	1	4
1966	9	16	14	15	11	4	12	8	12	5	17	3	7	10	6	2	1
1967	6	15	14	17	12	2	11	3	7	9	16	8	4	13	10	5	1
1968	8	14	3	16	5	2	6	9	10	13	4	12	15	17	11	7	1
1969	16	6	1	2	5	10	15	14	11	9	8	17	3	7	4	12	13
1970	7	12	2	17	10	1	3	15	16	14	11	13	5	9	7	6	4
1971	17	10	16	8	9	4	3	5	6	14	12	7	1	11	2	15	13
1972	17	5	13	3	9	2	15	6	8	4	14	11	12	16	1	7	10
1973	16	8	11	5	1	4	12	9	13	3	17	10	2	15	7	6	14
1974	17	12	16	14	2	10	8	4	6	3	15	5	7	13	9	1	11
1975	15	7	9	16	3	5	4	1	11	8	13	12	6	17	14	10	2
1976	15	6	17	3	12	14	16	4	1	2	13	7	9	10	5	11	8
1977	7	6	14	.3	11	1	16	5	1	9	17	4	14	8	10	13	12
1978	14	2	13	10	8	1	12	6	3	17	7	5	16	9	11	15	4
1979	16	1	17	10	12	5	13	6	14	11	9	8	3	4	15	2	7
1980	9	8	13	7	17	16	15	9	1	12	3	5	2	4	14	11	6
1981	12	5	14	13	7	9	16	8	4	15	1	3	6	2	17	11	10
1982	11	7	16	15	3	13	12	2	1	9	4	6	5	8	17	14	10

Derbyshire

Derbyshire, in Barry Wood's first full season as captain, finished 11th, improving by one place on their 1981 status. Their defeats were four fewer than in the past summer, but their wins remained constant, at four.

Their season began against a background of change in personnel — on the administrative side as well as in the playing staff. Mike Hendrick and Geoff Miller, who had relinquished the captaincy, asked to move, as did David Steele. Miller, however, had a change of heart as the new season approached and was welcomed back into the fold. By the measure of the runs he made in 1981, Steele would not be missed. But as a left-arm spinner, he was invaluable in that season in which Hendrick was not always available, and in which Miller was below par.

The team's balance was maintained by signing an experienced batsman in John Hampshire and by the presence on the staff of a young left-arm spinner in Scotsman Dallas Moir.

Despite problems, Derbyshire's followers were cheerfully optimistic about their team's prospects in 1982, their hopes no doubt founded on gains achieved after Wood took over the side in July 1981. Derbyshire had played attractive, purposeful cricket under Wood's direction, and there was the happy September memory of the NatWest triumph. Dreams of a happier future were symbolized by the hurried building of a new pavilion at their Derby headquarters.

True enough, Derbyshire had a notable win over Somerset in the season's early days. But the next one did not come until the end of June, marking the start of a purple patch in which they achieved the little success that was to follow.

The bluntness of their bowling, traditionally their stronger suit, was the principal reason for Derbyshire not making a better impact. The big disappointment in this area was the decline of Paul Newman. Possessing a high, rhythmic action, Newman, 23, began the season as a Test candidate. But he missed five matches through injury, his striking rate fell, and the cost of his wickets went up. Nor were Miller's talents as a current England all-rounder manifest in his contribution, particularly with the ball. The county's outstanding bowler of 1982 was Moir, who started the season with only four first-class games to his name. A giant of 6ft 8in, Moir obtained a high bounce, and took 75 wickets.

Derbyshire's batting was dominated by their overseas stars, Peter Kirsten and John Wright, although Hampshire was also prominent with a four-figure aggregate, his approach always appropriate to various situations. Kirsten (8) and Wright (7) both improved on the previous county record for centuries scored in one season as they accumulated 1,941 and 1,830 runs, respectively. Wood's performance would seem to have been affected by the weight of captaincy. Kirsten is taking a sabbatical next season and Wright will be away assisting the touring New Zealanders. Their absence will be conspicuous, but Ian Anderson, having made two hundreds in 1982, and Kim Barnett, having made his first, promise to mitigate the loss.

Schweppes County Championship:	11th	Won 4	Lost 3	Drawn 15	
All First-Class Matches:		Won 4	Lost 4	Drawn 15	
NatWest Bank Trophy:	Lost to Hampshire in 2nd round				
Benson & Hedges Cup:	Lost to Sussex in quarter-final				
John Player League:	12th	Won 6	Lost 9	No result 1	

Championship Averages   *not out

Batting/Fielding	M	I	NO	HS	R	Avge	100	50	Ct	St
P.N. Kirsten	21	37	7	164*	1941	64.70	8	6	12	—
J.G. Wright	21	39	6	190	1830	55-45	7	5	13	—
J.H. Hampshire	21	34	6	101*	1187	42.39	1	9	12	—
G. Miller	12	20	5	61	502	33.46	—	4	14	—
I.S. Anderson	16	24	4	103*	651	32.55	1	3	19	—
K.J. Barnett	17	23	5	120	578	32.11	2	1	11	—
B. Wood	20	36	4	124*	799	24.96	1	2	21	—
A. Hill	7	14	3	54	219	19.90	—	1	5	—
S. Oldham	20	17	9	35*	148	18.50	—	—	7	—
C.J. Tunnicliffe	16	19	2	40	273	16.05	—	—	8	—
P.G. Newman	17	21	4	39*	189	11.11	—	—	4	—
P.J. Hacker	8	4	2	10*	22	11.00	—	—	3	—
B.J.M. Maher	10	11	5	15*	49	8.16	—	—	13	—
R.W. Taylor	12	17	2	45	121	8.06	—	—	22	4
D.G. Moir	22	21	1	25	136	6.80	—	—	23	—

Also batted: R.J. Finney (1 match) 39 (1 ct); A. Watts (1 match) 0 (1 ct).

Bowling	O	M	R	W	Avge	Best	5w/I	10w/M
D.G. Moir	789.5	223	1990	75	26.53	6-63	4	—
P.J. Hacker	174.1	25	677	25	27.08	5-51	2	—
G. Miller	382.2	120	832	29	28.68	8-70	1	1
S. Oldham	486.5	98	1503	46	32.67	7-78	2	—
C.J. Tunnicliffe	383.1	92	1213	37	32.78	5-73	1	—
P.G. Newman	410.3	63	1494	37	40.37	4-59	—	—
B. Wood	225.2	53	659	10	65.90	2-0	—	—

Also bowled: I.S. Anderson 58.4-22-157-5; K.J. Barnett 42.3-8-139-0; R.J. Finney 14-5-40-1; J.H. Hampshire 4-1-26-0; A. Hill 1-0-4-0; P.N. Kirsten 121-28-348-9; A. Watts 9-1-31-0; J.G. Wright 3-0-29-0.

Hundreds (20)

8 **P.N. Kirsten:** 143 v Gloucs, Gloucester; 121* v Leics, Derby; 102 v Leics, Coalville; 113 v Essex, Southend; 164* and 123* v Surrey, Derby; 105* v Sussex, Chesterfield; 140* v Yorks, Scarborough.

7 **J.G. Wright:** 141* v Notts, Chesterfield; 103* v Middlesex, Lord's; 106 v Essex, Chesterfield; 190 v Yorks, Derby; 185* v Northants, Derby; 157 v Northants, Northampton; 107 v Hants, Derby.

2 **K.J. Barnett:** 120 v Warwicks, Birmingham; 100* v Glamorgan, Derby.

1 **I.S. Anderson:** 103* v Hants, Derby.

J.H. Hampshire: 101* v Lancs, Derby.

B. Wood: 124* v Notts, Nottingham.

Essex

Essex's strength in 1982 was less affected by requirements of the England selectors than for many years. Only Derek Pringle was called up, but his selection was a loss to Essex only during the latter part of the season. Under the circumstances, Essex, their side barely changed from 1979, when they won the Championship, must have been disappointed to have finished no higher than seventh, which was two places down on 1981.

If statistics are to be accepted as a guide, Essex should have been placed higher, as four of the counties above them suffered more defeats than the five Essex incurred. Moreover, Essex scored comprehensive wins over three of them. Four Essex batsmen, Gooch, Hardie, McEwan, and Fletcher, each aggregated well over a thousand runs, a mark that could have also been within the reach of Pont, had he enjoyed more opportunities.

In crises, runs invariably came from the two all-rounders, Turner or Phillip — sometimes from both — and the batting ability of wicket-keeper David East was not to be discounted. However, it was not until mid-July that Gooch reached prime form, and by then Essex had already scored three of their total of five wins. Clearly, Gooch took time to come to terms with the break in his international career. Fletcher made no secret of his acute disappointment at losing the England captaincy. But there was no trace of his emotions in his performance either as captain or as batsman.

Another statistic that suggested that Essex should have fared better was their tally of 75 bowling points, the highest by any county. Still, the overall impression was that their cause suffered from lack of penetration in their attack. Norbert Phillip, even though 34, was fit throughout and took 82 wickets, the most in his five seasons with the county. Lever's bag of 72 squashed the theory that he was over the hill. Judged by past standards, Stuart Turner had a lean season as a bowler, but many of his 30 wickets were valuable ones, and he often struck at crucial stages.

Gooch also made his presence felt as a bowler, taking 22 wickets, of which he seized 7 for only 14 runs in one innings. Pont too was useful in emergencies. When wickets were helpful, the spinners, Acfield and East, were seldom found wanting. All in all, the overworked Essex attack would have had greater firepower had Neil Foster not broken down. Foster, a 20-year-old pace bowler who spent the 1981-82 winter in Australia on a Whitbread Scholarship, was forced out by a fractured vertebra after playing only four matches.

Without doubt, Essex's bowlers — and their batsmen no less — would have appreciated more pace and bounce in the pitches at Chelmsford, where they played the majority of their home matches.

No end-of-term report on Essex would be complete without commendation of the wicket-keeping of David East in his first full season. With 74 victims, he was second amongst the season's most successful wicket-keepers.

Schweppes County Championship:	7th	Won 5	Lost 5	Drawn 12	
All First-Class Matches:		Won 6	Lost 5	Drawn 13	
NatWest Bank Trophy:	Lost to Yorkshire in quarter-final				
Benson & Hedges Cup:	Failed to qualify for Q-F (3rd in Group C)				
John Player League:	5th	Won 9	Lost 7		

Championship Averages   *not out

Batting/Fielding	M	I	NO	HS	R	Avge	100	50	Ct	St
G.A. Gooch	22	37	1	149	1597	44.36	3	12	25	—
K.S. McEwan	22	34	3	150*	1306	42.12	3	4	8	—
K.W.R. Fletcher	22	34	4	124	1221	40.70	3	6	12	—
B.R. Hardie	22	36	5	94	1207	38.93	—	8	16	—
K.R. Pont	14	21	6	89	576	38.40	—	5	11	—
S. Turner	21	26	4	83	661	30.04	—	5	7	—
N. Phillip	22	30	3	73	684	25.33	—	4	4	—
A.W. Lilley	8	11	1	67	236	23.60	—	1	3	—
D.R. Pringle	6	9	1	54	152	19.00	—	2	—	—
D.E. East	22	29	7	61	413	18.77	—	1	60	7
R.E. East	19	21	2	44	276	14.52	—	—	16	—
J.K. Lever	18	19	3	22*	89	5.56	—	—	5	—
D.L. Acfield	19	16	12	4*	20	5.00	—	—	8	—

Also batted: N.A. Foster (4 matches) 0, 7, 36*; R.J. Leiper (1 match) 3, 0 (2 ct).

Bowling	O	M	R	W	Avge	Best	5w/I	10w/M
K.R. Pont	53	10	120	10	12.00	5-17	1	—
D.R. Pringle	161.5	40	388	17	22.82	4-53	—	—
G.A. Gooch	225	72	510	22	23.18	7-14	1	—
J.K. Lever	543.5	112	1683	72	23.37	6-48	5	1
N. Phillip	537.2	98	1698	68	24.97	6-60	3	—
R.E. East	446.5	128	1130	41	27.56	6-80	2	—
D.L. Acfield	525.2	119	1247	45	27.71	4-35	—	—
S. Turner	418	109	984	26	37.84	4-53	—	—

Also bowled: K.W.R. Fletcher: 16.1-0-134-2; N.A. Foster 82-18-286-8; B.R. Hardie 7-1-20-0; A.W. Lilley 3-0-10-0; K.S. McEwan 11-0-94-1.

Hundreds (9)

3 K.W.R. Fletcher: 120 v Middlesex, Lord's; 122 v Surrey, Chelmsford; 124 v Northants, Northampton.

G.A. Gooch: 149 v Kent, Canterbury; 140 v Surrey, Oval; 127 v Kent, Chelmsford.

K.S. McEwan: 150* v Derbys, Chesterfield; 116 v Derbys, Southend; 128 v Warwicks, Colchester.

County Caps Awarded 1982

Derbyshire: K.J. Barnett, J.H.Hampshire; Essex: D.E. East, D.R. Pringle; Glamorgan: D.A. Francis, B.J. Lloyd; Hampshire: M.C.J. Nicholas, R.J. Parks; Kent: N.R. Taylor; Lancashire: J. Abrahams, C.E.H. Croft; Leicestershire: N.G.B. Cook; Nottinghamshire: M. Hendrick; Somerset: J.W. Lloyds; Surrey: M.A. Lynch, D.J. Thomas; Sussex: A.C.S. Pigott, C.M. Wells; Warwickshire: G.C. Small; Yorkshire: S.N. Hartley, K. Sharp.

Glamorgan

For the 10th time in the last 11 years, Glamorgan finished in the lower half of the Championship table. They were kept clear of bottom place by their solitary win of the season, over Gloucestershire, in the penultimate match.

Against this background, it is easy to see why Glamorgan were among the counties that had so staunchly opposed the newly introduced restriction on overseas players to one per county. Tom Cartwright, coach to Glamorgan as well as being National Coach for all Wales, believes that stronger counties would have felt the absence of a cricketer of Javed Miandad's calibre. The handicap would have been less severe, said Cartwright, if Glamorgan had been able to turn to Ezra Moseley, their other overseas player. In 1981, when the rules allowed both to play in the same team, Miandad contributed 2,083 runs and Moseley, having played only two-thirds of all matches, took 57 wickets. Miandad had scored 601 runs in 8 matches when he went off to join the Pakistani tourists. Cartwright says that he was missed not only for the runs that he would have made during the rest of the season, but also for the speed of their acquisition. 'Javed always seeks to dominate the bowling, and if he played a big innings we had two hours extra to bowl out the opposition', said Cartwright.

The operation of bowling the other side out became more arduous because of a drastic back injury to Moseley, whom Glamorgan had recruited in Barbados as a raw club cricketer but who, over two seasons, matured into a high-grade fast bowler. Glamorgan's talent scouts in the West Indies found them a splendid replacement in Winston Davis, from St Vincent. He, too, suffered from niggling injuries, but still took 42 wickets in only 12 matches.

In a season in which Glamorgan were so reliant on homegrown talent, they could make few calls on Hugh Morris, 18, a highly gifted left-hander before whom many records in schools cricket have crumbled. For much of the summer, Morris, from Blundells, was involved in representative cricket at under-19 level.

Whoever else in the Glamorgan side failed, Alan Jones, at 43, topped the thousand mark for the 22nd time. The two others to reach this level were Arthur Francis and Rodney Ontong, who was not only more prolific than before, but played a larger variety of shots and hit the ball more firmly. Ontong was valuable, too, as a medium-fast seam bowler. He did a lot of bowling and, with 62, took most wickets. He was the only bowler to exceed 50 wickets. Fitness problems enforced periods of inactivity on Malcolm Nash, now 37. A bowler who seldom took less than 70 wickets in a season, Nash managed only 31 in 1982.

Schweppes County Championship:	16th	Won 1	Lost 8	Drawn 13
All First-Class Matches:		Won 1	Lost 9	Drawn 14
NatWest Bank Trophy:	Lost to Warwickshire in 2nd round			
Benson & Hedges Cup:	Failed to qualify for Q-F (4th in Group D)			
John Player League:	10th	Won 6	Lost 7	No result 3

Championship Averages
*not out

Batting/Fielding	M	I	NO	HS	R	Avge	100	50	Ct	St
H. Morris	4	6	3	63	213	71.00	—	2	1	—
Javed Miandad	8	16	2	96*	601	42.92	—	6	10	—
D.A. Francis	18	31	5	142*	1064	40.92	2	7	9	—
A. Jones	22	42	5	146*	1242	33.56	3	5	4	—
C.J.C. Rowe	22	34	5	105	888	30.62	1	5	9	—
R.C. Ontong	22	39	3	152*	1019	28.30	2	4	11	—
J.A. Hopkins	21	38	5	124	923	27.96	1	4	15	—
A.L. Jones	19	33	1	88	839	26.21	—	6	9	—
T. Davies	8	13	3	66*	211	21.10	—	1	14	1
G.C. Holmes	5	8	1	46*	139	19.85	—	—	1	—
S.A.B. Daniels	9	13	5	73	151	18.87	—	1	3	—
E.W. Jones	14	20	3	65	268	15.76	—	2	34	3
B.J. Lloyd	22	28	8	48	278	13.90	—	—	13	—
J.G. Thomas	9	13	0	84	172	13.23	—	1	4	—
M.A. Nash	13	16	1	37	197	13.13	—	—	10	—
S.R. Barwick	12	13	5	23*	95	11.87	—	—	6	—
W.W. Davis	12	11	6	20*	52	10.40	—	—	3	—

Also batted: M.J. Llewellyn (1 match) 25, 0. M.N. Davies (1 match) did not bat.

Bowling	O	M	R	W	Avge	Best	5w/I	10w/M
J.G. Thomas	140	25	514	22	23.36	5-61	1	—
W.W. Davis	370.5	69	1222	42	29.09	7-101	1	—
S.R. Barwick	266.2	59	836	28	29.85	5-44	1	—
R.C. Ontong	615.1	128	1922	62	31.00	6-50	1	1
M.A. Nash	336.2	77	1048	31	33.80	5-35	1	—
B.J. Lloyd	564.5	96	1898	45	42.17	5-155	1	—
S.A.B. Daniels	187.4	33	737	15	49.13	3-65	—	—
C.J.C. Rowe	189.2	35	732	12	61.00	3-95	—	—

Also bowled: G.C. Holmes 10-3-31-0; Javed Miandad 101.4-31-293-7; A. Jones 1-1-0-0.

Hundreds (9)

3 A. Jones: 146* v Worcs, Worcester; 136* v Kent, Canterbury; 103 v Notts, Swansea.

2 D.A. Francis: 127 v Somerset, Taunton; 142* v Kent, Canterbury.
   R.C. Ontong: 152* v Gloucs, Swansea; 110 v Surrey, Guildford.

1 J.A. Hopkins: 124 v Surrey, Guildford.
   C.J.C. Rowe: 105 v Somerset, Taunton.

Gloucestershire

Even in Zaheer Abbas's great season of 1981, when he was the most prolific scorer in county cricket, Gloucestershire finished 13th. It was hardly surprising that they fared no better in 1982, when Zaheer made only six appearances for them.

Zaheer's absence, however, was not the only factor which limited Gloucestershire to just two Championship wins and caused them to be beaten nine times — more often than any other county. The previous season closed an era, with Mike Procter and Brian Brain leaving the staff. Bowling resources that were sorely depleted thus were reduced further by Alan Wilkins spending all season on the injured list. The new squeeze on overseas players also bit deep into Gloucestershire's flesh.

In mid-season, Gloucestershire were able to reinforce their bowling strength by acquiring the part-time services of the Barbados all-rounder Franklyn Stephenson, who was engaged in the Central Lancashire League. But when Stephenson, who bowled at a fearsome pace and took 25 wickets, turned out, Gloucestershire had by law to omit Sadiq, whose presence was vital to the stability of an erratic batting side.

Gloucestershire's problems were alleviated somewhat by the acquisition of Kent's veteran all-rounder John Shepherd. Despite his 38 years, Shepherd bowled more than 700 overs and was Gloucestershire's most damaging bowler. For a bowler who, even in the recent past, was regarded as an England prospect, John Childs had a poor season. David Graveney, also a left-arm spinner, fared marginally better.

But Graveney deserved much sympathy. At the best of times, it is not easy to combine the roles of captain and front-line bowler. Graveney's task, in his first season as captain, was complicated further by a large pile of adverse circumstances. Not the least of them was leading an unsettled and largely inexperienced team. To add to Gloucestershire's problems, the pitches at their Bristol headquarters rarely suited them. They tended to be uneven in bounce, and if they favoured bowlers at all, they were more amenable to seam bowling than spin, which really was Gloucestershire's stronger suit.

Things went wrong also at Cheltenham where, through history, Gloucestershire's spinners have proved irresistible and where the county has always reaped a rich harvest of points. In only one of the three matches at Cheltenham did the ball turn in the expected manner, and the benefit went to Hemmings and Nottinghamshire rather than to Gloucestershire.

A place in the last eight of the NatWest Bank Trophy provided one faint touch of prosperity to an otherwise flat season. They lost their quarter-final to Middlesex by a hair's breadth, which could probably be accounted for by the absence, through injury, of Philip Bainbridge.

Apart from the reliable Andy Stovold, Bainbridge was the only other Gloucestershire batsman to complete 1,000 runs. He and Tony Wright are among the young batsmen on whose talent the county bases its hopes for the future.

Schweppes County Championship:	15th	Won 2 Lost 9 Drawn 11
All First-Class Matches:		Won 4 Lost 9 Drawn 12
NatWest Bank Trophy:		Lost to Middlesex in quarter-final
Benson & Hedges Cup:		Failed to qualify for Q-F (3rd in Group D)
John Player League:	14th	Won 5 Lost 9 No result 2

Championship Averages

*not out

Batting/Fielding	M	I	NO	HS	R	Avge	100	50	Ct	St
Zaheer Abbas	6	12	1	162*	667	60.63	2	4	1	—
P. Bainbridge	17	31	7	103	1001	41.70	2	6	9	—
Sadiq Mohammad	14	27	0	91	974	36.07	—	9	8	—
A.W. Stovold	22	40	1	212*	1338	34.30	2	7	24	—
B. Dudleston	6	12	1	111	373	33.90	1	1	6	—
A.J. Hignell	15	28	6	72	664	30.18	—	4	9	—
P.W. Romaines	13	22	1	186	561	26.71	1	2	5	—
B.C. Broad	20	38	0	97	985	25.92	—	5	4	—
D.A. Graveney	21	28	9	55*	457	24.05	—	1	11	—
A.J. Wright	10	19	2	65	399	23.47	—	2	3	—
J.N. Shepherd	21	33	8	67*	533	21.32	—	2	12	—
R.C. Russell	4	6	1	41	81	16.20	—	—	4	2
M.W. Stovold	3	6	0	52	96	16.00	—	1	—	—
R.J. Doughty	5	5	1	29	58	14.50	—	—	2	—
A.J. Brassington	18	19	5	35	141	10.07	—	—	32	6
J.H. Childs	19	21	5	34*	132	8.25	—	—	6	—
D. Surridge	16	17	7	12	61	6.10	—	—	3	—
F.D. Stephenson	7	9	1	15	42	5.25	—	—	1	—
E.J. Cunningham	3	4	1	5	7	2.33	—	—	—	—

Also batted: D.P. Simpkins (1 match) 0, 1*; C.R. Trembath (1 match) 8*.

Bowling	O	M	R	W	Avge	Best	5w/I	10w/M
F.D. Stephenson	175.3	37	542	25	21.68	5-69	1	—
D.A. Graveney	430.4	118	1134	39	29.07	7-37	1	—
D. Surridge	491.2	134	1319	41	32.17	5-78	1	—
J.N. Shepherd	708.4	162	1962	60	32.70	6-75	2	—
R.J. Doughty	149.1	19	533	15	35.53	6-43	1	—
J.H. Childs	551.2	158	1514	33	45.87	5-112	1	—
P. Bainbridge	276	72	844	18	46.88	6-59	1	—

Also bowled: B.C. Broad 34-7-87-2; B. Dudleston 37-10-108-3; Sadiq Mohammad 101.4-20-305-7; D.P. Simpkins 2-0-15-0; C.R. Trembath 23.2-2-98-0; Zaheer Abbas 2-0-15-0.

Hundreds (8)

2 P. Bainbridge: 101* v Glamorgan, Swansea; 103 v Yorks, Bradford.

   A.W. Stovold: 100 v Warwicks, Nuneaton; 212* v Northants, Northampton.

   Zaheer Abbas: 162* and 107 v Lancs, Gloucester.

1 B. Dudleston: 111 v Hants, Bournemouth.

   P.W. Romaines: 186 v Warwicks, Nuneaton.

Hampshire

Hampshire, undeterred by two heavy losses in their first three matches, finished third in the Championship. It was the first time they had figured in the frame since 1974, when a series of wet days at Bournemouth deprived them of their second title in successive years.

Although they were among the front-runners for the second half of the season, Hampshire were never really in reach of the title. They might just have edged into second place had they won three of the matches that they narrowly lost. Still, considering that they had finished bottom only two years earlier, Hampshire must have been delighted at the outcome, specially as it was accompanied by reasonable performances in two of the one-day competitions. Hampshire were an exciting side in 1982 and one their opponents feared. Issuing brave challenges and readily picking up a gauntlet flung at their feet, they gave much pleasure to crowds everywhere.

Although by no means the only match-winners, Malcolm Marshall and Trevor Jesty were the main sources of Hampshire's inspiration. Marshall did not miss a single Championship match and took 134 wickets, 49 more than any other bowler in the country. By August 25, Marshall had become the first winner of *The Daily Telegraph* Swanton Trophy, the newly instituted award for the fastest hundred wickets in a season. Marshall reached the mark by taking 39 wickets in 4 matches. Not since the days of uncovered pitches had a bowler taken as many wickets in a season.

Fast bowlers hunt best in pairs, and an explanation for Marshall's outstanding success may lie in the fact that, for the first time since he joined Hampshire in 1979, he had a worthy comrade-in-arms in Kevin Emery. With 83 wickets, Emery, in his maiden season, was the most successful of all the English-born pace bowlers in the county game, and if his record is set among all fast bowlers, only Marshall and Surrey's Sylvester Clarke took more wickets.

Few cricketers in recent times have excelled during their benefit season, but Trevor Jesty, 34, rose to unprecedented heights. A batsman whose opportunities were restricted until Barry Richards left the county, Jesty had only 13 centuries to his name before last season. Yet, in 1982, he scored eight, including six in the Championship. All England was impressed except the Test selectors, and that in spite of Jesty's having sustained his form until the day they met to pick the party for Australia.

Of the four matches that Hampshire narrowly failed to win, one was against Surrey, at Portsmouth, which might just have been swayed in Hampshire's favour had Jesty not missed it from injury. Similarly, Gordon Greenidge's absence was vital when, towards the end of June, Hampshire lost by four wickets to Gloucestershire in a rain-affected match in which the rivals forfeited their first innings.

For all their other shortcomings, Hampshire might have been carried to the top by Marshall, Jesty, Emery, and Greenidge if the side had possessed one important ingredient — a spin bowler of real class.

Schweppes County Championship:	3rd	Won 8	Lost 6	Drawn 8
All First-Class Matches:		Won 10	Lost 7	Drawn 8
NatWest Bank Trophy:	Lost to Surrey in quarter-final			
Benson & Hedges Cup:	Failed to qualify for Q-F (5th in Group C)			
John Player League:	5th	Won 8	Lost 6	Tied 2

Championship Averages

*not out

Batting/Fielding	M	I	NO	HS	R	Avge	100	50	Ct	St
T.E. Jesty	20	32	5	135*	1302	48.22	6	4	11	—
C.G. Greenidge	20	39	8	183*	1366	44.06	2	4	23	—
M.C.J. Nicholas	21	37	6	127*	871	28.09	1	5	11	—
M.D. Marshall	22	31	3	116*	633	22.60	1	1	4	—
D.R. Turner	14	20	1	96	425	22.36	—	2	6	—
N.G. Cowley	20	27	1	104	571	21.96	1	2	6	—
J.W. Southern	16	21	7	50*	300	21.42	—	1	4	—
N.E.J. Pocock	20	27	0	164	548	20.29	1	3	20	—
J.M. Rice	21	40	4	69	728	20.22	—	5	26	—
R.E. Hayward	4	6	0	59	102	17.00	—	1	3	—
R.J. Parks	22	29	4	44	334	13.36	—	—	63	6
V.P. Terry	3	5	2	16*	35	11.66	—	—	3	—
T.M. Tremlett	14	20	3	48	190	11.17	—	—	11	—
S.J. Malone	3	5	2	4	13	4.33	—	—	—	—
K. St J.D. Emery	21	26	15	18*	37	3.36	—	—	3	—

Also batted: M.J. Bailey (1 match) 3.

Bowling	O	M	R	W	Avge	Best	5w/I	10w/M
M.D. Marshall	822	225	2108	134	15.73	8-71	12	4
T.E. Jesty	279.1	86	730	34	21.47	6-71	1	—
K. St J.D. Emery	598	146	1731	78	22.19	6-51	3	1
J.W. Southern	350.1	96	1024	44	23.27	5-51	2	—
T.M. Tremlett	299.3	89	665	24	27.70	5-59	1	—
N.G. Cowley	244.4	69	734	20	36.70	6-48	1	—

Also bowled: M.J. Bailey 18-4-76-2; S.J. Malone 58-12-194-6; N.E.J. Pocock 12.5-1-55-0; J.M. Rice 36.3-4-139-2; D.R. Turner 1-0-1-0.

Hundreds (12)

6 **T.E. Jesty:** 135* v Glamorgan, Portsmouth; 106 v Essex, Chelmsford; 123 v Worcs, Southampton; 121 v Gloucs, Bournemouth; 109 v Yorks, Bournemouth; 134 v Warwicks, Southampton.

2 **C.G. Greenidge:** 157* v Glamorgan, Cardiff; 183* v Glamorgan, Portsmouth

1 **N.G. Cowley:** 104 v Leics, Southampton.

　M.D. Marshall: 116* v Lancs, Southampton.

　M.C.J. Nicholas: 127* v Sussex, Basingstoke.

　N.E.J. Pocock: 164 v Lancs, Southampton.

Kent

Kent had a poor season, its most depressing feature being a marked fall in attendances. Most counties have become accustomed to, and budgeted for, small crowds. But Kent, in the previous few years, had been more fortunate. Sensitive to such public reaction, the club, even before the season ended, announced its intention to appoint a committee to effect economies and devise ways of improving facilities at its grounds.

They might not have set the Medway on fire, but Kent can take great pride in the fact that, in many of their matches during the season, they fielded teams comprised fully of county-born players, and that without the compulsion of statute or tradition, as in Yorkshire's case.

To an extent, Kent sacrificed success in the interests of reconstruction of their side. When it was established half-way through the season that success in the Championship was quite beyond them, Asif Iqbal, in his last season before retirement, withdrew from the side. The idea was to let Asif's possible successor as captain get a feel of the job, and also to give extended runs to several young batsmen who were waiting in the wings for their opportunity. At one time or another, these youngsters played big innings, but Asif was greatly missed.

Next season, finances may require Kent to prune their staff, and it may be in the interests of one or two players to move to counties where they might command a more regular place. But, to be realistic, the county will really need to hold on to most of the talent it has discovered and nurtured. Neil Taylor and Laurie Potter have both been spoken of in terms of being Test cricketers of the near future. Mark Benson, before and after a long absence through injury, scored runs with a consistency that has also attracted attention, especially as he is a left-hander.

Chris Tavaré looks established in the England side for a long time to come, which means that Kent must make provision for giving up three, even four, batsmen to England at the same time.

The most pressing matters before Kent are to decide on a new captain and to strengthen the bowling, which, in 1982, lacked depth — a weakness that was magnified by the prolonged period of Dilley's rehabilitation and Jarvis's poor form. The pretenders to the captaincy, Tavaré and Chris Cowdrey, both had turns at leading the side in the season, although Tavaré's opportunities to prove, or disqualify, himself were too few because of Test calls.

For the record, Kent won one match under each of the trialists. It must be said, however, that with the bowling resources they had, it was difficult to make an impact. Sporadically, the enigmatic Dilley inflicted damage. But day in, day out, Underwood, with 78 wickets at 22.44 apiece, was their most penetrative and economical bowler.

As for Underwood's great contemporary behind the stumps, Alan Knott, he wore his 36 years lightly. Agile, acrobatic, and sharp-eyed as ever, Knott missed no catch or stumping that he would have brought off ten years earlier. With the bat, too, he had one of his most productive seasons ever.

Schweppes County Championship:	13th	Won 3	Lost 4	Drawn 15					
All First-Class Matches:		Won 3	Lost 4	Drawn 17					
NatWest Bank Trophy:	Lost to Essex in 2nd round								
Benson & Hedges Cup:	Lost to Somerset in quarter-final								
John Player League:	4th	Won 9	Lost 7						

Championship Averages

*not out

Batting/Fielding	M	I	NO	HS	R	Avge	100	50	Ct	St
C.J. Tavaré	11	21	2	168*	790	41.57	2	4	12	—
M.R. Benson	14	27	4	137	930	40.43	2	7	7	—
R.A. Woolmer	12	21	3	203	683	37.94	1	4	12	—
Asif Iqbal	11	17	2	115*	558	37.20	1	4	7	—
A.P.E. Knott	21	32	5	115*	942	34.88	1	6	46	8
E.A. Baptiste	8	11	2	69*	305	33.88	—	2	7	—
L. Potter	11	19	2	108	561	33.00	1	4	5	—
N.R. Taylor	21	38	4	143*	1083	31.85	2	6	7	—
D.G. Aslett	15	27	2	82	743	29.72	—	6	11	—
C.S. Cowdrey	20	32	4	72*	726	25.92	—	4	25	—
R.M. Ellison	7	11	3	46*	179	22.37	—	—	3	—
G.W. Johnson	20	31	6	86	541	21.64	—	2	20	—
C. Penn	7	8	4	30	54	13.50	—	—	4	—
D.L. Underwood	22	22	11	30	129	11.72	—	—	3	—
S.G. Hinks	2	4	1	18	35	11.66	—	—	1	—
G.R. Dilley	19	26	7	32	166	8.73	—	—	9	—
K.B.S. Jarvis	20	15	4	6	21	1.90	—	—	6	—

Also batted: S. Marsh (1 match) 10* (2 ct).

Bowling	O	M	R	W	Avge	Best	5w/I	10w/M
D.L. Underwood	690.4	223	1751	78	22.44	7-79	5	1
R.M. Ellison	153.5	35	433	16	27.06	3-12	—	—
G.R. Dilley	466.2	96	1595	54	29.53	6-71	3	1
G.W. Johnson	286.4	69	796	25	31.84	5-36	2	—
C.S. Cowdrey	130.3	32	432	13	33.23	3-45	—	—
K.B.S. Jarvis	585	128	1961	49	40.02	5-94	1	—

Also bowled: D.G. Aslett 70.1-8-289-6; E.A. Baptiste 158.4-38-579-9; M.R. Benson 4-0-28-0; S.G. Hinks 1.4-1-5-0; C. Penn 93.4-17-327-7; L. Potter 8-3-13-1; N.R. Taylor 17-5-83-4; R.A. Woolmer 49-14-127-4.

Hundreds (10)

2 M.R. Benson: 107 v Worcs, Hereford; 137 v Sussex, Hove.

C.J. Tavaré: 122* v Somerset, Taunton; 168* v Essex, Chelmsford.

N.R. Taylor: 143* v Warwicks, Dartford; 100 v Middlesex, Tunbridge Wells.

1 Asif Iqbal: 115* v Warwicks, Dartford.

A.P.E. Knott: 115* v Essex, Chelmsford.

L. Potter: 108 v Middlesex, Lord's.

R.A. Woolmer: 203 v Sussex, Tunbridge Wells.

Lancashire

If Lancashire finished higher than in the two previous seasons, they still remained confined to the lower half of the table — for the seventh year in succession. Their consolation lay in producing a new Test player and scoring one of the most remarkable wins in the history of the game.

The new Test player was Graeme Fowler, left-handed opening batsman. Only a season after winning his county cap, he made an impressive England debut, against Pakistan in the final Test, and readily earned a tour place for Australia.

That unique win was against Warwickshire in mid-season. On a superb Southport pitch, Warwickshire amassed a total of 523 in well under a day and declared. But far from adopting a defensive posture in the face of such an overwhelming score, Lancashire themselves went on the rampage. At the head of the onslaught was Fowler, who reached his century in 109 minutes in spite of a thigh strain that forced him to use a runner. In exultant mood, Lancashire made the aggressive gesture of declaring 109 runs in arrears. The pitch remained sound, and Lancashire closed in anticipation of being set a target by Warwickshire. Instead — more to their glory — Lancashire bowled them out for 111 and proceeded to a comfortable, 10-wickets win. Les McFarlane, the West Indies-born fast bowler whom Lancashire had acquired from Northants, had softened up Warwickshire by taking two wickets on the evening of the second day and completed the rout just after lunch on the third. And the 221 runs required were knocked off by Fowler, who scored another hundred — once more with a runner — and David Lloyd, who had already left his mark on the day with a magnificent short-leg catch to dismiss Kallicharran.

It was appropriate that Fowler and Lloyd should have set the seal of victory on this momentous match, for they were the stalwarts of Lancashire's batting during the season. Without reaching great heights, Clive Lloyd was also consistent enough to score over a thousand. So did Hughes, who revelled in his promotion in the batting order. Abrahams responded splendidly to being capped at last, and O'Shaughnessy, once given a regular place, provided handsome returns.

The fact that Lancashire were beaten only three times proves that batting was not their weakness. Undoubtedly, they would have been an even greater force had Frank Hayes, whose early form had promised a prosperous season, not fractured his leg. The bone gave way while Hayes was taking a run during the Middlesex match at Lord's, in June.

Less plagued than usual by the notorious Old Trafford weather, Lancashire were not spared their other scourge — injuries! Hayes was only the first victim. The reunion with Croft worked to advantage until his back gave way, causing him to miss 10 matches. Lee made only a couple of appearances. Allott, too, was out for a period with a strain, and the indestructible Simmons, who was their main wicket-taker, missed five matches because of a broken finger.

Schweppes County Championship:	12th	Won 4	Lost 3	Drawn 15					
All First-Class Matches:		Won 4	Lost 4	Drawn 16					
NatWest Bank Trophy:	Lost to Middlesex in 2nd round								
Benson & Hedges Cup:	Lost to Nottinghamshire in semi-final								
John Player League:	10th	Won 6	Lost 7	Tied 1		No result 2			

Championship Averages

*not out

Batting/Fielding	M	I	NO	HS	R	Avge	100	50	Ct	St
J. Simmons	17	21	12	79*	487	54.11	—	4	14	—
D.P. Hughes	21	33	8	126*	1196	47.84	2	6	18	—
S.J. O'Shaughnessy	11	19	7	62	560	46.66	—	7	1	—
G. Fowler	18	30	2	150	1219	43.53	5	4	5	—
C.H. Lloyd	20	29	2	100	1135	42.03	1	9	19	—
D. Lloyd	20	32	2	114	1223	40.76	5	5	8	—
J. Abrahams	21	30	5	124	995	39.80	1	7	23	—
A. Kennedy	7	9	0	43	189	21.00	—	—	3	—
I. Cockbain	14	25	1	98	492	20.50	—	2	4	—
B.W. Reidy	8	11	2	33*	151	16.77	—	—	6	—
I. Folley	16	13	4	36	133	14.77	—	—	2	—
P.J.W. Allott	11	9	2	30	101	14.42	—	—	5	—
C.E.H. Croft	12	12	3	20	109	12.11	—	—	5	—
C. Maynard	15	18	3	37	181	12.06	—	—	18	5
C.J. Scott	6	6	1	15	29	5.80	—	—	11	1
L.L. McFarlane	11	8	3	8	16	3.20	—	—	1	—

Also batted: F.C. Hayes (2 matches) 43, 21*; K.A. Hayes (3 matches) 90, 4*, 9 (1 ct); P.G. Lee (2 matches) 0; G.J. Speak (2 matches) 1, 7 (2 ct); R.G. Watson (1 match) 11, 4; N.H. Fairbrother, T.J. Taylor, M.A. Wallwork and M. Watkinson (1 match each) did not bat.

Bowling	O	M	R	W	Avge	Best	5w/I	10w/M
J. Simmons	538.4	152	1284	49	26.20	5-57	2	—
S.J. O'Shaughnessy	209.2	34	710	27	26.29	4-66	—	—
D.P. Hughes	264.1	73	688	26	26.46	4-22	—	—
P.J.W. Allott	290	79	734	27	27.18	5-58	1	—
C.E.H. Croft	304	60	1003	33	30.39	7-88	1	—
L.L. McFarlane	198.5	38	855	27	31.66	6-59	1	—
I. Folley	280	67	694	21	33.04	3-20	—	—
D. Lloyd	288.2	67	784	21	37.33	4-36	—	—
B.W. Reidy	133	30	450	10	45.00	3-33	—	—
J. Abrahams	293.3	58	838	16	52.37	2-19	—	—

Also bowled: I. Cockbain 2-2-0-0; G. Fowler 7-2-13-0; A. Kennedy 9-2-28-1; P.G. Lee 27-2-84-2; G.J. Speak 43-4-144-1; T.J. Taylor 16-1-72-1; M. Watkinson 13-4-45-1.

Hundreds (14)

5 G. Fowler: 100 v Gloucs, Gloucester; 122 v Essex, Liverpool; 150 v Warwicks, Birmingham; 126 and 128* v Warwicks, Southport.

D. Lloyd: 114 v Derbys, Manchester; 108 v Gloucs, Gloucester; 112 v Hants, Southampton; 112* v Northants, Manchester; 103 v Kent, Manchester.

2 D.P. Hughes: 126* v Yorks, Leeds; 111 v Derbys, Derby.

1 J. Abrahams: 124 v Surrey, Manchester.

C.H. Lloyd: 100 v Yorks, Manchester.

Leicestershire

L eicestershire, over the last ten years, have never finished below the middle mark of ninth in the Championship, and five times during this period they have figured in the first five. Such a record projects them as the most consistent side of recent times.

However, 1982 was the first year since their Championship season of 1975 that Leicestershire were serious contenders for the title. They finished runners-up, and proof that they were worthy of this status lay in the fact their 10 wins included one over the ultimate champions, Middlesex.

In the final table, Leicestershire were 39 points adrift of Middlesex. But even at a stage as late as two matches from the finishing line, Leicestershire were as close as 2 points behind, having closed a gap of 45 in the previous fortnight. Leicestershire's chances were then crippled, almost extinguished, by a nightmare match at Trent Bridge against Nottinghamshire, whom they had beaten quite comprehensively at their earlier meeting.

It is interesting to contemplate how much stronger Leicestershire's challenge would have been if Andy Roberts had been a full-time member of the side, as he will be next season. Les Taylor was available throughout only because of the ban he incurred from being one of the 'rebel' team in South Africa. Leicestershire saw even less of their star batsman, David Gower, than of Roberts. His participation in the Championship was limited to a mere nine matches during a season when he was scoring freely. Fortunately, Leicestershire were cushioned against this handicap by the excellent form of Brian Davison and Chris Balderstone.

Davison, in his benefit year, scored seven hundreds, a season's record for the county. His 1,789 runs were of particularly high value, because the speed of his run-getting was always adjusted to the side's needs. Balderstone, again cast in the role of opening batsman, got 1,474 runs, including four hundreds, his consistency providing solidity to the top of the batting order.

The match-winning potential of a side is always in direct ratio with the depth of its bowling. Possessing two left-arm spinners who came on in the wake of a strong pace attack, Leicestershire were equipped for all conditions, as they proved by winning away as often as they did at home. Of the 329 wickets Leicestershire captured in the Championship, 141 fell to their spinners, in the main to Nick Cook (80) and John Steele (54). Flighting the ball bravely, Cook often took wickets when the pitch did not make spin readily available.

From want of enough bowling, Cook's form was low in May and June, when Championship matches were widely spread out. He took only 15 wickets in his first 7 games. It is not insignificant that the county's fortunes began to rise once Cook got among the wickets. The starting point of Cook's ascendancy — and Leicestershire's — was the match at Uxbridge, against the leaders, Middlesex. Cook took 6 for 32 in the first innings of this match, and he was to repeat the feat of capturing five

LEICESTERSHIRE

Schweppes County Championship:	2nd	Won 10	Lost 4	Drawn 8
All First-Class Matches:		Won 10	Lost 4	Drawn 11
NatWest Bank Trophy:	Lost to Somerset in 2nd round			
Benson & Hedges Cup:	Lost to Nottinghamshire in quarter-final			
John Player League:	3rd	Won 9	Lost 6	No result 1

Championship Averages

*not out

Batting/Fielding	M	I	NO	HS	R	Avge	100	50	Ct	St
B.F. Davison	21	35	4	172	1789	57.70	7	8	14	—
D.I. Gower	9	16	0	111	716	44.75	1	7	4	—
J.C. Balderstone	22	39	3	148	1474	40.94	4	8	16	—
N.E. Briers	22	37	4	106	1081	32.75	1	5	12	—
R.W. Tolchard	22	37	8	93*	782	26.96	—	6	43	7
M.A. Garnham	9	14	2	57	280	23.33	—	3	11	2
P.B. Clift	4	4	1	24	63	21.00	—	—	1	—
R.A. Cobb	19	31	1	63	600	20.00	—	3	10	—
A.M.E. Roberts	12	19	2	47	316	18.58	—	—	4	—
I.P. Butcher	4	5	1	31	71	17.75	—	—	4	—
J.F. Steele	19	29	5	58	423	17.62	—	1	26	—
N.G.B. Cook	21	23	7	37	263	16.43	—	—	16	—
G.J. Parsons	21	29	6	51	359	15.60	—	1	6	—
J.P. Agnew	8	11	0	56	122	11.09	—	1	1	—
L.B. Taylor	20	23	8	25	119	7.93	—	—	2	—
T.J. Boon	6	8	0	21	58	7.25	—	—	2	—

Also batted: G. Forster (1 match) 2 (1 ct); D.A. Wenlock (1 match) 4 (1 ct). K. Higgs (1 match) did not bat.

Bowling	O	M	R	W	Avge	Best	5w/I	10w/M
A.M.E. Roberts	410.2	109	1027	54	19.01	8-56	5	1
J.F. Steele	448.2	130	1026	50	20.52	5-4	3	—
L.B. Taylor	564.1	148	1411	66	21.37	5-24	3	—
N.G.B. Cook	767.2	240	1832	80	22.90	7-63	6	1
J.P. Agnew	157	24	609	18	33.83	4-55	—	—
G.J. Parsons	456.1	81	1649	44	37.47	5-25	1	—

Also bowled: J.C. Balderstone 75-22-177-7; N.E. Briers 19-2-75-2; P.B. Clift 77-21-194-3; R.A. Cobb 4-2-5-0; D.I. Gower 5-2-10-0; G. Forster 17-3-48-0; K. Higgs 19-5-64-1; D.A. Wenlock 2-0-8-0.

Hundreds (13)

7 **B.F. Davison:** 172 v Hants, Southampton; 111 v Surrey, Leicester; 100 v Middlesex, Uxbridge; 139* v Worcs, Worcester; 110* v Essex, Colchester; 119 v Glamorgan, Leicester; 100* v Kent, Canterbury.

4 **J.C. Balderstone:** 148 v Middlesex, Uxbridge; 103* v Gloucs, Leicester; 114* v Essex, Colchester; 118 v Glamorgan, Leicester.

1 **N.E. Briers:** 106 v Yorks, Hinkley. **D.I. Gower:** 111 v Somerset, Taunton.

wickets or more in an innings five times. Ironically, Cook failed to capitalise on a turning pitch at Coalville in the very next match, against Derbyshire, which Leicestershire lost. They won 7 of their next 10 games but, in retrospect, the lost opportunity at Coalville proved crucial.

Middlesex

Even if in smaller measures Middlesex suffered all the problems of their rivals — injuries, Test calls, and curtailment of matches by rain — still they made the running right through the 1982 Championship campaign, and won the title for the fourth time in seven years.

When the hour of victory arrived, on a mellow Saturday afternoon in Worcester, Middlesex's jubilation was mingled with sadness, for the curtain was soon to come down on the career of John Michael Brearley, who, having assumed the captaincy in a period of turmoil and mediocrity, had led them for 12 consecutive seasons. Brearley, with scholarship in philosophy and training in psychology behind him, was expert in man management. But that was only one of his attributes. Thanks to a brilliant mind, Brearley never lost time in reacting to changes in conditions and altering situations. Those big, flashing eyes studied every detail, and he was a master of the game's geometry.

Indeed, the talent under Brearley was abundant, much more than possessed contemporarily by any other county. But it would not be fair or accurate to say that any captain at all could have led so strong a team to victory. Often, a collection of brilliant individuals is harder to mould into a team than one of average players.

Of Middlesex's 12 wins, no less than 10 were gained from bowling out the opposition twice, and only on three occasions did they concede totals larger than 300. No more need be said in praise of Middlesex's bowling strength.

Having ruled himself out of Test cricket, John Emburey played in every Championship match, and with Daniel and Edmonds in the side, Middlesex had the most versatile attack any county has possessed in recent times. From midway through the season, when Norman Cowans came into the side, they had two bowlers of genuine pace to open the bowling. Cowans, who replaced another West Indian immigrant, the promising Neil Williams, twice captured five wickets in an innings, and in all took 33 wickets in 11 games. But it could not have been just this statistical record that earned him selection for Australia. The threat Cowans could pose the Australians was exhibited during a fiery opening spell he bowled on a tame pitch at Boycott and Lumb in the second innings of the Yorkshire match.

Middlesex's batting star of the summer was Mike Gatting, who aggregated more runs (1,651) than any English-born batsman except the redoubtable Boycott and Larkins. Fortunately for Middlesex, it was not until mid-July that the England selectors took note of his form.

As batsman, too, Brearley had a distinguished farewell season. He reached a thousand runs, as did Wilf Slack and Roland Butcher, who was tardy coming into form. When Gatting was absent and the middle of the batting sometimes collapsed, Emburey was always on hand to repair the damage. Of the non-regulars, Keith Tomlins played at least four innings of substance, and in the few opportunities that came their way Colin Cook and Richard Ellis, the Oxford captain, showed rich promise.

Schweppes County Championship:	1st	Won 12 Lost 2	Drawn 8
All First-Class Matches:		Won 14 Lost 2	Drawn 9
NatWest Bank Trophy:	Lost to Surrey in semi-final		
Benson & Hedges Cup:	Lost to Lancashire in quarter-final		
John Player League:	2nd	Won 11 Lost 4	No result 1

Championship Averages

*not out

Batting/Fielding

	M	I	NO	HS	R	Avge	100	50	Ct	St
M.W. Gatting	16	21	2	192	1273	67.00	5	5	23	—
J.M. Brearley	19	31	9	165	1023	46.50	3	3	18	—
R.O. Butcher	19	25	2	197	1013	44.04	3	2	20	—
W.N. Slack	22	36	5	85	1109	35.77	—	9	17	—
J.E. Emburey	22	26	4	100*	734	33.36	1	4	16	—
K.P. Tomlins	11	15	1	138	458	32.71	1	3	8	—
C.T. Radley	19	25	3	141*	697	31.68	2	1	20	—
R.G.P. Ellis	3	5	0	55	157	31.40	—	2	—	—
N.J. Kemp	4	5	2	46*	84	28.00	—	—	5	—
P.H. Edmonds	16	17	3	92	368	26.28	—	3	5	—
G.D. Barlow	4	7	2	37*	121	24.20	—	—	2	—
M.W.W. Selvey	9	6	1	36*	114	22.80	—	—	2	—
P.R. Downton	22	24	2	65	476	21.63	—	2	50	9
N.F. Williams	9	10	4	27*	106	17.66	—	—	2	—
W.W. Daniel	19	15	9	21	88	14.66	—	—	13	—
N.G. Cowans	11	10	1	16	63	7.00	—	—	8	—
S.P. Hughes	10	8	4	18	27	675	—	—	—	—

Also batted: C.R. Cook (2 matches) 2, 36 (1 ct); R.J. Maru (2 matches) 18, 12 (1 ct); J.D. Monteith (1 match) 36, 1; F.J. Titmus (1 match) 1*; W.G. Merry (1 match) did not bat.

Bowling

	O	M	R	W	Avge	Best	5w/I	10w/M
M.W. Gatting	111	32	283	19	14.89	5-34	1	—
W.W. Daniel	469.4	107	1245	71	17.53	9-61	5	1
P.H. Edmonds	635.1	195	1348	71	18.98	8-80	3	2
N.G. Cowans	222.3	50	721	33	21.84	5-28	2	—
J.E. Emburey	689.5	167	1629	74	22.01	5-50	2	—
W.N. Slack	81	18	225	10	22.50	3-17	—	—
S.P. Hughes	218.5	30	723	27	26.77	4-28	—	—
M.W.W. Selvey	223.5	65	524	17	30.82	3-47	—	—
N.F. Williams	173.4	24	622	15	41.46	4-40	—	—

Also bowled: J.M. Brearley 1-0-3-0; R.O. Butcher 1-0-10-0; N.J. Kemp 37-6-110-2; R.J.Maru 17-7-40-0; W.G. Merry 15.2-3-42-1; J.D. Monteith 6-1-18-0; C.T. Radley 4-0-27-0; K.P. Tomlins 10.3-1-59-2; F.J. Titmus 25-4-92-3.

Hundreds (15)

5 **M.W. Gatting:** 140 v Derbys, Lord's; 114 v Kent, Tunbridge Wells; 133* v Lancs, Lord's; 192 v Surrey, Oval; 141 v Yorks, Lord's.

3 **J.M. Brearley:** 165 v Northants, Lord's; 135 v Notts, Nottingham; 100* v Sussex, Hove.

R.O. Butcher: 122 v Glamorgan, Swansea; 173 v Gloucs, Cheltenham; 197 v Yorks, Lord's.

2 **C.T. Radley:** 141* v Kent, Tunbridge Wells; 106 v Warwicks, Coventry.

1 **J.E. Emburey:** 100* v Northants, Lord's.

K.P. Tomlins: 138 v Notts, Lord's.

Northamptonshire

All credit to Northamptonshire for rising to 9th place from the previous year's 15th, for the handicaps they bore were innumerable. But to count their blessings before listing their troubles, Larkins and Willey, two batsmen serving the three-year Test ban, had a season of plenty. There was also the return from Derbyshire of the prodigal son, David Steele, now 41, but as doughty as ever. Had Steele's left-arm spin not claimed 67 victims, Northamptonshire, desperately short of bowlers all season, would have found themselves positively distressed.

On the other side of the coin, they not only had to cope with Test calls on their English-registered players, Cook and Allan Lamb, but also had to contribute to the strength of the two touring sides. Sarfraz played only six matches before joining the Pakistanis. And their expectations of Kapil Dev playing continuously after the end of the Indian tour, on July 6, went unfulfilled. First, he went off on an informal tour of America with the Indians. Then, after playing just six Championship matches, and with two left, he returned home to play against Sri Lanka.

If Larkins and Willey, frequently called up by England in recent seasons, were available right through, Northants this time had to do without their captain, Geoff Cook, for 5 matches and Allan Lamb for as many as 12. Boyd-Moss was not available to them until after the Varsity match in late June, and then Capel was wanted for the Youth series between England and the West Indies.

But at least Northamptonshire had large reserves of batsmen. Their bowling resources, always limited, were strained further by a pre-season injury in the back to Tim Lamb. He had an operation and it was not until June 19 that he turned his arm over in anger. Jim Griffiths, their main wicket-taker in 1981, was also hampered by injury, and young Mallender's form was variable.

It was not until late July that Northants scored their first win. Hitherto, they had been beaten three times and played seven draws. To an extent, they were unlucky with their fixtures, in that most of their early matches were against the stronger sides. Each time their bowling was exposed, and except for Larkins, who scored 1,863 runs in the season, even their batsmen took time running into form. They were not helped by slow, uneven pitches at Northampton.

Cook, under pressure from various directions and suffering the disappointment of losing his England place, had a poor season by his own high standards. Nor did Williams do himself justice. Fortunately, Boyd-Moss brought his splendid Fenner's form to the county, and Steele, batting lower down the order than he used to, contributed many useful innings. When at last Kapil Dev became available, he did not take the wickets Northamptonshire badly needed from him, but he scored two centuries and an unbeaten 60, these innings all contributing to late-season wins over Sussex and Derbyshire, both worthy opponents.

Schweppes County Championship:	9th	Won 5	Lost 3	Drawn 14
All First-Class Matches:		Won 6	Lost 3	Drawn 16
NatWest Bank Trophy:	Lost to Surrey in 2nd round			
Benson & Hedges Cup:	Failed to qualify for Q-F (4th in Group B)			
John Player League:	8th	Won 8	Lost 7	No result 1

Championship Averages   *not out

Batting/Fielding

	M	I	NO	HS	R	Avge	100	50	Ct	St
A.J. Lamb	10	17	1	140	882	55.12	3	4	5	—
Kapil Dev	6	9	2	103	332	47.42	2	1	8	—
P. Willey	21	38	4	145	1605	47.20	4	7	10	—
W. Larkins	22	40	3	186	1728	46.70	5	8	13	—
R.J. Boyd-Moss	14	24	4	137	885	44.25	2	7	10	—
D.S. Steele	22	33	12	74*	775	36.90	—	3	18	—
G. Cook	17	31	2	125	1014	34.96	3	5	19	—
R.M. Carter	9	16	5	40	289	26.27	—	—	10	—
D.J. Wild	5	5	2	29	76	25.33	—	—	—	—
T.M. Lamb	12	12	7	39*	126	25.20	—	—	1	—
D.J. Capel	12	19	3	60*	402	25.12	—	1	6	—
R.G. Williams	21	35	3	87*	795	24.84	—	4	3	—
G. Sharp	22	24	7	58*	360	21.17	—	1	37	7
T.J. Yardley	3	5	0	39	89	17.80	—	—	3	—
N.A. Mallender	21	16	8	42	121	15.12	—	—	9	—
Sarfraz Nawaz	6	6	1	25	65	13.00	—	—	4	—
B.J. Griffiths	17	10	3	16	39	5.57	—	—	5	—

Also batted: R.J. Bailey (2 matches) 10, 4, 3 (1 ct).

Bowling

	O	M	R	W	Avge	Best	5w/I	10w/M
D.S. Steele	673.2	219	1623	67	24.22	6-59	6	1
B.J. Griffiths	367.1	81	1102	41	26.87	5-71	2	—
Sarfraz Nawaz	169.4	39	477	17	28.05	4-33	—	—
P. Willey	580.5	182	1211	41	29.53	6-17	1	—
N.A. Mallender	491.2	104	1670	47	35.53	7-41	3	1
R.G. Williams	208	54	596	16	37.25	3-23	—	—
T.M. Lamb	286.5	66	811	19	42.68	5-37	1	—

Also bowled: R.J. Boyd-Moss 2-0-26-0; D.J. Capel 79.5-5-373-3; R.M. Carter 32-5-127-2; G. Cook 2-0-7-0; Kapil Dev 139.4-32-404-9; W. Larkins 12-0-58-1; D.J. Wild 36.3-5-126-3.

Hundreds (19)

5 **W. Larkins:** 118* v Yorks, Northampton; 137 v Somerset, Northampton; 186 v Yorks, Middlesbrough; 110* v Worcs, Northampton; 105 v Derbys, Northampton.

4 **P. Willey:** 145 v Derbys, Derby; 140 v Essex, Northampton; 102 v Lancs, Manchester; 117 v Glamorgan, Swansea.

3 **G. Cook:** 125 v Leics, Leicester; 112* v Yorks, Middlesbrough; 101 v Gloucs, Bristol.

A.J. Lamb: 102 v Leics, Leicester; 140 v Hants, Northampton; 106 v Essex, Chelmsford

2 **R.J. Boyd-Moss:** 114* v Gloucs, Northampton; 137 v Derbys, Northampton.

Kapil Dev: 103 v Sussex, Eastbourne; 100* v Derbys, Northampton.

Nottinghamshire

Nottinghamshire began the season in the manner of champions, winning four of their first six matches. But rain destroyed their next two games, and they were unable to pick up the seam again. However, they had another good run in August and finished a very respectable fourth.

The defence of their title was affected firstly by Test calls, of which they had none in 1981. Randall had to miss 12 matches, many of them against the stronger counties. During the latter part of the season when pitches were turning, Hemmings missed six.

But worse than that, injuries took an exceptionally heavy toll of Nottinghamshire's strength. Rice arrived from South Africa with a neck injury that prevented him from bowling, except in the direst emergencies. Hadlee had two injuries, which forced him out of five matches and stopped him bowling in four others. There were several occasions when he bowled without being at all fit. Nevertheless, he took 59 wickets and headed the national averages. Notts had sought to strengthen their attack by signing Mike Hendrick from Derbyshire. But he was as prone to injury as ever, and bowled only 217 overs to get them just 27 wickets.

The period when Nottinghamshire were worst hit was in July, a month during which they had to play Essex, Middlesex (twice), Yorkshire, and Surrey, with the Benson & Hedges Cup final intervening. It was no coincidence that they lost every time.

In addition to unfit bowlers, their batsmen were going through a bad patch, and it is possible that their form was affected by the unsatisfactory pitches at Trent Bridge early in the season. As in 1981, Nottinghamshire's pitches came in for criticism. Hampshire, Worcestershire and Kent, who played successive matches at Trent Bridge, all expressed dissatisfaction. Not only did these pitches restrict the batsmen, but they also posed a physical threat. In the Hampshire match, Gordon Greenidge took a blow that forced him to retire. And Notts' own Basharat Hassan spent five days in hospital after mistiming a hook. His confidence unimpaired, however, he returned to the side and undertook the added responsibility of opening the innings, finishing the season with 970 runs.

Only Rice and Birch, who completed a thousand in all first-class matches, scored more for the county. Of course, Randall too had a good season, but only half his 1,308 runs were got in Notts' cause.

By his standards, Rice had a poor season. He made only one century and he rarely played with the authority and vigour of the previous season. The most trenchant batting came from Hadlee, who in Championship matches alone totalled 807 runs.

Schweppes County Championship:	4th	Won 7	Lost 7	Drawn 7	(Abandoned 1)
All First-Class Matches:		Won 8	Lost 7	Drawn 9	(Abandoned 1)
NatWest Bank Trophy:	Lost to Gloucestershire in 2nd round				
Benson & Hedges Cup:	Lost to Somerset in final				
John Player League:	5th	Won 8	Lost 6	Tied 1	No result 1

Championship Averages

*not out

Batting/Fielding	M	I	NO	HS	R	Avge	100	50	Ct	St
D.W. Randall	10	16	1	122	653	43.53	1	5	10	—
J.D. Birch	19	31	5	125	940	36.15	2	6	7	—
E.E. Hemmings	15	19	8	127*	385	35.00	1	—	11	—
B. Hassan	17	31	4	89*	918	34.00	—	7	14	—
C.E.B. Rice	21	35	3	144	1049	32.78	1	5	24	—
R.J. Hadlee	17	28	2	131	807	31.03	2	4	16	—
R.T. Robinson	19	34	2	109	879	27.46	1	4	11	—
B.N. French	21	33	6	79	681	25.22	—	5	56	3
M.K. Bore	6	7	5	23*	44	22.00	—	—	4	—
P.A. Todd	10	17	1	117*	305	19.06	1	—	9	—
M.A. Fell	10	18	0	108	315	17.50	1	—	9	—
K. Saxelby	13	14	4	59*	158	15.80	—	1	2	—
P. Johnson	4	7	1	37*	90	15.00	—	—	—	—
N.J.B. Illingworth	8	12	4	46*	109	13.62	—	—	3	—
K.E. Cooper	20	24	4	33*	190	9.50	—	—	7	—
M. Hendrick	9	10	4	29	54	9.00	—	—	6	—
I.L. Pont	4	7	1	16	32	5.33	—	—	1	—
P.M. Such	8	9	3	2	3	0.50	—	—	7	—

Bowling	O	M	R	W	Avge	Best	5w/I	10w/M
R.J. Hadlee	373.5	110	836	59	14.16	7-25	4	—
M. Hendrick	217.2	78	401	26	15.42	5-21	1	—
M.K. Bore	203.2	73	466	21	22.19	6-134	1	—
K. Saxelby	267.2	60	728	32	22.75	4-18	—	—
K.E. Cooper	586	163	1445	57	25.35	6-46	2	—
E.E. Hemmings	514.3	156	1241	48	25.85	6-76	2	—
P.M. Such	232.1	51	737	25	29.48	5-112	1	—
N.J.B. Illingworth	100.1	19	325	10	32.50	5-89	1	—

Also bowled: J.D. Birch 2.3-0-19-1; M.A. Fell 45-7-146-1; I.L. Pont 78.5-13-302-3; C.E.B. Rice 78.5-25-206-6; R.T. Robinson 3-0-22-1.

Hundreds (10)

2 J.D. Birch: 102* v Lancs, Nottingham; 125 v Leics, Nottingham.

R.J. Hadlee: 131 v Surrey, Oval; 100* v Worcs, Worcester.

1 M.A. Fell: 108 v Essex, Nottingham.

E.E.Hemmings: 127* v Yorks, Worksop.

D.W. Randall: 122 v Worcs, Worcester.

C.E.B. Rice: 144 v Derbys, Nottingham.

R.T. Robinson: 109 v Sussex, Hove.

P.A. Todd: 117* v Yorks, Worksop.

Somerset

Having finished third in 1981, which is as high as they have ever done, Somerset must have been disappointed not to have offered a stronger challenge. They finished sixth, having won six matches and lost the same number.

The reason for their not doing better was their inability to make the most of the weaker counties. Indeed, there were days when Somerset themselves looked fit to be ranked among the minnows. Yet there were others when they were quite irresistible. Invariably, such days of glory were those on which Botham, Richards, or Garner felt inspired.

Such occasions, however, were in short ration. In a season of four one-day internationals and six Test matches, Botham played as often under England's banner as under Somerset's. Garner had such acute problems with his knee that he missed the first eight matches and bowled well within himself in the next three, during which he took just one wicket. Only in eight Championship matches during the season was Garner firing on all cylinders. Richards played some masterly innings during the season — 146 in 160 minutes against Kent, 135 against Warwickshire, 178 against Lancashire, and 77 on a fiery pitch against Worcestershire. But these gems were separated by runs of very low scores. Following a winter that included a tour of Australia with the West Indies, and then a Shell Shield series, Richards could have been stale.

Between June 2, the day England played their first one-day international of the season, and the end of August, Botham played only four Championship matches. As an all-rounder who batted high in the middle order and did a considerable amount of bowling, the Test matches took a lot of his physical and mental stamina. Inevitably, he was below par in the intervening County games. But once the tension of international cricket was behind him, Botham turned in some memorable performances for Somerset. Against Warwickshire, he made the fastest century of the season, in 52 minutes, hitting 10 sixes and 12 fours. The very next time he batted, against Worcestershire, he scored 98 from 51 balls and, in the same match, took 8 wickets.

Brian Rose, the captain, dropped down the order to the advantage of the side as well as his own. He was able to make the switch because Roebuck settled comfortably into the opener's role, making nearly a thousand runs. So did the other opener, Jeremy Lloyds, who was capped during the season and also turned in several useful performances as an off-break bowler. His scope in this area was limited as Marks had a good season, taking 68 wickets in all first-class matches, among them his first Test match.

At the end of the season, Somerset parted company with their long-serving wicket-keeper, Derek Taylor, who, having caught 622 batsmen and stumped 84 in a career that began with Surrey, in 1966, hung up his gloves and went to live in Australia.

Schweppes County Championship:	6th	Won 6	Lost 6	Drawn 10
All First-Class Matches:		Won 6	Lost 6	Drawn 11
NatWest Bank Trophy:	Lost to Warwickshire in quarter-final			
Benson & Hedges Cup:	Winners			
John Player League:	9th	Won 8	Lost 8	

Championship Averages

*not out

Batting/Fielding

	M	I	NO	HS	R	Avge	100	50	Ct	St
B.C. Rose	20	31	8	173*	1079	46.91	2	5	9	—
I.V.A. Richards	19	30	1	178	1143	39.41	3	5	11	—
I.T. Botham	11	20	1	131*	675	35.52	1	4	5	—
N.A. Felton	8	12	0	71	346	28.83	—	3	4	—
J.W. Lloyds	22	37	3	132*	965	28.38	2	3	28	—
P.A. Slocombe	12	21	1	78	543	27.15	—	6	9	—
P.M. Roebuck	21	36	2	90	898	26.41	—	10	7	—
P.W. Denning	14	22	1	91*	541	25.76	—	3	6	—
N.F.M. Popplewell	15	22	4	55	422	23.44	—	1	8	—
V.J. Marks	18	28	2	67	507	19.50	—	4	10	—
H.R. Moseley	17	19	13	24*	113	18.83	—	—	6	—
J. Garner	10	11	5	40*	98	16.33	—	—	4	—
D.J.S. Taylor	17	26	5	67	334	15.90	—	2	41	4
C.H. Dredge	19	25	7	54*	283	15.72	—	1	8	—
T. Gard	5	4	1	31	37	12.33	—	—	8	2
M.R. Davis	8	12	2	21*	65	6.50	—	—	2	—

Also batted: M. Bryant (2 matches) 6, 0 (1 ct); R.J. McCool (1 match) 7, 12 (1 ct); R.L. Ollis (1 match) 1, 1 (1 ct); G.V. Palmer (1 match) 6, 27; N. Russom (1 match) did not bat.

Bowling

	O	M	R	W	Avge	Best	5w/I	10w/M
J. Garner	259.1	76	583	33	17.66	6-23	4	1
I.T. Botham	247.2	65	719	39	18.43	5-48	2	—
V.J. Marks	613	180	1699	63	26.96	7-51	4	—
H.R. Moseley	303	68	921	34	27.08	5-40	2	—
J.W. Lloyds	447.5	92	1384	43	32.18	7-88	3	—
M.R. Davis	125	17	394	12	32.83	3-36	—	—
C.H. Dredge	425.5	105	1154	33	34.96	3-33	—	—
I.V.A. Richards	251.3	72	623	16	38.93	3-6	—	—

Also bowled: M. Bryant 27-3-158-2; R.J. McCool 17-2-63-0; G.V. Palmer 17-3-57-0; N.F.M. Popplewell 82-16-258-6; P.M. Roebuck 39-5-109-1; B.C. Rose 1-0-5-0; N. Russom 16-2-64-3; P.A. Slocombe 3.2-0-10-1; D.J.S. Taylor 3-2-1-0.

Hundreds (8)

3 I.V.A. Richards: 146 v Kent, Taunton; 135 v Warwicks, Birmingham; 178 v Lancs, Taunton.

2 J.W. Lloyds: 132* and 102* v Northants, Northampton.

B.C. Rose: 102* v Warwicks, Birmingham; 173* v Gloucs, Bristol.

1 I.T. Botham: 131* v Warwicks, Taunton

Surrey

Surrey were fortunate in that for the first time since they signed Sylvester Clarke, one of the most lethal bowlers in contemporary cricket, he stayed fit right through the season, played every Championship match, and took 85 wickets. He played a considerable part, too, in Surrey's NatWest triumph. There were six times when Clarke took five wickets or more in an innings. His new-ball partner, Robin Jackman, performed such spectacular feats less often, but struck regularly enough to take 73 wickets and earn two Test caps.

In other seasons, such domination by the opening attack would have taken Surrey very close to the Championship. There were two factors, however, that limited them to fifth place. The more crucial was the lack of adequate support for Clarke and Jackman. This situation came about largely because Pat Pocock missed 15 consecutive games, leaving Surrey without a spinner of true experience.

The end-of-season averages give no clue to the batting problems that Surrey had early in the season. The summer was well advanced before they gained stability in this department, with injuries retarding the process. Butcher, Howarth, Lynch, and Smith each made a thousand runs, but rarely were two batsmen in prime form in the same match.

As Surrey strove to make their presence felt in the first stages of the Championship, all they had to be thankful for was that the Oval pitches were more conducive to decisive finishes than they used to be before Harry Brind began his renovation of the square. If a larger proportion of matches at the Oval remained unfinished, it was due partially to the weather's encroachments.

Surrey had a mixed start, losses alternating with wins during the first six matches. Ironically, the only match among these that yielded them full batting points was one they lost. It was significant, too, that the margin of one of their defeats — by Hampshire — was a mere 3 runs.

It was as early as in the fourth match that Pocock strained ligaments in his back. He turned to acupuncture as a cure and contracted a post-operation infection that delayed his return to the game until August. The fact that he took 21 wickets in 7 matches (one of which he did not complete) puts into focus the handicap his absence placed on Surrey.

Apart from Clarke and Jackman, David Thomas was the only other Surrey bowler to take more than 30 wickets. His availability, too, was restricted by injury. His finest hour, of course, came in the final of the NatWest Trophy. His figures for the season were not an accurate index of ability, for his reputation among the leading batsmen in the country (who make the best judges of a bowler) was very high.

As a hard-hitting batsman, Thomas played some useful innings in the lower order. One of them was the highlight of the run-chase at Portsmouth that got Surrey a thrilling two-wickets win. Jack Richards, too, batted in exciting fashion on many occasions, besides keeping wicket with sustained brilliance. Thomas, Richards, and Jackman, between them, did a lot to minimize Surrey's batting problems.

Schweppes County Championship:	5th	Won 6	Lost 6	Drawn 10
All First-Class Matches:		Won 6	Lost 6	Drawn 12
NatWest Bank Trophy:	Winners			
Benson & Hedges Cup:	Failed to qualify for Q-F (4th in Group C)			
John Player League:	12th	Won 6	Lost 9	Tied 1

Championship Averages

*not out

Batting/Fielding	M	I	NO	HS	R	Avge	100	50	Ct	St
D.M. Smith	13	23	4	160	1000	52.63	3	5	12	—
A.R. Butcher	20	37	5	187*	1293	40.40	3	6	12	—
G.P. Howarth	18	31	3	156*	1125	40.17	4	2	15	—
R.D. Jackman	17	18	8	68	350	35.00	—	2	3	—
M.A. Lynch	22	36	2	141*	1141	33.55	3	4	17	—
K.S. Mackintosh	10	9	6	31	93	31.00	—	—	4	—
G. Monkhouse	7	8	4	63*	122	30.50	—	1	3	—
G.R.J. Roope	13	23	6	108	480	28.23	1	1	13	—
D.J. Thomas	16	18	3	64	403	26.86	—	3	6	—
R.D.V. Knight	22	36	3	99	873	26.45	—	7	8	—
C.J. Richards	21	33	9	117*	597	24.87	1	3	47	2
G.S. Clinton	13	22	3	102	450	23.68	1	1	4	—
A. Needham	11	16	3	134*	282	21.69	1	—	7	—
S.T. Clarke	22	25	0	52	408	16.32	—	1	11	—
D.B. Pauline	2	4	0	26	51	12.75	—	—	—	—
P.H.L. Wilson	3	4	2	13	20	10.00	—	—	—	—
P.I. Pocock	7	8	2	10*	32	5.33	—	—	1	—

Also batted: R.G.L. Cheatle (4 matches) 27*, 1* (1 ct); A.J. Stewart (1 match) 9, 16 (4 ct).

Bowling	O	M	R	W	Avge	Best	5w/I	10w/M
S.T. Clarke	659.3	162	1696	85	19.95	6-63	6	1
R.D. Jackman	541.2	159	1429	61	23.42	6-28	2	—
K.S. Mackintosh	236.2	44	808	28	28.85	6-61	1	—
P.I. Pocock	233	64	632	21	30.09	5-73	1	—
D.J. Thomas	388.4	100	1154	32	36.06	4-39	—	—
A. Needham	309.3	56	1032	21	49.14	5-91	1	—
R.D.V. Knight	254.2	57	743	15	49.53	3-34	—	—

Also bowled: A.R. Butcher 83-12-367-4; R.G.L. Cheatle 49-9-183-3; M.A. Lynch 51.5-8-208-4; G. Monkhouse 95.3-14-297-9; D.B. Pauline 1-0-3-0; C.J. Richards 4-0-14-0; G.R.J. Roope 32-14-81-3; P.H.L. Wilson 73.4-18-209-4.

Hundreds (17)

4 G.P. Howarth: 121 v Derbys, Derby; 156* v Glamorgan, Guildford; 112 v Middlesex, Lord's; 126* v Yorks, Oval.

3 A.R. Butcher: 151* v Leics, Leicester; 187* v Warwicks, Birmingham; 162 v Worcs, Worcester.

  M.A. Lynch: 118 v Notts, Oval; 141* v Glamorgan, Guildford; 102 v Sussex, Oval.

  D.M. Smith: 105* v Warwicks, Birmingham; 160 v Worcs, Worcester, 100* v Yorks, Oval.

1 G.S. Clinton: 102 v Leics, Leicester.

  A. Needham: 134* v Lancs, Manchester.

  C.J. Richards: 117* v Notts, Oval.

  G.R.J. Roope: 108 v Northants, Northampton.

Sussex

With Imran Khan due to tour with Pakistan and therefore available for only the first seven Championship matches, Sussex were not expected to fare as well as in 1981, when they were runners-up. But a drop of six places was a poor reflection of their talent and flair.

It is interesting to compare Sussex's achievements during the short span that Imran played, and afterwards. In the initial period, they won consecutive matches, over Essex and Gloucestershire, and also beat Warwickshire and Worcestershire. Meanwhile, they lost to Middlesex and suffered a heavy defeat by Kent. After Imran's departure, they were beaten five more times and achieved only two more wins, with an interval of eight matches between them. Indeed, the second was against the ultimate champions, Middlesex, and it was achieved in a manner that did Sussex proud.

No doubt, Imran played important parts in two of the three early matches. But they were not so substantial as to leave the impression that Sussex would cease to be a force when he went away. Sussex did not so much miss the runs Imran might have scored, or the wickets he might have taken. It is very probable, though, that they missed him as a source of inspiration and self-assurance. Another factor that could have deflected Sussex from a steady course was the pressure of maintaining their position in a tightly contested John Player League, which they won so handsomely.

Hypotheses apart, Sussex's prospects in the Championship were undermined by the indifferent form of the more established batsmen. Their main run-scorer was Collin Wells, engaged in only his second full season. The only other batsman to reach a thousand — no one else was within 150 runs of the mark — was Mendis. Even Mendis was nowhere near as confident, perky, or prolific as in 1981.

Barclay, who formed so reliable an opening partnership with Mendis in the previous season, was in indifferent form and was forced to drop himself down the order. Innings of substance from Parker were isolated, and Greig made many fewer runs that in 1981. Barclay sought a solution for their batting difficulties in frequent changes in the batting order, which only compounded their problem. However, the crisis brought out the fighter in Le Roux, as well as a batting talent that had not before been seen to its fullest extent. Gould also played several good innings, some of them as an opener.

The bowling did not suffer overmuch from Imran's absence, mainly because Tony Pigott came good at last and took 61 wickets, only 4 fewer than Le Roux, who was the season's outstanding bowler. Greig also topped the 60 mark, and Waller, who did an immense amount of bowling, took 55. Virtually no other county enjoyed the luxury of four bowlers taking 244 wickets between them. Such bowling strength should have been a springboard at least to one of the first three places.

Happily, there were signs that problems with their batting need not continue. Two uncapped youngsters, Alan Wells and Allan Green,

Schweppes County Championship:	8th	Won 6	Lost 7	Drawn 9						
All First-Class Matches:		Won 6	Lost 8	Drawn 9						
NatWest Bank Trophy:	Lost to Nottinghamshire in 1st round									
Benson & Hedges Cup:	Lost to Somerset in semi-final									
John Player League:	1st	Won 14	Lost 1	No result 1						

Championship Averages   *not out

Batting/Fielding	M	I	NO	HS	R	Avge	100	50	Ct	St
A.P. Wells	4	7	3	70	212	53.00	—	1	1	—
Imran Khan	7	12	3	85	297	33.00	—	1	2	—
A.M. Green	13	24	1	99	743	32.30	—	6	7	—
C.M. Wells	22	39	3	126	1161	32.25	3	4	6	—
G.S. le Roux	20	28	5	83	737	32.04	—	6	15	—
G.D. Mendis	22	40	2	104	1078	28.36	1	7	5	—
J.R.T. Barclay	22	33	6	95	761	28.18	—	6	25	—
P.W.G. Parker	22	39	7	106	845	26.40	1	5	20	—
I.J. Gould	18	30	3	94	652	24.14	—	5	40	5
I.A. Greig	18	23	1	109	477	21.68	1	3	18	—
C.P. Phillipson	15	20	3	64	254	14.94	—	1	23	—
C.E. Waller	22	25	11	50	172	12.28	—	1	17	—
A.C.S. Pigott	22	21	6	40	165	11.00	—	—	9	—
G.G. Arnold	3	5	4	8*	11	11.00	—	—	—	—

Also batted: R.S. Cowan (1 match) 0, 18* (1 ct); J.R.P. Heath (2 matches) 17, 3, 19; A.N. Jones (3 matches) 29, 5, 5; D.J. Smith (5 matches) 1, 0, 0 (6 ct); A. Willows (1 match) 0*, 4.

Bowling	O	M	R	W	Avge	Best	5w/I	10w/M
Imran Khan	194.1	58	458	29	15.79	4-26	—	—
G.S. le Roux	467	116	1210	65	18.61	5-15	3	—
I.A. Greig	535.5	122	1578	63	25.04	5-46	2	—
A.C.S. Pigott	454	88	1597	61	26.18	7-74	4	—
C.E. Waller	571	165	1527	55	27.76	7-67	1	—
J.R.T. Barclay	230.2	58	702	11	63.81	3-44	—	—

Also bowled: G.G. Arnold 59-23-89-6; R.S. Cowan 9-0-34-0; I.J. Gould 5.4-2-18-0; A.M. Green 36-4-182-6; A.N. Jones 26-5-89-4; P.W.G. Parker 5-0-16-0; C.M. Wells 56.3-9-175-5; A. Willows 17-4-39-0.

Hundreds (6)
3 **C.M. Wells:** 100* v Gloucs, Bristol; 126 v Kent, Hove; 123* v Notts, Hove.
1 **I.A. Greig:** 109 v Warwicks, Birmingham.
  G.D. Mendis: 104 v Lancs, Manchester.
  P.W.G. Parker: 106 v Leics, Hove.

looked magnificent strikers of the ball as Sussex chased runs to beat Middlesex, late in the summer. It is to be hoped that their development is not impaired by bad habits cultivated from an excess of one-day cricket.

Warwickshire

There was a curious irony in Warwickshire's plight of ending the Championship without a single win — and, naturally, at the bottom of the table — for their ranks contained the season's highest-scoring batsman, Alvin Kallicharran. Furthermore, their season's run aggregate was the highest of any county except Northamptonshire.

Warwickshire were also the only other county besides Northamptonshire to acquire more bonus points for batting than bowling, which is regarded the baser currency. This state of affairs was at once a tribute to Warwickshire's batting strength and a commentary on their bowling resources, which took the full blast of their injury problems. Three times in the season, Warwickshire compiled totals well above 400, but to no avail. Paradoxically, their best, 523 for 4 declared, which no county equalled during the season, was prelude to a heavy defeat by Lancashire. There was no previous instance in English cricket of a side scoring 500 and losing.

There were several indignities inflicted on Warwickshire's outcricket during the season. In a very early match, a rare one of low scores at Edgbaston, they had reduced Yorkshire to 143 for 9. But Yorkshire's last man, Stevenson, made a lightning hundred and the tenth wicket put on 149. In the very next match, Glenn Turner made 311 not out in a day, and Worcestershire declared at 501 for only one wicket. On another occasion, Warwickshire fielded to a score of 502 by Essex.

At such times, it could have been no consolation to Warwickshire that they themselves had wrought havoc of high proportions on others, with the brilliant Kallicharran bending the bowling to his will. The little left-hander, now 33, had his best ever season, scoring over 2,000 runs for the first time in 11 seasons of county cricket. Kallicharran hit three double centuries, narrowly missing a fourth, and made four other three-figure scores. Amiss, Andy Lloyd, and Humpage also topped the thousand mark and, on the occasion when Warwickshire made 523 at Southport, Humpage hit 13 sixes in the second double-century of the innings.

Such feats came to nothing when only one Warwickshire bowler, Gladstone Small, could take 50 wickets. Small's average was undistinguished, but allowances must be made because he had no support to speak of, not even on the occasions when Willis was spearheading the attack. Willis paced himself to stay fit and fresh for Test matches. For Warwickshire, Willis was not — and has not been for some seasons — the bowler he is for England.

Under the circumstances, Warwickshire were utterly distressed when first Ferreira broke down with an Achilles' tendon injury, followed by Hogg, whose ankle gave way. Cumbes was a third casualty with an illness that hastened his retirement from the game. Ferreira missed almost three months of cricket, returning only just in time to help Warwickshire into the NatWest final.

Schweppes County Championship:	17th	Won 0	Lost 8	Drawn 14
All First-Class Matches:		Won 1	Lost 8	Drawn 16
NatWest Bank Trophy:	Lost to Surrey in final			
Benson & Hedges Cup:	Failed to qualify for Q-F (3rd in Group B)			
John Player League	17th	Won 3	Lost 11	No result 2

Championship Averages

*not out

Batting/Fielding	M	I	NO	HS	R	Avge	100	50	Ct	St
A.I. Kallicharran	21	36	5	235	2118	68.32	8	5	7	—
D.L. Amiss	21	38	1	156	1404	37.94	1	9	12	—
G.W. Humpage	22	38	3	254	1264	36.11	3	5	45	1
P.J. Lewington	4	5	4	15*	35	35.00	—	—	—	—
T.A. Lloyd	22	40	4	122	1156	32.11	2	6	9	—
C. Lethbridge	15	20	5	87*	369	24.60	—	1	7	—
K.D. Smith	17	30	5	67	604	24.16	—	4	10	—
A.M. Ferreira	6	9	1	41	191	23.87	—	—	4	—
P.A. Smith	8	14	0	68	329	23.50	—	2	7	—
Asif Din	21	30	0	102	681	22.70	1	1	14	—
R.G.D. Willis	12	15	5	63*	215	21.50	—	1	4	—
G.A. Tedstone	2	4	2	18*	36	18.00	—	—	1	1
P.R. Oliver	5	7	0	46	115	16.42	—	—	3	—
R.I.H.B. Dyer	5	5	1	31*	58	14.50	—	—	1	—
G.C. Small	22	28	4	36	252	10.50	—	—	6	—
P.J. Hartley	3	4	1	16	31	10.33	—	—	1	—
J. Cumbes	11	14	7	7*	33	4.71	—	—	5	—
W. Hogg	3	4	2	8	9	4.50	—	—	2	—
S.P. Sutcliffe	13	16	6	20	35	3.50	—	—	2	—

Also batted: D.J. Brown (3 matches†) 7* (1 ct); K.R. Maguire (3 matches) 2, 1, 0; D.M. Smith (1 match) 0; S.H. Wootton (3 matches) 3, 0.

† *Includes one match as temporary substitute for G.C. Small (Test stand-by) when he bowled.*

Bowling	O	M	R	W	Avge	Best	5w/I	10w/M
A.M. Ferreira	175.2	41	568	19	29.89	5-109	1	—
G.C. Small	500.4	86	1646	51	32.27	7-68	1	—
C. Lethbridge	301.3	67	961	29	33.13	5-68	1	—
R.G.D. Willis	262	58	842	24	35.08	6-45	1	—
A.I. Kallicharran	154.2	21	578	14	41.28	3-32	—	—
S.P. Sutcliffe	533.4	107	1755	37	47.43	5-151	1	—
Asif Din	252.1	55	999	20	49.95	5-100	1	—
J. Cumbes	228.1	50	654	12	54.50	3-65	—	—

Also bowled: D.L. Amiss 2.1-0-18-0; D.J. Brown 51-8-204-4 *(including 13-3-47-1 when substituting for G.C. Small)*; R.I.H.B. Dyer 1-0-2-0; P.J. Hartley 57-11-215-2; W. Hogg 58.3-9-198-4; G.W. Humpage 27-6-74-2; P.J. Lewington 89.1-19-294-3; T.A. Lloyd 80-23-266-3; K.R. Maguire 35-6-123-1; D.M. Smith 4-0-14-0; P.A. Smith 94-16-362-7.

Hundreds (15)

8 A.I. Kallicharran: 105 v Kent, Dartford; 235 v Worcs, Worcester; 210 v Leics, Leicester; 173 v Gloucs, Nuneaton; 230* v Lancs, Southport; 195 v Surrey, Birmingham; 109* v Worcs, Birmingham; 131 v Hants, Southampton.

3 G.W. Humpage: 254 v Lancs, Southport; 113 v Somerset, Taunton; 146 v Northants, Birmingham.

2 T.A. Lloyd: 122 v Glamorgan, Cardiff; 120 v Worcs, Birmingham.

1 D.L. Amiss: 156 v Somerset, Birmingham. **Asif Din:** 102 v Middlesex, Coventry.

Worcestershire

The season of 1982 closed an era in Worcestershire cricket, for among several players who were due to leave at the end of it were two who had become part of the county's cricket history — Norman Gifford and Glenn Turner. Gifford, a Lancastrian by birth, had been on the staff for a quarter of a century and been associated with all their three Championships, the last of which was gained under his captaincy. Turner, a New Zealander, joined them in 1967 as a replacement for Don Kenyon.

Turner had quite a void to fill, for Kenyon had made more runs (30,000) for the county than any other batsman. Dour and dull in his initial years, Turner blossomed into a magnificent player. He left the county's record book filled with his name, and contributed 22,298 runs, including 72 centuries.

Gifford, who took 1,620 of his 1,712 wickets for the county, faded gently from the scene, playing 12 matches in his last season. Turner, too, had planned to play less than a full season. But, whatever his intentions, the end came with dramatic suddenness when, towards the end of July, he was rushed into hospital with appendicitis. As a result, having made hundreds in his last three matches, he went out in a blaze of glory. His final innings was a dazzling one of 66 against Kent on a bleak, blustery day at Hereford, before a small crowd.

Turner did a lap of honour with a fleeting appearance in the last Sunday league match of the season. But the most abiding memory at Worcester of Turner's last season will be his amazing innings at the Spring Holiday weekend, when he laid on a feast of 311 runs in a day against poor Warwickshire. Such a marvel had been seen only once since World War II — strangely enough, at the same ground — when Jack Robertson of Middlesex made 331, in 1949. Turner finished out on his own at the head of the English first-class averages.

In view of their long associations, Gifford, Turner, and Ted Hemsley, no less, will regret that their last season was not a successful one for the county. Worcestershire made no mark in the one-day competitions and finished 14th in the Championship. They were strong enough not to lose more than four times, but too weak to win more than three.

In common with most counties in the bottom half of the table, Worcestershire had the batting to take them higher, but were woefully short of bowling. The only one among their regular bowlers who was enjoying a reasonable amount of success, John Inchmore, did not stay fit right through. In the end, their main wicket-taker was an all-rounder, Dipak Patel, with his off-breaks.

Patel also confirmed his advance as a polished batsman, completing his thousand runs for the second year running. Despite missing six matches, Younis was the only other to top four figures in the Championship, as Turner's 1,171 included a double century against Oxford. Ormrod came to the fore against Gloucestershire when he laid the basis of a win with an unbeaten double century and helped to complete it with another fine innings of 93.

Schweppes County Championship:	14th	Won 3	Lost 5	Drawn 14
All First-Class Matches:		Won 3	Lost 6	Drawn 16
NatWest Bank Trophy:	Lost to Yorkshire in 2nd round			
Benson & Hedges Cup:	Failed to qualify for Q-F (3rd in Group A)			
John Player League:	15th	Won 5	Lost 10	No result 1

Championship Averages

*not out

Batting/Fielding	M	I	NO	HS	R	Avge	100	50	Ct	St
G.M. Turner	8	15	2	311*	932	71.69	4	3	8	—
Younis Ahmed	16	26	4	122	1039	47.22	4	4	11	—
D.N. Patel	22	38	1	133	1085	29.32	1	4	20	—
D.J. Humphries	22	33	5	98	784	28.00	—	7	36	4
T.S. Curtis	10	17	4	59*	359	27.61	—	2	5	—
P.A. Neale	22	37	6	79*	851	27.45	—	4	8	—
J.A. Ormrod	20	37	2	200*	915	26.14	1	3	7	—
A.E. Warner	10	15	2	67	268	20.61	—	1	2	—
M.J. Weston	15	27	1	68	526	20.23	—	4	4	—
H.L. Alleyne	7	8	2	32	121	20.16	—	—	1	—
N. Gifford	12	15	7	31*	155	19.37	—	—	9	—
J.D. Inchmore	13	18	3	68	273	18.20	—	2	5	—
E.J.O. Hemsley	13	20	1	49	336	17.68	—	—	8	—
R.K. Illingworth	9	12	2	47*	171	17.10	—	—	3	—
A.J. Webster	8	10	5	25	75	15.00	—	—	3	—
M.S. Scott	4	7	0	37	100	14.28	—	—	1	—
A.P. Pridgeon	14	16	4	21	110	9.16	—	—	4	—
S.P. Perryman	12	16	8	14	56	7.00	—	—	5	—

Also batted: D.B. D'Oliveira (2 matches) 10, 4, 18* (2 ct); R.M. Ellcock (1 match) 0, 13*;
P.A. Newport (2 matches) 6, 11, 6* (1 ct).

Bowling	O	M	R	W	Avge	Best	5w/I	10w/M
J.D. Inchmore	289.4	57	778	32	24.31	7-53	2	—
D.N. Patel	490.2	124	1328	46	28.86	7-46	2	—
S.P. Perryman	350.1	82	1027	31	33.12	6-49	3	—
A.E. Warner	190.1	33	643	19	33.84	4-73	—	—
R.K. Illingworth	219.4	55	638	17	37.52	4-85	—	—
A.P. Pridgeon	424	92	1109	29	38.24	4-39	—	—
H.L. Alleyne	193.3	42	558	14	39.85	4-92	—	—
N. Gifford	417	121	944	23	41.04	6-48	1	—
A.J. Webster	202.1	36	716	15	47.73	5-87	1	—

Also bowled: T.S. Curtis 2-0-7-0; R.M. Ellcock 26.1-2-90-3; E.J.O. Hemsley 20.4-1-80-1;
P.A. Neale 4-0-16-0; J.A. Ormrod 1-0-5-0; P.A. Newport 36-1-174-6; M.J. Weston
57.3-8-215-5; Younis Ahmed 5-1-14-0.

Hundreds (10)

4 G.M. Turner: 311* v Warwicks, Worcester; 115 v Lancs, Worcester; 112 v Yorks, Sheffield; 118 v Kent, Hereford.
  Younis Ahmed: 114* v Gloucs, Worcester; 122 v Leics, Worcester; 110 v Warwicks, Birmingham; 114 v Notts, Worcester.
1 J.A. Ormrod: 200* v Gloucs, Worcester.
  D.N. Patel: 133 v Surrey, Worcester.

Yorkshire

The season was not quite six weeks old when Yorkshire, in a dramatic move, installed Ray Illingworth as captain in place of Chris Old, who had had a turbulent time in the job. After all the in-fighting during the close season, and the attempted coup against the central figure of the row, Geoff Boycott, there had been absolute peace. And when Old gave up the captaincy, nothing had gone too wrong for Yorkshire in the Championship. But their failures in the one-day competitions were reaching intolerable limits.

That Yorkshire offered Illingworth the captaincy was no great shock. Illingworth's acceptance, however, at 50 and when he had not played first-class cricket for three years, was more surprising. Perhaps he found the honour — which he could have had many years earlier had he not left the county — too great to resist.

With the bowling at his disposal, there was not much Illingworth could do to turn the tide of fortune. At his age, he could make no great contribution with personal performance. And he could exert no more authority in matters of discipline — for, as manager, he already possessed the power and scope. What Illingworth could achieve, however, by sacrificing the comfort of the deckchair was to apply his matchless judgement of field placings and his unique ability to motivate his bowlers.

The legend is that Yorkshiremen have an intense dislike of defeat, and on this count pride must have been satisfied because they lost just one match in the Championship, a degree of invincibility that was beyond all the other 16 counties. If Brian Close, a man who played over two decades for Yorkshire, is to be believed, however, the desire of his compatriots to win is stronger than their aversion to defeat. In this respect, Yorkshire got no farther than in the previous, stormy season, with five victories.

To put the record straight, Yorkshire had already scored one of their wins before Old stepped down. The first five matches under Illingworth were all drawn, and then they had a run of three wins. At the end of this sequence — and, indeed, when the summer of 1982 had faded — Yorkshire must have been relieved that they did not send Boycott packing, for he played at least one major innings in every match Yorkshire won. He played several others and finished the season with 1913 runs, a total exceeded only by Kallicharran and Kirsten.

Bill Athey, too, had a profitable season, his aggregate of 1,339 runs, which included four centuries, being his best ever. Boycott and he were the only two to reach a thousand. Graham Stevenson made a heroic century against Warwickshire, turning adversity into a famous victory. It was also one of those rare ones made by a number eleven. Stevenson was 115 when his partner succumbed, the partner being one G. Boycott, who had opened the innings and scored 79!

Schweppes County Championship:	10th	Won 5	Lost 1	Drawn 15	(Abandoned 1)
All First-Class Matches:		Won 5	Lost 1	Drawn 16	(Abandoned 1)
NatWest Bank Trophy:	Lost to Warwickshire in semi-final				
Benson & Hedges Cup:	Failed to qualify for Q-F (5th in Group A)				
John Player League:	16th	Won 3	Lost 10	Tied 1	No result 2

Championship Averages

*not out

Batting/Fielding	M	I	NO	HS	R	Avge	100	50	Ct	St
G. Boycott	21	37	6	159	1913	61.70	6	10	10	—
M.D. Moxon	2	4	0	67	197	49.25	—	2	—	—
C.W.J. Athey	21	37	6	134	1278	41.22	4	7	20	—
J.D. Love	17	28	5	123	770	33.47	2	4	7	—
S.N. Hartley	19	29	9	114	619	30.95	1	4	6	—
D.L. Bairstow	21	28	8	77	599	29.95	—	4	51	3
R.G. Lumb	19	31	0	81	777	25.06	—	6	9	—
G.B. Stevenson	16	19	4	115*	356	23.73	1	—	6	—
P. Carrick	19	21	3	93	423	23.50	—	2	7	—
A. Sidebottom	19	18	8	44*	233	23.30	—	—	4	—
K. Sharp	9	16	1	52	343	22.86	—	1	2	—
R. Illingworth	13	6	2	33	86	21.50	—	—	3	—
C.M. Old	16	18	3	32	207	13.80	—	—	9	—

Also batted: P.A. Booth (1 match) 0*; S.J. Dennis (2 matches) 5*; P.W. Jarvis (6 matches) 0*, 7, 0 (5 ct); A. Ramage (4 matches) 4*, 0; N.S. Taylor (3 matches) 0*; J.P. Whiteley (3 matches) 1, 5* (3 ct).

Bowling	O	M	R	W	Avge	Best	5w/I	10w/M
A. Sidebottom	495.2	95	1538	62	24.80	6-31	3	—
S.J. Dennis	66	10	262	10	26.20	5-42	1	—
C.M. Old	458.2	125	1229	46	26.71	6-76	1	—
G.B. Stevenson	422.4	87	1423	45	31.62	5-72	1	—
P. Carrick	532.5	135	1329	40	33.22	6-90	1	—

Also bowled: C.W.J. Athey 27.1-1-98-0; P.A. Booth 10-3-22-0; G. Boycott 57.2-13-120-8; S.N. Hartley 116-27-373-6; R. Illingworth 223.4-66-587-9; P.W. Jarvis 132-25-434-8; J.D. Love 3-3-0-0; A. Ramage 90-14-381-5; N.S. Taylor 62.3-14-186-6; J.P. Whiteley 16-0-71-1.

Hundreds (14)

6 G. Boycott: 138 v Northants, Northampton; 134 v Glamorgan, Leeds; 159 v Worcs, Sheffield; 152* v Warwicks, Leeds; 122* v Sussex, Scarborough; 129 v Somerset, Weston-super-Mare.

4 C.W.J. Athey: 100 v Glamorgan, Leeds; 134 v Derbys, Derby; 100 v Kent, Leeds; 114* v Surrey, Oval.

2 J.D. Love: 110 v Derbys, Derbys; 123 v Surrey, Oval.

1 S.N. Hartley: 114 v Gloucs, Bradford.

G.B. Stevenson: 115* v Warwicks, Birmingham.

University Cricket

The Oxford and Cambridge batsmen took full advantage of some markedly true and fast wickets in the Parks and at Fenners last season, and their powers were handsomely evident in the 138th University Match — with bat well on top of ball.

The loss at Lord's of the Cambridge captain, all-rounder Derek Pringle, to England duty was, of course, a blow. But their batsmen certainly excelled themselves in the second innings when set 272 to win in 210 minutes. Boyd-Moss scored a hundred, Henderson fifty, and Cambridge beat Oxford by 7 wickets. So often in the past has the University Match concluded in an inevitable draw, but this time Oxford's captain, Ellis, earned much more than just Light Blue praise for issuing a sporting challenge.

Cambridge had come to Lord's having enjoyed some notable triumphs at Fenners, including victory over Lancashire by 7 wickets. This was their first county success since 1971, when, under the captaincy of Majid Khan, the University also defeated the Pakistani tourists.

On the first day of the season, Hodgson, at accurate medium pace, took 8 for 68 against Glamorgan — the best analysis by a Cambridge bowler since A.J.G. Pearson captured all 10 wickets against Leicestershire, at Loughborough, in 1961. Pringle hit a majestic hundred on the second day of this Glamorgan match and set an English batting record for the month of April by scoring 361 runs in his 6 innings. The outstanding all-round skills of Pringle were clearly reflected by his heading of both the batting (77.42) and the bowling (22.15) averages.

Boyd-Moss was second in the batting averages, with an aggregate of 717 runs. It was against Warwickshire that he became only the seventh Cambridge batsman to have scored a hundred in each innings of a match, joining D.S. Sheppard, R.M. Prideaux, and A.J. Hignell as the fourth to record this feat since the war. In the previous match at Fenners, the left-handed freshman Henderson had impudently attacked the Middlesex bowling to score 209 not out. Henderson, son of the 1950 Oxford Blue D. Henderson, is to be Cambridge captain next season.

Oxford's captain Ellis scored 666 runs, with many a handsome straight drive, but their leading batsman was undoubtedly Cowan. He had an average of 46.81, having started the season in prolific form, with hundreds off Northants and Kent and an innings of 76 against Worcestershire in the first three matches. Toogood, next year's captain, also impressed with flowing stroke-play for 83 runs in this Worcestershire match, although he never quite confirmed such quality batting in the second half of term.

The batting prowess of both teams sufficed to ensure a most encouraging season for University cricket. And the Test match appearances of such Blues as Tavaré, Edmonds, Ian Greig, Marks, and Pringle — to say nothing of their Pakistani opponents Imran Khan and Majid Khan — further emphasized the fruitful contribution that Oxford and Cambridge continue to make towards the first-class game.

Oxford University v Cambridge University
Cambridge won by 7 wickets
Played at Lord's, June 26, 28, 29
Toss: Oxford. Umpires: J. Birken Shaw and W.L. Budd

Oxford

*R.G.P. Ellis	c Goldie b Hodgson	86	c Henderson b Pollock	14
R. Marsden	lbw b Palmer	13	b Boyd-Moss	39
K.A. Hayes	retired hurt	13		
R.S. Cowan	c Goldie b Hodgson	33	(3) c Mills b Pollock	4
G.J. Toogood	c Henderson b Hodgson	31	(4) c Barrington b Boyd-Moss	38
†R.S. Luddington	b Boyd-Moss	6	(7) c Henderson b Boyd-Moss	7
R.P. Moulding	not out	20	(5) c Mills b Boyd-Moss	8
J.G. Varey	not out	32	(6) not out	12
S.P. Ridge			(8) not out	2
I.J. Curtis	did not bat			
T.J. Taylor				
Extras	(lb 10, w 1, nb 4)	15	(b 6, lb 4, nb 2)	12
Total	(5 wickets declared)	**249**	(6 wickets declared)	**136**

Cambridge

*J.P.C. Mills	c sub b Ellis	9	lbw b Ridge	11
D.W. Varey	c Cowan b Varey	22	retired hurt	16
R.J. Boyd-Moss	not out	41	c sub b Curtis	100
S.P. Henderson	not out	39	c Ridge b Taylor	50
W.E.J. Barrington			not out	48
K.I. Hodgson			not out	36
S.J.G. Doggart				
†C.F.E. Goldie	did not bat			
A.J. Pollock				
C.C. Ellison				
R.W.M. Palmer				
Extras	(lb 1, w 1, nb 1)	3	(b 1, lb 9, nb 1)	11
Total	(2 wickets declared)	**114**	(3 wickets)	**272**

Cambridge	O	M	R	W	O	M	R	W
Palmer	17	2	52	1	10	0	35	0
Pollock	3	1	19	0	7	1	16	2
Hodgson	26	4	89	3	3	0	20	0
Ellison	6	1	23	0	2	0	7	0
Boyd-Moss	11	1	51	1	9	0	42	4
Varey					1	0	4	0

Oxford	O	M	R	W	O	M	R	W
Cowan	7	0	49	0	6	0	42	0
Ridge	6	0	14	0	8	1	33	1
Ellis	4	0	18	1	1	0	2	0
Taylor	5	0	17	0	16	4	46	1
Varey	2	0	13	1	3	0	19	0
Curtis					22	2	119	1

Fall of Wickets

	OU	CU	OU	CU
Wkt	1st	1st	2nd	2nd
1st	58	19	17	26
2nd	125	50	25	178
3rd	188	—	64	190
4th	189	—	104	—
5th	199	—	113	—
6th	—	—	127	—
7th	—	—	—	—
8th	—	—	—	—
9th	—	—	—	—
10th	—	—	—	—

* Captain   † Wicket-keeper

Cambridge University

Results: Played 9 Won 2 Lost 4 Drawn 3
First-Class Averages

Batting/Fielding	M	I	NO	HS	R	Avge
D.R. Pringle	6	10	3	127	521	74.42
†R.J. Boyd-Moss	9	17	1	123	717	44.81
†S.P. Henderson	9	16	3	209*	531	40.84
†D.W. Varey	9	17	3	156*	548	39.14
†W.E.J. Barrington	4	6	1	59	174	34.80
†K.I. Hodgson	8	10	1	50	213	23.66
†J.P.C. Mills	9	17	0	98	389	22.88
†S.J.G. Doggart	9	13	1	64	242	20.16
†C.C. Ellison	7	7	4	16	56	18.66
†C.F.E. Goldie	9	9	0	31	115	12.77
†A.J. Pollock	7	8	2	19	63	10.50
†R.W.M. Palmer	9	8	5	12	20	6.66

Also batted: A.G. Davies (1 match) 13, 4 (3 ct);
R.S. Dutton (2 matches) 0, 0*, 0; P.D. Griffiths (1
match) 1, 0.

Bowling	O	M	R	W	Avge
D.R. Pringle	117.2	37	288	13	22.15
†R.J. Boyd-Moss	64	15	233	9	25.88
†K.I. Hodgson	198.1	42	625	23	27.17
†A.J. Pollock	115.5	18	483	14	34.50
†R.W.M. Palmer	219.4	34	849	14	60.64
†C.C. Ellison	96.5	20	314	5	62.80
†S.J.G. Doggart	182.4	29	623	7	89.00

Also bowled: R.S. Dutton 19-1-130-0; P.D.
Griffiths 9-2-39-0; †S.P. Henderson 6-3-8-0;
†D.W. Varey 1-0-4-0.

Hundreds (6)
3 R.J. Boyd-Moss: 123 and 119 v Warwicks,
   Cambridge; 100 v Oxford U., Lord's.
1 S.P. Henderson: 209* v Middlesex, Cambridge.
   D.R. Pringle: 127 v Glamorgan, Cambridge.
   D.W. Varey: 156* v Northants, Cambridge.

* not out   † Blue 1982

Oxford University

Results: Played 10 Won 0 Lost 5 Drawn 5
First-Class Averages

Batting/Fielding	M	I	NO	HS	R	Avge
†R.S. Cowan	7	14	3	143*	515	46.81
S.J. Halliday	4	7	1	113*	213	35.50
†R.G.P. Ellis	10	20	1	105*	666	35.05
†J.G. Varey	7	12	5	68	239	34.14
†R. Marsden	5	10	1	60	264	29.33
†K.A. Hayes	10	19	2	152	491	28.88
†G.J. Toogood	9	18	4	83	392	28.00
J.R. Chessher	3	4	1	47	67	22.33
†R.S. Luddington	10	14	1	65	290	22.30
†R.P. Moulding	10	20	2	67	242	13.44
A.D. Gilfillan	3	4	1	31	40	13.33
†S.P. Ridge	10	13	5	22	64	8.00
M.P. Lawrence	4	5	2	18	20	6.66
H.T. Rawlinson	4	6	0	21	30	5.00

Also batted: P.A.N. Armstrong (1 match) 34, 0;
J.J. Cassidy (1 match) 0; P.J. Crowe (1 match) 11,
0; †I.J. Curtis (5 matches) 0*, 20*, 0 (1 ct); R.
Edrooke (1 match) 84*, 16; A.J.T. Miller (1
match) 0, 20; †T.J. Taylor (4 matches) 0, 20, 17*.

Bowling	O	M	R	W	Avge
†I.J. Curtis	214.4	45	659	15	43.93
†T.J. Taylor	149	24	469	9	52.11
†S.P. Ridge	240.1	32	829	13	63.76
H.T. Rawlinson	96.1	9	435	5	87.00
†R.S. Cowan	131	18	559	6	93.16

Also bowled: J.J. Cassidy 4-2-12-0; P.J. Crowe 36-
4-121-1; †R.G.P. Ellis 61-14-182-4; A.D.
Gilfillan 51-5-218-2; †K.A. Hayes 21-1-96-0;
M.P. Lawrence 99-20-366-2; †G.J. Toogood 3-0-
22-0; †J.G. Varey 132-15-550-3.

Hundreds (5)
2 R.S. Cowan: 143* v Northants, Oxford;
   108 v Kent, Oxford.
1 R.G.P. Ellis: 105* v Surrey, Oxford.
   S.J. Halliday: 113* v Kent, Oxford.
   K.A. Hayes: 152 v Warwicks, Oxford.

* not out   † Blue 1982

First-Class Averages

Batting (Qualifications: 8 innings, average 10.00)

(* not out)	M	I	NO	HS	Runs	Avge	100	50
G.M. Turner	9	16	3	311*	1171	90.07	5	3
Zaheer Abbas	16	25	4	162*	1475	70.23	5	8
A.I. Kallicharran	23	37	5	235	2120	66.25	8	5
P.N. Kirsten	21	37	7	164*	1941	64.70	8	6
G. Boycott	21	37	6	159	1913	61.70	6	10
M.W. Gatting	23	34	6	192	1651	58.96	6	5
T.E. Jesty	22	36	8	164*	1645	58.75	8	4
J.G. Wright	21	39	6	190	1830	55.45	7	5
B.F. Davison	22	37	4	172	1800	54.54	7	8
Younis Ahmed	18	29	6	122	1247	54.21	4	7
J. Simmons	18	21	12	79*	487	54.11	—	4
P. Willey	23	41	6	145	1783	50.94	5	8
D.M. Smith (Sy)	14	25	4	160	1065	50.71	3	5
Javed Miandad	18	29	8	105*	1051	50.04	1	9
D.P. Hughes	23	36	9	126*	1303	48.25	3	6
C.J. Tavaré	20	36	4	168*	1522	47.56	3	10
D.W. Randall	20	33	4	130*	1369	47.20	4	8
J.M. Brearley	20	32	9	165	1083	47.08	3	4
S.J.O'Shaughnessy	11	19	7	62	560	46.66	—	7
A.J. Lamb	18	30	2	140	1302	46.50	5	4
D.I. Gower	20	35	2	176*	1530	46.36	2	12
C.G. Greenidge	21	41	8	183*	1526	46.24	3	4
I.V.A. Richards	20	31	2	181*	1324	45.65	4	5
W. Larkins	24	44	3	186	1863	45.43	5	9
B.C. Rose	21	32	8	173*	1090	45.41	2	5
Imran Khan	16	20	7	85	588	45.23	—	3
R.J. Boyd-Moss	23	41	5	137	1602	44.50	5	10
R.S. Cowan	8	16	4	143*	533	44.41	2	2
I.T. Botham	17	29	1	208	1241	44.32	3	7
G.A. Gooch	23	38	1	149	1632	44.10	3	12
W.N. Slack	25	40	6	203*	1499	44.08	2	10
M.R. Benson	16	30	5	137	1100	44.00	3	7
C.W.J. Athey	22	38	7	134	1339	43.19	4	8
Kapil Dev	14	20	2	103	770	42.77	2	4
P. Bainbridge	18	33	8	103	1069	42.76	2	7
R.A. Woolmer	13	22	3	203	809	42.57	2	4
R.O. Butcher	21	28	3	197	1058	42.32	3	2
J.H. Hampshire	22	36	6	101*	1264	42.13	1	9
B.R. Hardie	24	39	5	161	1432	42.11	1	8
G. Fowler	21	35	2	150	1387	42.03	5	5
C.H. Lloyd	21	29	2	100	1135	42.03	1	9
K.S. McEwan	24	37	3	150*	1421	41.79	3	6
S.P. Henderson	9	16	3	209*	531	40.84	1	2
L. Potter	12	21	2	118	775	40.78	2	5
G. Miller	16	26	7	98	772	40.63	—	6
K.R. Pont	16	24	7	89	687	40.41	—	6
D. Lloyd	23	36	2	114	1371	40.32	5	7
G.P. Howarth	19	32	3	156*	1158	39.93	4	2
A.R. Butcher	23	43	5	187*	1514	39.84	4	6
M.C.J. Nicholas	24	42	9	206*	1312	39.75	3	7

(* not out)	M	I	NO	HS	Runs	Avge	100	50
D.W. Varey	9	17	3	156*	548	39.14	1	3
K.W.R. Fletcher	24	36	4	124	1249	39.03	3	6
J.C. Balderstone	23	41	3	148	1482	39.00	4	8
A.P. Wells	5	9	3	70	233	38.83	—	1
D.A. Francis	19	33	5	142*	1076	38.42	2	7
G.W. Humpage	24	41	4	254	1407	38.02	4	5
D.L. Amiss	21	38	1	156	1404	37.94	1	9
K.P. Tomlins	13	17	1	146	607	37.93	2	3
A.M. Ferreira	8	10	2	112*	303	37.87	1	—
J. Abrahams	23	32	5	124	1013	37.51	1	7
Asif Iqbal	11	17	2	115*	558	37.20	1	4
D.S. Steele	25	36	13	74*	853	37.08	—	4
T.A. Lloyd	25	45	5	122	1432	35.80	2	9
Sadiq Mohammad	15	29	1	91	998	35.64	—	9
A. Jones	25	47	5	146*	1491	35.50	4	6
E.A. Baptiste	9	12	3	69*	319	35.44	—	2
A.P.E. Knott	21	32	5	115*	942	34.88	1	6
J.D. Birch	22	35	6	125	1011	34.86	2	6
N.E. Briers	23	38	4	106	1175	34.55	1	6
N.R. Taylor	24	43	4	143*	1340	34.35	3	7
R.G.P. Ellis	13	25	1	105*	823	34.29	1	5
J.E. Emburey	24	27	5	100*	752	34.18	1	4
J.G. Varey	7	12	5	68	239	34.14	—	1
B. Dudleston	6	12	1	111	373	33.90	1	1
D.R. Pringle	18	26	4	127	741	33.68	1	6
J.D. Love	18	29	6	123	773	33.60	2	4
C.E.B. Rice	22	36	3	144	1095	33.18	1	5
A.W. Stovold	23	42	1	212*	1350	32.92	2	7
C.M. Wells	23	41	3	126	1248	32.84	3	5
G.S. Clinton	14	23	4	172*	622	32.73	2	1
C.J.C. Rowe	25	39	6	105	1071	32.45	1	6
B. Hassan	19	34	4	89*	970	32.33	—	7
K.J. Barnett	18	25	5	120	642	32.10	2	1
M.A. Lynch	23	38	2	141*	1155	32.08	3	4
G.S. le Roux	20	28	5	83	737	32.04	—	6
D.G. Aslett	16	28	3	82	794	31.76	—	7
R.M. Carter	11	19	6	79	411	31.61	—	1
G. Cook	24	43	2	125	1285	31.34	3	7
K.S. Mackintosh	12	10	7	31	94	31.33	—	—
K.A. Hayes	13	22	3	152	594	31.26	1	3
G.R.J. Roope	14	25	7	108	560	31.11	1	1
R.G. Williams	24	39	4	141	1087	31.05	2	4
A.M. Green	14	26	1	99	776	31.04	—	6
R.J. Hadlee	18	28	2	131	807	31.03	2	4
G.D. Mendis	23	42	2	114	1240	31.00	2	7
R.D.V. Knight	24	40	4	111	1114	30.94	2	7
C.T. Radley	21	28	3	141*	773	30.92	2	2
R.C. Ontong	24	43	4	152*	1205	30.89	3	4
R.D. Jackman	20	22	8	68	430	30.71	—	3
I.S. Anderson	17	26	4	103*	671	30.50	1	3
I.P. Butcher	6	9	3	71*	182	30.33	—	1
S.N. Hartley	20	30	9	114	635	30.23	1	4

(* not out)	M	I	NO	HS	Runs	Avge	100	50
A.J. Hignell	15	28	6	72	664	30.18	—	4
K. Sharp	10	18	2	115	478	29.87	1	1
R. Marsden	5	10	1	60	264	29.33	—	1
N.A. Felton	8	12	0	71	346	28.83	—	3
D.L. Bairstow	23	30	9	77	603	28.71	—	4
S. Turner	23	28	4	83	679	28.29	—	5
J.R.T. Barclay	22	33	6	95	761	28.18	—	6
B.C. Broad	22	41	0	97	1153	28.12	—	7
R.T. Robinson	21	38	3	109	984	28.11	1	5
R.W. Tolchard	23	38	8	93*	843	28.10	—	7
P.H. Edmonds	21	22	4	92	505	28.05	—	4
G.J. Toogood	9	18	4	83	392	28.00	—	2
P.A. Neale	26	44	8	79*	1006	27.94	—	6
P.W. Romaines	14	24	2	186	609	27.68	1	2
T.S. Curtis	10	17	4	59*	359	27.61	—	2
T.M. Lamb	13	13	8	39*	137	27.40	—	—
G. Monkhouse	8	10	5	63*	137	27.40	—	1
J.W. Lloyds	23	39	3	132*	981	27.25	2	3
J.A. Ormrod	21	38	2	200*	981	27.25	1	4
J.A. Hopkins	23	41	5	124	978	27.16	1	4
N. Phillip	24	32	3	79	783	27.00	—	5
R.G.D. Willis	18	22	9	72	351	27.00	—	2
D.N. Patel	25	42	1	133	1104	26.92	1	4
Asif Din	24	34	2	102	855	26.71	1	2
D.J. Humphries	25	37	5	98	852	26.62	—	7
R.G. Lumb	20	33	1	81	844	26.37	—	7
P.W.G. Parker	25	43	9	106	896	26.35	1	5
P.A. Slocombe	13	23	1	78	579	26.31	—	6
P.M. Roebuck	23	40	3	90	958	25.89	—	10
P.W. Denning	14	22	1	91*	541	25.76	—	3
B.N. French	23	34	6	79	721	25.75	—	5
D.A. Graveney	23	30	11	55*	489	25.73	—	1
C.S. Cowdrey	22	35	4	72*	794	25.61	—	4
D.J. Capel	14	22	4	60*	460	25.55	—	1
P.A. Smith	10	16	1	68	383	25.53	—	2
E.E. Hemmings	20	25	8	127*	432	25.41	1	—
B. Wood	21	38	4	124*	851	25.02	1	2
A.L. Jones	22	38	2	88	900	25.00	—	6
C.J. Richards	25	38	9	117*	716	24.68	1	4
K.D. Smith	20	34	6	67	691	24.67	—	5
P.A. Todd	12	21	2	117*	461	24.26	2	1
D.J. Thomas	17	20	3	64	409	24.05	—	3
I.J. Gould	20	32	3	94	695	23.96	—	5
N.F.M. Popplewell	16	24	5	55	451	23.73	—	1
G.B. Stevenson	17	19	4	115*	356	23.73	1	—
K.I. Hodgson	8	10	1	50	213	23.66	—	1
J.N. Shepherd	22	34	9	67*	590	23.60	—	3
T. Davies	10	16	4	66*	283	23.58	—	2
P. Carrick	20	21	3	93	423	23.50	—	2
A.J. Wright	10	19	2	65	399	23.47	—	2
M.J. Weston	17	31	1	93	704	23.46	—	6
G.C. Holmes	7	10	1	68	210	23.33	—	1

(* not out)	M	I	NO	HS	Runs	Avge	100	50
A. Sidebottom	19	18	8	44*	233	23.30	—	—
C. Lethbridge	16	21	5	87*	369	23.06	—	1
D.R. Turner	15	21	1	96	459	22.95	—	2
J.P.C. Mills	9	17	0	98	389	22.88	—	3
A. Needham	13	20	6	134*	319	22.78	1	—
M.D. Marshall	22	31	3	116*	633	22.60	1	1
R.M. Ellison	7	11	3	46*	179	22.37	—	—
R.S. Luddington	10	14	1	65	290	22.30	—	2
G.D. Barlow	7	12	3	37*	199	22.11	—	—
P.J.W. Allott	18	15	5	41*	220	22.00	—	—
A. Kennedy	9	12	1	43	242	22.00	—	—
N.E.J. Pocock	22	30	2	164	616	22.00	1	3
S.A.B. Daniels	11	15	6	73	197	21.88	—	1
D.E. East	24	32	8	78	525	21.87	—	2
H.L. Alleyne	8	9	3	32	130	21.66	—	—
N.G. Cowley	23	28	1	104	584	21.62	1	2
G.W. Johnson	22	34	7	86	582	21.55	—	2
J.W. Southern	19	21	7	50*	300	21.42	—	1
V.J. Marks	23	33	5	71*	599	21.39	—	5
A.W. Lilley	10	14	1	67	276	21.23	—	1
R.E. Hayward	6	9	1	59	169	21.12	—	1
R.A. Cobb	22	37	1	64	760	21.11	—	4
G. Sharp	25	26	7	58*	401	21.10	—	1
P.R. Downton	25	25	2	65	483	21.00	—	2
I. Cockbain	14	25	1	98	492	20.50	—	2
S.J.G. Doggart	9	13	1	64	242	20.16	—	1
A. Hill	7	14	3	54	219	19.90	—	1
A.M.E. Roberts	13	20	3	47	338	19.88	—	—
M.A. Garnham	11	17	2	57	298	19.86	—	3
J.F. Steele	20	31	6	63	496	19.84	—	2
S. Oldham	21	18	10	35*	156	19.50	—	—
J.M. Rice	23	44	4	69	777	19.42	—	5
N. Gifford	14	15	7	31*	155	19.37	—	—
A.E. Warner	11	17	2	67	287	19.13	—	1
H.R. Moseley	18	19	13	24*	113	18.83	—	—
I.A. Greig	21	28	1	109	507	18.77	1	3
N.F. Williams	12	11	5	27*	112	18.66	—	—
J.D. Inchmore	15	19	3	68	294	18.37	—	2
B.W. Reidy	9	13	2	37	199	18.09	—	—
C.H. Dredge	20	26	8	54*	317	17.61	—	1
M.A. Fell	10	18	0	108	315	17.50	1	—
M.W. Stovold	5	9	0	52	154	17.11	—	1
E.J.O. Hemsley	16	24	1	49	393	17.08	—	—
N.G.B. Cook	25	25	8	37	284	16.70	—	—
R.E. East	21	23	2	58	344	16.38	—	1
J. Garner	10	11	5	40*	98	16.33	—	—
S.T. Clarke	22	25	0	52	408	16.32	—	1
T.J. Boon	9	14	1	90	210	16.15	—	1
C.J. Tunnicliffe	16	19	2	40	273	16.05	—	—
K. Saxelby	14	15	5	59*	160	16.00	—	1
R.K. Illingworth	11	16	4	47*	191	15.91	—	—
D.J.S. Taylor	17	26	5	67	334	15.90	—	2

(* not out)	M	I	NO	HS	Runs	Avge	100	50
P.R. Oliver	7	9	0	46	143	15.88	—	—
N.J.B. Illingworth	11	14	4	49	158	15.80	—	—
G.J. Parsons	24	32	7	51	392	15.68	—	1
I. Folley	17	15	4	36	165	15.00	—	—
A.J. Webster	8	10	5	25	75	15.00	—	—
E.W. Jones	15	21	3	65	268	14.88	—	2
M.K. Bore	8	8	5	23*	44	14.66	—	—
W.W. Daniel	19	15	9	21	88	14.66	—	—
C.P. Phillipson	16	22	3	64	274	14.42	—	1
Sarfraz Nawaz	14	9	1	26	115	14.37	—	—
R.J. Parks	25	30	5	44	350	14.00	—	—
C.M. Old	16	18	3	32	207	13.80	—	—
C. Penn	7	8	4	30	54	13.50	—	—
N.A. Mallender	24	17	8	42	121	13.44	—	—
R.P. Moulding	10	20	2	67	242	13.44	—	1
C. Maynard	17	20	3	40	227	13.35	—	—
B.J. Lloyd	25	32	8	48	318	13.25	—	—
J.G. Thomas	9	13	0	84	172	13.23	—	1
G.C. Small	25	29	5	57*	309	12.87	—	1
C.F.E. Goldie	9	9	0	31	115	12.77	—	—
C.E.H. Croft	12	12	3	20	109	12.11	—	—
C.E. Waller	23	27	12	50	181	12.06	—	1
R.W. Taylor	19	29	5	54	286	11.91	—	1
K.E. Cooper	23	26	5	38*	247	11.76	—	—
D.L. Underwood	22	22	11	30	129	11.72	—	—
F.D. Stephenson	8	10	1	63	105	11.66	—	1
S.R. Barwick	15	17	6	24	126	11.45	—	—
M.A. Nash	16	20	1	37	216	11.36	—	—
J.P. Agnew	10	12	1	56	122	11.09	—	1
T.M. Tremlett	16	22	3	48	209	11.00	—	—
P.G. Newman	19	22	4	39*	196	10.88	—	—
M.S. Scott	6	11	0	37	118	10.72	—	—
A.J. Pollock	7	8	2	19	63	10.50	—	—
A.C.S. Pigott	23	23	7	40	167	10.43	—	—

Bowling (Qualification: 10 wickets in 10 innings)

	O	M	R	W	Avge	Best	5w/I
R.J. Hadlee	403.5	122	889	61	14.57	7-25	4
M.D. Marshall	822	225	2108	134	15.73	8-71	12
M.W. Gatting	135	40	343	21	16.33	5-34	1
Imran Khan	484.4	134	1079	64	16.85	7-52	2
W.W. Daniel	469.4	107	1245	71	17.53	9-61	5
J. Garner	259.1	76	583	33	17.66	6-23	4
M. Hendrick	244.2	86	473	26	18.19	5-21	1
G.S. le Roux	467	116	1210	65	18.61	5-15	3
A.M.E. Roberts	428.2	114	1081	55	19.65	8-56	5
F.D. Stephenson	197.3	40	632	32	19.75	5-64	2
S.T. Clarke	659.3	162	1696	85	19.95	6-63	6
J.F. Steele	470.2	134	1075	52	20.67	5-4	3

	O	M	R	W	Avge	Best	5w/I
T.E. Jesty	288.1	89	750	35	21.42	6-71	1
K. Saxelby	291.4	68	799	37	21.59	4-18	—
M.K. Bore	279.1	104	609	28	21.75	6-134	1
N.G. Cowans	222.3	50	721	33	21.84	5-28	2
L.B. Taylor	582.1	153	1465	67	21.86	5-24	3
P.H. Edmonds	789	242	1768	80	22.10	8-80	3
D.L. Underwood	690.4	223	1751	78	22.44	7-79	5
N. Phillip	584.1	107	1842	82	22.46	6-50	5
W.N. Slack	81	18	225	10	22.50	3-17	—
S.J. Malone	150.5	35	505	22	22.95	7-55	2
I.T. Botham	491.4	114	1517	66	22.98	5-46	4
J.E. Emburey	764.5	198	1787	77	23.20	5-50	2
N.G.B. Cook	847.1	257	2093	90	23.25	7-63	6
J.G. Thomas	140	25	514	22	23.36	5-61	1
J.K. Lever	543.5	112	1683	72	23.37	6-48	5
D.R. Pringle	433.1	122	1087	46	23.63	6-33	2
K. St J.D. Emery	659	152	1969	83	23.72	6-51	3
J.W. Southern	439.5	118	1314	55	23.89	5-51	2
T.M. Tremlett	353.3	114	766	32	23.93	5-59	1
R.D. Jackman	674.1	196	1751	73	23.98	6-28	2
J.D. Inchmore	326.2	68	841	35	24.02	7-53	2
G.A. Gooch	230	72	541	22	24.59	7-14	1
A. Sidebottom	495.2	95	1538	62	24.80	6-31	3
E.E. Hemmings	666.1	198	1611	64	25.17	6-76	3
K.E. Cooper	685	191	1719	68	25.27	6-46	2
I.A. Greig	581.1	131	1723	68	25.33	5-46	2
D.P. Hughes	292.3	79	789	31	25.45	4-22	—
Sarfraz Nawaz	327.4	72	920	36	25.55	6-92	1
B.J. Griffiths	411.1	91	1200	46	26.08	5-71	2
J. Simmons	538.4	152	1284	49	26.20	5-57	2
S.J. O'Shaughnessy	209.2	34	710	27	26.29	4-66	—
D.S. Steele	755	245	1846	70	26.37	6-59	6
C.M. Old	458.2	125	1229	46	26.71	6-76	1
S.P. Hughes	218.5	30	723	27	26.77	4-28	—
P. Willey	670.1	223	1371	51	26.88	6-17	1
R.M. Ellison	153.5	35	433	16	27.06	3-12	—
P.J. Hacker	174.1	25	677	25	27.08	5-51	2
K.I. Hodgson	198.1	42	625	23	27.17	8-68	1
D.G. Moir	811.5	228	2076	76	27.31	6-63	4
R.E. East	490.5	141	1231	45	27.35	6-80	2
A.C.S. Pigott	477	92	1684	61	27.60	7-74	4
I. Folley	309	76	758	27	28.07	4-40	—
H.R. Moseley	320	68	985	35	28.14	5-40	2
D.A. Graveney	498.4	145	1242	44	28.22	7-37	1
R.G.D. Willis	446	89	1444	51	28.31	6-45	2
V.J. Marks	700.4	199	1951	68	28.69	7-51	4
G.R. Dilley	563.2	124	1839	64	28.73	6-71	4
P.M. Such	232.1	51	737	25	29.48	5-112	1
C.E. Waller	605	171	1627	55	29.58	7-67	1
D.L. Acfield	565.2	129	1332	45	29.60	4-35	—
M.W.W. Selvey	254.5	74	597	20	29.85	3-47	—
K.S. Mackintosh	304.2	59	1023	34	30.08	6-61	1

	O	M	R	W	Avge	Best	5w/I
P.I. Pocock	233	64	632	21	30.09	5-73	1
G. Miller	455.3	135	1058	35	30.22	8-70	1
A.M. Ferreira	243.3	49	789	26	30.34	5-109	1
C.E.H. Croft	304	60	1003	33	30.39	7-88	1
G.C. Small	589.1	106	1925	63	30.55	7-68	1
D.N. Patel	572.2	146	1531	50	30.62	7-46	2
S.R. Barwick	323.2	79	981	32	30.65	5-44	1
W.W. Davis	390.5	70	1296	42	30.85	7-101	1
J.W. Lloyds	468.3	96	1463	46	31.80	7-88	3
D. Surridge	561	159	1507	47	32.06	5-78	1
J.N. Shepherd	742.4	175	2026	63	32.15	6-75	2
S. Oldham	502.5	98	1544	48	32.16	7-78	2
R.C. Ontong	639.1	130	2059	64	32.17	6-50	1
P.J.W. Allott	453	128	1172	36	32.55	5-58	1
G.B. Stevenson	443.4	95	1474	45	32.75	5-72	1
C.J. Tunnicliffe	383.1	92	1213	37	32.78	5-73	1
G. Monkhouse	131.3	27	395	12	32.91	3-40	—
M.A. Nash	418.2	103	1276	38	33.57	5-35	1
C. Lethbridge	304.3	68	977	29	33.68	5-68	1
R.G. Williams	274	75	747	22	33.95	4-25	—
G.W. Johnson	330.4	84	892	26	34.30	5-36	2
A.J. Pollock	115.5	18	483	14	34.50	5-108	1
C.H. Dredge	446.5	109	1214	35	34.68	3-33	—
S.P. Perryman	430.1	111	1216	35	34.74	6-49	3
P. Carrick	568.5	144	1425	41	34.75	6-90	1
N. Gifford	500	157	1080	31	34.83	6-48	1
L.L. McFarlane	223.5	43	946	27	35.03	6-59	1
R.J. Doughty	149.1	19	533	15	35.53	6-43	1
N.F. Williams	236.4	33	819	23	35.60	4-38	—
D.J. Thomas	426.4	109	1284	36	35.66	4-39	2
S. Turner	453	117	1080	30	36.00	4-53	—
A.P. Pridgeon	463	103	1184	32	37.00	4-39	—
N.A. Mallender	562.2	130	1860	50	37.20	7-41	3
A.E. Warner	202.1	34	707	19	37.21	4-73	—
N.G. Cowley	310.1	86	895	24	37.29	6-48	1
H.L. Alleyne	207.3	44	599	16	37.43	4-92	—
C.S. Cowdrey	166.3	39	533	14	38.07	3-45	—
D. Lloyd	297.2	68	801	21	38.14	4-36	—
K.B.S. Jarvis	636	145	2078	54	38.48	5-94	1
G.J. Parsons	518.1	89	1931	50	38.62	5-25	1
B.J. Lloyd	687.2	138	2201	55	40.01	5-58	2
M.R. Davis	145	19	481	12	40.08	3-36	—
N.J.B. Illingworth	164.1	29	565	14	40.35	5-89	1
A.I. Kallicharran	154.2	21	578	14	41.28	3-32	—
P.G. Newman	458.3	73	1661	40	41.52	4-59	—
S.A.B. Daniels	223.2	37	836	20	41.80	3-49	—
Kapil Dev	395.2	77	1214	29	41.86	5-39	2
I.V.A. Richards	265.3	75	671	16	41.93	3-6	—
T.M. Lamb	308.5	77	850	20	42.50	5-37	1
J.P. Agnew	203.5	27	816	19	42.94	4-55	—
J.H. Childs	656.3	201	1681	38	44.23	5-112	1
R.K. Illingworth	260.4	59	811	18	45.05	4-85	—

	O	M	R	W	Avge	Best	5w/I
B.W. Reidy	137	32	457	10	45.70	3-33	—
C.J.C. Rowe	265.2	57	898	19	47.26	3-67	—
J. Cumbes	349.1	71	993	21	47.28	4-47	—
A.J. Webster	202.1	36	716	15	47.73	5-87	1
P. Bainbridge	301	77	915	19	48.15	6-59	1
S.P. Sutcliffe	554.4	114	1799	37	48.62	5-151	1
R.D.V. Knight	266.2	61	762	15	50.80	3-34	—
A. Needham	357	72	1167	22	53.04	5-91	1
P.A. Smith	136	21	536	10	53.60	2-12	—
E.A. Baptiste	186.4	45	671	12	55.91	3-41	—
Asif Din	284.1	60	1128	20	56.40	5-100	1
J. Abrahams	316.1	61	921	16	57.56	2-19	—
R.W.M. Palmer	219.4	34	849	14	60.64	4-96	—
S.P. Ridge	240.1	32	829	13	63.76	4-128	—
J.R.T. Barclay	230.2	58	702	11	63.81	3-44	—
B. Wood	231.2	54	690	10	69.00	2-0	—

The following bowlers took 10 wickets but bowled in fewer than 10 innings:

	O	M	R	W	Avge	Best	5w/I
K.R. Pont	62	11	158	10	15.80	5-17	1
S.J. Dennis	95	16	365	12	30.41	5-42	1
N.A. Foster	125	29	425	12	35.41	3-32	—
I.J. Curtis	214.4	45	659	15	43.93	5-140	1
T.J. Taylor	165	27	541	10	54.10	5-118	1

Fielding Statistics

Wicket-keepers

76 R.J. Parks (70ct, 6st)
74 D.E. East (65ct, 9st)
64 B.N. French (61ct, 3st)
61 D.L. Bairstow (57ct, 4st)
61 P.R. Downton (51ct, 10st)
55 C.J. Richards (52ct, 3st)
55 G. Sharp (48ct, 7st)
54 A.P.E. Knott (46ct, 8st)
52 R.W. Taylor (48ct, 4st)
52 R.W. Tolchard (45ct, 7st)
50 G.W. Humpage (49ct, 1st)
48 I.J. Gould (43ct, 5st)
46 D.J. Humphries (41ct, 5st)
45 A.J. Brassington (37ct, 8st)
45 D.J.S. Taylor (41ct, 4st)
41 E.W. Jones (37ct, 4st)
25 C. Maynard (20ct, 5st)
23 C.F.E. Goldie (19ct, 4st)
21 T. Davies (20ct, 1st)

Tolchard's total includes
10 catches taken as a fielder.

Fieldsmen

30 J.W. Lloyds
28 M.W. Gatting
26 G. Cook
26 C.S. Cowdrey
26 J.M. Rice
26 J.F. Steele
25 J.R.T. Barclay
25 C.E.B. Rice
25 G.A. Gooch
24 J. Abrahams
24 Javed Miandad
24 D.G. Moir
24 C.P. Phillipson
24 A.W. Stovold
23 C.G. Greenidge
21 C.W.J. Athey
21 R.O. Butcher
21 R.E. East
21 P.W.G. Parker
21 W.N. Slack
21 B. Wood
20 N.G.B. Cook

20 G.W. Johnson
20 D.N. Patel
20 N.E.J. Pocock
20 C.T. Radley

Benson & Hedges Cup

Somerset became the first county to win the 11-year-old Benson and Hedges Cup competition twice in succession, though, interestingly, they were heavily beaten by Middlesex in a group tie. Middlesex, who won all their group matches, fell in the quarter-finals to Lancashire — their first defeat of the season in any competition. Nottinghamshire, the only other 100 per cent side in the groups, were beaten finalists — the nearest that they had ever come to winning any of the one-day competitions.

In the group matches, results tended to reflect form in the County Championship. The strongest group was 'C', containing three former champions in Kent, Essex, and Surrey, besides Sussex, who had started the season on a buoyant note, and Hampshire, whose past one-day record belied their potential. Essex were collectively out of form in the early weeks of the season and did not really come into the race. Hampshire again disappointed, failing to win a single match. The crucial tie in the group proved to be Surrey v Sussex, at the Oval, which was spread over three days. Sussex showed great resilience in winning it from an impossible position of 106 for 6 in reply to Surrey's 231. Kent and Sussex were level on points at the top of the group, as were Derbyshire and Leicestershire, in Group 'A'.

The one blot on Leicestershire's copybook was a defeat in their last match at the hands of Minor Counties, at Wellington. Batting second, Leicestershire were shot out for 56, the lowest-ever score in the history of the competition. Equally embarrassing was the margin of defeat — 131 runs. 'It was a dreadful wicket, but it played no worse than when Minor Counties batted on it', said Roger Tolchard.

Middlesex were never seriously challenged in any of their group matches — not even by Somerset, who suffered from Viv Richards's indifferent form and, more so, from the absence through injury of Joel Garner. Somerset were fully extended by Glamorgan in a match they could not afford to lose.

When it came to the quarter-finals, Leicestershire had cause to regret their loss to the Minor Counties, which had deprived them of a match at home. Instead, they played Notts on a dubious Trent Bridge pitch, and lost by a mere 2 runs. Somerset had Garner back for the quarter-finals, and he played a leading part in the last-over defeat of Kent, despite a valiant century by Taylor and Cowdrey's 40. A slow Derby pitch produced a low-scoring match between Derbyshire and Sussex. But the finish was exciting, Sussex winning in the penultimate over. Lancashire recaptured their old mastery at one-day cricket to score a comfortable win over Middlesex at Lord's.

Against Notts, in the semi-finals, Lancashire's bowlers performed with great credit, and Lancashire seemed to be well set to win when Notts, replying to their 182, were 116 for 6 with only 11 overs remaining. But Hadlee was allowed an early escape and he, with a belligerent 55 not out, tilted the balance. Without Imran Khan, who, by then, had taken up his duties as captain of the touring Pakistanis, and Parker, who was injured, Sussex were no match for Somerset in the other semi-final, which was decided before tea.

Somerset had no more difficulty beating Notts in the most one-sided final ever. Notts' main bowlers were all unfit. But that was hardly the deciding factor. The issue was decided before Notts took the field to defend a total of 130. Clearly, they were undermined by the nerves of first-time Lord's finalists.

Zonal Results

Group A	P	W	L	Pts
DERBYSHIRE	4	3	1	6
LEICESTERSHIRE	4	3	1	6
Worcestershire	4	2	2	4
Minor Counties	4	1	3	2
Yorkshire	4	1	3	2

Group B	P	W	L	Pts
NOTTINGHAMSHIRE	4	4	0	8
LANCASHIRE	4	3	1	6
Warwickshire	4	2	2	4
Northamptonshire	4	1	3	2
Scotland	4	0	4	0

Group C	P	W	L	Pts
KENT	4	3	1	6
SUSSEX	4	3	1	6
Essex	4	2	2	4
Surrey	4	2	2	4
Hampshire	4	0	4	0

Group D	P	W	L	Pts
MIDDLESEX	4	4	0	8
SOMERSET	4	3	1	6
Gloucestershire	4	2	2	4
Glamorgan	4	1	3	2
Combined Universities	4	0	4	0

Final Rounds

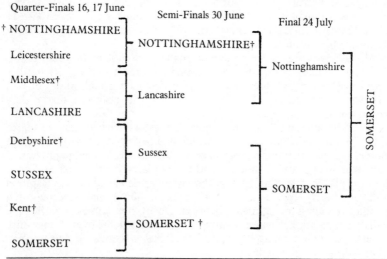

Benson & Hedges Cup Winners

1972	Leicestershire	1978	Kent
1973	Kent	1979	Essex
1974	Surrey	1980	Northamptonshire
1975	Leicestershire	1981	Somerset
1976	Kent	1982	Somerset
1977	Gloucestershire		

Nottinghamshire v Somerset 1982 Benson & Hedges Cup Final
Somerset won by 9 wickets
Played at Lord's, July 24
Toss: Somerset. Umpires: D.J. Constant and D.G.L. Evans
Gold Award: V.J. Marks

Nottinghamshire		Runs	Mins	Balls	6s	4s
P.A. Todd	*b* Garner	2	9	11	—	—
R.T. Robinson	*c* Richards *b* Dredge	13	65	51	—	—
D.W. Randall	*b* Marks	19	58	42	—	3
B. Hassan	*c* Taylor *b* Dredge	26	89	60	—	2
*C.E.B. Rice	*b* Marks	27	50	51	1	3
J.D. Birch	*b* Moseley	7	28	24	—	—
R.J. Hadlee	*b* Garner	11	27	17	—	1
†B.N. French	*c* Taylor *b* Botham	8	39	32	—	—
E.E. Hemmings	*b* Botham	1	4	8	—	—
K.E. Cooper	*b* Garner	3	11	6	—	—
M. Hendrick	*not out*	0	1	—	—	—
Extras	(*lb* 5, *w* 7, *nb* 1)	13				
Total	(50.1 overs; 199 minutes)	**130**				

Somerset		Runs	Mins	Balls	6s	4s
P.W. Denning	*c* French *b* Hendrick	22	29	36	—	3
P.M. Roebuck	*not out*	53	115	108	—	7
I.V.A. Richards	*not out*	51	84	55	—	8
*B.C. Rose						
I.T. Botham						
V.J. Marks						
N.F.M. Popplewell	*did not bat*					
†D.J.S. Taylor						
J. Garner						
C.H. Dredge						
H.R. Moseley						
Extras	(*lb* 5, *w* 1)	6				
Total	(33.1 overs; 115 minutes)	**132**				

Somerset	O	M	R	W
Garner	8.1	1	13	3
Botham	9	3	19	2
Dredge	11	2	35	2
Moseley	11	2	26	1
Marks	11	4	24	2

Nottinghamshire	O	M	R	W
Hadlee	9	0	37	0
Hendrick	8	1	26	1
Cooper	5.1	0	41	0
Rice	6	2	11	0
Hemmings	5	0	11	0

Fall of Wickets

Wkt	N	S
1st	3	27
2nd	40	—
3rd	40	—
4th	86	—
5th	102	—
6th	106	—
7th	122	—
8th	123	—
9th	130	—
10th	130	—

* Captain   † Wicket-keeper

NatWest Bank Trophy

The most lasting memory of the 1982 NatWest Bank Trophy competition, won by Surrey, will be the controversy over the 10.00 a.m. start to all matches from the quarter-final stage onwards. Starting so early on dewy August mornings was found to give the side winning the toss a disproportionate advantage. Indeed, of the seven matches that started at 10 o'clock, six were won by counties favoured by the coin, and there was only one instance of a side that was made to bat first emerging the winner.

The five Minor Counties and Ireland were all devoured in the opening round. The second round coincided with a spell of unfriendly weather and took three days to complete. Mainly thanks to the efforts of their two overseas batsmen, Wright and Kirsten, who made a brilliant century, Derbyshire, the holders, raised a handsome total of 239. But they lacked the bowling to contain Greenidge, and went down to Hampshire. Northamptonshire, runners-up in 1981, included Kapil Dev for the first time in the season, but could not hold off Surrey. At Chelmsford, Essex accounted for Kent more easily than expected.

The most remarkable second-round win was Yorkshire's, at Headingley, over Worcestershire. A masterly century by Turner led to Worcestershire's acquiring an imposing total of 286. When bad weather ended the first day's play, Yorkshire had lost 4 wickets (all to Inchmore) for 40 runs. However, Bairstow, one of the most redoubtable fighters of lost causes, played a dazzling innings of 92, supported by Hartley and Old, and took Yorkshire within 48 runs of their objective. Stevenson, another robust hitter, then completed the task.

Norman Cowans, newly risen to fame, prevented Lancashire from repeating their Benson & Hedges success over Middlesex, at Lord's. Middlesex won in a photo-finish. The remaining matches were all decided by wide margins.

Quarter-finals day started off cloudy at Headingley and misty at Southampton, where the pitch retained considerable moisture. The plight of Essex and Hampshire when they lost the toss and were sent in brought into sharp focus the disadvantage of a 10 o'clock start. Against Yorkshire, Essex were 51 for 9 before the cavalry, in the form of Turner and Ray East, arrived to provide token resistance. Hampshire's innings against Surrey was laid waste by Jackman.

At Bristol, Middlesex, who had preferred to bat first against Gloucestershire, scraped home by 3 runs, ending a fine innings by Broad (98) in the nick of time. An epic innings of 141 by Kallicharran achieved an unlikely win for Warwickshire, who, in aiming for a target of 260 against Somerset, at Taunton, had lost 2 wickets scoring the first 30.

Kallicharran failed to score in the semi-final, at Edgbaston, against Yorkshire. But Warwickshire prevailed through a fine century by David Smith. The other semi-final, at the Oval, broke the pattern of victory accompanying success with the toss. The option lay with Middlesex, but batting second in easier conditions was no help. Sylvester Clarke was too fast and hostile for the top order, and Jackman rammed home the advantage.

So to the final. Too much had been written and spoken about the perils of batting first for Warwickshire not to perform apprehensively when Surrey sent them in. They were soon 74 for 8. In Surrey's reply, Butcher played a polished innings of 86, and another Lord's final came to an early and disappointing end.

Gillette Cup Winners

1963	Sussex	1969	Yorkshire	1975	Lancashire
1964	Sussex	1970	Lancashire	1976	Northamptonshire
1965	Yorkshire	1971	Lancashire	1977	Middlesex
1966	Warwickshire	1972	Lancashire	1978	Sussex
1967	Kent	1973	Gloucestershire	1979	Somerset
1968	Warwickshire	1974	Kent	1980	Middlesex

NatWest Bank Trophy Winners

1981	Derbyshire	1982	Surrey

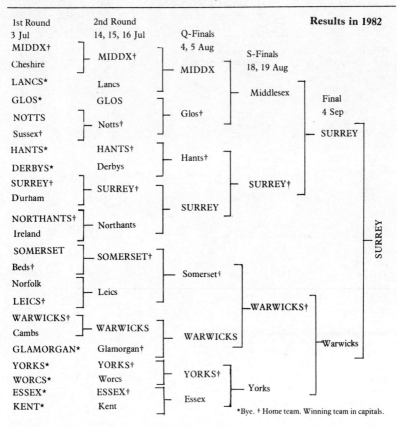

Surrey v Warwickshire 1982 NatWest Bank Trophy Final
Surrey won by 9 wickets
Played at Lord's, September 4
Toss: Surrey. Umpires: H.D. Bird and B.J. Meyer
Man of the Match: D.J. Thomas

Warwickshire		Runs	Min.	Balls	6s	4s
T.A. Lloyd	*lbw b* Jackman	2	12	13	—	—
K.D. Smith	*hit wkt b* Thomas	12	54	34	—	2
A.I. Kallicharran	*c* Howarth *b* Knight	19	71	50	—	2
D.L. Amiss	*b* Thomas	0	5	3	—	—
†G.W. Humpage	*c* Richards *b* Thomas	0	8	9	—	—
P.R. Oliver	*run out* (Butcher/Richards)	2	4	5	—	—
Asif Din	*lbw b* Jackman	45	128	111	—	6
A.M. Ferreira	*lbw b* Clarke	8	13	11	—	1
C. Lethbridge	*c* Howarth *b* Knight	4	15	15	—	—
G.C. Small	*c* Richards *b* Clarke	33	113	88	—	2
*R.G.D. Willis	*not out*	8	23	12	—	—
Extras	(*b* 8, *lb* 11, *nb* 6)	25				
Total	(57.2 overs; 232 minutes)	**158**				

Surrey		Runs	Min.	Balls	6s	4s
A.R. Butcher	*not out*	86	130	128	—	12
G.P. Howarth	*c* Oliver *b* Lethbridge	31	75	49	—	2
D.M. Smith	*not out*	28	53	40	—	3
*R.D.V. Knight						
M.A. Lynch						
†C.J. Richards						
D.J. Thomas	*did not bat*					
G. Monkhouse						
S.T. Clarke						
R.D. Jackman						
K.S. Mackintosh						
Extras	(*lb* 4, *nb* 10)	14				
Total	(33.4 overs; 130 minutes)	**159-1**				

Surrey	O	M	R	W
Clarke	11.2	5	17	2
Jackman	12	2	27	2
Thomas	11	1	26	3
Monkhouse	8	0	36	0
Knight	12	3	14	2
Mackintosh	3	0	13	0

Warwickshire	O	M	R	W
Willis	7	0	23	0
Small	8	0	60	0
Ferreira	6	0	16	0
Lethbridge	6	1	23	1
Kallicharran	6.4	1	23	0

Fall of Wickets

Wkt	Wa	Sy
1st	3	80
2nd	32	—
3rd	42	—
4th	48	—
5th	51	—
6th	52	—
7th	67	—
8th	74	—
9th	136	—
10th	158	—

* Captain   † Wicket-keeper

John Player League

Sussex, who were left holding the wooden spoon for the first two years of the competition and whose best previous standing was fourth, in 1977, became John Player League champions for the first time.

It was paradoxical that Sussex, the early masters of overs-limit cricket, should have had to wait 14 seasons to win the league. In this time, they had five times finished in the lower half of the table. When at last Sussex laid the bogey, they won in the grand manner, accumulating a record 58 points from 14 wins. Sussex, who lost just once, to Worcester in mid-June, clinched the issue with two matches to spare. The decisive win was over their nearest rivals, Middlesex, who headed the table for a large part of the season. It was a testimony to Sussex's strength in depth that they kept their impetus after losing the services of Imran Khan to the Pakistan tourists before the campaign had gone half-way.

A substantial gap separated the champions and Middlesex, who also left a lot of daylight between themselves and Leicestershire in third place. Nevertheless, the competition was strongly contested. Until mid-August, no less than nine counties had at least a mathematical chance of winning. For all their consistency, Sussex might have put themselves under a lot of pressure had they not got home on the day they did, for their next match was rained off.

Middlesex also had bad luck with the weather in one match, but that was early in the season when they had plenty of scope to recoup. Middlesex, in fact, remained undefeated until they had played half their matches. Then they lost three games in a row, the second of them to Glamorgan who, until then, had just one win. Glamorgan beat the leaders quite easily, as did Derbyshire, to start the rot.

Essex, very worthy champions in 1981, took so long to settle that they lost their first four matches, all but one of them by some distance. Resilient as ever, though, they won the next eight in a row and soared from bottom to a challenging sixth place. Lowly Gloucestershire ended this run, and before Essex knotted up the broken ends, they were beaten by Warwickshire, the bottom team, in one of the most remarkable matches in the history of the competition.

In this match, no less than five records were broken. So hectic were the events leading to a gripping climax that the match seemed almost fictional. Essex scored 299 for 4, their innings ending in a rousing crescendo as McEwan (156 not out) took 24 runs from the final over. But they still could not win. After a superb start of 135, Warwickshire were powered ahead by a fourth-wicket partnership between Humpage and Asif Din which added 94 in a mere 9 overs, taking them well past the highest score ever made by a side batting second.

It seems incredible that Warwickshire, a side with such batting potential, could win no more than three times in 1982, and sink, in the span of two seasons, from championship to bottom place.

Final Table	P	W	L	T	NR	Pts	6s	4w
1 SUSSEX (5)	16	14	1	0	1	58	50	4
2 Middlesex (15)	16	11	4	0	1	46	22	6
3 Leicestershire (14)	16	9	6	0	1	38	17	6
4 Kent (7)	16	9	7	0	0	36	17	3
5 Essex (1)	16	9	7	0	0	36	43	2
Hampshire (6)	16	8	6	2	0	36	29	3
Nottinghamshire (10)	16	8	6	1	1	36	34	2
8 Northamptonshire (17)	16	8	7	0	1	34	54	2
9 Somerset (2)	16	8	8	0	0	32	54	5
10 Glamorgan (10)	16	6	7	0	3	30	14	2
Lancashire (10)	16	6	7	1	2	30	28	4
12 Derbyshire (4)	16	6	9	0	1	26	26	3
Surrey (7)	16	6	9	1	0	26	44	3
14 Gloucestershire (16)	16	5	9	0	2	24	9	1
15 Worcestershire (10)	16	5	10	0	1	22	36	2
16 Yorkshire (7)	16	3	10	1	2	18	38	1
17 Warwickshire (3)	16	3	11	0	2	16	26	1

Kent gained fourth place over Essex by achieving more away wins (applicable to first four places only).

1981 final positions are shown in brackets.

Winners

1969	Lancashire	1974	Leicestershire	1979	Somerset
1970	Lancashire	1975	Hampshire	1980	Warwickshire
1971	Worcestershire	1976	Kent	1981	Essex
1972	Kent	1977	Leicestershire	1982	Sussex
1973	Kent	1978	Hampshire		

1982 Awards and Distribution of Prize Money

£12,000 and League Trophy to champions — SUSSEX

£5,500 to runners-up — Middlesex

£2,500 to third-placing — Leicestershire

£1,300 to fourth-placing — Kent

£250 to winner of each match (shared in event of 'no results' and ties)

£350 to the batsman hitting most sixes in the season:

W. Larkins (Northamptonshire) — 17

£350 to the bowler taking four or more wickets most times in the season:

G.J. Parsons (Leicestershire) — 3

£250 to the batsman scoring the fastest 50 in a match televised on BBC2:

M.W. Gatting (Middlesex) — 38 balls v Somerset at Weston-super-Mare on August 8.

Notable Records

The match between Essex and Warwicks at Colchester produced a record aggregate of 600 runs, with Warwicks establishing a record total for any side batting second, 301-6 off 39.3 overs. A.M. Ferreira (Warwicks) conceded a record 85 runs in his 8 overs.

J.A. Ormrod (92*) and D.N. Patel (125) shared a 1st-wicket partnership of 224 for Worcs v Hants at Southampton to set a new JPL record for *any* wicket.

D.M. Smith (Surrey) became the first batsman to be dismissed 'Handled the Ball' in this competition, against Hampshire at The Oval.

A total of 541 sixes eclipsed the previous record of 438 in 1970, while the 54 struck by Northants and Somerset broke Kent's record of 53 in 1970.

Minor Counties and 2nd XI

Minor Counties Championship 1982 — Final Table

			P	W	L	D	NR	Points	Avge
1	OXFORDSHIRE (14)	NW	10	4	2†	4	—	56	5.60
2	Wiltshire (7)	NW	10	4	4*‡	2	—	51	5.10
3	Dorset (20)	NW	10	4	1	4	1	48	4.80
4	Berkshire (14)	NW	10	3	4†‡	3	—	47	4.70
	Hertfordshire (17)	NW	10	3	—	6	1	47	4.70
6	Suffolk (10)	NW	10	3	2†	5	—	46	4.60
7	Cambridgeshire (3)	NW	10	3	2*	5	—	44	4.40
8	Somerset II (4)		8	2	—	5	1	31	3.87
9	Durham (1)	NW	10	1	1*	8	—	37	3.70
10	Lincolnshire (14)	NW	8	2	2	4	—	26	3.25
11	Shropshire (7)	NW	10	1	—	7	2	31	3.10
12	Lancashire II (18)		8	1	—	4	3	24	3.00
13	Devon (21)	NW	10	2	3	3	2	29	2.90
	Norfolk (2)	NW	10	1	2*	6	1	29	2.90
15	Cheshire (6)	NW	12	2	1	8	1	34	2.83
16	Staffordshire (12)		10	1	—	7	2	25	2.50
17	Bedfordshire (5)		10	1	3*	6	—	23	2.30
18	Northumberland (13)		12	—	2*	7	3	23	1.91
19	Buckinghamshire (11)		12	1	5*	6	—	19	1.58
20	Cornwall (19)		10	—	3	5	2	13	1.30
21	Cumberland (9)		8	—	2	5	1	10	1.25

1981 final positions are shown in brackets. * Signifies first innings lead in one match lost. † Signifies first innings lead in two matches lost. ‡ Signifies tie on first innings in one match lost. NW Signifies qualified for NatWest Bank Trophy in 1983 (expanded to accommodate 13 minor counties instead of 5. No Challenge Match was held in 1982 as Oxfordshire and Wiltshire had already met in the competition. Oxfordshire gained their third title since this Championship was inaugurated in 1895, the others being in 1929 and 1974.

Second XI Championship 1982 — Final Table

		P	W	L	D	Bonus Points Batting	Bowling	Total Points	Avge
1	WORCESTERSHIRE (14)	15	6	1	8	36	52	184	12.2
2	Lancashire (16)	14	5	1	8	34	46	160	11.4
3	Kent (7)	16	6	3	7	39	35	170	10.6
4	Middlesex (3)	13	4	2	7	28	33	125	9.6
5	Hampshire (1)	13	3	1	9	38	39	125	9.6
6	Warwickshire (8)	18	5	5	8	34	53	167	9.2
7	Surrey (2)	14	4	2	8	25	39	128	9.1
8	Gloucestershire (13)	11	2	3	6	31	38	101	9.1
9	Derbyshire (4)	13	3	2	8	31	37	116	8.9
10	Leicestershire (10)	10	1	2	7	33	33	82	8.2
11	Nottinghamshire (9)	18	3	6	9	49	48	145	8.0
12	Essex (5)	12	2	4	6	27	30	89	7.4
13	Northamptonshire (17)	13	2	2	9	30	30	92	7.0
14	Yorkshire (11)	16	2	3	11	37	42	111	6.9
	Somerset (6)	12	2	4	6	18	30	80	6.6
16	Sussex (12)	13	1	6	6	27	34	77	5.9
17	Glamorgan (15)	13	0	4	9	23	40	63	4.8

1981 final positions are shown in brackets. The following matches were abandoned without a ball being bowled: 23, 24, 25 June — Middlesex v Leicestershire, Nottinghamshire v Warwickshire, Worcestershire v Glamorgan. Worcestershire gained their third title since this championship was inaugurated in 1959, the others being in 1962 and 1963.

Village and Club Cricket

The last weekend of August was gloriously sunny at Lord's, and good, if vociferously partisan, crowds enjoyed the finals of the two national club championships — the John Haig Trophy for senior sides and the Samuel Whitbread Village event. Experience of 'headquarters' on big-match days proved a valuable asset, and both 1981 victors won for the second successive year. In all, more than 1,200 clubs entered the competitions.

In the John Haig Trophy, Scarborough recorded their fourth victory since 1976, although both they and Finchley, the Middlesex 'local' side, suffered self-inflicted wounds with 8 of the 15 batsmen dismissed falling to run-outs. William Younger, the brewers, have taken over the sponsorship of the competition, which will continue to be organized by the National Cricket Association.

John Haig Trophy (45 overs). Lord's, 28 August; Scarborough won toss.
Scarborough: 150-7 (W.L. Pincher 61 not, A.J. Moor 30, D. Byas 23; M.E. Milton 2-20, J.S. Alldis 2-53); *Finchley:* 146-8 (T. Selwood 49, Milton 39; Pincher 2-16). *Scarborough won by 4 runs.*

The Sunday 40-overs Village final for the Samuel Whitbread Challenge Trophy was a triumph of captaincy. It was won by St Fagans from Cardiff, who beat Collingham (Notts) by 6 wickets and with 2.2 overs in hand. Ricky Needham, solicitor and a former captain of Harrow School XI, put the opposition in, and by judicious field placings, and his personal bag of 3 wickets for 21 runs off 9 overs, held Collingham to 148 for 9.

St Fagans paced their reply skilfully, and while Painter — captain in 1981 — held one end steady, Needham hit out strongly, so that Stevens, the self-acknowledged slogger of the side, could come to the crease to crash 16 runs from 5 deliveries to gain victory in the 38th over. This competition, since its inception in 1972 (by John Haig), has been organized by *The Cricketer*.

Samuel Whitbread Village Championship (40 overs). Lord's, 29 August; St Fagans won toss.
Collingham: 148-9 (G. Driscoll 63 not, R. England 42, J. Kirkham 25; P.J. Needham 3-21, S. Robertson 2-19); *St Fagans* (37.4 overs): 149-4 (D. Mason 43, D. Painter 39 not, P.J. Needham 21). *St Fagans won by 6 wickets.*

At the end of each final, G.H.G. Doggart, President of MCC, presented the trophies. Scarborough received £800 towards club funds and St Fagans £500, the runners-up getting £450 and £250, respectively.

(Statistics by John Fogg)

Schools Cricket

Every season produces its young stars, and if there were such a distinction as *Wisden's* Five Cricketers of the Year at school level, the choice for 1982 might well include two sons of former first-class batsmen, Graham Cowdrey and Neil Lenham. Cowdrey, in his fifth and last year in the Tonbridge XI, scored 691 runs, took 29 wickets, and was a commanding figure in every department. Lenham, still only 16, had the remarkable aggregate of 1,073 runs (average 76.6) at Brighton.

These two schools were among the most successful in England. Tonbridge, unbeaten in all matches, won eight and drew two against schools: while Brighton began with eight consecutive victories and gained 12 in all out of 16 matches.

Lancing, the only school to overcome Brighton, set a new record by winning 12 games. Other schools to produce outstanding figures were Felsted (W10, D4, L1), King's, Taunton (W9, D5, L1), and three undefeated teams, Bablake, Coventry (W11, D6), Merchant Taylors', Northwood (W11, D3), and Sutton Valence (W12, D6).

In the North, St Peter's, York, had a fine season, winning six and drawing five out of 11 matches completed against schools. Durham's figures (W10, D6, L1) were by far their best ever.

Among the famous names, Eton were unbeaten in all matches, with seven wins and seven draws. Malvern's four victories in a season without defeat were all against schools, and they possessed a potent weapon in the exceptional pace of a 17-year-old Barbadian, Ricardo Ellcock, who took 55 wickets. Harrow did not lose to another school, but drew seven of their eight games against their rivals.

The MCC Schools XI selected after the trials to play the National Association of Young Cricketers was:

M. Gouldstone (Braintree College)
W.J.P. Matthews (Bablake)
*H. Morris (Blundell's)
N.H. Fairbrother (Oughtrington HS, Lymm)
G.R. Cowdrey (Tonbridge)
G.D. Rose (Northumberland Park HS, Tottenham)
R.C. Talbot (Richard Huish College, Taunton)
A. Golding (Colchester RGS)
†P. Gill (Grange School, Oldham)
R.A. Pick (High Pavement Sixth Form Coll., Nottingham)
R.M. Ellcock (Malvern)

ICC Trophy

It is easy, when speaking of international cricket these days, to think only of the Test-playing nations and forget just how broadly international the game is. Such forgetfulness was, however, hard to excuse last summer, when all but two of the International Cricket Conference's 18 associate members assembled in England for the 'mini World Cup.' The absentees were Argentina and Denmark.

Zimbabwe, recently admitted to membership after splitting from South African cricket, earned the prize of a place in the 1983 World Cup by defeating Bermuda by five wickets at Leicestershire's Grace Road ground in the final. The two participants had been regarded as the favourites from the start.

Bermuda scored an enterprising 231-8 in 60 overs with useful contributions from Gladstone Brown, Colin Blades, and Steven Lightbourne, all of them falling when half-centuries seemed within their reach. Duncan Fletcher's brisk medium-pace earned him 3-34, and Bermuda suffered a severe blow early in the Zimbabwe innings when their opening bowler King, once rated a likely West Indian Test player, limped off with a leg injury.

Thereafter Zimbabwe's progress was relatively serene, with Andy Pycroft earning the Man of the Match award for a fluent 82 and Hodgson lending aggressive support with an unbeaten 57.

Glorious sunshine made the final a colourful affair, but the earlier stages of the competition had been treated less kindly by the weather, 22 of the 56 group games being abandoned, 15 of them without a ball being bowled. The first ICC Trophy competition in 1979 had been almost equally disrupted by the weather.

Nor was the competition, played on club grounds throughout the Midlands, spared controversy. Israel were left with only half a team when their manager and several players went home early in protest. 'A series of incidents before and during the tour opened a rift between the management and several of the senior players,' said Geoffrey Davis, Israel's UK representative to the ICC.

Papua New Guinea won the third-place play-off against the other semi-finalists Bangladesh. As winners, Zimbabwe qualified for the chance to test their claims for full Test status against the major cricketing nations in next summer's World Cup.

International Cricket Conference Trophy 1982
Group One — Final Table

	P	W	L	NR	Points
ZIMBABWE	7	5	—	2	24
PAPUA NEW GUINEA	7	4	2	1	18
Canada	7	3	1	3	18
Kenya	7	3	2	2	16
Hong Kong	7	2	3	2	12
United States	7	1	2	4	8
Gibraltar	7	—	3	4	8
Israel	7	—	5	2	4

Papua New Guinea gained second place by winning more matches than Canada.

Group Two — Final Table

	P	W	L	NR	Points
BERMUDA	7	6	—	1	26
BANGLADESH	7	4	1	2	20
Holland	7	3	1	3	18
Singapore	7	1	2	4	12
Fiji	7	1	3	3	10
East Africa	7	1	3	3	10
West Africa	7	—	2	5	10
Malaysia	7	—	4	3	6

Semi-Finals
7 July. ZIMBABWE beat BANGLADESH by 8 wickets at West Bromwich Dartmouth. Bangladesh 124 (55.2 overs) (K.M. Curran 4-28); Zimbabwe 126-2 (29.5 overs) (J.G. Heron 63★).
7 July. BERMUDA beat PAPUA NEW GUINEA by 6 wickets at Mitchell & Butler's. Papua New Guinea 153 (39.1 overs) (Vavine Pala 72); Bermuda 155-4 (42.4 overs) (C.F. Blades 69★).

Play-off for Third Place
9 July. PAPUA NEW GUINEA beat BANGLADESH by 3 wickets at Bournville. Bangladesh 224 (57.5 overs) (Yousuf Rahman 115, Nazem Shirazi 52; La'a Aukopi 5-14); Papua New Guinea 225-7 (57 overs) (W. Maha 60).

Final
Scorecard is on page 192.

Bermuda v Zimbabwe ICC Trophy Final
Zimbabwe won by 5 wickets
Played at Grace Road, Leicester, July 10
Toss: Zimbabwe.
Man of the Match: A.J. Pycroft

Bermuda

G. Brown	c Traicos b Rawson	48
W. Reid	b Hogg	13
S. Lightbourne	b Fletcher	32
N.A. Gibbons	b Fletcher	1
*C. Blades	c Curran b Rawson	45
E.G. James	run out (Heron)	8
J. Tucker	lbw b Hogg	18
†A. Douglas	not out	36
J.L.O. Bailey	c Hough b Fletcher	4
A. King	not out	5
W.H. Trott	did not bat	
Extras	(b 1, lb 15, w 1, nb 4)	21
Total	(60 overs; 211 minutes)	**231-8**

Zimbabwe

†D.L. Houghton	lbw b Trott	8
J.G. Heron	c and b Gibbons	9
K.M. Curran	lbw b Blades	30
A.J. Pycroft	c Lightbourne b Gibbons	82
*D.A.G. Fletcher	c Douglas b Blades	13
C.A.T. Hodgson	not out	57
R.D. Brown	not out	12
P.W. Rawson		
A.J. Traicos	did not bat	
E.J. Hough		
V.R. Hogg		
Extras	(b 1, lb 8, w 10, nb 2)	21
Total	(54.3 overs; 188 minutes)	**232-5**

Zimbabwe	O	M	R	W
Hogg	10	0	35	2
Hough	8	3	28	0
Rawson	12	1	48	2
Traicos	12	3	25	0
Fletcher	9	1	34	3
Curran	9	1	40	0

Bermuda	O	M	R	W
Trott	11.3	1	27	1
King	3	0	10	0
James	11	1	41	0
Gibbons	12	0	64	2
Blades	12	2	39	2
Bailey	5	0	30	0

Fall of Wickets

Wkt	B	Z
1st	27	22
2nd	74	30
3rd	78	78
4th	135	110
5th	151	177
6th	161	—
7th	197	—
8th	210	—
9th	—	—
10th	—	—

* Captain   † Wicket-keeper

Young West Indies Tour

The West Indies Young Cricketers' 15-match programme included three four-day 'Tests' for the Agatha Christie Trophy and two one-day international matches. The tourists lost only the two internationals, spin bowling playing a vital role in important victories.

Rhodil Clarke from Tobago managed the side, with Seymour Nurse as coach and assistant-manager; sponsorship was by Agatha Christie Ltd. In Roger Harper from Guyana, the West Indians had a captain of gentle firmness, mature beyond his years and much respected.

Laurie Potter of Kent, an opening batsman of infinite promise, captained the England Young Cricketers, though the burdens of leadership may have been placed too early on his shoulders. Outstanding on the England side were Yorkshire-born Richard Illingworth from Worcestershire (slow left-arm), batsman David Capel (Northants), and quicker bowlers Ian Folley (Lancashire) and Paul Jarvis (Yorkshire), left-arm and right-arm respectively.

For the first Test, Northamptonshire produced a poor pitch on which the toss, won by Harper, proved decisive. Illingworth took 10 wickets in the match for 82 runs, but West Indies' spinners Shervan Pragg, left-arm chinaman and googly, and Robert Haynes, leg-spin, baffled England's batsmen, and West Indies won by 62 runs in just over two days.

Pragg spent the second Test at Scarborough in an isolation ward with mumps. A fine innings of 117 by Capel enabled England to lead by 74 on first innings, but foul weather claimed 12 hours' playing time and no result was possible.

The first day's play of the final Test at Hove was limited by rain to 10 minutes, the main events being West Indies' decision to put England in and the news that George Ferris, 17, was to join fellow Antiguan Andy Roberts with Leicestershire. Though Pragg stole the show on the second day with 4 wickets for 21, Potter played authoritatively for 43 and Penn and Folley had a fast bowlers' frolic in a ninth-wicket stand of 51, which helped England towards a total of 226.

West Indies were let off the hook on the third day, recovering from 90 for 7 at lunch to 211. Potter used only four bowlers during the match, which, with a day to go, was still evenly poised, England 113 ahead with 6 wickets left.

On the last day, however, the England innings subsided, the fiery Ferris taking 5 for 45. West Indies needed 168, which they duly made with 4 wickets to spare, but not without surviving two dropped catches. Harper again steadied his ship and Haynes added a buccaneering 51 not out to his first-innings 80.

A tragic postscript to the tour was the sudden death a fortnight afterwards of Neil Lloyd, a very promising 17-year-old left-hander who opened the Young England innings in the third Test.

The West Indies touring party: R. Harper (capt, Guyana), M. Bowers, G. Ferris, A. Merrick (Antigua), D.A. Cumberbatch, R.O. Denny (Barbados), H. Edgings (St Kitts), R. Haynes, P. Harris, C. Walsh (Jamaica), D. Persaud, A. Jackman (vice-capt, Guyana), S.A. Pragg, P. Simmons, D. Williams (wicket-keeper, Trinidad & Tobago).

The following represented Young England: L. Potter (capt, Kent, 5 matches), D.J. Capel, D.J. Wild (Northants, each 5), I. Folley (Lancs, 5), P.W. Jarvis (Yorks, 5), R.K. Illingworth (Worcs, 5), C. Penn (Kent, 4), R.C. Russell (wicket-keeper, Glos, 4), H. Morris (Glamorgan, 4), P.J. Prichard (Essex, 5), C.K. Bullen (Surrey, 2). Appeared in one match: C.P. Metson (wicket-keeper, Middlesex), N. Lloyd (Yorks), K.A. Kayes (Lancs, injured in 1st Test).

Women's Cricket

Jan Southgate, 26-year-old Civil Servant, is the new England Women's Cricket Captain. She succeeds Sue Goatman (Kent), a primary school teacher from Eltham, who announced her retirement from international cricket at the beginning of the season, having led England since 1979.

Jan Southgate, who lives in Chessington and whose husband David plays for Beddington CC, has had an excellent season with the bat. In the first England trials at Oakham School, captaining the South against the East, she scored a record 201 not out — and combined with Jackie Court (Middlesex) in a third-wicket stand of 246, with 'JC' finishing on 105 not out. Four other centuries were scored in the Oakham trials: by England veteran Enid Bakewell (111), Lancashire all-rounder Carole Hodges (139), former England opener and Welsh hockey international Lynne Thomas (133 not out), and Janet Tedstone (122), sister of Geoff Tedstone who appeared for Warwickshire CCC during the season.

England's domestic season, with no home Test series, had further trial matches at Reading and Cambridge, culminating in the selection of the England touring team to the West Indies (Feb. 16—Mar. 19 1983).

There are four changes from the squad who played in the World Cup in New Zealand in February. Newcomers are Sarah Potter, left-arm pace bowler (daughter of TV and film writer Dennis Potter); wicket-keeper Joan Lee; all-rounder Ros Heggs; and Jill Stockdale (18), the youngest member of the party.

Rachael Flint (43), who has played for England since 1960, with 51 appearances to her name, was omitted from the touring team after an indifferent season, but has been named as a reserve and will be assistant manager on the tour to Pam Crain (East Anglia).

England Touring Team: Jan Southgate (Sussex, captain), Shirley Hodges (Sussex, vice-captain), Enid Bakewell (E. Midlands), Janette Brittin (Surrey), Jackie Court (Middx), Ros Heggs (Middx), Helen Stother (Middx), Carole Hodges (Lancs & Cheshire), Avril Starling (Lancs & Cheshire), Megan Lear (East Anglia), Joan Lee (Yorks), Jill Stockdale (Yorks), Sarah Potter (West), Janet Tedstone (W. Midlands), Chris Watmough (Surrey).

Other Highlights: Janette Brittin, Young England's captain, scored 1,175 runs in club, county, and representative cricket in the 1982 season; 17 innings, 7 not out, average 117.50, 3 hundreds. Sarah Potter has been playing for Hereford Men's CC 2nd XI in the Three Counties League — selected on merit. Jill Powell, former Young England captain, who failed to get chosen for the West Indies Tour, will play grade cricket for South Perth Women's Cricket Club as a contracted player — the first English cricketer to take up such an appointment.

Oakham Trials Weekend: (May 29, 30, 31)
East 166 (M. Lear 56, M. Peear 60) and 143-6 (K. Brown 60); South 410-2 dec. (J. Southgate 201 not, J. Court 105 not, J. Brittin 55). *Drawn.*
North 279-6 dec. (E. Bakewell 111, C. Hodges 73) and 300-5 dec. (C. Hodges 139, S. Minto 79); West 282-1 dec. (L. Thomas 133 not, J. Tedstone 122) and 111-8 (L. Thomas 62; C. Hodges 4-44). *Drawn.*
Reading Trial Matches: (June 12/13)
(46 overs) England 168-8 (J. Southgate 58; E. Wulcko 3-43); Rest 123-9 (C. Hodges 38; A. Bainbridge 4-28). *England won by 45 runs.*
(51 overs, Sunday) England 188-5 (J. Court 60 not, E. Bakewell 41); Rest 153 (J. Powell 43; A. Starling 4-22). *England won by 35 runs.*
Cambridge Three-Day Trial Match (July 17, 18, 19)
Rest 257-6 dec. (J. Brittin 144, R. Heggs 56; A. Starling 3-53) and 176-2 dec. (J. Court 74 not, E. Bakewell 50); England 117 and 231-7 (M. Lear 71 not, S. Potter 38; R. Heggs 3-29). *Drawn.*

(Statistics by R. Heyhoe-Flint)

Notes on the season

Test Career Averages

The following individual career averages and records include all official Test matches played before September 1982. A dagger (†) indicates a left-handed batsman.

Key to bowling categories:

RF	Right-arm fast	LM	Left-arm medium
RFM	Right-arm fast-medium	OB	Right-arm slow off-breaks
RM	Right-arm medium	LB	Right-arm slow leg-breaks
LF	Left-arm fast	SLA	Left-arm slow leg-breaks
LFM	Left-arm fast-medium		

Australia

Batting and Fielding

	M	I	NO	HS	R	Avge	100	50	Ct	St
T.M. Alderman	14	19	11	12*	44	5.50	—	—	16	—
A.R. Border†	42	75	12	162	3057	48.52	9	17	50	—
R.J. Bright	14	23	4	33	269	14.15	—	—	7	—
I.W. Callen†	1	2	2	22*	26	—	—	—	1	—
G.S. Chappell	76	134	16	247*	6291	53.31	20	29	106	—
T.M. Chappell	3	6	1	27	79	15.80	—	—	2	—
W.M. Darling	14	27	1	91	697	26.80	—	6	5	—
J. Dyson	19	36	5	127*	779	25.12	2	1	6	—
J.D. Higgs	22	36	16	16	111	5.55	—	—	3	—
R.M. Hogg	22	36	4	36	246	7.68	—	—	5	—
K.J. Hughes	48	86	5	213	3121	38.53	7	15	36	—
M.F. Kent	3	6	0	54	171	28.50	—	2	6	—
B.M. Laird	18	34	2	92	1204	37.62	—	10	12	—
G.F. Lawson	5	8	2	16	56	9.33	—	—	1	—
D.K. Lillee	63	85	21	73*	872	13.62	—	1	19	—
R.W. Marsh†	83	131	11	132	3362	28.01	3	15	291	11
L.S. Pascoe	14	19	9	30*	106	10.60	—	—	2	—
P.R. Sleep	3	6	0	64	95	15.83	—	1	—	—
J.R. Thomson	42	57	13	49	550	12.50	—	—	18	—
K.D. Walters	74	125	14	250	5357	48.26	15	33	43	—
D.M. Wellham	4	7	0	103	221	31.57	1	—	1	—
M.R. Whitney	2	4	0	4	4	1.00	—	—	—	—
G.M. Wood†	37	72	5	126	2318	34.59	7	10	31	—
K.J. Wright	10	18	5	55*	219	16.84	—	1	31	4
G.N. Yallop†	32	61	3	172	2101	36.22	6	7	16	—
B. Yardley	25	43	4	74	776	19.89	—	3	22	—

Bowling

	Type	Balls	R	W	Avge	Best	5w/I	10w/M
T.M. Alderman	RFM	3631	1652	63	26.22	6-135	4	—
A.R. Border	SLA	1097	368	12	30.66	3-20	—	—
R.J. Bright	SLA	3106	1126	34	33.11	7-87	3	1
I.W. Callen	RFM	440	191	6	31.83	3-83	—	—
G.S. Chappell	RM	4850	1712	46	37.21	5-61	1	—
J.D. Higgs	LB	4752	2057	66	31.16	7-143	2	—
R.M. Hogg	RFM	4652	1937	82	23.62	6-74	5	2
K.J. Hughes	LB	84	22	0	—	—	—	—
B.M. Laird	OB	18	12	0	—	—	—	—
G.F. Lawson	RFM	913	414	16	25.87	7-81	1	—
D.K. Lillee	RFM	16478	7568	328	23.07	7-83	22	7

Bowling	Type	Balls	R	W	Avge	Best	5w/I	10w/M
R.W. Marsh	OB	60	51	0	—	—	—	—
L.S. Pascoe	RFM	3403	1668	64	26.06	5-59	1	—
P.R. Sleep	LB	373	223	2	111.50	1-16	—	—
J.R. Thomson	RF	8959	4620	172	26.86	6-46	6	—
K.D. Walters	RM	3295	1425	49	29.08	5-66	1	—
M.R. Whitney	LFM	468	246	5	49.20	2-50	—	—
G.N. Yallop	LM	192	116	1	116.00	1-21	—	—
B. Yardley	OB	6531	2818	95	29.66	7-98	4	1

England

Batting and Fielding	M	I	NO	HS	R	Avge	100	50	Ct	St
P.J.W. Allott	5	6	2	52	119	29.75	—	1	2	—
C.W.J. Athey	3	6	0	9	17	2.83	—	—	2	—
D.L. Bairstow	4	7	1	59*	125	20.83	—	1	12	1
I.T. Botham	54	82	3	208	2996	37.92	11	12	60	—
G. Boycott	108	193	23	246*	8114	47.72	22	42	33	—
J.M. Brearley	39	66	3	91	1442	22.88	—	9	52	—
R.O. Butcher	3	5	0	32	71	14.20	—	—	3	—
G. Cook	4	7	0	66	149	21.28	—	2	8	—
G.R. Dilley†	16	25	7	56	313	17.38	—	2	4	—
P.R. Downton	4	7	1	26*	59	9.83	—	—	8	—
P.H. Edmonds	21	24	5	64	367	19.31	—	2	22	—
J.E. Emburey	22	33	6	57	326	12.07	—	1	15	—
K.W.R. Fletcher	59	96	14	216	3272	39.90	7	19	54	—
G. Fowler†	1	2	0	86	95	47.50	—	1	1	—
M.W. Gatting	22	38	3	59	797	22.77	—	6	17	—
G.A. Gooch	42	75	4	153	2540	35.77	4	15	36	—
D.I. Gower†	44	75	7	200*	2897	42.60	4	15	24	—
I.A. Greig	2	4	0	14	26	6.50	—	—	—	—
E.E. Hemmings	2	4	0	19	41	10.25	—	—	2	—
M. Hendrick	30	35	15	15	128	6.40	—	—	25	—
R.D. Jackman	4	6	0	17	42	7.00	—	—	—	—
A.P.E. Knott	95	149	15	135	4389	32.75	5	30	250	19
A.J. Lamb	6	11	1	107	255	25.50	1	—	1	—
W. Larkins	6	11	0	34	176	16.00	—	—	3	—
J.K. Lever	20	29	4	53	306	12.24	—	1	11	—
V.J. Marks	1	2	1	12*	19	19.00	—	—	—	—
G. Miller	27	37	3	98*	978	28.76	—	6	12	—
C.M. Old†	46	66	9	65	845	14.82	—	2	22	—
P.W.G. Parker	1	2	0	13	13	6.50	—	—	—	—
D.R. Pringle	4	5	0	23	58	11.60	—	—	—	—
D.W. Randall	33	54	4	174	1514	30.28	4	7	22	—
B.C. Rose†	9	16	2	70	358	25.57	—	2	4	—
G.B. Stevenson	2	2	1	27*	28	28.00	—	—	—	—
C.J. Tavaré	17	30	1	149	1072	36.96	1	8	13	—
R.W. Taylor	42	57	8	97	875	17.85	—	3	131	7
D.L. Underwood	86	116	35	45*	937	11.56	—	—	44	—
P. Willey	20	38	5	102*	923	27.96	2	4	3	—
R.G.D. Willis	74	101	46	28*	645	11.72	—	—	29	—
R.A. Woolmer	19	34	2	149	1059	33.09	3	2	10	—

England (contd)

Bowling	Type	Balls	R	W	Avge	Best	5w/I	10w/M
P.J.W. Allott	RFM	696	414	6	69.00	2-17	—	—
I.T. Botham	RFM	12762	5807	249	23.32	8-34	20	4
G. Boycott	RM	944	382	7	54.57	3-47	—	—
G. Cook	SLA	6	4	0	—	—	—	—
G.R. Dilley	RF	2758	1401	45	31.13	4-24	—	—
P.H. Edmonds	SLA	4697	1512	55	27.49	7-66	2	—
J.E. Emburey	OB	4981	1696	56	30.28	6-33	2	—
K.W.R. Fletcher	LB	285	193	2	96.50	1-6	—	—
M.W. Gatting	RM	92	39	0	—	—	—	—
G.A. Gooch	RM	937	348	8	43.50	2-12	—	—
D.I. Gower	OB	12	2	1	2.00	1-1	—	—
I.A. Greig	RM	188	114	4	28.50	4-53	—	—
E.E. Hemmings	OB	337	149	3	49.66	2-56	—	—
M. Hendrick	RFM	6208	2248	87	25.83	4-28	—	—
R.D. Jackman	RFM	1070	445	14	31.78	4-110	—	—
J.K. Lever	LFM	4115	1785	67	26.64	7-46	3	1
V.J. Marks	OB	42	31	1	31.00	1-8	—	—
G. Miller	OB	3955	1320	46	28.69	5-44	1	—
C.M. Old	RFM	8858	4020	143	28.11	7-50	4	—
D.R. Pringle	RM	648	281	7	40.14	2-16	—	—
D.W. Randall	RM	16	3	0	—	—	—	—
G.B. Stevenson	RFM	312	183	5	36.60	3-111	—	—
C.J. Tavaré	RM	12	11	0	—	—	—	—
R.W. Taylor	RM	12	6	0	—	—	—	—
D.L. Underwood	LM	21862	7674	297	25.83	8-51	17	6
P. Willey	OB	1067	441	6	73.50	2-73	—	—
R.G.D. Willis	RF	14302	6712	267	25.13	8-43	14	—
R.A. Woolmer	RM	546	299	4	74.75	1-8	—	—

West Indies

Batting and Fielding	M	I	NO	HS	R	Avge	100	50	Ct	St
S.F.A.F. Bacchus	19	30	0	250	782	26.06	1	3	17	—
S.T. Clarke	11	16	5	35*	172	15.63	—	—	2	—
C.E.H. Croft	27	37	22	33	158	10.53	—	—	8	—
W.W. Daniel	5	5	2	11	29	9.66	—	—	2	—
P.J. Dujon	3	6	1	51	227	45.40	—	1	9	—
J. Garner	28	36	2	60	400	11.76	—	1	22	—
H.A. Gomes†	22	35	2	126	1418	42.96	4	8	4	—
C.G. Greenidge	36	63	3	134	2569	42.81	5	19	39	—
D.L. Haynes	24	38	1	184	1431	38.67	3	8	13	—
M.A. Holding	31	44	8	58*	434	12.05	—	2	9	—
A.I. Kallicharran†	66	109	10	187	4399	44.43	12	21	51	—
C.H. Lloyd†	85	143	10	242*	5831	43.84	14	30	63	—
M.D. Marshall	12	16	1	45	126	8.40	—	—	5	—
E.H. Mattis	4	5	0	71	145	29.00	—	1	3	—
D.A. Murray	19	31	3	84	601	21.46	—	3	57	5
R. Nanan	1	2	0	8	16	8.00	—	—	2	—

Batting and Fielding		M	I	NO	HS	R	Avge	100	50	Ct	St
D.R. Parry		12	20	3	65	381	22.41	—	3	4	—
I.V.A. Richards		47	74	4	291	4129	58.98	13	17	48	—
A.M.E. Roberts		40	54	9	54	610	13.55	—	2	8	—
L.G. Rowe		30	49	2	302	2047	43.55	7	7	17	—

Bowling	Type	Balls	R	W	Avge	Best	5w/I	10w/M
S.F.A.F. Bacchus	RM	6	3	0	—	—	—	—
S.T. Clarke	RF	2477	1171	42	27.88	5-126	1	—
C.E.H. Croft	RF	6165	2913	125	23.30	8-29	3	—
W.W. Daniel	RF	788	381	15	25.40	4-53	—	—
J. Garner	RFM	6648	2560	124	20.64	6-56	2	—
H.A. Gomes	RM/OB	744	266	5	53.20	2-20	—	—
C.G. Greenidge	RM	26	4	0	—	—	—	—
D.L. Haynes	RM/LB	18	8	1	8.00	1-2	—	—
M.A. Holding	RF	7162	3194	139	22.97	8-92	10	2
A.I. Kallicharran	LB	406	158	4	39.50	2-16	—	—
C.H. Lloyd	RM	1716	622	10	62.20	2-13	—	—
M.D. Marshall	RF	2220	1083	34	31.85	4-25	—	—
E.H. Mattis	OB	36	14	0	—	—	—	—
R. Nanan	OB	216	91	4	22.75	2-37	—	—
D.R. Parry	OB	1909	936	23	40.69	5-15	1	—
I.V.A. Richards	OB	1924	703	13	54.07	2-19	—	—
A.M.E. Roberts	RF	9674	4481	173	25.90	7-54	10	2
L.G. Rowe	OB	86	44	0	—	—	—	—

New Zealand

Batting and Fielding	M	I	NO	HS	R	Avge	100	50	Ct	St
S.L. Boock	12	19	6	8	37	2.84	—	—	8	—
B.P. Bracewell	5	10	2	8	17	2.12	—	—	1	—
J.G. Bracewell	4	6	1	16	29	5.80	—	—	2	—
M.G. Burgess	50	92	6	119*	2684	31.20	5	14	34	—
B.L. Cairns	26	42	6	52*	575	15.97	—	1	19	—
E.J. Chatfield	5	7	3	13*	31	7.75	—	—	—	—
J.V. Coney	18	31	5	82	805	30.96	—	7	18	—
M.D. Crowe	3	4	0	9	20	5.00	—	—	3	—
B.A. Edgar†	18	32	1	161	1049	33.83	3	4	11	—
G.N. Edwards	8	15	0	55	377	25.13	—	3	7	—
R.J. Hadlee†	38	66	8	103	1241	21.39	1	5	20	—
G.P. Howarth	28	51	5	147	1788	38.86	6	7	14	—
W.K. Lees	17	31	3	152	642	22.92	1	—	35	7
P.E. McEwan	3	6	0	21	56	9.33	—	—	3	—
J.F.M. Morrison	17	29	0	117	656	22.62	1	3	9	—
J.M. Parker	36	63	2	121	1498	24.55	3	5	30	—
J.F. Reid†	4	7	1	123*	269	44.83	1	1	2	—
I.D.S. Smith	7	10	2	20	86	10.75	—	—	19	—
M.C. Snedden†	6	6	2	32	72	18.00	—	—	2	—
G.B. Troup	12	15	6	13*	43	4.77	—	—	2	—
G.M. Turner	39	70	6	259	2920	45.62	7	14	40	—
J.G. Wright†	20	36	1	141	976	27.88	2	3	8	—

New Zealand (contd)

Bowling	Type	Balls	R	W	Avge	Best	5w/I	10w/M
S.L. Boock	SLA	2107	706	19	37.15	5-67	1	—
B.P. Bracewell	RFM	838	456	10	45.60	3-110	—	—
J.G. Bracewell	OB	837	290	11	26.36	5-75	1	—
M.G. Burgess	OB	498	212	6	35.33	3-23	—	—
B.L. Cairns	RM	6529	2478	72	34.41	6-85	4	—
E.J. Chatfield	RFM	1102	492	8	61.50	4-100	—	—
J.V. Coney	RM	1107	360	10	36.00	3-28	—	—
M.D. Crowe	RM	27	14	0	—	—	—	—
R.J. Hadlee	RFM	9498	4464	169	26.41	7-23	13	3
G.P. Howarth	OB	500	235	3	78.33	1-13	—	—
W.K. Lees	RM	5	4	0	—	—	—	—
J.F.M. Morrison	SLA	264	71	2	35.50	2-52	—	—
J.M. Parker	OB	40	24	1	24.00	1-24	—	—
M.C. Snedden	RFM	870	426	11	38.72	2-39	—	—
G.B. Troup	LFM	2601	1114	34	32.76	6-95	1	1
G.M. Turner	OB	12	5	0	—	—	—	—
J.G. Wright	RM	6	2	0	—	—	—	—

India

Batting and Fielding	M	I	NO	HS	R	Avge	100	50	Ct	St
K Azad	4	6	0	24	107	17.83	—	—	2	—
R.M.H. Binny	9	15	2	46	198	15.23	—	—	7	—
C.P.S. Chauhan	40	68	2	97	2084	31.57	—	16	38	—
D.R. Doshi†	27	30	9	20	108	5.14	—	—	10	—
S.M. Gavaskar	78	137	9	221	6792	53.06	24	30	69	—
K.D. Ghavri†	39	57	14	86	913	21.23	—	2	16	—
Kapil Dev	41	59	6	126★	1760	33.20	2	10	15	—
S.M.H. Kirmani	57	83	14	101★	1884	27.30	1	9	106	30
Madan Lal	25	39	8	55★	549	17.70	—	1	11	—
A. Malhotra	3	4	0	31	36	9.00	—	—	2	—
S.V. Nayak†	2	3	1	11	19	9.50	—	—	1	—
G.A. Parkar	1	2	0	6	7	3.50	—	—	1	—
S.M. Patil	15	24	3	174	921	43.85	2	5	6	—
P. Roy	2	3	1	60★	71	35.50	—	1	1	—
R.J. Shastri	12	16	3	93	281	21.61	—	2	7	—
K. Srikkanth	4	6	0	65	119	19.83	—	1	1	—
T.E. Srinivasan	1	2	0	29	48	24.00	—	—	—	—
D.B. Vengsarkar	51	83	8	157★	2869	38.25	6	14	41	—
G.R. Viswanath	84	145	10	222	5935	43.96	14	34	61	—
N.S. Yadav	15	19	6	43	207	15.92	—	—	4	—
Yashpal Sharma	25	39	6	140	1169	35.42	2	6	5	—
Yograj Singh	1	2	0	6	10	5.00	—	—	—	—

Bowling	Type	Balls	R	W	Avge	Best	5w/I	10w/M
K. Azad	OB	294	158	1	158.00	1-35	—	—
R.M.H. Binny	RM	1133	632	15	42.13	3-53	—	—
C.P.S. Chauhan	RM	174	106	2	53.00	1-4	—	—

Bowling	Type	Balls	R	W	Avge	Best	5w/I	10w/M
D.R. Doshi	SLA	7979	2730	97	28.14	6-102	4	—
S.M. Gavaskar	RM	304	163	1	163.00	1-34	—	—
K.D. Ghavri	LM/SLA	7042	3656	109	33.54	5-33	4	—
Kapil Dev	RFM	9139	4620	157	29.42	7-56	11	1
Madan Lal	RFM	4024	1700	49	34.69	5-23	4	—
S.V. Nayak	RM	231	132	1	132.00	1-16	—	—
S.M. Patil	RM	621	225	9	25.00	2-28	—	—
R.J. Shastri	SLA	2979	1014	31	32.70	5-125	1	—
K. Srikkanth	RM	36	10	0	—	—	—	—
D.B. Vengsarkar	RM	23	13	0	—	—	—	—
G.R. Viswanath	LB	70	46	1	46.00	1-11	—	—
N.S. Yadav	OB	3137	1449	41	35.34	4-35	—	—
Yashpal Sharma	RM	18	1	0	—	—	—	—
Yograj Singh	RFM	90	63	1	63.00	1-63	—	—

Pakistan

Batting and Fielding	M	I	NO	HS	R	Avge	100	50	Ct	St
Abdul Qadir	11	17	3	29*	187	13.35	—	—	6	—
Ashraf Ali	2	3	2	58	132	132.00	—	1	3	2
Ehtesham Uddin	5	3	1	2	2	1.00	—	—	2	—
Haroon Rashid	19	32	1	153	1069	34.48	3	3	11	—
Ijaz Faqih	2	4	0	34	63	15.75	—	—	—	—
Imran Khan	40	65	8	123	1542	27.05	1	5	11	—
Iqbal Qasim†	32	39	11	56	267	9.53	—	1	26	—
Javed Miandad	43	74	13	206	3222	52.81	7	20	43	1
Majid Khan	62	105	5	167	3931	39.31	8	19	70	—
Mansoor Akhtar	7	13	0	58	261	20.07	—	2	6	—
Mohammad Nazir	8	11	7	29*	89	22.25	—	—	2	—
Mohsin Khan	13	22	1	200	878	41.80	2	1	14	—
Mudassar Nazar	26	41	1	126	1179	29.47	2	6	17	—
Rashid Khan	2	3	2	59	105	105.00	—	1	1	—
Rizwanuz Zaman	3	6	0	42	112	18.66	—	—	1	—
Sadiq Mohammad†	41	74	2	166	2579	35.81	5	10	28	—
Salim Malik	2	4	1	100*	139	46.33	1	—	4	—
Salim Yousuf	1	1	0	4	4	4.00	—	—	5	2
Sarfraz Nawaz	43	57	8	55	760	15.51	—	3	24	—
Shafiq Ahmed	6	10	1	27*	99	11.00	—	—	—	—
Sikander Bakht	25	34	12	22*	137	6.22	—	—	6	—
Tahir Naqqash	5	7	1	57	125	20.83	—	1	—	—
Taslim Arif	6	10	2	210*	501	62.62	1	2	6	3
Tausif Ahmed	6	3	1	18	23	11.50	—	—	3	—
Wasim Bari	64	96	24	85	1191	16.54	—	5	153	20
Wasim Raja†	44	73	12	117*	2311	37.88	2	16	12	—
Zaheer Abbas	49	85	6	274	3154	39.92	7	12	27	—

Bowling	Type	Balls	R	W	Avge	Best	5w/I	10w/M
Abdul Qadir	LB	2820	1109	32	34.65	6-44	1	—
Ehtesham Uddin	RM	940	375	16	23.43	5-47	1	—
Haroon Rashid	RM	8	3	0	—	—	—	—
Ijaz Faqih	OB	156	85	1	85.00	1-76	—	—

Pakistan (contd)

Bowling	Type	Balls	R	W	Avge	Best	5w/I	10w/M
Imran Khan	RF	10598	4589	179	25.63	8-58	12	2
Iqbal Qasim	SLA	8269	3073	104	29.54	7-49	4	2
Javed Miandad	LB	1350	621	17	36.52	3-74	—	—
Majid Khan	OB	3578	1452	27	53.77	4-45	—	—
Mohammad Nazir	OB	1798	635	26	24.42	7-99	2	—
Mohsin Khan	LB	8	3	0	—	—	—	—
Mudassar Nazar	RM	1481	603	21	28.71	6-32	1	—
Rashid Khan	RM	288	134	3	44.66	2-53	—	—
Rizwanuz Zaman	LB	102	39	3	13.00	3-26	—	—
Sadiq Mohammad	LB	199	98	0	—	—	—	—
Sarfraz Nawaz	RFM	10581	4386	136	32.25	9-86	4	1
Shafiq Ahmed	RM	8	1	0	—	—	—	—
Sikander Bakht	RFM	4738	2305	66	34.92	8-69	3	1
Tahir Naqqash	RFM	888	471	14	33.64	5-40	1	—
Taslim Arif	RM	30	28	1	28.00	1-28	—	—
Tausif Ahmed	OB	1446	620	23	26.95	4-58	—	—
Wasim Bari	RM	8	2	0	—	—	—	—
Wasim Raja	LB	3055	1412	39	36.20	4-68	—	—
Zaheer Abbas	OB	20	2	0	—	—	—	—

Sri Lanka

Batting and Fielding	M	I	NO	HS	R	Avge	100	50	Ct	St
A.L.F. de Mel	4	8	1	34	95	13.57	—	—	3	—
D.S. de Silva	4	8	1	36*	118	16.85	—	—	—	—
G.R.A. de Silva†	3	5	2	12	27	9.00	—	—	—	—
R.L. Dias	4	8	0	109	372	46.50	1	3	1	—
H.M. Goonatillake	4	8	2	56	170	28.33	—	1	7	3
R.S.A. Jayasekera	1	2	0	2	2	1.00	—	—	—	—
L.W. Kaluperuma	2	4	1	11*	12	4.00	—	—	2	—
R.S. Madugalle	4	8	1	91*	223	31.85	—	2	5	—
L.R.D. Mendis	4	8	0	54	160	20.00	—	1	4	—
A.N. Ranasinghe	1	2	0	6	11	5.50	—	—	—	—
A. Ranatunga	3	6	0	54	104	17.33	—	1	1	—
J.R. Ratnayeke†	2	4	1	24	25	8.33	—	—	—	—
B. Warnapura	3	6	0	38	86	14.33	—	—	1	—
S. Wettimuny	4	8	0	157	331	41.37	1	1	2	—
R.G.C.E. Wijesuriya	1	2	0	3	3	1.50	—	—	—	—

Bowling	Type	Balls	R	W	Avge	Best	5w/I	10w/M
A.L.F. de Mel	RFM	897	591	16	36.93	4-70	—	—
D.S. de Silva	LBG	1175	584	20	29.20	5-59	1	—
G.R.A. de Silva	SLA	854	307	7	43.85	2-38	—	—
L.W. Kaluperuma	OB	162	93	0	—	—	—	—
A.N. Ranasinghe	LM	72	40	1	40.00	1-23	—	—
J.R. Ratnayeke	RFM	298	190	4	47.50	3-121	—	—
B. Warnapura	RM	36	19	0	—	—	—	—
S. Wettimuny	RM	12	21	0	—	—	—	—
R.G.C.E. Wijesuriya	SLA	144	105	0	—	—	—	—

Newcomers Guide

Register of New Players 1982

The following players made their first appearances in English first-class cricket during the 1982 season. Four of them (A.J. Wright of Gloucestershire, and M.A. Fell, P. Johnson, and I.L. Pont of Nottinghamshire) had appeared in limited-overs matches for their counties in previous seasons. Players marked with a dagger (†) had already made their debuts in first-class cricket overseas.

Key to categories:

RH	Right-handed batsman	LFM	Left-arm fast-medium
LH	Left-handed batsman	LM	Left-arm medium
RF	Right-arm fast	OB	Right-arm slow off-breaks
RFM	Right-arm fast-medium	LB	Right-arm slow leg-breaks
RM	Right-arm medium	SLA	Left-arm slow leg-breaks
LF	Left-arm fast	WK	Wicket-keeper

Surname	Given Names	Birthdate	Place of Birth	Bat	Ball
Derbyshire					
Finney	Roger John	2 Aug 60	Darley Dale, Derbyshire	RH	LM
Jefferies†	Stephen Thomas	8 Dec 59	Cape Town, S. Africa	LH	LFM
Morris	John Edward	1 Apr 64	Crewe, Cheshire	RH	RM
Watts	Andrew	4 Oct 60	Chapeltown, Yorkshire	LH	RM
Glamorgan					
Davies	Mark Nicholas	28 Dec 59	Maesteg, Glamorgan	LH	—
Davis†	Winston Walter	18 Sep 58	St Vincent, WI	RH	RFM
Gloucestershire					
Cunningham	Edward James	16 May 62	Oxford, Oxon.	LH	OB
Simpkins	David Paul	28 Mar 62	Chippenham, Wiltshire	RH	OB
Stephenson†	Franklyn Dacosta	8 Apr 59	St James, Barbados, WI	RH	RF
Trembath	Christopher Richard	27 Sep 61	London	RH	RM
Wright	Anthony John	27 Jun 62	Stevenage, Herts	RH	RM
Hampshire					
Emery	Kevin St John Dennis	28 Feb 60	Swindon, Wiltshire	RH	RFM
Smith†	Robin Arnold	13 Sep 63	Durban, South Africa	RH	LB
Kent					
Hinks	Simon Graham	12 Oct 60	Northfleet, Kent	LH	LM/WK
Marsh	Steven	27 Jan 61	Westminster, London	RH	WK
Penn	Christopher	19 Jun 63	Dover, Kent	LH	RFM
Lancashire					
Fairbrother	Neil Harvey	9 Sep 63	Warrington, Lancashire	LH	—
Folley	Ian	9 Jan 63	Burnley, Lancashire	RH	LFM
Wallwork	Mark Andrew	14 Dec 60	Urmston, Lancashire	RH	WK
Watkinson	Michael	1 Aug 61	Westhoughton, Lancs	RH	RM
Watson	Roger Graeme	14 Jan 64	Rawtenstall, Lancashire	RH	OB
Middlesex					
Williams	Neil FitzGerald	2 Jul 62	Hope Well, St Vincent, WI	RH	RFM
Northamptonshire					
Bailey	Robert	28 Oct 63	Stoke-on-Trent, Staffs	RH	OB
Bamber	Martin John	7 Jan 61	Cheam, Surrey	RH	RM
Nottinghamshire					
Fell	Mark Andrew	17 Nov 60	Newark, Notts	RH	SLA
Johnson	Paul	24 Apr 65	Newark, Notts	RH	RM
Pont	Ian Leslie	28 Aug 61	Brentwood, Essex	RH	RFM
Such	Peter Mark	12 Jun 64	Helensburgh, Scotland	RH	OB
Somerset					
Bryant	Michael	5 Apr 59	Camborne, Cornwall	RH	RFM
Davis	Mark Richard	26 Feb 62	Kilve, Somerset	LH	LFM
Felton	Nigel Alfred	24 Oct 60	Guildford, Surrey	LH	—
McCool	Russel John	4 Dec 59	Taunton, Somerset	RH	LB
Palmer	Gary Vincent	11 Jan 65	Taunton, Somerset	RH	RM

Surname	Given Names	Birthdate	Place of Birth	Bat	Ball
Surrey					
Bullen	Christopher Keith	5 Nov 62	Clapham, London	RH	OB
Butcher	Martin Simon	17 May 58	Thornton Heath, Surrey	RH	RM
Warwickshire					
Hartley	Peter John	18 Apr 60	Keighley, Yorkshire	RH	RM
Maguire	Keith Robert	20 Mar 61	Marston Grn, B'ham	RH	RFM
Smith	Paul Andrew	15 Apr 64	Jesmond, Northumberland	RH	RM
Tedstone	Geoffrey Alan	19 Jan 61	Southport, Lancashire	RH	WK
Worcestershire					
D'Oliveira	Damian Basil	19 Oct 60	Cape Town, S. Africa	RH	RM/WK
Ellcock	Ricardo McDonald	17 Jun 65	Bridgetown, Barbados	RH	RF
Illingworth	Richard Keith	23 Aug 63	Bradford, Yorkshire	RH	SLA
Newport	Philip John	11 Oct 62	High Wycombe, Bucks	RH	RFM
Warner	Alan Esmond	12 May 57	Birmingham	RH	RFM
Yorkshire					
Booth	Paul Antony	5 Sep 65	Huddersfield, Yorkshire	LH	SLA
Taylor	Nicholas Simon	2 Jun 63	Holmfirth, Yorkshire	RH	RF
Cambridge University					
Barrington	William Edward James	4 Jan 60	Carshalton, Surrey	RH	—
Davies	Andrew George	15 May 62	Altrincham, Cheshire	RH	WK
Ellison	Charles Christopher	11 Feb 62	Pembury, Kent	RH	RM
Griffiths	Peter David	13 Jul 61	Bulawayo, S. Rhodesia	RH	SLA
Pollock	Angus John	19 Apr 62	Liversedge, Yorkshire	RH	RM
Oxford University					
Armstrong	Philip Alexander Nikolas	23 Jan 62	Lambeth, London	RH	RM
Cassidy	John Joseph	31 Jan 63		RH	RM
Chessher	John Robert	21 Aug 62	Banstead, Surrey	RH	RM
Crowe	Philip John	27 Oct 55	London	LH	LM
Edbrooke	Roger	30 Dec 60		RH	RM
Gilfillan	Andrew Douglas	21 Aug 59	Johannesburg, S. Africa	RH	LB
Lawrence	Mark Philip	6 May 62	Warrington, Lancashire	LH	SLA
Luddington	Richard Simon	8 Apr 60	Kingston upon Thames, Surrey	RH	WK
Miller	Andrew John Trevor	30 May 63	Chesham, Bucks	LH	RM
Rawlinson	Henry Thomas	21 Jan 63	Edgware, Middlesex	RH	RM
Toogood	Giles John	19 Nov 61	West Bromwich, Staffs	RH	OB
Varey	Jonathan Guy	15 Oct 61	Darlington, Co Durham	RH	RM

The following players made their first appearances in county cricket during 1982 but in limited-over matches only. They have still to make their debuts in first-class cricket.

Surname	Given Names	Birthdate	Place of Birth	Bat	Ball
Derbyshire					
Fowler†	William Peter	13 Mar 59	St Helens, Lancashire	RH	SLA
Essex					
Prichard	Paul John	7 Jan 65	Billericay, Essex	RH	—
Worcestershire					
Banks	David Andrew	11 Jan 65	Brierley Hill, Staffs	RH	RM
Yorkshire					
Metcalfe	Ashley Anthony	25 Dec 63	Horsforth, Yorkshire	RH	OB

Newcomers Record in English First-Class Cricket

Batting and Fielding

Team		M	I	NO	HS	R	Avge	100	50	Ct	St
Derbys	R.J. Finney	1	1	0	39	39	39.00	—	—	1	—
	S.T. Jefferies	1	2	1	14*	14	14.00	—	—	—	—
	J.E. Morris	1	2	0	12	18	9.00	—	—	—	—
	A. Watts	1	1	0	0	0	0.00	—	—	1	—
Glam	M.N. Davies	2	1	0	0	0	0.00	—	—	1	—
	W.W. Davis	13	13	6	20*	58	8.28	—	—	3	—
Glos	E.J. Cunningham	4	6	2	11*	27	6.75	—	—	—	—
	D.P. Simpkins	1	2	1	1*	1	1.00	—	—	—	—
	F.D. Stephenson	8	10	1	63	105	11.66	—	1	2	—
	C.R. Trembath	2	1	1	8*	8	—	—	—	1	—
	A.J. Wright	10	19	2	65	399	23.47	—	2	3	—
Hants	K. St J.D. Emery	24	26	15	18*	37	3.36	—	—	4	—
	R.A. Smith	1	2	0	8	9	4.50	—	—	2	—
Kent	S.G. Hinks	2	4	1	18	35	11.66	—	—	1	—
	S. Marsh	2	1	1	10*	10	—	—	—	6	—
	C. Penn	7	8	4	30	54	13.50	—	—	4	—
Lancs	N.H. Fairbrother	1	—	—	—	—	—	—	—	—	—
	I. Folley	17	15	4	36	165	15.00	—	—	3	—
	M.A. Wallwork	1	—	—	—	—	—	—	—	3	—
	M. Watkinson	1	—	—	—	—	—	—	—	—	—
	R.G. Watson	1	2	0	11	15	7.50	—	—	—	—
Middx	N.F. Williams	12	11	5	27*	112	18.66	—	—	2	—
N'hants	R. Bailey	2	3	0	10	17	5.66	—	—	1	1
	M.J. Bamber	1	2	0	31	58	29.00	—	—	—	—
Notts	M.A. Fell	10	18	0	108	315	17.50	1	—	9	—
	P. Johnson	4	7	1	37*	90	15.00	—	—	—	—
	I.L. Pont	4	7	1	16	32	5.33	—	—	1	—
	P.M. Such	8	9	3	2	3	0.50	—	—	7	—
Som't	M. Bryant	2	2	0	6	6	3.00	—	—	1	—
	M.R. Davis	9	12	2	21*	65	6.50	—	—	4	—
	N.A. Felton	8	12	0	71	346	28.83	—	3	4	—
	R.J. McCool	1	2	0	12	19	9.50	—	—	1	—
	G.V. Palmer	1	2	0	27	33	16.50	—	—	—	—
Surrey	C.K. Bullen	1	—	—	—	—	—	—	—	1	—
	M.S. Butcher	1	—	—	—	—	—	—	—	1	—
Warw	P.J. Hartley	3	4	1	16	31	10.33	—	—	1	—
	K.R. Maguire	3	3	0	2	3	1.00	—	—	—	—
	P.A. Smith	10	16	1	68	383	25.53	—	2	7	—
	G.A. Tedstone	3	5	2	18*	45	15.00	—	—	4	1
Worcs	D.B. D'Oliveira	4	7	1	21	65	10.83	—	—	2	—
	R.M. Ellcock	1	2	1	13*	13	13.00	—	—	—	—
	R.K. Illingworth	11	16	4	47*	191	15.91	—	—	5	—
	P.J. Newport	3	5	1	11	38	9.50	—	—	1	—
	A.E. Warner	11	17	2	67	287	19.13	—	1	2	—
Yorks	P.A. Booth	1	1	1	0*	0	—	—	—	—	—
	N.S. Taylor	4	1	1	0*	0	—	—	—	1	—
CU	W.E.J. Barrington	4	6	1	59	174	34.80	—	1	1	—
	A.G. Davies	1	2	0	13	17	8.50	—	—	3	—
	C.C. Ellison	7	7	4	16	56	18.66	—	—	1	—
	P.D. Griffiths	1	2	0	1	1	0.50	—	—	—	—
	A.J. Pollock	7	8	2	19	63	10.50	—	—	—	—
OU	P.A.N. Armstrong	1	2	0	34	34	17.00	—	—	—	—
	J.J. Cassidy	1	1	0	0	0	0.00	—	—	—	—
	J.R. Chessher	3	4	1	47	67	22.33	—	—	—	—
	P.J. Crowe	1	2	0	11	11	5.50	—	—	—	—

Batting and Fielding (contd)

Team		M	I	NO	HS	R	Avge	100	50	Ct	St
OU	R. Edbrooke	1	2	1	84*	100	100.00	—	1	—	—
(contd)	A.D. Gilfillan	3	4	1	31	40	13.33	—	—	—	—
	M.P. Lawrence	4	5	2	18	20	6.66	—	—	—	—
	R.S. Luddington	10	14	1	65	290	22.30	—	2	5	1
	A.J.T. Miller	1	2	0	20	20	10.00	—	—	—	—
	H.T. Rawlinson	4	6	0	21	30	5.00	—	—	1	—
	G.J. Toogood	9	18	4	83	392	28.00	—	2	4	—
	J.G. Varey	7	12	5	68	239	34.14	—	1	2	—

Bowling

Team		O	M	R	W	Avge	Best	5w/I	10w/M
Derbys	R.J. Finney	14	5	40	1	40.00	1-37	—	—
	S.T. Jefferies†	28	3	109	5	21.80	3-57	—	—
	A. Watts	9	1	31	0	—	—	—	—
Glam	W.W. Davis†	390.5	70	1296	42	30.85	7-101	1	—
Glos	E.J. Cunningham	4	0	13	0	—	—	—	—
	D.P. Simpkins	2	0	15	0	—	—	—	—
	F.D. Stephenson†	197.3	40	632	32	19.75	5-64	2	—
	C.R. Trembath	49.3	7	219	6	36.50	5-91	1	—
Hants	K. St J.D. Emery	659	152	1969	83	23.72	6-51	3	1
Kent	S.G. Hinks	1.4	1	5	0	—	—	—	—
	C. Penn	93.4	17	327	7	46.71	2-11	—	—
Lancs	I. Folley	309	76	758	27	28.07	4-40	—	—
	M. Watkinson	13	4	45	1	45.00	1-24	—	—
Middx	N.F. Williams	236.4	33	819	23	35.60	4-38	—	—
	M.A. Fell	45	7	146	1	146.00	1-20	—	—
	I.L. Pont	78.5	13	302	3	100.66	2-107	—	—
Notts	P.M. Such	232.1	51	737	25	29.48	5-112	1	—
Som't	M. Bryant	27	3	158	2	79.00	1-29	—	—
	M.R. Davis	145	19	481	12	40.08	3-36	—	—
	R.J. McCool	27	2	63	0	—	—	—	—
	G.V. Palmer	17	3	57	0	—	—	—	—
Surrey	C.K. Bullen	9	0	22	0	—	—	—	—
	M.S. Butcher	1	0	2	0	—	—	—	—
Warw	P.J. Hartley	57	11	215	2	107.50	2-45	—	—
	K.R. Maguire	35	6	123	1	123.00	1-32	—	—
	P.A. Smith	136	21	536	10	53.60	2-12	—	—
Worcs	R.M. Ellcock	26.1	2	90	3	30.00	3-80	—	—
	R.K. Illingworth	260.4	59	811	18	45.05	4-85	—	—
	P.J. Newport	47	1	238	6	39.66	4-76	—	—
	A.E. Warner	202.1	34	707	19	37.21	4-73	—	—
Yorks	P.A. Booth	10	3	22	0	—	—	—	—
	N.S. Taylor	84.1	16	293	8	36.62	2-45	—	—
CU	C.C. Ellison	96.5	20	314	5	62.80	3-30	—	—
	P.D. Griffiths	9	2	39	0	—	—	—	—
	A.J. Pollock	115.5	18	483	14	34.50	5-108	1	—
OU	J.J. Cassidy	4	2	12	0	—	—	—	—
	P.J. Crowe	36	4	121	1	121.00	1-105	—	—
	A.D. Gilfillan	51	5	218	2	109.00	2-177	—	—
	M.P. Lawrence	99	20	366	2	183.00	1-32	—	—
	H.T. Rawlinson	96.1	9	435	5	87.00	2-102	—	—
	G.J. Toogood	3	0	22	0	—	—	—	—
	J.G. Varey	132	15	550	3	183.33	1-13	—	—

Obituaries 1981-82

In writing just a little on each of the foremost cricketers who have died in the year coinciding with the end of the 1982 season, I have one qualification which I record with mixed feelings: I either knew them and/or saw them all play. With several I even took the field. Seniority of age is an unexceptionable batting order, and it has the advantage, as it happens, of putting in first *Andrew Sandham*, no less, coupled inseparably and always with Sir Jack Hobbs. One of the great opening pairs of history they were, and as men most modest, a pattern to all aspiring sportsmen. Andrew died at 91, not long after *Lord Cornwallis* (89), Kent's captain 1924-26 and a man so devoted to county affairs and institutions that he was called 'The Spirit of Kent'.

Geoffrey Lowndes (84) in his middle thirties answered Hampshire's call to the captaincy, as good cricketers in those days sometimes could, for two summers and is remembered for making a sparkling 140 against the Australians. The name of *Hal Hooker* (83) is secure as joint holder with Alan Kippax of the world's 10th-wicket record of 307 for NSW v Victoria. When we were fellow-broadcasters in Australia Hal liked to tell how Victoria's captain, when his opponents were 157 for 9 at lunch needing another 60 to avoid the danger of following on, sought the opinion of Hugh Trumble, the Melbourne CC secretary, as to whether to enforce. Trumble said he'd better get them out first — which they did the day after next.

Norman Partridge (81) was a talented part-time amateur between the wars. *'Nobby' Clark* (79) was much more than that, with 8 England caps as a fast left-arm bowler, deadly one day but wayward the next. *Harry Crabtree* (76) was a good cricketer, who was also a pioneer of modern coaching, under the aegis of MCC. *Tom Longfield* (75) was a notable player and administrator in India when it was in its early days as a Test — playing country. *Jack Stephenson* (74) had 'temperament' of the right kind, bred of intense enthusiasm. Many a worse bowler has worn England's colours. *Jack Fingleton* (73) was a doughty, uncompromising performer both with bat and pen. A cricketer-journalist, he spoke 'having authority and not as the scribes'. *Eddie Watts* (70) decorated the Oval with a fine, high action and cheerful demeanour. Geoff Chubb (71), an opening bowler, was the oldest man to be first capped by South Africa, but ever young at heart. *Meyer-Homji* (70) was India's reserve wicket-keeper on their 1936 tour. *Tom Reddick* (70) was an admirable coach, in both England and South Africa, and a stylish batsman.

Derek Sealy (69) was at the other end of the scale from Chubb, at 17⅓ the youngest man (apart from four precocious Pakistanis) ever to be chosen for a Test match. *Charlie Grove* (69) helped Warwickshire to their 1951 Championship, a fastish, cheerful bowler built for hard work. *Alan Skinner* (68) was also concerned with a midland title, that of Derbyshire in 1936. A member of a third Championship-winning team was *Len Muncer* (68), whose off-breaks were crucial to the Glamorgan victory of 1948. He was later head coach at Lord's.

Ken Mackay (56) was the youngest cricketer of high distinction to die during the year under review, an idiosyncratic all-rounder and — like all the foregoing, with only minor qualifications — a model sportsman, widely popular.

Finally, a select list of those who have served the game with distinction off the field. *Marjorie Pollard* (81) was a pioneer of both the Women's Cricket Association and of women games-writers. *Edmund King* (75) gave 45 years of committee service to Warwickshire, and was one of the most important and respected architects in 1968 of the new TCCB. *Ray Robinson* (73) was perhaps the most widely read and respected of all Australian cricket-writers pure and simple. *Harold Burnett* (64) was secretary of the West Indian Board of Control at his death, a zealous worker for harmony in cricket as, finally, was *Rashid Varachia* (64), President of the recently formed non-racial South African Cricket Union — which could indeed ill afford to lose him.

E.W. Swanton

Career Details (b — born; d — died; F-c — first-class career)

BEARD, Donald Derek; b Palmerston North 14 Jan 1920; d in England 15 Jul 82. Central Districts, N. Districts and New Zealand. F-c (1945-65): 2166 runs (22.10); 278 wkts (21.58).

BESSANT, John; b New Forest, Hants, 11 Nov 1892; d Bristol 18 Jan 82. Glos. F-c (1921-28): 1200 runs (10.26); 130 wkts (35.50).

BROUGHTON, Ernest Alfred; b Wigston, Leics, 22 Apr 1905; d 19 Feb 82. Leics. F-c (1928-33): 482 runs (13.03).

CHUBB, Geoffrey Walter Ashton; b E. London, SA, 12 Apr 1911; d E. London, 28 Aug 82. Border, Transvaal, and South Africa. F-c (1931-51): 835 runs (18.15); 160 wkts (23.91). Test debut aged 40 years 56 days.

CLARK, Edward Winchester ('Nobby'); b nr Peterborough 9 Aug 1902; d nr King's Lynn, Norfolk, 28 Apr 82. Northants and England. F-c (1922-47): 1963 runs (6.25); 1203 wkts (21.54).

CORNWALLIS, Capt. Hon. Wykeham Stanley, KCVO, KBE, MC, 2nd Baron Cornwallis of Linton; b Linton Park, Maidstone, 14 Mar 1892; d Linton Park 4 Jan 82. Kent (capt. 1924-26). F-c (1919-26): 994 runs (11.55); 118 wkts (32.39).

CRABTREE, Harry Pollard, MBE; b Barnoldswick, Yorks (now Lancs), 30 Apr 1906; d Brentwood, Essex, 28 May 82. Essex. F-c (1931-47): 1281 runs (32.02), 4 hundreds.

FINGLETON, John Henry Webb, OBE; b Waverley, Sydney, 28 Apr 1908; d Killara, Sydney, 22 Nov 81. NSW and Australia. F-c (1928-29 to 1939-40): 6816 runs (44.54), 22 hundreds.

GROVE, Charles William; b Yardley, Birmingham, 16 Dec 1912; d Solihull, Warwicks, 15 Feb 82. Warwicks (1938-53) and Worcs (1954). F-c: 3161 runs (11.58), 1 hundred; 744 wkts (22.67).

HILL-WOOD, Denis John Charles Hill; b Hoxne, Norfolk, 25 Jun 1906; d Hartley Wintney, Hants, 4 May 82. Derbys. F-c (1928-29): 453 runs (22.65); 3 wkts (41.00).

HOOKER, John Edward Halford ('Hal'); b Summer Hill, Sydney, 6 Mar 1898; d Mosman, Sydney, 12 Feb 82. NSW. F-c (1924-25 to 1931-32): 421 runs (20.04); 271 wkts (24.40).

HUSSAIN, Syed Mohammad; b Hyderabad 8 Dec 1902; d Hyderabad 2 July 82. Hyderabad, Moslems, and All-India (toured UK 1936). Ranji Trophy (1934-43): 449 runs (29.93).

LEE, Frank Stanley; b Marylebone, London, 24 Jul 1905; d 30 Mar 82. Middx (1925) and Somerset (1929-47). Umpired 29 Tests. F-c: 15,310 runs (27.93), 23 hundreds: 25 wkts (30.48).

LONGFIELD, Thomas Cuthbert; b 12 May 1906; d 21 Dec 81. Cambridge U. (Blue 1927 and 1928), Kent, Bengal, and Europeans. Kent (1927-39): 731 runs (19.75); 23 wkts (66.26).

LOWNDES, William Geoffrey Lowndes Frith; b 24 Jan 1898; d Newbury, Berks, 23 May 82. Oxford U. (Blue 1921) and Hants (1924-35, capt. 1934-35). F-c (1921-36): 3257 runs (23.94), 5 hundreds; 75 wkts (39.16).

MACKAY, Kenneth Donald ('Slasher'), MBE: b Windsor, Brisbane, 24 Oct 1925; d   Stradbroke Island 13 Jun 82. Queensland and Australia. F-c (1946-47 to 1963-64): 10,823 runs (43.64), 23 hundreds; 251 wkts (33.31).

MEHERHOMJI, Khurshed Rustomji; b Bombay 9 Aug 1911; d Bombay 10 Feb 82. W. India, Bombay, Freelooters, Parsees, and India. Toured UK 1936. Wicket-keeper.

MUNCER, Bernard Leonard; b Hampstead, London, 23 Oct 1913; d 18 Jan 82. Middx (1933-46) and Glam (1947-54). F-c (1933-57): 8646 runs (20.88), 4 hundreds; 755 wkts (20.91).

NICOLSON, Frank ('Nipper'); b Millom, Cumberland, 9 Sep 1909; d Port Elizabeth 30 Jul 82. Griqualand West and South Africa. F-c (1927-28 to 1946-47): 4 hundreds; 32 ct, 32 st.

PARTRIDGE, Norman Ernest; b Great Barr, Staffs, 10 Aug 1900; d Aberystwyth 10 Mar 82. Cambridge U. (Blue 1920) and Warwicks. F-c (1920-37): 2719 runs (18.61) 1 hundred; 393 wkts (23.02).

POWELL, Adam Gordon; b Boxted, Essex, 17 Aug 1912; d Sandwich, Kent, 7 Jun 82. Cambridge U. (Blue 1934), Essex and Suffolk. MCC tour to Australia and New Zealand 1935-36. F-c (1932-37): 768 runs (14.37); 59 ct, 14 st.

REDDICK, Tom Bockenham; b Shanghai, China, 17 Feb 1912; d Cape Town 1 Jun 82. Middx (1931), Notts (1946-47), and W. Province. F-c (1931-51): 2688 runs (30.55), 2 hundreds; 6 wkts (78.00).

SANDHAM, Andrew; b Streatham, London, ꜜ Jul 1890; d 20 Apr 82. Surrey and England. First to score 300 in Test — 325 v West Indies, Kingston, 1929-30. Shared 63 century 1st-wicket partnerships with J.B. Hobbs. F-c (1911-37); 41,284 runs (44.83), 107 hundreds.

SEALY, James Edward Derek; b Barbados 11 Sep 1912; d Trinidad Feb 82. Barbados, Trinidad, and West Indies (debut aged 17 years 122 days). F-c: 3831 runs (30.40); 63 wkts (28.60).

SIEDLE, Ivan Julian ('Jack'); b Durban 11 Jan 1903; d Durban 24 Aug 82. Natal and South Africa. F-c (1922-23 to 1936-37): 7730 (40.05), 17 hundreds.

SKINNER, Alan Frank, OBE: b Brighton, Sussex, 22 Apr 1913; d Bury St Edmunds, Suffolk, 28 Feb 82. Cambridge U. (1934 — no Blue), Derbys (1931-38), and Northants (1949). F-c (1931-49): 3537 runs (26.20), 1 hundred; 6 wkts (41.67).

STEPHENSON, Lt Col John William Arthur, DSO; b Hong Kong 1 Aug 1907; d Pulborough, Sussex 20 May 82. Army, Europeans, Essex (1934-39), Worcs (1947), and Bucks (1927-32). Took 9-46 for Gentlemen v Players, Lord's, 1936. F-c (1931-48): 2582 runs (21.34), 2 hundreds; 311 wkts (23.99).

WATTS, Edward Alfred; b Peckham, London, 1 Aug 1911; d Cheam 2 May 82. Surrey. Took 10-67 for Surrey v Warwicks, Birmingham, 1939. F-c (1933-49): 6158 runs (21.29), 2 hundreds; 729 wkts (26.07).

Their Record in Tests

Batting and Fielding

	M	I	NO	HS	R	Avge	100	50	Ct	St
E.W. Clark† (Eng.)	8	9	5	10	36	9.00	—	—	—	—
A. Sandham (Eng.)	14	23	0	325	879	38.21	2	3	4	—
J.H.W. Fingleton (Aus.)	18	29	1	136	1189	42.46	5	3	13	—
K.D. Mackay† (Aus.)	37	52	7	89	1507	33.48	—	13	16	—
G.W.A. Chubb (SA)	5	9	3	15*	63	10.50	—	—	—	—
F. Nicholson (SA)	4	8	1	29	76	10.85	—	—	3	—
I.J. Siedle (SA)	18	34	0	141	977	28.73	1	5	7	—
J.E.D. Sealy (WI)	11	19	2	92	478	28.11	—	3	6	1
D.D. Beard (NZ)	4	7	2	31	101	20.20	—	—	2	—
K.R. Meherhomji (Ind.)	1	1	1	0*	0	—	—	—	1	—

† Left-handed batsman.

Bowling

	Type	Balls	R	W	Avge	Best	5w/I	10w/M
E.W. Clark (Eng.)	LF	1931	899	32	28.09	5-98	1	—
K.D. Mackay (Aus.)	RM	5792	1721	50	34.42	6-42	2	—
G.W.A. Chubb (SA)	RM	1425	577	21	27.47	6-51	2	—
I.J. Siedle (SA)		19	7	1	7.00	1-7	—	—
J.E.D. Sealy (WI)	RM	156	94	3	31.33	2-7	—	—
D.D. Beard (NZ)	RM	812	302	9	33.55	3-22	—	—

Two Great Milestones

Two world Test records were set during the 1981-82 season. Geoffrey Boycott became the leading scorer in Test cricket on 23 December in Delhi during his century for England in the third Test against India. Four days later in Melbourne, Dennis Lillee became the most successful wicket-taker at official international level during Australia's first Test against West Indies.

Geoffrey Boycott
The highest individual aggregate of runs in Test cricket is 8,114 (average 47.72) by Geoffrey Boycott for England in 108 Tests (193 innings) between 4 June 1964 and 6 January 1982. Boycott's first scoring stroke in Test cricket was a boundary four off the bowling of Australia's Graham McKenzie from the 16th ball he had faced in the first Test at Trent Bridge. He broke the previous record of 8,032 runs, scored for West Indies by Sir Garfield Sobers in 160 innings, with another boundary, off Dilip Doshi of India, at 4.23 p.m. on 23 December 1981 at Delhi. Boycott's record aggregate was the result of batting for 27,332 minutes (455 hr 32 min), or the equivalent of being at the crease throughout 76 six-hour match days or 15 complete five-day Tests. He hit 793 fours, 7 fives, and 9 sixes — the last six coming from a hook off Keith Boyce (West Indies) at The Oval at 12.12 p.m. on 28 July 1973. Boycott scored his runs at an average rate of 17.8 per hour.

In addition to setting new records for the most runs and longest batting time in a Test career, Boycott had more innings (193) and scored more fifties (64, including 22 hundreds) than any other batsman. Only Cowdrey played in more Tests (114), and only Bradman, Sobers, and Gavaskar scored more centuries. Boycott also shared in more century partnerships in Test matches than any other batsman, 20 of the 47 being for the first wicket.

Runs Distribution

Australia	South Africa	West Indies	New Zealand	India	Pakistan
2,945	373	2,205	916	1,084	591

Dennis Lillee
At 2.55 p.m. on 27 December 1981, Dennis Lillee induced an edged stroke from Larry Gomes which was caught by Greg Chappell at first slip. It was the second day of the Melbourne Test between Australia and West Indies, and Lillee had overhauled the world record of 309 Test wickets held by Lance Gibbs for almost six years. By a remarkable coincidence, Lillee had gained the record on the very ground where, on 31 January 1976, Gibbs had beaten the previous highest aggregate (Trueman's 307), and just four days after Boycott had exceeded the record batting aggregate established by Sobers.

	Wkts	Tests	Innings	Balls	5 Wkts
D.K. Lillee	310	58	110	15,389†	22
L.R. Gibbs	309	79	148	27,115	18
F.S. Trueman	307	67	127	15,178	17

† Up to and including the ball with which he took his 310th wicket.

Lillee has subsequently extended his record for the most wickets in Test matches to 328 from 29 January 1971 until 22 March 1982. His method of dismissal reads: 88 caught by Rodney Marsh (Test record for individual catches off one bowler), 130 caught by other fieldsmen, 58 leg before wicket, 51 bowled, and just one caught-and-bowled (Dilley at Headingley in 1981).

Wickets Distribution

England	West Indies	New Zealand	India	Pakistan
163	55	38	21	51

The above extracts are from Bill Frindall's *Guinness Book of Cricket Facts and Feats* to be published by Guinness Superlatives in 1983.

Looking forward

England on Tour 1982-83

England's Tour Party

	Age	Caps
Bob Willis, capt. (Warwicks)	33	74
Ian Botham (Somerset)	26	54
Geoff Cook (Northants)	31	4
Norman Cowans (Middx)	21	0
Graeme Fowler (Lancs)	25	1
Ian Gould (Sussex)	25	0
David Gower (Leics)	25	44
Eddie Hemmings (Notts)	33	2
Robin Jackman (Surrey)	37	4
Allan Lamb (Northants)	28	6
Vic Marks (Somerset)	27	1
Geoff Miller (Derbys)	30	27
Derek Pringle (Essex)	24	4
Derek Randall (Notts)	31	33
Chris Tavaré (Kent)	27	17
Bob Taylor (Derbys)	41	42

Tour manager, Doug Insole; asst. mngr., Norman Gifford; physiotherapist, Bernard Thomas; scorer, Geoffrey Saulez.

Tour Itinerary
In Australia
Oct.	22-25	Queensland (Brisbane)
	27-29	New South Wales (Newcastle)
	31-3 Nov.	South Australia (Adelaide)
Nov.	5-8	Western Australia (Perth)
	12-17	AUSTRALIA (Perth), 1st Test
	20-23	New South Wales (Sydney)
	26-1 Dec.	AUSTRALIA (Brisbane), 2nd Test
Dec.	4-7	Victoria (Melbourne)
	10-15	AUSTRALIA (Adelaide), 3rd Test
	18-20	Tasmania (Hobart)
	22	Tasmania (Launceston)
	26-30	AUSTRALIA (Melbourne), 4th Test
Jan.	2-7	AUSTRALIA (Sydney), 5th Test

Benson & Hedges World Series Cup
Three-cornered series of one-day internationals, with top two meeting in best-of-three final; Australia (A), England (E), New Zealand (N).

Jan. 9 A v N (Melbourne), 11 A v E (Sydney), 13 E v N (Melbourne), 15 E v N (Brisbane), 16 A v E (Brisbane), 18 A v N (Sydney), 20 E v N (Sydney), 22 A v N (Melbourne), 23 A v E (Melbourne), 26 A v E (Sydney), 29 E v N (Adelaide), 30 A v E (Adelaide), 31 A v N (Adelaide), Feb. 5 E v N (Perth), 6 A v N (Perth). Finals: Feb. 9 (Sydney), 13 (Melbourne), 16 (Sydney).

In New Zealand:
One-day internationals, New Zealand v England: Feb. 19 (Auckland), 23 (Wellington), 26 (Christchurch).

The 1983 Season

Not everything comes more easily with experience, and the staging of the World Cup, which will be the main event of the 1983 season in England, was scarcely facilitated by the two previous Prudential jamborees in 1975 and 1979. For a long time it was by no means certain to come off.

The chief debating-point this time was the distribution of the loot. One reason for starting the World Cup in the first place was to help the funds of the associate member-countries of the ICC who had few sources of income of their own. With the passing years and the growing commercialism of cricket, this noble purpose was rivalled by other financial aims. The Australian players are said not to have been happy with what they received in 1979, and if Australia did not send a team, or a fully representative one, the World Cup, already lacking one of the strongest cricketing nations, South Africa, would scarcely justify the name.

More difficult to settle was the English dissatisfaction with previous arrangements. The TCCB wanted compensation for the loss of one Test match and three one-day international matches, which would otherwise have been played against New Zealand and from which they would have earned more than their share of the World Cup profits.

There was also a feeling among some associate member-countries that three of them, not just one, should take part in the World Cup, bringing the field up to 10. This idea was rejected, presumably because the competition occupies long enough already.

Eventually agreement was reached over a share-out, sighs of relief were heaved, and the World Cup 1983 goes ahead. Since then, it has been greatly helped by the fact that the draw has worked out very well.

The tough opposition offered by Pakistan last summer was a reminder that England are in a competitive group in which they have no room for error against either New Zealand or Sri Lanka, even though all opponents are to be met twice. The ease with which the stalwart Zimbabweans (formerly the 'wicked' Rhodesians) swept aside opponents in the ICC Trophy last summer suggests that they may be no push-over in the other group for Australia, West Indies, and India. They have, after all, a background of many years first-class cricket in the Currie Cup in South Africa.

After the World Cup comes the four-match Test series between England and New Zealand, who have improved steadily in recent years with wider experience, more confidence, and such redoubtable full-time professionals as Glenn Turner, Richard Hadlee, and John Wright.

England last played New Zealand in 1978. Now they are playing them in one-day matches in Australia this winter, in a Test series in England next summer, and again in New Zealand next winter. Recently England and India met twice within a few months. In 1980 and 1981, England and West Indies played 11 Tests against each other in 11 months.

This is the age of 'marketing', and presumably the planners know what they are about. But I wish they would answer the innumerable readers' letters on the subject received over the last few years.

Domestic Fixtures 1983

Duration of Matches (* including play on Sunday)

Cornhill Tests	5 days		Prudential Cup	1 day
Schweppes Championship	3 days		NatWest Bank Trophy	1 day
Tourist matches	3 days or as stated		Benson & Hedges Cup	1 day
			John Player League	1 day
University matches	3 days		Other matches	as stated

Sun 8		**JPL**	
	Southampton	Hants v Essex	
	Canterbury	Kent v Surrey	
	Old Trafford	Lancs v Derby	
	Leicester	Leics v Worcs	
	Lord's	Middx v Glam	
	Northampton	Northants v Notts	
	Taunton	Somerset v Sussex	
	Edgbaston	Warw v Yorks	
Wed 11		**Championship**	
	Chesterfield	Derby v Lancs	
	Chelmsford	Essex v Kent	
	Gloucester	Glos v Sussex	
	Southampton	Hants v Warw	
	Lord's	Middx v Yorks	
	Northampton	Northants v Notts	
	The Oval	Surrey v Leics	
	Worcester	Worcs v Somerset	
		Other match	
	Oxford	Univ v Glam	
Sat 14		**B & H Cup**	
	Chelmsford	Essex v Somerset	
	Gloucester	Glos v Leics	
	Canterbury	Kent v Middx	
	Hove	Sussex v Minor Cts	
	Edgbaston	Warw v Derby	
	Bradford	Yorks v Notts	
		Scotland v Worcs	
	Oxford	Combined Univ v Glam	
Sun 15		**JPL**	
	Derby	Derby v Northants	
	Chelmsford	Essex v Lancs	
	Swansea	Glam v Warw	
	Gloucester	Glos v Leics	
	Lord's	Middx v Hampshire	
	Trent Bridge	Notts v Somerset	
	Hove	Sussex v Kent	
	Headingley	Yorks v Surrey	
Tue 17		**B & H Cup**	
	Canterbury	Kent v Surrey	
	Leicester	Leics v Northants	
	Lord's	Middlesex v Glam	
	Trent Bridge	Notts v Derby	
	Taunton	Somerset v Hampshire	
	Headingley	Yorks v Lancs	
		Scotland v Glos	
	Slough	Minor Cts v Essex	

April			
Wed 20	Cambridge	Univ v Glam	
Sat 23	Cambridge	Univ v Leics	
	Oxford	Univ v Lancs	
Wed 27	Lord's	MCC v Middx	
	Cambridge	Univ v Essex	
	Oxford	Univ v Somerset	
Sat 30		**Championship**	
	Derby	Derby v Glos	
	Old Trafford	Lancs v Glam	
	Leicester	Leics v Hants	
	Lord's	Middx v Essex	
	Trent Bridge	Notts v Somerset	
	The Oval	Surrey v Kent	
	Edgbaston	Warw v Northants	
	Worcester	Worcs v Yorks	
		Other match	
	Oxford	Univ v Sussex	
May			
Sun 1	Old Trafford	Lancs v Glam (1 day)	
Wed 4		**Championship**	
	Cardiff	Glam v Essex	
	Bristol	Glos v Surrey	
	Leicester	Leics v Derby	
	Lord's	Middx v Lancs	
	Northampton	Northants v Hants	
	Taunton	Somerset v Worcs	
	Hove	Sussex v Notts	
	Headingley	Yorks v Warw	
		Other Match	
	Cambridge	Univ v Kent	
Sat 7		**B & H Cup**	
	Chesterfield	Derby v Yorks	
	Southampton	Hants v Essex	
	Old Trafford	Lancs v Warw	
	Northampton	Northants v Glos	
	Taunton	Somerset v Sussex	
	The Oval	Surrey v Middx	
	Worcester	Worcs v Leics	
	Cambridge	Combined Univ v Ker	

May (contd)		

Thu 19		**B & H Cup**	Wed 1		**B & H Cup**
	Derby	Derby v Lancs			*(Quarter-Finals)*
	Chelmsford	Essex v Sussex			
	Cardiff	Glam v Surrey	Sat 4		**Championship**
	Bournemouth	Hampshire v Minor Cts		Derby	Derby v Hampshire
	Leicester	Leics v Scotland		Dartford	Kent v Middlesex
	Lord's	Middlesex v Combined		Trent Bridge	Notts v Leics
		Universities		Taunton	Somerset v Essex
	Trent Bridge	Notts v Warw		Hove	Sussex v Worcs
	Worcester	Worcs v Northants		Edgbaston	Warw v Lancs
				Middlesbrough	Yorks v Glam
Sat 21		**B & H Cup**			
	Swansea	Glam v Kent	Sun 5		**JPL**
	Bristol	Glos v Worcs		Bristol	Glos v Surrey
	Old Trafford	Lancs v Notts		Old Trafford	Lancs v Northants
	Northampton	Northants v Scotland		Lord's	Middx v Worcs
	The Oval	Surrey v Combined		Trent Bridge	Notts v Glam
		Univs		Taunton	Somerset v Essex
	Hove	Sussex v Hampshire		Edgbaston	Warw v Derby
	Edgbaston	Warw v Yorks		Middlesbrough	Yorks v Hampshire
	Slough	Minor Cts v Somerset			
			Wed 8		**Championship**
Sun 22		**JPL**		Chelmsford	Essex v Notts
	Chelmsford	Essex v Derbyshire		Bristol	Glos v Somerset
	Bournemouth	Hampshire v Northants		Bournemouth	Hampshire v Lancs
	Leicester	Leics v Kent		Leicester	Leics v Yorks
	The Oval	Surrey v Somerset		Uxbridge	Middx v Derby
	Edgbaston	Warw v Lancs		Hove	Sussex v Kent
	Worcs	Worcs v Glos		Worcester	Worcs v Surrey
		Yorks v Middx			
					Other matches
Wed 25		**Championship**		Cambridge	Univ v Warw
	Southampton	Hampshire v Worcs		Oxford	Univ v Northants
	Leicester	Leics v Essex			
	Lord's	Middx v Glam	Thu 9		**Prudential Cup**
	Taunton	Somerset v Sussex		Trent Bridge	Australia v Zimbabwe
	The Oval	Surrey v Lancs		The Oval	England v New Zealand
	Edgbaston	Warw v Glos		Swansea	Pakistan v Sri Lanka
	Bradford	Yorks v Northants		Old Trafford	West Indies v India
Sat 28		**Championship**	Sat 11		**Prudential Cup**
	Chelmsford	Essex v Surrey		Taunton	England v Sri Lanka
	Swansea	Glam v Glos		Leicester	India v Zimbabwe
	Canterbury	Kent v Hampshire		Edgbaston	Pakistan v New Zealand
	Old Trafford	Lancs v Yorks		Headingley	West Indies v Australia
	Lord's	Middx v Sussex			
	Northampton	Northants v Leics			**Championship**
	Trent Bridge	Notts v Derby		Derby	Derby v Leics
	Worcester	Worcs v Warw		Cardiff	Glam v Warw
				Tunbridge	Kent v Essex
Sun 29		**JPL**		Wells	
	Swansea	Glam v Lancs		Old Trafford	Lancs v Notts
	Canterbury	Kent v Hampshire		Northampton	Northants v Glos
	Lord's	Middx v Sussex		The Oval	Surrey v Middx
	Northampton	Northants v Leics		Hove	Sussex v Somerset
	Trent Bridge	Notts v Surrey			
	Bradford	Yorks v Somerset			**Other match**
				Oxford	Univ v Hampshire

June (contd)

Sun 12		**JPL**
Derby	Derby v Leics
Chelmsford	Essex v Kent
Cardiff	Glam v Yorks
Old Trafford	Lancashire v Notts
Northampton	Northants v Glos
The Oval	Surrey v Middx
Hove	Sussex v Warw

Mon 13		**Prudential Cup**
Lord's	England v Pakistan
Trent Bridge	India v Australia
Bristol	New Zealand v Sri Lanka
Worcester	West Indies v Zimbabwe

Wed 15		**Prudential Cup**
Edgbaston	England v New Zealand
The Oval	West Indies v India
	Championship
Derby	Derby v Essex
Swansea	Glam v Somerset
Tunbridge Wells	Kent v Sussex
Old Trafford	Lancs v Warw
Leicester	Leics v Glos
Uxbridge	Middx v Hampshire
Trent Bridge	Notts v Surrey
	Other matches
Cambridge	Univ v Northants
Oxford	Univ v Worcs

Thu 16		**Prudential Cup**
Southampton	Australia v Zimbabwe
Headingley	Pakistan v Sri Lanka

Sat 18		**Prudential Cup**
Old Trafford	England v Pakistan India v Zimbabwe
Derby	New Zealand v Sri Lanka
Lord's	West Indies v Australia
	Championship
Bristol	Glos v Kent
Southampton	Hampshire v Yorks
Northampton	Northants v Warw
Bath	Somerset v Derby
Horsham	Sussex v Lancs
Worcs	Worcs v Middlesex
	Other matches
Cambridge	Univ v Notts Surrey v Oxford

Sun 19		**JPL**
Bristol	Glos v Kent
Basingstoke	Hampshire v Leics
Luton	Northants v Warw
Bath	Somerset v Glam
Horsham	Sussex v Lancs
Worcester	Worcs v Essex

Mon 20		**Prudential Cup**
Chelmsford	Australia v India
Headingley	England v Sri Lanka
Trent Bridge	New Zealand v Pakistan
Edgbaston	West Indies v Zimbabwe

Wed 22	Old Trafford and The Oval	**Prudential Cup** *(Semi-Finals)*
	Championship
Ilford	Essex v Northants
Abergavenny	Glam v Worcs
Basingstoke	Hampshire v Sussex
Leicester	Leics v Surrey
Trent Bridge	Notts v Kent
Bath	Somerset v Glos
Sheffield	Yorks v Derby
	Other matches
Cambridge	Univ v Middx
Edgbaston	Warw v Oxford

Sat 25	Lord's	**Prudential Cup Final**
	Championship
Chesterfield	Derby v Middx
Ilford	Essex v Sussex
Bristol	Glos v Hampshire
Leicester	Leics v Glam
Trent Bridge	Notts v Lancashire
The Oval	Surrey v Northants
Edgbaston	Warw v Yorks
	Other match
Worcester	Worcs v Cambridge

Sun 26		**JPL**
Chesterfield	Derby v Middx
Ilford	Essex v Sussex
Canterbury	Kent v Notts
Leicester	Leics v Glam
Bath	Somerset v Glos
East Molesey	Surrey v Northants
Edgbaston	Warw v Hampshire
Worcester	Worcs v Yorks

June (contd)

Wed 29

NatWest Trophy
(1st Round)
Berks v Yorks
Cambs v Middx
Dorset v Essex
Durham v Lancs
Glos v Scotland
Herts v Hants
Ireland v Sussex

Canterbury — Kent v Cheshire
Leicester — Leics v Devon
Lincs v Surrey
Norfolk v Glam
Shrops v Somerset
Suffolk v Derby
Edgbaston — Warw v Oxon
Wilts v Northants
Worcester — Worcs v Notts

Other match
Lord's — Oxford v Cambridge

Thu 30 Portsmouth — Combined Services v
New Zealand (2 days)

July

Sat 2

Championship
Derby — Derbyshire v Worcs
Canterbury — Kent v Glam
Liverpool — Lancs v Hampshire
Trent Bridge — Notts v Essex
The Oval — Surrey v Glos
Hove — Sussex v Northants
Edgbaston — Warw v Middx
Harrogate — Yorks v Leics

Tourist match
*Taunton — Somerset v New Zealand

Sun 3

JPL
Derby — Derby v Worcs
Old Trafford — Lancs v Hampshire
Lord's — Middx v Glos
Trent Bridge — Notts v Essex
Hove — Sussex v Northants
Scarborough — Yorks v Leics

Wed 6

B & H Cup
(Semi-Finals)

Tourist match
Bristol — Glos v New Zealand
(or another county if
Glos in B & H
semi-final)

Other match
Harrogate — Tilcon Trophy (3 days)

July (contd)

Sat 9

Championship
Cardiff — Glam v Sussex
Bristol — Glos v Derby
Southampton — Hampshire v Surrey
Maidstone — Kent v Lancs
Leicester — Leics v Somerset
Northampton — Northants v Yorks
Edgbaston — Warw v Essex
Worcester — Worcs v Notts

Tourist match
*Lord's — Middx v New Zealand

Sun 10

JPL
Cardiff — Glam v Sussex
Bristol — Glos v Derby
Portsmouth — Hampshire v Surrey
Maidstone — Kent v Lancashire
Leicester — Leics v Somerset
Tring — Northants v Yorks
Edgbaston — Warw v Essex
Worcester — Worcs v Notts

Wed 13

Championship
Southend — Essex v Hampshire
Swansea — Glam v Lancashire
Bristol — Glos v Middlesex
Maidstone — Kent v Somerset
Trent Bridge — Notts v Northants
Edgbaston — Warw v Derby
Worcester — Worcs v Leics
Headingley — Yorks v Sussex

Thu 14

Cornhill Series
(1st Test)
The Oval — ENGLAND v NEW
ZEALAND

Sat 16

Championship
Derby — Derby v Northants
Southend — Essex v Glam
Bournemouth — Hampshire v Notts
Old Trafford — Lancs v Worcs
Lord's — Middlesex v Leics
Taunton — Somerset v Surrey
Sheffield — Yorks v Kent

Sun 17

JPL
Southend — Essex v Glam
Bristol — Glos v Warw
Portsmouth — Hampshire v Notts
Old Trafford — Lancs v Worcs
Lord's — Middx v Leics
Hull — Yorks v Kent

July (contd)

Wed 20		**NatWest Trophy**
		(2nd Round)
		Berks or Yorks v Wilts
		or Northants
		Dorset or Essex v Kent
		or Cheshire
		Durham or Lancs v
		Shrops or Somerset
		Ireland or Sussex v
		Worcs or Notts
		Leics or Devon v
		Glos or Scotland
		Lincs or Surrey v
		Warw or Oxon
		Norfolk or Glam v
		Herts or Hants
		Suffolk or Derby v
		Cambs or Middx
		Tourist match
	Trent Bridge	Notts or Worcs v New
	or Worcester	Zealand (loser of
		NatWest Trophy
		1st Round Match)
Sat 23	Lord's	**B & H Cup Final**
		Tourist match
	Edgbaston	Warw v New Zealand
		(or another county if
		Warw in B & H Final)
Sun 24		**JPL**
	Derby	Derby v Notts
	Canterbury	Kent v Middx
	Leicester	Leics v Essex
	Northampton	Northants v Glam
	Taunton	Somerset v Hampshire
	The Oval	Surrey v Lancs
	Hastings	Sussex v Yorks
	Edgbaston	Warw v Worcs
Wed 27		**Championship**
	Portsmouth	Hampshire v Derby
	Southport	Lancs v Glos
	Northampton	Northants v Somerset
	The Oval	Surrey v Notts
	Hove	Sussex v Essex
	Edgbaston	Warw v Kent
	Worcester	Worcs v Glam
Thu 28		**Cornhill Series**
		(2nd Test)
	Headingley	ENGLAND v NEW
		ZEALAND

Sat 30		**Championship**
	Chesterfield	Derby v Kent
	Swansea	Glam v Surrey
	Portsmouth	Hampshire v Glos
	Old Trafford	Lancs v Somerset
	Hinckley	Leics v Sussex
	Lord's	Middx v Warw
	Northampton	Northants v Worcs
	Worksop	Notts v Yorks
Sun 31		**JPL**
	Chesterfield	Derby v Kent
	Swansea	Glam v Surrey
	Bournemouth	Hampshire v Glos
	Old Trafford	Lancs v Somerset
	Leicester	Leics v Sussex
	Lord's	Middx v Warw
	Trent Bridge	Notts v Yorks
	Worcester	Worcs v Northants

August

Wed 3		**NatWest Trophy**
		(Quarter-Finals)
		Tourist match
	Northampton	Northants v New
		Zealand (or another
		county if
		Northants in
		NatWest quarter-
		finals)
Sat 6		**Championship**
	Chelmsford	Essex v Middx
	Cheltenham	Glos v Glam
	Canterbury	Kent v Worcs
	Leics	Leics v Notts
	Weston-super-	Somerset v Northants
	Mare	
	The Oval	Surrey v Warw
	Eastbourne	Sussex v Derby
	Headingley	Yorks v Lancs
		Tourist match
	*Bournemouth	Hampshire v New
		Zealand
Sun 7		**JPL**
	Chelmsford	Essex v Middx
	Cheltenham	Glos v Glam
	Canterbury	Kent v Worcs
	Leicester	Leics v Notts
	Weston-super-	Somerset v Northants
	Mare	
	The Oval	Surrey v Warw
	Eastbourne	Sussex v Derby
	Headingley	Yorks v Lancs

August (contd)

Sun 7
                  Other matches
                  Warwick Under-25
                  semi-finals (1 day)
                  (or Sun, 14 Aug)

Wed 10
	Championship
Chelmsford	Essex v Leics
Ebbw Vale	Glam v Notts
Cheltenham	Glos v Warw
Canterbury	Kent v Surrey
Northampton	Northants v Middx
Weston-super-Mare	Somerset v Yorks
Eastbourne	Sussex v Hampshire
Worcester	Worcs v Lancs

Thu 11
	Cornhill Series (3rd Test)
Lord's	ENGLAND v NEW ZEALAND

Sat 13
	Championship
Derby	Derby v Somerset
Cardiff	Glam v Kent
Cheltenham	Glos v Yorks
Old Trafford	Lancs v Middx
Wellingborough	Northants v Essex
Trent Bridge	Notts v Hampshire
Guildford	Surrey v Worcs
Edgbaston	Warw v Leics

Sun 14
	JPL
Heanor	Derby v Somerset
Cardiff	Glam v Kent
Cheltenham	Glos v Yorks
Old Trafford	Lancs v Middx
Wellingborough	Northants v Essex
Trent Bridge	Notts v Sussex
Guildford	Surrey v Worcs
Edgbaston	Warw v Leics

                  Other matches
                  Warwick Under-25
                  semi-finals (1 day)
                  (if not played on
                  Sun, 7 August)

Wed 17
                  NatWest Trophy
                  (Semi-Finals)

	Tourist match
Chelmsford	Essex v New Zealand (or another county if Essex in NatWest semi-final)

Sat 20
	Championship
Colchester	Essex v Glos
Swansea	Glam v Derby
Folkestone	Kent v Warw
Lord's	Middx v Somerset
Northampton	Northants v Lancs
Hove	Sussex v Surrey
Worcester	Worcs v Hampshire
Headingley	Yorks v Notts

	Tourist match
*Leicester	Leics v New Zealand

Sun 21
	JPL
Colchester	Essex v Glos
Swansea	Glam v Derby
Folkestone	Kent v Warw
Lord's	Middlesex v Somerset
Hove	Sussex v Surrey
Worcester	Worcs v Hampshire

	Other match
Edgbaston	Warwick Under-25 final (1 day)

Wed 24
	Championship
Colchester	Essex v Worcs
Bournemouth	Hampshire v Somerset
Folkestone	Kent v Leics
Blackpool	Lancs v Derby
Lord's	Middx v Surrey
Northampton	Northants v Glam
Edgbaston	Warw v Sussex
Scarborough	Yorks v Glos

Thu 25
	Cornhill Series *(4th Test)*
Trent Bridge	ENGLAND v NEW ZEALAND

Sat 27
	Championship
Chesterfield	Derby v Yorks
Bristol	Glos v Notts
Bournemouth	Hampshire v Kent
Leicester	Leics v Northants
Taunton	Somerset v Glam
The Oval	Surrey v Essex
Hove	Sussex v Middx
Edgbaston	Warw v Worcs

Sun 28
	JPL
Cardiff	Glam v Worcs
Bristol	Glos v Lancs
Southampton	Hampshire v Sussex
Milton Keynes	Northants v Middx
Taunton	Somerset v Kent
The Oval	Surrey v Essex
Edgbaston	Warw v Notts
Bradford	Yorks v Derby

August (contd)

Wed 31

	Championship
Cardiff	Glam v Northants
Bristol	Glos v Worcs
Old Trafford	Lancs v Essex
Leicester	Leics v Kent
Trent Bridge	Notts v Warw
Taunton	Somerset v Hampshire
The Oval	Surrey v Sussex
	Yorks v Middx
	Tourist match
Scarborough	Yorks & New Zealand

September

Sat 3　Lord's　　**NatWest Final**

Sun 4

	JPL
Derby	Derby v Hampshire
Leicester	Leics v Surrey
Trent Bridge	Notts v Middx
Hove	Sussex v Glos
Worcester	Worcs v Somerset
	Other matches
Scarborough	ASDA Cricket
	Challenge (3 days)

Wed 7

	Championship
Derby	Derby v Notts
Lord's	Middx v Northants
Taunton	Somerset v Kent
Hove	Sussex v Leics
Edgbaston	Warw v Glam
Worcs	Worcs v Glos
Scarborough	Yorks v Surrey

Sat 10

	Championship
Chelmsford	Essex v Yorks
Southampton	Hampshire v Glam
Canterbury	Kent v Northants
Old Trafford	Lancs v Leics
Trent Bridge	Notts v Middx
Taunton	Somerset v Warw
The Oval	Surrey v Derby
Worcester	Worcs v Sussex

Sun 11

	JPL
Chelmsford	Essex v Yorks
Bournemouth	Hampshire v Glam
Canterbury	Kent v Northants
Old Trafford	Lancs v Leics
Trent Bridge	Notts v Glos
Taunton	Somerset v Warw
The Oval	Surrey v Derby
Worcester	Worcs v Sussex

Clerical Medical Awards 1982

The men who matched us for consistency

The Clerical Medical Awards are made annually to the batsman and bowler making the most consistent contribution to Surrey and Yorkshire County Cricket. The Awards are competed for on a points system covering all first-class matches.

The 1982 winners were:

Surrey	**Yorkshire**
batting – Alan Butcher	batting – Geoff Boycott
bowling – Sylvester Clarke	bowling – Arnie Sidebottom

Clerical Medical is a leading life assurance and pensions office well known for its own consistent performance in producing high investment returns for policyholders.

Turn Black

JPS 85 DTC

MIDDLE TAR As defined in H.M. Government Tables
DANGER: H.M. Government Health Departments' WARNING:
THINK ABOUT THE HEALTH RISKS BEFORE SMOKING

This isn't a bouncer!

Congratulations to Surrey on winning the NatWest Bank Trophy.